WHAT INDIA THINKS

BEING A SYMPOSIUM OF THOUGHT, CONTRIBUTED IN 1939, BY 50 EMINENT WOMEN AND MEN HAVING INDIA'S INTERESTS AT HEART

RABINDRA NATH TAGORE
KT., D. LITT.

WHAT INDIA THINKS

BEING A SYMPOSIUM OF THOUGHT, CONTRIBUTED IN 1939, BY 50 EMINENT WOMEN AND MEN HAVING INDIA'S INTERESTS AT HEART

COMPILED AND EDITED BY

C. ROBERTS

GYAN

Published by

Gyan Publishing House
5, Ansari Road
Daryaganj, New Delhi-110002
Phone: 011-47034999, 9811692060
E-mail: books@gyanbooks.com

Distribution Network
gyanbooks.com
India, USA, Canada, UK, Australia, France

ISBN : 978-81-212-4215-8 (PB)
First Published, Calcutta, 1939

2nd Impression 2020

Printed at: Gyan Press, Delhi.

What India Thinks
Edited by: C. Roberts

WHAT INDIA THINKS

*Being a Symposium of Thought
Contributed by 50 Eminent
Men and Women
having India's
Interests at
Heart*

Compiled and Edited by
C. ROBERTS

THE NATIONAL LITERATURE COMPANY
CALCUTTA.

First Published.............................1939.

Printed by Fakir Das Chandra at the Moti Press Ltd., 50 Pataldanga St., Calcutta, and Published by the same on behalf of the Proprietor. Editor :—C. Roberts.

TO THE YOUTH OF INDIA AND ALL OTHERS WHO HAVE THE WELFARE OF INDIA AT HEART THIS VOLUME IS RESPECTFULLY DEDICATED IN THE FERVENT HOPE THAT ITS CONTENTS WILL BE A SOURCE OF INSPIRATION AND GUIDANCE.

CONTENTS

Publication of an article does not necessarily imply agreement with the sentiments expressed or the arguments propounded.

The Publishers and the Editor take this opportunity af recording their very sincere thanks to all who have contributed to this volume and to express their regret to those whose articles have not been published therein. These, it is hoped, will form the nucleus of a companion volume which is to be published in the near future.

ILLUSTRATIONS

WHAT INDIA THINKS

DR. RABINDRA NATH TAGORE

KT., D. LITT.,

There are many reasons why the name of Rabindra Nath Tagore will go down in history as one of Bengal's greatest sons, not the least being his work for the preservation of the language of Bengal and its literature. Any holder of a Nobel award deserves an entry on his country's scroll of fame and when to this is added a life vigorously devoted to the cultural uplift of his fellow men irrespective of caste, creed or background posterity itself will do him the honour which the present generation already recognises as his due.

This recognition of a great man is no mere matter of confinement within the limits of his own country, nor is it bounded by this vast sub-continent of India. National fame is an intangible asset which many attempt to secure but which few attain. International respect is on a different plane entirely and connotes a breadth of vision and a depth of feeling outside the ken of ordinary man. Such is the fame of "The Poet" as he is affectionately called.

Born in 1861 his father Maharshi Debendranath Tagore was the founder of Adi Brahma Samaj which inculcated a new faith among the Hindus. Rabindra Nath Tagore gave glimpses of his genius as a poet from early boyhood. In 1912, by which time he came to be known all over the world as a poet of outstanding merit, he was awarded the Nobel prize for literature. In the same year Calcutta University conferred upon him the degree of Doctor of Literature and in 1913 the Government honoured him with a knighthood. Dr. Tagore surrendered this as a protest against the Jhilianwalla affair and his fearless and impassioned statement in that connection stands out as a remarkable document.

In his younger days he was often in the limelight of the Swadeshi movement and many of his patriotic songs composed during those years are a source of undying inspiration to the young men and women of this country. He is the founder of Visva-Bharati an international centre of art and culture which aims at the cultural uplift of man and where the best talents of the world, attracted by the personality and genius of Dr. Tagore, are teaching a cosmopolitan gathering of students. Many professors of international repute are attached to this University. Dr. Tagore's genius knows no limit and he has enriched Bengali literature in all its aspects. He has written about 50 dramas, nearly 100 books of verses (about 3000 in number), about 40 works of fiction and short stories, innumerable songs with notations, about 50 books of literary, political and religious essays and scores of others on travel and children's stories.

He is a master in the science of music and has given a new interpretation to the musical renderings prevalent in Bengal. Although a man nearing eighty his ever sparkling genius still puts forth new creations every day. His books have been translated into every language of the world and during his birthday celebrations some eight years ago a special volume was brought out named *The Golden Book of Tagore* in which litterateurs and great thinkers of the world paid homage to him. During the last ten years the Poet has taken to painting. His interpretation is as unorthodox as it is unique and symbolises the mood of the artist in various phases. His paintings have earned unstinted praise in Moscow, Berlin, Paris, New York, Munich and Birmingham art exhibitions.

Dr. Tagore is a very widely travelled man and has visited almost all the countries of the world. Besides being a great poet and dramatist he is a great actor, and has been seen many times on the stage, appearing in roles created by him. His histrionic presentations have been considered by the critics to be of the highest order and were aided in his younger days with a rich ringing voice.

RELIGIOUS EDUCATION

ATTAINMENTS, which do not have their origin in external habit but are the result of the unfolding of the inner nature of man, cannot be gained by artificial methods. They depend on favourable conditions. If religious feeling is not considered a mere sectarian accomplishment, but rather the fulfilment of humanity itself, then it must have a suitable environment for its exercise, and sufficient leisure for its growth. The surrounding light and air must be so ample that the soul may gain fresh life with every breath it draws. This amplitude is what the forest universities of ancient India offered for the spiritual education of her children. The ideal of perfection preached by the forest dwellers of ancient India runs through the heart of our classical literature and still dominates our mind.

The forest *Asram* was the sacred abode, where human activity, in cadence with that reposefulness which is in universal nature, mingled in the discipline of man's pure disinterested endeavour. The spirit of the universe and the soul of man united to build up a temple for worship. This worship itself was service, unfettered by the bonds of self-seeking. It is this spiritual unity which was set forth so truly and so purely by the great thinkers and teachers of ancient India in their forest *Asramas* ; and it is this same ideal which we need for our religious growth today.

The religion of the modern time which does not ascribe any particular form to the subject of its worship, nor attribute any special efficacy to particular rites, but rather believes that outward observances carry with them a certain danger to man's intellect as well as to his moral nature,—such religion cannot be expected to keep a permanent hold over the minds of men by the mere preaching of its ideals.

The atmosphere of the *Asrama* is needed if the religious spirit in the modern age is to find its inner harmony and its living power. For, in the *Asrama* life, such a harmony exists. There are no artificial barriers between man and nature. Men, women and little children come naturally to regard bird and beast, tree and creeper, as their kith and kin. The subtle allurements and endless appurtenances of worldly comforts do not constantly distract the mind. The search after God is not merely an act of meditation, but is continued throughout the daily life in acts of sacrifice and compassion. Conscience is not imprisoned by any personal consideration of expediency. Its urgence is ever towards the higher ideal of universal good as the only final sanction.

There are truths, which are of the nature of information, that can be added to our stock of knowledge from the outside. But there are other truths, of the nature of inspiration, which cannot be used to swell the number of our accomplishments. These latter are not like food, but are rather the appetite itself, that can only be strengthened by inducing harmony in our bodily functions. Religion is such a truth. It establishes the right centre for life's activities, giving them an eternal meaning; maintains the true standard of value for the objects of our striving; inspires in us the spirit of renunciation which is the spirit of humanity. It cannot be doled out in regulated measure, nor administered through the academic machinery of education. It must come immediate from the burning flame of spiritual life, in surroundings suitable for such life. The *Asrama*, the Forest University of ancient India, gave for our country the answer to the question as to how this religion can be imparted.

It was in the *Asrama* where the harvest of religious thoughts, reaped in a great period of Indian history, was garnered in the Upanishads. These had nothing to do with any institution;

they never harboured any creeds, nor built rigid walls round them of logical consistency; and therefore people brought up in the atmosphere of some sectarian religion consider the texts contained in them merely as so many seeds of religious philosophy. But there can be no doubt that these seeds came out of the fruit of a true life of religion, fully lived. Such religion, contains the true spirit of liberation in its essence of spiritual truth because it is free from the bondage of sect.

What is significant about the religion of the Upanishads is that, though it was worked out by individuals who were not tied to each other by a common bond of conformity, a natural cord of unity nevertheless runs through their different thoughts of all variety of shades. For myself, I believe in such freedom of spiritual realisation, and I feel that the habit of obedience produced by the constant guidance of fixed creeds and everwatchful sects enfeebles the spiritual instinct of man and gives rise to materialistic ideas and practices disguised in religious phraseology.

What is most remarkable in the history of our religion is the fact that the people belonging to the despised community in this country, banished from the barricaded shrines of worship exclusively owned by the prouder castes have reached a religion which with its simple dignity transcends all boundaries of caste arrogance. These people had no scriptures, no schools, no temples, they only had their unfenced atmosphere of freedom kept pure by the helpful contempt of the learned orthodoxy and their unsophisticated devotion naturally came to the altar of *advaitam* the one supreme soul comprehending the souls of all beings.

Let me conclude my paper with the translation of a characteristic poem by a Baul poet by the name of Madan whose courage to decry the conventional paths of the pious as leading to spiritual futility is made evident in this song :—

Thy path, O Lord, is hidden by mosque and temple.
I hear thine own call, but the guru stops the way.
What gives peace to my mind, sets the world ablaze,
The cult of the One dies in the conflict of the many.
The door to it is closed by many a lock, of Koran,
Purna and Rosary.
Even the way of renunciation is full of tribulation,
Wherefore weeps Madan in despair.

THE RT. HON'BLE SIR AKBAR HYDARI
NAWAB HYDER NAWAZ JUNG BAHADUR

K.T., P.C., B.A. LL.D., D. C. L. HONORARY LL.D. (OSMANIA) HONORARY LL.D. (MADRAS)

President, H. E. H. the Nizam's Executive Council
(with Railway, Mines and Constitutional Affairs Portfolios)

Son of Nazerally Hydari of Cambay, India and Amena Najmuddin Tyabji (First class, Kaiser-i-Hind Gold Medal) daughter of Najmuddin Tyabji, Bombay was born on 8th November 1869. He has four sons and two daughters. Educated at St. Xavier's College, Bombay he joined the Indian Finance Department in 1888, and has been Assistant Accountant General U.P. in 1890 and Deputy Accountant General, Bombay in 1897 and in Madras in 1900. Examiner of Government Press Accounts in 1901. Controller of Indian Treasuries and was lent as Ac countant General to Hyderabad State in 1905. Financial Secretary and Secretary to Government Home Department (Judicial, Police, Medical, Education etc) in 1911. Acting Director-General of Commerce and Industries in 1919. Accountant General, Bombay and the Finance and Railway Member of Hyderabad State Executive Council. Also a Member for Co-operative Credit and Mines Department in 1927. Official Director of Singareni Collieries Co., Ltd and Mining Boards, in 1925. Director of the Shahabad Cement Co, Ltd., The Indian Cement Co., Ltd., The Indian Industrial and General Trust Ltd., The Central Bank of India Ltd., The Osmanshah Mills Ltd., and the Azamjahi Mills Ltd., and the Chairman of the Inter-University Board, in 1925. First President of the Hyderabad Educational Conference in 1915 and the President of the All India Muhammadan Educational Conference, Calcutta in 1917.

He delivered the Punjab University Convocation Address in 1925. Is a Fellow of the Bombay, Dacca, Aligarh Muslim and Hyderabad Osmania Universities and conceived and organised the Osmania University, Hyderabad, the first University of its kind in India, imparting higher education through the medium of the vernacular (Urdu) while retaining English as a compulsory second language throughout ; the Urdu Nastaliq type marks a new era in Urdu printing and the development of Urdu literature. He organised the State Archæological Department and negotiated the purchase for the State of the N. G. S. Railway. He led the Hydreabad Delegation to the three Round Table Conferences in London at which he was a Member of the Business, Federal Structure and Finance Sub-Committees. He has been a Member of the Parliamentary Joint Select Committee 1933 at which he was a member of the Reserve Bank and Railway Authority Sub-Committee and Advisor to the League of Nation's Monetary and Economic Conference held in London. Also President of the Muslim Educational Conference (Bombay Presidency) in 1934 and the Vice-President of the Nizam's Executive Council and Chairman of the Informal Committee of Indian States' Ministers. He is specially interested in Ajanta frescoes and Indian paintings. His publications include *Hyderabad State Budgets* and *Educational Addresses*.

Sir Akbar Hydari's contribution to *What India Thinks* takes the form of a lecture which he delivered to the Nizam's College Union on the faculty of seeing things as they are presented to us—clearly, without prejudice or partisanship.

OBJECTIVITY

OBJECTIVITY is the faculty to see things as they are presented to us clearly, without prejudice or partisanship. It is to see things with the eye of the artist who finds all forms, even ugly forms, interesting; it is to see things with the eye of the connoisseur who knows the relative worth of things and judges every article placed before him on its merits without importing his personal likes and dislikes into the field of judgment. This mental attitude is now the accepted attitude of the scientist, and is now admitted as the proper attitude for the historian.

The ancient Greeks and the Romans cultivated it. Europe in the Middle Ages had no place for it; in those days it was cultivated in the East—in Baghdad, Cairo and Damascus and in the universities of Spain. The Muslims recommended it to the Europe of the Renaissance and it has now become standard of that modern civilisation which derives from East and West both.

I ask you to read Gibbon—that great example of objective vision in the field of history—on the subject of the origins of the Reformation and the Renaissance, to read, either in Arabic or in a translation, Ibn Khaldun's *History* and his *Prolegomena*, remembering that these great works were written quite five hundred years before the critical study of history began to be undertaken in Christendom, and to remember that centuries before Copernicus and Galileo, Al-Biruni was aware, from his experiments, that the earth was revolving round the sun, and was not persecuted for expressing that opinion. And let me remind you that Al-Biruni, among others, was the means of conveying the old Hindu learning, especially in mathematics and astronomy, into the Arab symposium whence it passed on into the thought of modern Europe, which owes much more to the East than is generally admitted or supposed. If the Arabs derived a great deal of their learning and culture from the ancient Greeks, they also derived a great deal from Indians, Budhists and Hindus.

The gift of this objective vision in an individual is not so noticeable in his lifetime as it becomes to posterity, when he and his contemporaries can be seen as the relative height of mountains can be seen, from a distance. The great Napoleon in the estimation of his contemporaries was nothing like so great or so lonely a figure as we now see him. Many of his contemporaries thought themselves as great as he was, and most of them considered him an impudent upstart and impostor. We now know him as a man of ruthlessly objective vision who saw the world as it then was very clearly, who saw the needs of Europe as we see them now, and not as most of his contemporaries full of national and dynastic prejudices saw them.

Cervantes, the author of *Don Quixote*, was only one of many Spanish authors of his time, but to-day the world knows him and has forgotten his contemporary writers. The world knows him as the author of a singularly objective work of fiction. This gift of objectivity enables the writer to criticise his own work, the statesman to criticise his own programme, so as to exclude from it unworthy, perishable matter. Objective vision is to be found in the writings of the French encyclopaedists, and particularly in the works of Voltaire. Many people objected and still object to Voltaire's writings because he (Voltaire) was, they say, an atheist. Such people lack the golden gift of objectivity for what is laid before them for their judgment in the case of Voltaire is no ecclesiastical or theological matter, but a purely literary one, and Voltaire was a very great writer. For us to-day he outshines Rousseau and other contemporaries of his solely on account of his objective vision of humanity, unlike Rousseau's sentimental outlook. I have already mentioned Gibbon as a giant in this respect. In his day he was regarded much as Voltaire was regarded, and there are still some people who think his "*Decline and Fall of the Roman Empire*" reprehensible because it explodes historic fallacies and fables dear to them. Disraeli had this gift; and Gladstone, who was his rival was conspicuously lacking in it in his outlook on world politics. They appeared equal in the sight of their contemporaries, but today Disraeli, as a statesman, is without a rival in his times. To show you what I mean: Disraeli, as a Jew who had become a Protestant had every reason to dislike the Roman Catholic Church; but for a sympathetic appreciation of the Roman Catholic Church, I commend to you his novel *Sybil*; and in the same book by the leader of the Conservative Party, the Tory of Tories, you will find a wonderfully clear and candid picture of the wrongs the English poor were suffering, and a thoroughly respectful treatment of their claims.

The gift of objectivity is not common; few individuals possess it completely, but it is the gain of modern civilisation that it does extol this gift and does set it up as an ideal for every thinker.

I am told that the dispute between the Romanticists and the Classsicists among imaginative writers of a century ago in Europe was once described as a dispute as to which was the most important thing about an orange, the history of Spain or the orange-skin; a very good hit at the mentality of those who lack the gift of objectivity, for the most important thing about an orange is the fruit itself, its quality and flavour.

Most people, whether in the East or West, are more or less strongly influenced in their judgment by traditions, environment, heredity, personal prejudice and some are so impulsive, so unreasoning, that every new or old phenomenon is not for them an object to be observed and studied, but a subject for liking or disliking; and the reasons for their liking or disliking, if we probe down to them, are irrational. What would you think of a man who, if some magnificent monument of the days of old were shown to him, should say: I must think it ugly because the men who built it were meat-eaters or vegetarians? What would you think of a man who, when advised to read some classic work of literature, should say; I cannot endure it because the man who wrote it disagreed with my great grandfather? Yet most of the judgments which we form unthinking, and carry with us all through life as prejudice are no better than those.

Cultivate objective vision while you are still young ; when you grow old it will be too late to do so, for your minds will have hardened, each in the mould in which you have allowed it to set. It will enable you to see things as they really are, and so to help to make them as they ought to be. If we do not see things as they really are through prejudice or careless vision, how can we ever hope to set them right. Above all it will enable you to see yourselves, occasionally and when you choose, as others see you. Most of us go through life comfortably wrapped up in a good opinion of ourselves ; no matter what we do we find excuses for it because we do it. And often it comes as a terrible and painful shock to a man who has thus lived wrapped up in self-satisfaction, when he finds that other people think his character absurd, his conduct blameworthy. Turn the searchlight on yourself occasionally ; all the better if you are displeased with what it shows you for that will make you eager to improve.

The need of the kind of vision I am recommending to you is particularly great in our own country just now. India has just made a lofty claim before the world and her claim is being favourably heard. Indians have got to justify that claim by their behaviour. Communalism, the worst product of the un-objective mind, will, if we indulge in it, ruin and disgrace our country in the eyes of the whole world. Hindus have their virtues and their special gifts and so have Muslims. Both have contributed greatly to the culture, art and thought of India and of the world. They have their separate histories well deserving to be studied ; but what I would impress upon you here, you students of the Nizam College, is that Muslims and Hindus have a *common history and a splendid common history*, here in India extending over several hundred years. For centuries they lived together amicably in an Empire which made India great among the nations of the world—an Empire in which Hindus and Muslims equally shared—an Empire of which our Hyderabad is the sole surviving remnant. No one is more conscious than I am that our country is still backward in some ways but Muslims please remember, and Hindus please remember, there is nothing in the world so backward as the blind, mad communal hatred which is being cultivated, I am sorry to say, in some other parts of India. It is the will of His Exalted Highness The Nizam to reform and improve the administration and to raise the people of these Dominions, so that Hyderabad may become the model of of an Indian modern State, and His Exalted Highness expects Hindus and Muslims both, loyally to help his Government in this great and by no means easy work of progress.

Hyderabad is as big as many countries of Europe. It is bigger than several countries of Europe which have won renown by their achievements. It is for you, the people of Hyderabad, to make Hyderabad great in prosperity and renowned for peacefull progress, to make it culturally and economically what it is geographically—the heart of India. The Government can only provide you with a framework allowing of your great and rapid progress and that Government is doing as quickly as it can. And Government can do no more than that without your active help. It is for you to fill in that framework using the materials with which the State provides you, with the myriad cells of the activity of a happy, peaceful and well-protected people and to store those cells with the honey of a nation's wealth. It is owing to the absence of objective vision that young men see no career save Government service. Government service may have certain advantages for the individual, and it may be useful to the community but that depends entirely on the zeal and conscience of the individual. From the nation's point of view it is at best only like the service of the man who looks after the ground on which the match is played, the service of the man who keeps the house in which the work is done and sees to it that the workers have all that they require to make the product of their work the best possible. It is the agriculturist first and foremost, and then in connection with the agriculturist, the merchant, the manufacturer, the miner, the weaver, the inventor of new means for using natural products of our country to increase the nation's wealth and to reduce the number of the destitute who is the real worker for the country, and it is he and such as he for whose welfare our gracious Ruler and all who have the honour to serve him in his Government are mainly concerned. Productive workers *only* can fill in the framework. Their work is of incalculable value, and the whole framework of Government exists only to secure, protect, help and encourage their work. It is on its young men that a country depends.

I know that it is distasteful to youth to be patient. They would like to crowd the achievements of a decade in a year. Nor can I find it in my heart to blame the impatience of youthful enthusiasm for it is that which makes a man want to do one better. On the other hand, let not your impatience make you unfair in assessing the value of what has so far been achieved. I make bold to say that, no dispassionate observer of our land would fail to regard the steady progress in all directions which Hyderabad has registered in recent times and especially during the reign of our present gracious Sovereign the Nizam I would ask you to have a pride in the achievements of Hyderabad and its well-being, willing to learn whatever others may have to teach you for good, because something is happening beyond our borders that is good and should be copied.

One of the tendencies of to-day in British India is to bring religious differences into regions where they have no right to exist; into politics, education; into matters which ought to be common ground where men of all religions can meet on equal terms, agree as good citizens. We in Hyderabad must be careful to avoid that tendency which proceeds from nothing else than lack of objectivity. We have to notice and avoid the errors which our neighbours make. We have derived much benefit from European education, but we must remember that we are still Indians and that Indians have a different genius from Europeans and that to adopt a European framework for the life of India might tend to cramp, and not develop and expand that genius. We want to create conditions which will give that genius free play here in Hyderabad and, without objective vision, we can never do so. We have first of all to see Hyderabad as it is and then imagine it as a unit of a future Federation of all India. In order to become a unit it must first become a unity. We have a model for the future unity of Hyderabad in a European country, Switzerland, which is often held up as a pattern of good Government. In Switzerland people of three nations, Germans, Italians and Frenchmen live side by side, preserving and developing their several cultures, all equally proud of their Swiss citizenship and two different religions, Roman Catholic and Protestant exist together without clash of interests. In order to make such unity for Hyderabad an accomplished fact within a little while, I want you to conceive it as your object and to keep it ever in your mind. We have to develop and cultivate State consciousness, State patriotism, and in order to do that we must have objective vision which means a clear and true vision of our country's needs. We must resolutely shut our ears to the suggestions of outsiders who tempt us to view our problems "un-objectively." We have to make Hyderabad a united country and as we have always had an Indian Government in Hyderabad, we cannot, we need not adopt the prejudices formed in people who have lived for years under other conditions. Though I am growing old I have always tried to be sufficiently objective to keep my mind in sympathy with the mind and ideals of youth. I place very high hopes in the young men of Hyderabad. It is for this reason that on the point of leaving Hyderabad to undertake a great and arduous service for the State I have tried to put aside all engagements in order to come here and talk earnestly to the students of the Nizam College. I shall be absent for the next few months, but you will still be here in Hyderabad. I want you in my absence to be the missionaries of the high objective, the high ideal, the noble ideal I tried to place before you this morning.

DR. GEORGE SYDNEY ARUNDALE

D. LITT., M.A., LL.B., F.R. HIST. S.

President of The Theosophical Society in succession to Dr. Annie Besant since June 1934, elected for 7 years; educated in Italy and Germany, graduating from St. John's College, Cambridge, B. A., with honours in Moral Science, LL.B. with honours, and M. A., in 1902 doing research work on the French Revolution at the Achives Nationales, Paris. Came to India in 1903 at Dr. Besant's request as Professor of History at the Central Hindu College, Benares, later becoming examiner to the Allahabad University and the U. P. Government; Headmaster, Central Hindu College 1907, Principal 1909.

Served in the British Red Cross Society during the Great War 1915, and was for some time in the charge of Commissariat, Endsleigh Palace Hospital for Officers, London. Returned to India in 1916 and joind Dr. Besant in her political and national education work. Organizing Secretary, All-India Home Rule League, interned with Dr. Besant in 1917 under Defence of India Act. In the same year was founded, in Madras, the Society for the Promotion of National Education in connection with which he established schools and stimulated interest in national education by extensive touring, lecturing and writing in the Press. Principal, National University, Madras, and head of the Teachers' Training Department. For his services to education the National University (Chancellor Dr. Rabindranath Tagore) conferred upon him the degree of D. Litt..

Married Shrimati Rukmini Devi 1920 (who is deeply interested in music, art and the dance, specially the classical Indian Bharata Natya, and working for India's artistic and cultural renaissance). 1920 Education Minister to H. H. the Holkar Saheb of Indore. Travelled extensively in Europe in 1925, lecturing and studying educational, political and social conditions.

Visited Australia 1926 and founded Australia-India League, *Advance Australia* journal, and 2GB Theosophical Broadcasting Station. Travelled Europe and United States of America in 1927 and returned in 1929 to Australia and inspired "Who's for Australia League" devoted to Australia's political regeneration.

Visited Europe and America every year from 1931-34, and after election as President of The Theosophical Society spent 1935 at Adyar reorganizing the administration, developing his Seven-Year Plan, and organizing World Theosophical Campaigns.

Dr. Arundale's contribution to "What India Thinks" stresses the need for a different form of education if India is to be built anew. In this he has drawn upon his long experience of Indian youth to set forth those aspects of their nature which differ from the aspect of youth elsewhere in the world.

DYNAMIC EDUCATION

Educational reconstruction in India will take some considerable time, for a century and more has been required to bring the existing system to its present stagnation point.

I do not think we shall need anything like a century to substitute an Indian system of education. But we shall need less or more time according to the one-pointedness of those in whose hands must lie the very real orientation that will be required.

Obviously, the existing foreign system of education in India would have to be scrapped at the earliest possible moment, for no education which is in any way foreign can ever be true or right for any country. As Sir James Barrie said many years ago to the students of St. Andrew's University in Scotland, the supreme objective of education is courage—courage to face life's difficulties, troubles and frustrations, serenely, strongly and cheerfully. Unless education is designed to help achieve this it is not education, whatever else it may be. To courage I would add enthusiasm of fire—enthusiasm for truth, for reverence, for goodwill and understanding, for compassion, for tolerance and all possible appreciation.

And right education would lay immense stress on creative activity along all lines congenial to the individual student, not mere appreciation or power to reproduce, but also originality and inventiveness. The creative spirit is one of the universal signs of our essential divinity, and its disregard is directly productive of that degradation of our several functions so terribly prevalent throughout the world.

DYNAMIC EDUCATION

If education were for living and not merely for livelihood; if education were for joy and happiness and not merely for temporal success; if education were for self-expression and not so exclusively for imitation; if education were as much for service as it is for selfseeking ; if education were as much for wisdom and truth as it is for so-called facts ; if education were as much for the soul as it is supposed to be for the mind ; then, indeed, would the younger generation be well-equipped for life. But education tends to be static. Only here and there, and now and then, is it dynamic. It makes its pupils far more respectable than real. By reason of the fact that this is an age of mind, education, concentrating on the mind, has practically forgotten, if it ever knew, the emotions, and is only now remembering the physical body. Yet of infinitely greater importance than the mind are the emotions, and of no less importance than the physical body. Were the emotions educated as they should be educated, many of the world's acutest problems would cease to be. The problems of war, of sex, of poverty, of disease, would, I make bold to say, be far nearer to understanding, and therefore to solution, than they are today.

EDUCATION FOR ORDERED FREEDOM

The right education of the emotions is the direct route to brotherliness, to the spirit of unity, to all that makes for generosity and compassion, to happiness and peace. To neglect the emotions is to leave brotherliness to its fate ; to grow as best it can untended, to make unity the slave of individuality ; to yield to selfseeking and to force happiness and peace to make room for worry and anxiety. Without the wise co-operation of the mind the emotions tend to become aimless and uncontrolled. Freedom I demand for mind, emotions and for the physical body. That true freedom which is ordered because it is loftily purposeful ; and that these may be thus ordered purposefully they need education, that is, unfoldment, wise nurture and noble direction from within aided by understanding sympathy from without.

THE TRUE HOME OF EDUCATION

May I now turn to education in India ? No more splendid background is there in the world for education than India, the true home of education, where the deepest principles of education lie imbedded in her eternity for those to find who seek the real in regions eternal rather than in realms of time. I look over the world and I see education everywhere in the melting pot. I see everywhere problems, everywhere plans and methods, schemes and projects. I see education extending sway over the prenatal, delving into psychological temperament, penetrating almost up to the very soul itself. But is it not mostly tinkering ? Is it not mostly taking the child as he is, as a child, as an emptiness, more as a vase to be filled than, as Madame Montessori so truly wishes him to be, a spark to be fanned into a flame ?

What is really understood today of the child's eternal nature, of the great pilgrimage of life at a particular stage of which he stands before us ? What is known of the many-coloured spectrum of human diversity as the manifestation of the white light of divine unity ? Who is able to assign to a child his individuality-colour with all its wondrous significance ? What is known or surmised as to the reason why a child is born in this country or in that, in this faith or in that, in these surroundings or in those ? What is realized as to the differing notes of the various faiths, of the various nationalities, of the various temperaments, in the great harmony of universal life ? What is perceived as to the true relationship between the various kingdoms of nature—human, non-human, super-human, and as to the need of recognizing the obligations of such relationship for co-operative and therefore for mutually helpful living ? How little do we realize that education is everywhere ; is the universal process of life, and that there is no isolation in education ; that education at one point affects education at all points ; that education here or there is affecting education everywhere.

A WATCHWORD OF MODERN EDUCATION

Do we not need to realise that just as all life must grow together, and does grow together, therefore should all life as far as possible be educated together, so that it may grow beautifully together. That word "together" might well be a watchword of modern education. How long shall we be before we realize that where the younger kingdoms of nature are neglected, the human kingdom must inevitably remain stunted. Nothing can grow at the expense of one, apart from, other things. Nothing can grow through tyranny, through cruelty, through neglect, through indifference. Neither can the tyrant grow, nor that over which he tyrannizes. And the suffering of one member of the family is the weakness of the rest. There is no limit to the length to which we may not carry the implications of that universal brotherhood which enfolds all life.

We are one with the trees, the flowers, the shrubs, the very weeds themselves. We are one with the rocks, the earth, the stones. We are one with the waters and the seas. We are one with gods and angels and men. For all is divinity in process of achieving self-consciousness, and the ladder of growth is unbroken from unconsciousness in the mineral kingdom to wakefulness in the human kingdom, to full consciousness in glorious regions beyond the human. Oh ! that education could give us, thrill us, with such truths as these through its facts and figures, through its subjects and schemes ! Oh ! that education could put its votaries in the way of understanding the major problems of life, instead of leaving them most carefully alone ! That it could strengthen its votaries against all fear, evolving in them their natural heritage of courage ! That it could take away from them the fear of death by disclosing to them the true nature of death ! That it could take away from them the fear of failure by demonstrating all absence of failure where effort still remains ! That it could make life more than endurable, delightful, by showing that pain and suffering are but the birth-pangs of power and joy ! that it could draw the veil which separates present from future and disclose the splendour of our destiny !

Why should not education do these things, or at least move in the direction of doing these things ? Not, perhaps, so much education of the mass variety, but certainly education in the hands of pioneers, visionaries and fanatics of the right kind. Let books be written on education's larger issues. Let public opinion be aroused to demand from education that it shall show the way to wisdom as well as point out roads of lesser import. Education needs to be idealistic if it is to be wisely practical. Education needs to be full of beauty if it is to be true. Education needs to be full of vision and eternity if it is to serve the true purposes of time.

THE SOUL OF INDIAN EDUCATION

What an opportunity we have here in India, an opportunity that I am afraid the existence of an alien spirit in education causes us most terribly to miss. In very truth we have but to lift up our eyes unto the hills whence cometh all help to know of what nature Indian education should be. I am guilty of no flight of fancy when I say that in the glorious Himalayas, the root-base of eternal India, we have the keynote to the whole of Indian life, and therefore to the soul of Indian education. Does not India draw from these mighty mountain beings much of the faith in which a large majority of her peoples live ? Does she not almost draw from them her protection ? Does she not draw down from them much, very much, of her material wellbeing ? True, we have among us our Mussalman brethren whose life immediately came from Arabia where their great prophet stood forth in such unique magnificence. True, we have our Parsi brethren whose life is more immediately traceable to Persia, and our Christian brethren who come, as it were, from Palestine. We have our Buddhist brethren, but they are of our own land.

Yet will not all surely reverence the Himalaya mountain brotherhood for a grandeur which, though physical, must come from some inner power of which the brotherhood is the outer form ? For what do the Himalayas stand so far as regards education ? Above all, they stand for power, for unity, for lofty purpose. They are a very embodiment of all these, and because of all these India is. Because of all these India, like the phœnix, is rising today from the ashes of her past, those glorious ashes yet smouldering, which the devotion of her children shall fan into a fire more splendid than has ever been. And our education, therefore, must be a Himalayan education. We do not look, we need not look, let us not look, to the west for power in our education, for unity in our

DR GEORGE SYDNEY ARUNDALE
D.LTT., M.A., LL.B., F.R. HIST. S.

education, for lofty purpose in our education, for truth in our education. Let us cease to believe that the education of the west is the ideal for the east. Far from it! Let us look into the India of bygone days, let us look into the splendid culture of our Mussalman brethren, itself the father of much of the culture in the west; let us lift up our eyes unto the Himalayas and we shall find ourselves listening to the song India has ever sung, the song she shall sing today, the song her children must learn to sing with all their hearts.

For some parts of the *body* of our education we may well go to the west. But for the *soul* never. Indeed, I boldly and emphatically say that the soul of all education throughout the world is to be sought and found in this ancient land of ours, and that only as our educational brethren of the west gain the wise humility which will turn their eyes to the east shall they begin to find the solutions of many of the problems which perplex them today. But if great things are to be done in the educational field in India there must be unrestricted freedom. Under a foreign system of education no youth of any land can truly grow. Only with an education full of Indian ideals, full of Indian spirit, full of Indian power, full of Indian unity, full of Indian simplicity, full of Indian purpose, full, that is, of Indian life, can Indian youth grow into Indian manhood, can India be herself. You ask: "*Where are these Indian ideals, where is this Indian spirit, where is this Indian unity, where is this Indian purpose, where is this Indian life*?" I say they are everywhere. And I say that you have but to look up to the Himalayas, the guardians of India, to know that all these things still live, are at the worst asleep, are to awake once more to the glory of the mother of all lands and to the peace and happiness of the world.

RECONSTRUCTION

How are we to begin the reconstruction? By organizing it. We must first of all disentangle ourselves from the immediate past, and this is one of the greater difficulties in reconstruction, since most of us are products of the very system from which we have to escape and we do not at all like to think that the education we have undergone has not been productive of very good results. It has produced us, and this ought to be sufficient refutation, we think, of Sir Radhakrishnan's slashing denunciation of our foreign education that it is making barbarians of civilized people.

But we have to try to be impersonal, and consider if a national type of education could not produce results *even better*, (this is in italics as a sop to any self-satisfaction we may possess) than those of the foreign system itself. We must gather together material upon which to base our reconstruction, instead of plunging impulsively, as we are now doing, into spectacular activities which may or may not have practical value in a scheme which has been the subject of the most careful preparation.

The subject of our educational reconstruction is the Indian child from birth onwards, through youth and adolescence, into maturity and, who knows, perhaps even beyond.

NATURE OF AN INDIAN CHILD

How does such nature vary ? What is his, and her, background ? How does the background vary ? What is the setting, and how does this vary ? What do we expect the Indian child and youth and adult respectively to be and to do ? What is the relationship of the state, the motherland, to her citizens of either sex and of all ages and capacities ?

We have to remember that the Indian child differs from all other children, and that we must take this into account and profit from such difference. We must, therefore, remember that only an Indian system of education can benefit an Indian child ; an Italian system an Italian child ; a Chinese system a Chinese child, or a Japanese system a Japanese child. Essentially, India's education must be Indian. Nothing short of this can give her her own strength and her own wisdom.

It is for this reason that we must insist on knowing all we can about the Indian child in those differences from other children which give him his own national and individual uniqueness. We tend far too much to assume that a child is just a child all the world over, and that the system which fulfils the needs of one particular class of child fulfils the needs of any other class.

I am, therefore, often asked to sum up my long experience of Indian youth, and to set forth those aspects of their nature which differ from the aspects of youth elsewhere in the world.

REVERENCE

First, I would assert that an Indian youth, boy or girl, is, practically without exception, animated by that spirit of reverence which causes him to fit harmoniously with his surroundings. In him, be he Hindu or Mussalman, the quality of *Dharma* is actively functioning in the sense that he has an instinctive perception of his own due righteousness. He tends to react rightly to his surroundings, be these family, friends, or other external circumstances.

Given a truly Indian education this spirit of reverence would splendidly develop, endowing him with that true freedom which exists only when the individual and his surroundings tend to be in a condition of perfectly harmonious relationship. But the Indian youth is not given an Indian education. He is compelled to undergo an education designed for another type of youth altogether, a foreign education, with the result that his own essential spirit is either quenched altogether or distorted out of all recognition. The result is the chaos we see around us—a denationalized youth yearning after nationalism, and not knowing what true nationalism is, knowing nationalism only in its foreign aspect.

How greatly I yearn for the restoration to Indian youth of such education as shall give back to him his wonderful heritage of reverence, a realization of his true relationship with all his surroundings.

Even as it is, this spirit of reverence has not entirely disappeared. My experience of Indian young people is that they still possess their heritage of reverence, overlaid though it has been by the sands of foreign futilities. Indian young people still show forth, at all events until the foreign education has gained its hold over them after a period of years, the reverence which is graciousness, which is fine manners, which is respect and eager service, which is dignity and even a reflection of India's eternal majesty. I say all this knowing of what I speak.

INSTINCTIVE GENTILITY

Innate in this reverence are its complements of kindliness and goodwill towards all, and of very real tenderness toward all suffering and unhappiness. In a single phrase, an Indian youth is instinct with that gentility, with that refinement, with that courtliness, which are the mark of an age-old race dwelling in an atmosphere sanctified and made fragrant by a veritable pantheon of greatness.

But let me add that this gentlemanliness is to be found in flower not only in Indian youth in schools and colleges, but even more, I would venture to insist, in the Indian peasant, in the Indian worker, poor, half-starved, miserable, helpless and almost hopeless, as he generally is. In my experience with the Indian worker during my trade union activities, I was amazed at the example he set me of a graciousness and a deference animated by the finest courtesies.

Look at western civilization as it is, and then look at the Indian poor and at the Indian child. The Indian poor have fortunately escaped modern education, and therefore have remained simple, natural, and in possession of their natural heritage of reverence and courtesy. The Indian child! He retains his spirit of reverence and grace till his education overwhelms him. And then he is delivered over into the clutches of the western time-spirit and he ceases to be Indian while being unable to become anything else. So we see him in the higher reaches of his school and in his college a really forlorn individual, a hybrid of west and east, and receiving every encouragement from agitators who are walking tragedies of Indian souls vainly seeking release from imprisonment in bodies stretched to fit the bed of a western Procrustes. There is no greater tragedy in the whole world today than the selling of India's splendid birthright for a mess of western pottage.

How many voices are there to cry, in this wilderness, of India's uniqueness in every department of life, of her power to give far more than she need ever receive, how in every field she can give to the west more, far more, than the west can ever give to her ?

AN INDIAN HERITAGE

I think of the Indian child and of all I know of him. The little I have written is only a little revealing of what he is, of what my experience has shown him to be. And then I think of the almost desecrating treatment which even our patriots are content to mete out to him.

I, for one, shall feel that we have betrayed India if we do not fashion an education which shall cause to burn brightly in every Indian youth the heritage of his race and of his land. And so far we have not heard a single word of all the greater things of Indian education.

SIMPLICITY - CONTENTMENT

I would then assert that the Indian youth has in him the quality of great simplicity. He has in him a spirit of contentment which tends to render him indifferent to the call of luxury, even of comfort. He generally does live simply, and is quite able to reconcile simplicity with all his needs. An Indian youth is quite able to "rough it" and has no instinctive taste for the enjoyments of western civilization. These tastes are very definitely acquired, partly through the pressure of western civilization round about him, with its many uglinesses and few refinements, partly through the absence of simplicity in his forms of education, and partly through the very influence of the foreign system of education itself, the whole tendency of which is to divorce him from simplicity and to incline him to desire expensiveness.

Given a true system of Indian education, this spirit of simplicity might develop along very beautiful lines, gradually tending to release the whole country from the bleak and generally ugly spots of large cities. The Indian youth would once more gain his satisfactions partly from within, his education developing in him self-contentment and thus simplicity, and partly from nature unenslaved to man. He would find his happiness and unfolding growth in nature, in close intimacy with nature, in helping nature, in rejoicing in nature, in sharing together his life and the richness of nature's life. He would belong to mother earth and gradually learn to draw from her her godliness to increase his own.

IDEALISM—LOYALTY—HONOUR

Furthermore, perhaps as an offspring of his reverence, the Indian youth is for the most part an idealist. While his lot is largely cast in difficult circumstances, idealism is rarely altogether lost. He reacts instantly and finely to ideals of whatever kind, but most of all, of course, to those ideals with which, if he be a Hindu, his past is fabulously rich. His spirit of loyalty and honour, also qualities marked in the Indian youth, go out to the great ideals of his ancient history and to the towering figures of those who gave such ideals form. Nay more. His spirit of loyalty and honour tends even to create ideals and to be very true to them, rather to persons than to principles. His teachers, even his foreign teachers, are very often ideals to him, and throughout his whole life receive his homage and his allegiance. I know this from my own experience as a teacher in the Central Hindu College at Benares. The Indian youth, indeed, is such an indealist that he is easily influenced by any adventurer who will call to him in the name of an ideal. India is the world's richest home of ideals, and young India cherishes them deeply even if it cannot, as India is today, incarnate them.

So we have as characteristics of the Indian youth reverence, kindness, goodwill, tenderness, simplicity, idealism, loyalty and honour. I know these to exist in the average Indian youth for the very reason that I have intimately contacted thousands of them, and in each, *given an Indian atmosphere*, those qualities glow. But the teacher himself must be deeply inspired by India, by her mightiness, by the splendours of her many faiths, by the great traditions which are her eternal background, by the glory of the future that awaits her. In other words, he must in India be as other true teachers are in every country in the world. Let him be indifferent to all these, let him be a teacher just for the sake of money, let him be as ashes and not as a fire ; then will the fires of the Indian youth burn low and, perhaps for this incarnation, remain asleep in darkness.

INDIAN WOMANHOOD

I have been writing of Indian youth generally. But while all I have written I believe to be true of Indian youth still more is it true of the Indian girl. In all the world there is no woman as is the Indian woman. And the Indian girl is a beautiful shadow of what she is to be. All the virtues I have enumerated are true of her, and to them she adds her purity, her modesty and her unrivalled grace. The Indian woman ought to be a compelling example to her foreign sisters, reminding them of what a woman ought to be and, save exceptionally, is not in most other parts of the world. Look at the degradation of womanhood in the west, as portrayed in the press, in the theatre, in the cinema houses, in her slavery to fashion and to a hundred conventionalities, some of them even cruel and, many of them, ugly. As are the woman of a nation, so is the nation. The nation is mirrored in its women. India is so far safe in this respect. But already we hear of fashions in sarees, and of other signs of loss of freedom on the part of the less Indian women.

WHERE IS AN INDIAN LEADER ?

Where is the leader who stands for India, for India's eternal greatness, for the protection of a greatness which still endures today, against the ravages of ugly modernism ?

Where is the leader who calls his Indian people to remain true to themselves, be they of whatever faith, of whatever community ? There may be that to which we cannot go back. But what are we going to provide to take the place of that which, for whatever reason, has become worn out. What is to take the place of the caste system as it was originally planned ? How are we to give to the India of today the inherent greatness of the caste system without those evils which have caused its downfall ? How are we to give to the India of today all that is so wonderful in temple worship without that narrowness which has caused the downfall of its self-centred pride ? How are we, in the midst of the onrush of the spirit of equality with all its inconoclasms, to retain the truth that in nature there is no equality, no equality is intended, for in truth it is hierarchy which is the law of nature and of growth, and not equality, since there is only equality in terms of the goal, not in terms of reaching it ?

How are we so to exalt inequality that it is not swept away under the tidal wave of equality with all its democratic implications ? Inequality is true. Aristocracy is true. Hierarchy is true. Difference is true. How are we so to purify them that they are strong to serve and to guide the spirit of the times ?

This is the problem before us as we build India anew, and nowhere is the problem more insistent than in the field of education.

PROFESSOR NICHOLAS K. DE ROERICH

Commander of the Imperial Russian order of St. Stanislaus, St. Anna and St. Vladimir; Commander I. Cl. of the Royal Swedish Order of the Northern Stat; French Legion d'Honneur; Yugoslavian St. Sava I. Cl. Grand Cross; Honorary President Roerich Museum, and Master of the Institute of United Arts, New-York; Honorary President of the Union International, pour le Pacte Roerich, Burges and of the Pact Committee, U. S. A.; Honorary Member of the Bose Institute and the Maha Bodhi Society of Calcutta and the Yugoslavian Academy of Art and Science. Is a Life Member of the French Red Cross Society and the Asiatic Society of Bengal; Vice-President of the Archaeological Institute of America and a member of the Academy of Rheims Societaire of Salone d'Automne, Paris; Honorary Member of Secession Wien; and the Honorary Protector and President of 55 Roerich Societies in the world. Academician of the Imperial Academy of Fine Arts, St. Petersburg.

Born at St. Petersburg, 10 Oct. 1874 he is the son of Konstantin Roerich and Marie V. Kalashnikoff. In 1901 he married Helena Ivanovna Shaposhnikov and has two sons Dr. George de Roerich (Harvard) and Svetoslav de Roerich (Artist). Professor Roerich was educated at the Department of Law, University of St. Petersburgh and studied painting under Kuindjy at the Academy of Fine Arts, St. Petersburgh and also under Cormon and Puvis de Chavannes, Paris. Was Professor at the Imperial Archaeological Institute, St. Petersburg and was General Secretary, Imperial Society of Fine Arts 1898-1906 and Director in 1906-1917.

Undertook archeological excavations at Novgorod and exhibitions and lecture tours in Sweden, Denmark, Finland and England in 1917-1919 and the United States in 1920. He headed the Central Asiatic Roerich Expedition, making 500 paintings and collecting data on Asiatic Culture and Philosophy in 1923-1929 and the Roerich Museum was established in his honour in New York in 1923. It contains over 1000 of his paintings. There are Roerich Halls in Paris, Belgrade, Zagreb, Benares, Bruges, Riga, Allahabad, Buenos-Aires, and Kyoto and over 2000 of his paintings are hung in leading museums and art collections of the world. He is the President-Founder of the Urusvati Himalayan Research Institute, Naggar, Kulu, Punjab, started in 1928.

Roerich Pact, International Conferences were held at Bruges, 1931 and 1932; Washington, 1933 and the Roerich Pact for the protection of the world's cultural treasures was signed on April 15, 1935 by 21 governments of America. He headed the Central Asiatic U. S. expedition in China, Mongolia in 1934-36. Publications include his complete works in 1914; Adamant, 1924: Paths of Blessing, 1925; Altai-Himalaya, 1929, Heart of Asia, 1930, Flame in Chalice, 1930; Shambhala, 1930; Realm of Light, 1931; Fiery Stronghold, 1933; Sacred Vigil, 1934; Gates into the Future, 1936 (in English, Russian, Spanish French, etc.)

HIMALAYA

Athanasius Nikitin Tveritin, a Moscovite of the XV-th century, after his journey to India, exclaimed : *"And I, out of the midst of many troubles, went to India"*.

The most excellent Hali, the Arabian, mentioned by Paracelsus, said : *"Vade, filii, ad Montes Indiae et ad cavernas suas, et accipe ex cis lapides honoratos !"*—"Go, my son to the Mountains of India, and to their quarries and take from there those precious stones !" Let us go the Mountains of India !

From all parts of the world people want to know about the Himalayas. The best people are striving in heart towards this jewel of India. They ask to send at least a small sketch, or a snapshot, which they could keep on their desk for inspiration. In all ages there was this attraction to the Himalayas. People know that when anyone seeks spiritual uplift he has to look towards the Himalayas.

Many expeditions have striven to conquer the gorgeous peaks of the Himalayas. Severely the unconquered giants meet the daring intruders. Again Everest refuses to welcome the new-comers. And Nanga Parbat does not facilitate matters in the attempted conquest. And the Kinchanjunga peak is not even contested. And yet from all sides various nations aspire to reach the resplendent Himalayan summits. Such a procession turns into a homage of pilgrims to the highest of the world.

The local lamas smile mysteriously when they hear that yet another attempt has been defeated. If they have confidence in you they will tell you in whispers some ancient prophecies which assert that certain sacred summits will never be defiled. Not long ago a well-known lama, who is now dead, told us : *"Curious people are the pelings, why do they undertake such dangers in the physical body, when we can visit these summits and do so in our subtle body ?"*

Indeed in every striving to the summits, in every ascent, is contained an untold joy. An inner impulse irresistibly calls people towards the heights.

A DIVERSE HERITAGE

If someone would begin to trace historically these aspirations, having the Himalayas as their goal, an unusually significant study would result. Truly if one could trace back the force of attraction of these heights for a thousand years one could readily see why the Himalayas have been called "Incomparable". Since time immemorial innumerable tokens of divinity have been connected with this country of mountains. Even in the dark middle ages remote countries dreamt of beautiful India, which was epitomised in the imagination of people by the mysterious sacred snowy giants.

Let us mentally compare all these beautiful legends, which could only be conceived in the Himalayas. First of all, we will be astonished at the amazing diversity of this heritage. It is true that this wealth of legends has originated in the accumulations of many tribes, becoming more bounteous through the grateful contributions, and are crowned by the achievements of great seekers after truth. All this is so. But for such supreme achievements a magnificent environment is necessary, and what could be more majestic than the unconquered mountains with all their inexpressible radiance and all their exquisite variations of forms ?

It would be a rather unfortunate and feeble effort to compare the Himalayas with any of the other splendid mountain ranges of the world. The Andes, the Caucasus, the Alps, the Altai—all the most beautiful heights will appear to be but single peaks in comparison.

What does it not encompass, this multiform beauty ? Tropical approaches, alpine slopes and, finally, all the incalculable glaciers, powdered with meteoric dust. No one describes the Himalayas as overwhelming ; no one would dare to call them gloomy portals, nor mention the word monotony, in thinking of the Himalayas. Truly a great part of the human vocabulary must be forgotten when you enter the realm of the Himalayan snow—the part of one's vocabulary comprising its sinister and effete expressions.

TRIBUTE ?

The human spirit, seeking to overcome all obstacles, is filled with a yearning, which irresistibly impels one towards the conquest of these summits, and the very difficulties which at times loom so dangerously become only the most necessary and the most desired steps of ascent, overcoming earthly conventionality. All the dangerous bamboo bridges over the thundering mountain torrents ; all the slippery steps on the age-old glaciers over perilous precipices, all the unavoidable inclines before each successive ascent ; and the storms, thunder and cold and heat are surmounted, when the chalice of achievement is full.

Not the feelings of ambition nor boastfulness alone could inspire so many travellers and searchers to go to the Himalayas. Other difficult peaks could be found for competition and contests. But above all thoughts of competition and contests is a yearning towards these world magnets ; that ineffable holy aspiration, of which heroes are born.

The true magnets are not competitive laurels of contests nor the fleeting front pages of books and newspapers, but the attraction to this surpassing grandeur which sustains the spirit ; and in such striving there can be no harm.

"Is this another tribute to the Himalayas ?" One may ask.

But does the solemn grandeur of the Himalayas need any tributes ?

In this case tributes are out of place ; and any of them, even the most excellent, can be but feeble echoes. But why does one think of the Himalayas, why are we seemingly compelled to think of them, remember them and strive towards them ?

Because even mental communion with their solemn grandeur provides one of the best tonics. Everything is impelled towards the beautiful in its own way. Everyone thinks about beauty and feels an impulse to say something or other about it. The thought of beauty is so powerful and moving, that man cannot contain it silently within himself, but always tries to clothe it in words. Perhaps in song or in some other expression of his being, man must manifest and record his thought of the beautiful.

TRUE BEAUTY

From the tiniest flower, from the wing of a butterfly, from the glow of a crystal and on, further and higher, through beautiful human forms, through the mysterious sublime touch, man wants to fortify himself by the immutably beautiful. Wherever on earth there are beautiful creations of human hands, the pilgrim will come to them, He will find calm under their created vaults, and in the radiance of their frescoes and stained glass. And, if the pilgrim is captivated by mirages of nature's far-off horizons, he will set out towards them. And if, at last, he becomes aware of these lofty peaks shining afar off, he will be drawn to them and, in this very striving, he will become stronger, purer and inspired to achievements for good, for beauty and for uplift.

The pilgrim is always listened to with special attention near the camp fire or at a gathering of men. And not only in ancient chronicles does one read of the respect accorded to those who came from afar. Even now, despite all the speedy ways of communication, when the world has already become small, when people strive into higher strata or down towards the centre of the planet, even now, the narrative of the pilgrim still remains the highlight of every gathering.

"Are the Himalayas truly so beautiful ?"

"Are they really incomparable ?"

"Tell us something about the Himalayas and whether anything unusual is to be found there ?"

People expect something unusual in every narrative of a pilgrim. Customs, habits, immovability due to attachments, depresses even the coarsest heart. Even a depressed spirit strives towards movement. After all, no one thinks of movement as directed downward only.

I recall the story that a traveller, once related, having begun the descent of the Grand Canyon in Arizona ; surrounded by most beautiful colours, he was oppressed by the very thought of such endless descent : *"We went lower and lower and this thought of descending even prevented our admiring the country."*

Of course exaltation and transport is primarily connected with ascent. During ascent there is the urgent desire to look beyond the snowy peaks that soar before. But when you descend, each parting summit pronounces a sad "goodbye". Therefore, it is so joyous not only to ascend a summit, but at least to follow the ways of ascent in thought. When we hear of new travellers to the Himalayas, we are thankful even for that, for they remind us of the summits, of the call ever-beautiful and ever necessary.

Himalayas, let me send once more my heartfelt admiration !

Likewise, India, all-beautiful, let me send thee another greeting for all the greatness and inspiration, which fill thy meadows, thy forests, thy ancient cities and sacred rivers !

Kailasa, Manasarowar, Badrinath, Kedarnath, Triloknath, Ravalsar—these glorious gems of the Highest always fill the heart with a specially blissful tremor. When we were within a day's journey of Manasarowar the entire caravan already became uplifted—thus far does the aura of a holy *ashram* act.

Another vivid recollection arises from the path to Triloknath. A long line of sadhus and lamas stretches along this road—the old sanctuary, the site of pilgrimage and prayer. These pilgrims have met here from any different roads. Some, already completing their spiritual journeyings, are walking along with a trident ; some carry bamboo staffs ; others are without anything, some even are without clothing. And the snow of the Rotang Pass is no impediment to them.

The pilgrims proceed, knowing that the *Rishis* and the *Pandavas* dwelt here. Here is the *Beas* of Vyas ; here is *Vyasakund*—the place of the fulfilment of all wishes. Here Vyasa Rishi compiled the *Mahabharata*.

Not in legend alone, but in reality, did the great *Rishis* live here. Their presence breathes life into the cliffs which are crowned with glaciers, into the emerald pastures where the yaks graze and into the caves and the roaring torrents. From here were sent forth those spiritual calls which humanity has heard through all ages. These calls are taught in schools; they have been translated into many languages—and this crystal of acquisitions has been stratified on the cliffs of the Himalayas.

THE GIFT OF GOD

"*Where can one find words with which to praise the Creator, after seeing the incomparable beauty of the Himalayas?*" sings the Hindu. Along the paths of *Guru*, along the peaks of the *Rishi*, along the mountain paths of the pilgrims of the spirit, lies that treasure, which no torrent of rain can wear away, nor any lightning turn to ashes. He who walks towards the Good is blessed on all paths. How touching are all the narratives which tell of the meeting of the righteous ones of various nations. The tops of the deodars in the forest touch each other in the wind. Thus, everything that is of the highest meets without injury and harm. Time was when quarrels were settled by single combat and decisions were reached by a conference of chiefs.. So do the deodars discuss matters between themselves. What a meaningful word: deodar—the gift of God. And this significant name is not without reason: for the resin of the deodar has healing powers. Deodar, musk, valerian, roses and other similar substances comprise the beneficent medicines of the *Rishis*. Some have wanted to do away with these medicines by substituting an invasion of new discoveries; however, humanity again reverts to the foundations.

Here is a photograph of a man who walks through fire without harming himself. This is not a fiction. Witnesses will tell you of the same trials by fire in Madras, Lucknow, Benares. And not only does the *sadhu* walk harmlessly on the flaming coals, but he leads behind him those who desire to follow him and hold on to him.

In Benares a *sadhu* sits in sacred posture upon the water of the Ganges. His crossed legs are covered by the brim of the water. The people flock to the banks, amazed at the holy man.

Still another *sadhu* has been buried alive for many days; another swallows various poisons without any harm. Here is a *lama*, who can levitate himself; another *lama* by means of *tumo* can generate his own heat, thus protecting himself against snow and mountain glaciers; there a *lama* can give the death stroke with his deadly eye to a mad dog. A venerated *lama* from Bhutan relates, how during his stay in the Tzang district in Tibet, a *lama* asked the ferryman to take him across from Tzampo free of charge, but the cunning man replied: *"I will gladly take you over, if you can prove that you are a great lama. A mad dog is running about here, doing great harm—kill it."* The *lama* said nothing; but looking at the dog, he raised his hand and said a few words and the dog fell dead! The Bhutanese *lama* saw this himself. One hears frequently in Tibet and in India of the same 'deadly eye' and the 'eye of *Kapila*' and on a map of the XVIIth century printed in Antwerp by authority of the Catholic clergy, is mentioned the name of the country Shambhala.

TRANSMUTATION

If one can walk through fire, and another can sit on water, and a third remain suspended in the air, and a fourth repose on nails, and a fifth swallow poison and a sixth kill with a glance and a seventh lie buried without harm, then one may collect all those grains of knowledge in himself and the obstacles of lower matter thus can be transmuted! Not in a remote age, but now, right here, where Millikan's cosmic rays, Rhine's thought transference and the reality of the finest psychic energy are being studied and affirmed.

Every *Rishi* pronounced in his own language the sacred pledge for the construction of a revived, refined and beautiful world!

For the sake of a single righteous being, a whole city was saved. As beacons, lightning rods and citadels of God, stood the *Rishis* of various nations, of various creeds, of various ages, yet one in the spirit of salvation and ascension for all!

Whether the *Rishi* came upon fire, whether he arrived upon a stone, whether he came upon the whirlwind—he always hastened for the general good. Whether he prayed on mountain summits, or on a steep river-bank or in a hidden cave, he always sent out his prayers for the unknown, for the stranger, for the labourer, for the sick and the crippled.

Whether the *Rishi* sent out white horses to save unknown pilgrims, or whether he blessed unknown seafarers, or guarded a city by night, he always stood as a pillar of light for all, without condemnation and without extinguishing the flame. Without condemnation, without mutual suspicion, without weakening each other; ever onwards the *Rishis* ascended the eternal Mount Meru.

Before us is the road to Kailas. There rises one of the fifteen wonders described in Tibetan books: The Mount of the Bell! Along sharp ridges one climbs to its summit. It stands higher than the last junipers, higher than the last yellow and white mountain ranges. There Padma Sambhava once walked—this is recorded in the ancient monastery Gando-la. It is here that the caves of Milaraspa are situated and not one, but many, have been sanctified with the name of the hermit, who hearkened before dawn to the voices of the Devas. Not far away are also legends which surround Pahari Baba. Here are the spiritual strongholds of Gautam Rishi. Many *Rishis* walked here and he who gave the mountain its enticing name "Mount of the Bell", also thought of the call of the Bell for all, of helping all, of the Universal Good!

Here *Rishis* lived for Universal Good!

TOWARDS THE GOOD

When *Rishis* meet on the mountain paths they do not ask each other: *"From where do you come? Is it from the East, or West, or South or North?"* This is quite apparent: they have come from the Good and go to the Good. An exalted, refined, flaming heart knows where the Good is and in what it can be found.

Some of the travellers in our caravan were once discussing the qualities of the various *Rishis.* But a grey-haired pilgrim, pointing to snowy peaks, effulgent in their complete beauty said : "*Are we to judge the qualities of these summits ? We can but bow in admiration before their unattainable splendour* !

"*Satyam, Shivam, Sundaram*".

The *Upanishads* affirm that there is no joy without infiniteness. There is no joy in the finite. Joy is infinity. But it is needful to wish to cognize infinity.

The lofty and spiritual mood in which a Hindu recites the words of the sacred tradition is something not easily forgotten. The great poet Tagore, whose sensitive heart is a storehouse of these great rhythms, knows how to evoke all their beauties.

In India when the verses of the *Mahabharata,* the *Upanishads* and the *Puranas* are being recited, there is joy despite of all troubles ; and even if the modernization of India is inevitable, the beauty of such sacred poetry will live for ever.

The inner joy of the heart is something that we have to cultivate and learn to retain so that it takes up its abode in the heart, and this beneficent joy of the heart becomes a lasting power to disperse all the forces of darkness. Whether we think of those sublime temples of Southern India, the grandeur of Chittur and Gwalior, the great strongholds of Rajputana, or the solemn spirit of the Himalayas, we shall find the joy of great thoughts. On the moonlit Ganges, in the mystery of Benares seen at night, and in the great cadences of the Himalayan waterfalls, we shall find the same lofty sense of joy. In the repetition of such ancient names as Manu, Arjuna, Krishna of the *Pandavas, Rishis,* heroes, creators and great constructors, we recognize a loving respect for the past.

From the Mother of the World, from the Queen of Peace, we receive this delicate flower-like joy of the heart.

Marvellous India ! Splendid in outer beauty, most beautiful in its secret inner life.

Beautiful, beloved India !

ASIT KUMAR HALDER

PRINCIPAL

GOVERNMENT SCHOOL OF ARTS & CRAFTS, LUCKNOW.

Born in Calcutta on the 10th of September 1890 Mr. Asit Kumar Halder is one of the foremost disciples of Dr. Abanindra Nath Tagore, C. I. E., the father of modern art movement in India.

A one time Fellow of the Royal Society of Arts some of Mr. Halder's more widely known works are his copies of the fresco paintings of the Ajanta and Bagh Caves and the cave paintings of Jogimara at Ramgarh.

During his career he has been the Principal at Kalabhavana, Santiniketan, Visva-Bharati; and Maharaja's School of Arts and Crafts, Jaipur and the Adhar Chandra Mukerjee Lecturer of Calcutta University.

A copious writer, Mr. Halder is the author of several plays and story books for children in Bengali, his more serious writings taking the form of contributions on Indian art in the *Burlington Magazine*, *Modern Review*, *Prabasi*, *Vichitra*, *Bharatbarsha*, *Bharati* etc., a noted publication in English being his *Art and Tradition*. Calcutta University publications include his *Bagh Cave and Ramgarh Cave Paintings*, *Ajanta Cave Paintings* and two books on Indian and Western Art all in Bengali. Volumes of poems which he has published show him to be a poet of great merit and originality.

Mr. Halder's great aim is shown in his contribution to this volume which takes the form of an appeal for the preservation and development of Indian arts and crafts.

INDIAN ARTS AND CRAFTS

THE urge of nationalism has spread to all departments of life and one of its expressions is to be found in the love of Indian art. The crafts of India have yet to win the same esteem as the arts but here too the influence is felt. For the improvement of certain industries a study of art is necessary. We now desire calico printing to have Indian designs though, unless there is a certain amount of training in distinguishing them, it is not possible to say which design is Indian and which is not. The blouse is now cut after the Indian Kanchali pattern and the border of the sari has a lotus or swan design ; even ornaments are being designed after the old Indian style.

It was Sj. Abanindra Nath Tagore and his school that first drew the attention of the country to Indian art.

Magazines are full of their pictures and, unnoticed, a taste for Indian art has been gradually created. By imbibing the spirit of the Ajanta caves in the fine arts and in sculpture they were able to turn the taste of the public towards Indian art. In this way the dress and furniture painted in their pictures are being introduced in Indian homes and are becoming the fashion. I believe the nude pictures in the art galleries of Europe are responsible largely for the reaction against clothes shown by ladies in the west. When Greek civilization and Greek art became defunct, and with them the beautiful robes of the Greeks, painters rather than paint the ulgy dress which is to-day the fashion, have taken more and more to painting nude pictures. It is art that moulds the taste of a nation and there is no denying that the fine arts exert a great influence, not only on the crafts, but also on certain industries.

Lord Eustace Percy, President of the Board of Education of Great Britain has said, "*Broadly speaking the nation would have a higher standard of industrial art if it had a Greek school in fine arts. If we had a national school of painting, sculpture and architecture, its influence would be felt throughout the art schools and in every branch of industry.*" In our country we have partly realised this ideal.

The artists of Bengal have opened up the treasures of Indian art to the artists of the rest of India. Now everywhere Indian art is being cultured only keeping the provincial traits of the different provinces. In most of the art schools of India the art disciples of the master painter Abanindra Nath Tagore are at the head. From this we can understand that the influence of the Bengal School of Indian Art is being exerted on the fine arts and crafts of the rest of India, and this will lead to a revival of Indian art in the country.

In the art schools of other provinces crafts find an important place, and this is leading to the artistic revival of the crafts of India. It is necessary that in Bengal, too, there should be a revival of the old crafts. I should like to draw the attention of the Government and specially the city corporations to this.

THE POWER OF GROWTH

In this country, in lectures on art, it is the custom to lament over the degeneration of Indian crafts and to assign the reason that we have not now the patience to do delicate and fine handiwork. The real reason, however, has not been sought. We get the true reason of this in a long memorandum on the subject by Sir Walter Crane, Sir Alfred East, Sir Edward Buck and Mr. T. W. Rolleston in the *Journal of Indian Art and Industry Vol XV*, written on the occasion of the Festival of Empire and Imperial Exhibition of 1911. It is a pity our art directors are not acquainted with this piece of writing but indulge in vague despondency and false reasonings, looking back to a past Utopia in art.

Before referring to the memorandum mentioned above we must remember that the human mind is dynamic. It cannot be bound by any particular style. That is why the designs introduced in the period of Shah Alam, or even before, and which find expression in Indian crafts, although they may have some value as curios, cannot satisfy or limit the modern taste in art in India. Growth and a desire for the new is such a characteristic of the time that it will not do to say whatever our ancestors did was good. That is why the want of handicrafts which are based on Indian designs have yet the power of growth and have led to the introduction of cheap European manufactures which try to imitate Indian handicrafts.

In the report of the judging committee of the Festival of Empire Exhibition of 1911 we get the following passage :—

> "The art is influenced by some cause. which was not present in the past, at least not to the same extent. This influence may arise from various causes, the tendency to commercialise art, the quickness and cheapness of production, the increasing value of time, the loss of patronage and the other causes but I think the chief cause is the desire of craftsman to conform to a demand and the demand to-day is such that it prefers to select articles which show an infinity of labour and an extraordinary amount of industry. In the particular way I fear, the Indian craftsman has been influenced by European purchasers."

ART AND COMMERCE

If art has to be commercialised then art becomes an article of commerce only and has to conform to the laws of demand and supply. Apart from supplying the needs of the market there is nothing to be done and the desire for improvement becomes non-existent. In the times of the East India Company Indian handicrafts found a market all over the world. The result was that, whilst our handicrafts were appreciated all over the world, they began at the same time to conform to the needs of the west and many goods were produced such as vases, tables, etc., according to European models. We have now become so used to them that we have now forgotten their western origin.

Western critics have ascribed the degeneration of our handicrafts to the following reasons (1) bad design (2) too much detail and consequent overcrowding (3) the random mixture of the designs of the various provinces and consequent lack of unity in design (4) careless work (5) hurried work (6) lack of usefulness of articles designed (7) lack of proper instruments and (8) lack of proper material.

Our first complaint about Indian handicrafts is lack of imagination. The provincial art schools are there to remedy these defects. On the excellence of the imagination depends the excellence of handicrafts. It is not necessary to go into details on this point. This lack of imagination has led to the same nature of handicrafts with the same design being sent to Europe as Indian handicrafts. So Walter Crane said, "*The nature of the exhibits confirms the opinion that native designs and handicrafts have greatly suffered from European influence, which always appears to have a confusing effect upon the native artist and craftsman, destructive of his natural taste and feeling.*" If our art directors realise the above point and, instead of seeking foreign appreciation, try to popularise Indian handicrafts in India they will be working on the right lines.

WAYS AND MEANS

In the following ways we can popularise Indian handicrafts (1) To arrange for exhibitions of old Indian handicrafts and keep them in the museums (2) by giving prizes in annual exhibitions to encourage imagination in the designs of the handicrafts (3) to give lantern lectures on the comparative study of Indian and foreign handicrafts (4) the establishment of handicraft associations in the various provinces which would give orders to the craftsmen of beautiful designs and which would help to popularise their products (5) make catalogues of new designs of the various handicrafts (6) to publish illustrated articles on handicrafts in the various magazines in different languages in order to create a taste for these wares.

If thus by associations and exhibitions Indian handicrafts are supported they will be able to rehabilitate themselves. Recently in an exhibition at Lucknow we decorated a model house in Indian style i.e., the drawing and dining rooms, office, bed-room etc., were furnished with articles designed in Indian style. The result was that all the visitors wanted furniture made after those designs. Exhibitions can be thus utilised to enlist sympathy towards Indian handicrafts. We all know that by the creation of societies and the arrangement of exhibitions Indian art was popularised. The Indian Society of Oriental Art was established in 1907. Sj. Abanindra Nath Tagore and his late lamented brother Sj. Gaganendra Nath Tagore with a few friends (Indian and English) started this society. At first these paintings in Indian style were made fun of by everyone as certain periodicals of that time bear witness. Indian handicrafts might, at first, meet with opposition but if, through exhibitions and through newspapers and magazines, these handicrafts are popularised they will undoubtedly improve our economic conditions by helping Indian craftsmen.

Victorian and Georgian furniture are not in fashion even in Europe for oriental influence, specially Chinese and Japanese, is distinctly seen in European furniture and decorations. The room is no longer filled with heavy furniture and crowded with bric-a-brac. All furniture according to the Japanese style is unobtrusive and in Japan the furniture does not obtrude on the notice ; but a visit to the Louvre of Versailles will prove the opposite. Every piece of furniture draws the attention of the visitors. We are still charmed by the art and crafts of Europe. It is true that we are not self-conscious. If Indian art becomes the fashion in Europe we will undoubtedly imitate the fashion.

AN EXPERT CRITICISM

Until and unless our belief in ourselves is re-established and Indian handicrafts are re-introduced, I see no future for Indian art. If we take painting, sculpture and architecture it is only modern Indian painting which has made a substantial contribution towards Indian art. There is still much to be done in order to revive Indian sculpture and architecture. It is pleasing to note the efforts in these directions. The time has come for a revival of Indian handicrafts too. Let the nationalist not forget that beautiful handicrafts are the pride of the nation. If our handicrafts have to depend for their existence on foreign markets then it is better for those handicrafts to die. Because the handicraft of every nation depends for its existence on its fame in the land of its birth, otherwise its downfall is assured. European experts have said that—

> "Commercialism, facility of communication and, in consequence, the great increase in patronage of tourists, have led to an enormous demand for all kinds of curios and for specimens of Indian art work at the different centres on lines of communication, and especially of such as are portable and can be taken home or sent to friends as reminiscences of travel. The dealer demands and the workman provides for the rush of purchasers which every winter brings to the east, and both are eager to suit all pockets and to meet all wants. Prices are so cut down that crafts cannot afford to waste labour or material, for which reasons they are not able to reject imperfect specimens ; and thus the standard is lowered and the world is flooded with bad work, which in time, moreover, leads to the decay and abandonment, perhaps, of what once were beautiful and profitable art industries."

When our critics learn to analyse the position in this way, then alone can a regeneration take place. Once we are asked to increase the supply and again we are told that the handicrafts no longer show the minuteness of detail that it showed of old. Are we indeed so ignorant about the fine arts ?

If we try to disturb the old handicrafts which go by the name of curios, the suppliers will at once object on the ground that any change will effect the sale adversely. The handicrafts we have inherited from our fathers and which are appreciated so much by foreigners should in no way be touched. We cannot, therefore, depend on foreign sales for that is a bar to any improvement. Prof. Jost Hoffman, Art Director (Vienna) has recently written in the "*Studio*".

"Industry had become the prey of the manufacturer who now began to produce almost exclusively bad designs. Beautiful tradition had gone already. The most important factor in the

big enterprises of the manufactures was to calculate how to conquer big markets. To do this they began to pander to the thoroughly degenerate taste of the masses."

BLIND IMITATION

We cannot say that we have no art traditions in this country. If that were so and if we were like the Africans then perhaps we could imitate the art of some foreign country. If we proceed on the basis of our older traditions then alone will our handicrafts have a national stamp. Otherwise, we shall have to imitate the ultra-modern artists like Paul Klee, Pavlo Picasso, Jaen Jris, Andre Masson and thus free our art from any national stamp. This ultra-modern art of Europe has been reflected in European handicrafts and this has in some cases added to its beauty. These ultra-modern paintings, however, only require that we should blindfold our eyes and with the canvas before us dab on colours and draw lines in a haphazard way. Ultra-modern art is a reaction against a blind imitation of nature.

But why should we imitate ? Our paintings were never a blind imitation of nature as can be seen in the old paintings of Ajanta, Bagh and Singuria caves. We must try to recapture the note in these paintings. It is a difficult task. Revolt in art is a mere revolt—it is not art. Art is intuition. The more we try to analyse it the more we move away from it. If the new is not spontaneous but is only for the sake of revolt, it can never be the basis either of fine art or of handicrafts.

MADAME SOPHIA WADIA

THEOSOPHIST

A member of the United Lodge of Theosophists and the Royal Asiatic Society. Was born on September 13th. 1901 and was educated in Paris and Columbia University, the U. S. A., Is an International lecturer and writer and is the Editor of Indian P. E. N. which centre she founded in 1933.

Was delegate from India Centre to International P. E. N. Congress in Barcelona, Spain 1935, and Buenos Aires, Argentina, 1936. Represented India and spoke at International Writers' Congress Paris, 1935. Contributor to leading periodicals.

Madame Sophia Wadia's contributions to this publication take the form of a Lecture delivered under the auspices of the Bombay Ladies' Branch of the National Indian Association on January 28th. 1935, and monographs.

THE JOY OF LIVING

EVERY member of this our Women's Association, I feel sure, desires to enjoy life. I am equally certain that very few indeed would call their lives a continuous song of joy. There are ups and downs, moods of elation and of depression, conditions of health and of disease, birthdays and death-days, in the lives of all of us. Unalloyed satisfaction with the events of life is rare ; even happy events have their unhappy aspects ; and most people can repeat with truth the wonderful words of Shelley

We look before and after,
And pine for what is not ;
Our sincerest laughter
With some pain is fraught ;
Our sweetest songs are those
That tell of saddest thought.

People like ourselves, however, must consider ourselves fortunate ; for when we look around us we find millions of our fellow men steeped in ghastly poverty, suffering awful diseases, surrounded by stupendous ignorance. When we contact and contemplate the sad lives of those millions, we are struck with the tragedy of life, and we then are likely to exclaim that life cannot have any great meaning or any divine purpose.

And yet, have you known any man, even in most abject poverty, who is utterly devoid of hope ? And have you not found that in the heart of the most fallen woman there is a spot of purity ; and that the hand of the greediest miser sometimes extends itself in charity ? Constantly, and very consistently, do we find in nature joy superseding sorrow, beauty overcoming ugliness. When we look at nature superficially we see her tooth and her claw ; but when we probe deep we come upon her heart, ever throbbing with compassion. We call nature "Mother Nature", and not without good reason : like a true mother, nature gives us birth and nourishes us ; she loves every child of hers, and her love is not partial or foolish or selfish like that of so many women ; no, her love is ever and always educative. Every act of nature is creative, and out of ugliness beauty is born, out of pain power comes. This was so clearly understood by our ancient Indian philosophers that they described cosmic manifestation as a dance, and the whole of life's process as Lila, a gorgeous play, and the highest aspect of deity they named bliss, Ananda, the great joy.

JOY ABOVE PLEASURE

We are apt to judge life by the many comedies which please or the numerous tragedies which depress, both of which are alternately experienced by each and all of us. We must learn to look deeper ; not only to look at the surface, but to go to the core within every comic incident of life. within every little tragedy that wounds our heart or confuses our mind. It is because we do not look deep that we miss the meaning and the purpose of life. The end of life is not pain and death ; nor should we judge the bliss, Ananda or the joy of life, by the fleeting pleasures which gladden us in their coming and sadden us when they depart.

Most people enjoy their pleasures and suffer from their pains, but fail to learn from either. Our ancient philosophers taught that the joy of life is ours only when we are able to distil out of all incidents, whether pleasurable or painful, the perfume they contain. Real joy cannot be experienced merely by passing through some incident which brings a smile to our lips and a sparkle to our eyes and which thrills our blood. For soon we come upon other incidents which tighten those lips, bring tears to our eyes, and congeal the blood with depression or with fear. Both these types of events come and go, and we endure them without learning from them. That is why real joy, abiding and continuous, is absent from the lives of most people. Real joy is above pleasures as it is above pains, for it is made of the essence of these both.

This philosophical truth was very simply but effectively demonstrated to me one day by a tall, handsome, aged Toda at Ootacamund. We were out walking and came upon this Toda who could talk a little English. On our asking him when he enjoyed life most—when the rains poured as in August, or when the sky was blue and the sun blazed as in February, he smiled and thought for a moment. Then his eyes sparkled ; he showed us a lime he was carrying and he asked : "Can I get the juice without the peel ? The juice of life is both in rain and in sun. Look for it in rain only and you are not satisfied ; look for it in the shining of the sun only and you are not satisfied. Put them together and you enjoy them both. No, *Dorosani,*" he said, "neither joy nor happiness is really in this lime ; it is in my fingers, if I can squeeze the hard peel along with the soft pulp ; and remember—to taste the juice I must take it with my food, not throw it away."

PERSONAL ANALYSIS

We who think ourselves civilized and educated have a lot of philosophy to learn from simple-minded people who live in the company of nature. Let us see what the old Toda has

PROFESSOR NICHOLAS K. DE ROERICH

to impart to us. There are three things to be noted : (1) Real joy is to be felt not only through happy incidents, but also through the unhappy ones, through sunshine, yes, but also through rain ; the happy incidents are like the pulp of the lime, the unhappy ones like the peel of the lime ; both must be joined before true joy is experienced. (2) But we must squeeze the lime, *i.e.* squeeze the juice of joy through all our life events. And finally, (3) we must not throw away the juice of joy, but taste it and enjoy it.

Now, all of us have happy and unhappy experiences, but only a few of us know how to squeeze the joy out of them ; and fewer still are those who drink that joy. Why is this ? Because in our schools and colleges we are not taught how to extract the essence of joy every day, every hour. We go through experiences, but we do not learn from them and therefore are not able to enjoy them. Our wish is father to our efforts, and we desire to get rid of all pain and sorrow, believing that thus we shall be happy. In other words, we want the juice of the lime without squeezing it, and even without being bothered with its peel ! In our civilization we are not taught how actually to value pain and suffering. Our many kinds of reformers are trying to devise ways and means to get rid of pain and suffering. They will not succeed, though their motive is noble, because we simply cannot have happiness without suffering. Life itself is joy, Ananda, but that joy cannot manifest without the wall of resistance which we call pain. The old philosophers taught people to value pain, to appreciate suffering, to go to the heart of sorrow. The great Buddha taught four noble truths, and the very first of them was—that sorrow is. The cause and the cure of sorrow he also taught, but he began by asserting—sorrow is.

For without sorrow how could we know pleasure ? Does not joy itself demand the contrast of pain ? As one of our French poets has beautifully put it :—

Les moissons pour mûrir ont besoin de rosée,
Pour vivre et pour sentir, l'homme a besoin des pleurs.

La Joie a pour symbole une plante brisée,
Humide encore de pluie et couverte de fleurs.

The harvests to ripen are in need of the dew,
To live and to feel, man is in need of tears.
Joy has for its symbol a broken plant,
Still dampened by the rain, and yet covered with blossoms.

APPLICATION

Let us now turn to consider in a practical manner how we can best apply these truths, and what we should do to enjoy life in a real way, and to fill our hours and days with joy. Three things we are called upon to do, and we must learn the art of doing them. What are the three ? (1) Take both the good and the bad, the pleasant and the unpleasant, with equal grace and with an equal mind—please note the two qualities : equal grace and equal mind. (2) Extract the lesson of each event, of every experience, in silence and by study. (3) Apply that lesson by creativeness, which is always a joyous process.

To examine this threefold practice which would make life joyous it is necessary for us to note that it is the soul in us who is the real enjoyer. In our ancient philosophy one of the names of the soul is the enjoyer, *Bhokta*. Do you remember the famous verse of the *Bhagavad Gita ?*

> The Spirit in this body is called Maheshwara, the Great Lord, the Spectator, the Admonisher, the Sustainer, the Enjoyer, and also the Paramatma, the highest Soul.

The soul is the true *Bhokta,* the enjoyer. And unless we take this fact into account, we are going to be confused, for there are pleasures which produce pain, there are joys which are not real joys, there are attractions and attachments which turn to dust and ashes in no time. Look upon the soul as the great enjoyer, but please remember that the soul does not enjoy, cannot enjoy, any and everything. Just as you cannot carve a statue out of mud, so the soul cannot create with anger and greed, with malice and jealousy. Just as you cannot write with a broken pen, so the soul cannot create with a broken conscience. Just as a composer full of music cannot make others listen to it if he has not an appropriate instrument, so also the soul is not able to pour out its great song of life without a pure mind, without an intelligent heart. So in learning to enjoy life truly we must ever take into account the Soul who is the real *Bhokta*, the enjoyer.

It is with the aid of the soul that we have to adopt the threefold exercise we mentioned. Let us study it in detail.

THE MILLS OF GOD

We must learn to take the unpleasant with the pleasant with both equal grace and equal mind. Most of us are apt to seek the pleasant and to shun the unpleasant. If we do not check ourselves in time, if we let ourselves go after the so-called pleasant, we shall go from bad to worse ; we shall weaken our characters, shall dull and even kill the voice of our conscience, and then—diseases and suffering will overtake us in a short time, or after a long time, to-morrow or in another life ; but come they will—diseases of body, mind, heart, and suffering of every description.

Though the mills of God grind slowly
Yet they grind exceeding small ;
Though with patience He stands waiting,
With exactness grinds He all.

Yes, people are fooled because the grinding mills of *Karma* are slow, but they are slow because they are exact. Our difficulties do not begin in wickedness, but in folly ; wickedness grows on the bush of folly ; stop folly and wickedness will stop itself. It is the folly of sense-life and sense-indulgence which we have to stop ; but do not make the mistake that some people have made. Having found out that sense-life and sense-indulgence are the cause of human misery, they go to the other extreme. In the name of soul and of spirit they discard the pleasant and the beautiful and despise their bodies and their senses, instead of training them ; and thus they dwarf and distort their faculty of experiencing the joy of life.

They also are wrong. The exaggerated ascetic is as wrong as the foolish hedonist. Real and practical philosophy says: Neglect neither the senses nor the soul; spirit and matter are equally valuable to nature and to life.

To enjoy life really we need to develop an active faculty and not a passive resignation. There are people who go through their troubles with resignation, but in the process their faces become long, their tempers become sour, their whole outlook becomes bitter. Merely to say "God's will", and to resign ourselves to what we call the inevitable, is to take the wrong way with life. What we need is the power to look at every event of life with equal grace and equal mind. Graciousness and equanimity enable us not merely to go through life, but to enjoy it. When people lose themselves in the excitement and the thrill of happiness they are also bound to be knocked over by a single gust of ill-wind. Happiness is like champagne; it often goes to the head; people do not really enjoy their happiness, for through it they develop pride and foster egotism. That is why to enjoy our happiness we must possess both graciousness and equanimity.

LEARNING THE LESSON

What are they? What is graciousness? It is that attitude of the soul which enables us to be content and gracious with all people and with all events, because we are able to learn from all and to see the good and the noble which is hidden in what looks ugly and crooked. Please do not misunderstand: it does not mean that we have to call impurity purity and be sentimentally stupid and repeat and reiterate: "*There is no disease, there is no evil, there is no folly.*" Alas! There is plenty of all these! The fact must be recognized that sorrow is. But we must not let evil frighten us. We must learn to turn the forces of evil into good by learning the lesson back of every painful event or experience. In our daily life, in all events as they occur hour after hour, we must look for the hidden meaning, the hidden beauty, the hidden good. To do this is to be truly gracious. And what is equanimity? Equal-mindedness is that quality which does not allow our minds to be swayed by our feelings. I admit that this is very difficult, but it *can* be done. To us women who have never done it, the feat of the village maiden who carries one pot full of water on her head, and another adjusted on hip and hand looks almost miraculous, for she does not spill the water ! So with our mind. We need that poise and balance necessary not to spill our experiences !

And that brings us to our next item. We must extract the lessons from each event by careful study and silent examination. That habit of silence is a rare one these days. Our civilization is all noise, all talk. Do not rush with your pleasures and your pains to this friend and that relative. You often thereby lose their lessons and their charm. When you are in some difficulty, do not run to all and sundry exclaiming : "See what has happened ! What shall I do ? What shall I do ?" When some painful and alarming experience comes your way, don't go about crying : "How dreadful !" You will not help yourself or mend matters in that way. Instead of rushing about complaining, sit down and become quiet, and read something which will compose your excitement. And do you know what will then happen ? Half of your difficulties will evaporate. When we are excited our trouble looks very grave ; face it quietly and half of its seriousness vanishes ! Never rush, never be hasty or impulsive. Sit down and say to yourself : "Let us see what has happened." And try to use your mind to ascertain if such a thing did not happen to you before ; and if not, if it did not happen to some one you know. It is a surprising fact, but there is not a single trouble of any one of us which is new and unique. Other people before us have gone through the very *same* troubles, and you may be sure other people will go through them in the future. Now, here it is that the use of study comes in. People want to go through the serious business of life without knowledge. To play the piano, you must study ; to paint or to carve you must study ; to be a doctor, a lawyer, an engineer, you must study. But for the most serious of all occupations—the day-to-day living—we want to do without study ! That is why we fail to enjoy life.

For what does study of human events and human problems do ? It develops the true sense of humour. Without a sense of humour not only is life difficult, life becomes very dangerous. This sense of humour is not the mere capacity to laugh at jokes and to make other people laugh ! No, the real sense of humour uncovers for us the real meaning of any event, of any experience. If we sit down and become quiet when misery assails us or when happiness encompasses us, and if we study, our sense of humour will come to our rescue, and we shall laugh at our own childishness in being elated over the soap-bubbles of life, and we shall smile at our own weaknesses in being depressed because somebody said something nasty about us !

BE CALM

If we remain calm in pleasant circumstances, we shall be able to maintain our composure in painful events. But to secure that faculty of gracious equal-mindedness we must acquire the habit of daily study, of remaining silent every day for a while—for an hour, for half-an-hour. That enables us to create joy in the routine of life. In playing with her children the mother often forgets the worries which those very children cause ! Similarly, in playing with the sorrows of life we overcome them ; nay, more, we learn their meaning and hence we soon learn to enjoy them.

Thus, retaining our mental balance, calmly studying our problems, and able to see the humour of every situation, we are capable of applying the lesson learnt—the third aspect of our exercise—and thus of creating joy in the small duties as in the great ones. The greatest possibility of the human soul is that of creation. Creation implies love and joy and expansion. In the small plain duties of life we must use the creative faculty. In saying "Good Morning" we can create happiness ; in preparing our menus for the day we can create health ; in giving and seeking advice we can create knowledge ; in calling on friends and in receiving them we can create nobility ; not only in receiving gifts can we create gratitude, but in giving presents we can feel grateful that we have people whom we love; and similarly, we can create charity in giving and in receiving; in coming to such meetings as these we can create usefulness.

All day long, all life long, we can create a picture full of beauty and strength and sacrifice, on the smooth canvas of happiness and with the paints with unpleasant odours, for within us is the creator of joy, the enjoyer of bliss. And when death comes, with its help we also can create a new life. For the soul is deathless and birthless, and ever and ever progresses, going from joy to greater joy, from one bliss to another grander bliss, till that soul realises that life itself and the whole universe are the expressions of unfading and unfailing joy.

REINCARNATION AND PUBLIC SERVICES

THEODORA Bosanquet wrote the "Notes on the Way" in the issue of *Time and Tide* for the 17th of September last. *Time and Tide* is a great weekly which serves its readers most usefully without failing to provide them with entertainment. It deserves to be better known and more widely read in our country, not so much for its own sake as for that of Indians who aspire to serve intelligently the great Motherland.

In these "Notes" the writer comments upon reincarnation and on the post-physical theories advanced by Gerald Heard and Aldous Huxley. We shall take this opportunity to draw the readers' attention once more to two most excellent volumes *The Third Morality* by Gerald Heard and *Ends and Means* by Aldous Huxley. About reincarnation Theodora Bosanquet writes :—

> Some one...I think it was Michæl Roberts...once said in a broadcast talk that if Cabinet Ministers knew for certain that they would be reborn soon after death into London slum families social reform would be pushed forward with astonishing speed. It would indeed ! But up to date few people of the Western democracies have taken the idea of reincarnation very seriously. The outlook for the next birth gives almost nobody really cold feet.

There is truth in the remark that few westerners have taken the idea of reincarnation very seriously. This is because, generally speaking, westerners are unpractical people. They look upon philosophical ideas as of no value in their profession or trade or in the political life of their country. They have not taken very seriously the doctrines of Plato or the sayings of Jesus. Ideas and teachings which are most practical are discarded by them ; as, for example, the teaching of "*Resist not evil*" which Jesus stressed, is not believed in although so many of them still look upon Jesus as the only begotten Son of God ; or take the doctrine of ideas put forward by Plato ; or the profound statement of the Great Buddha :— "*Hatred ceaseth not by hatred ; but by love. This is an ancient truth.*" These and many other most practical principles are relegated to the realm of utopias and abstractions. This is because western culture is founded upon an altogether false premise, namely, the supremacy of matter over spirit, of body over soul. Thus spirit is not looked upon as the basic, primary principle, but merely as a secondary by-product, an emanation of matter ; soul is born of the sensorium ; mind is the fruit growing out of the activity of the brain ; psychology is rooted in physiology ; and so on.

DEGENERATION

But it is not only most westerners who, discarding philosophical truths, have become most impractical men and women ; here in our India too, so-called educated people, living mostly in our large cities, also have learnt not to take very seriously the idea of reincarnation and other spiritual facts. They boast about their disbelief, rooted in crass ignorance, while fancying themselves civilized! Many are the sins of omission and commission committed by the foreign rulers of India; but none has been so drastic in its effects as the sin which they committed, perhaps unconsciously to themselves, that of inoculating into the minds of school and college boys and girls the virus of the delusion that an unphilosophical basis of life is practical, useful and correct. British soldiers and civil servants, foreign missionaries and tradesmen all have contributed to the degeneration of the Indian mind, till to-day the sorriest sight in India is presented by the Eurasian mentality of Hindus, Muslims and Parsis; all Indians who adopt ill-suited European habits and manners, and try to pass off as reformed and civilized characters.

But let us turn to reincarnation. Theodora Bosanquet remarks that *"the outlook for the next birth gives almost nobody really cold feet"*; that is also true, and it is not unnatural since the idea is not taken seriously. Those of us who do not believe in the eternal damnation of certain Christian denominations do not shiver when we are consigned to perpetual hell-fire for our opinions. But the credulous and the superstitious who do believe in a heaven of harps and golden streets, and in a hell of ever-continuing torments, do warm up to talk of the singing of the angels, and do get very cold feet indeed at the picture of the sulphurous flames. Similarly, we know of many, the writer herself is one of them, to whom reincarnation is not a mere matter of belief, but one of conviction rooted in reason, and for whom, in consequence, the lines of Sir Edwin Arnold, who translated Buddhist philosophy into English poetry, contain a profound verity :—

> Who toiled a slave may come anew a Prince
> For gentle worthiness and merit won;
> Who ruled a King may wander earth in rags
> For things done and undone.

It is necessary, however, to point out that the teaching of reincarnation is one which inspires hope, and more. As a European friend born and brought up in the Roman Catholic faith recently said to me: *"The idea that this is not the only life on earth, that we shall come back, that there will be another chance, is certainly more humane than that of eternal heaven and hell.*" And after a few moments of silence he added : "*How I wish I could have faith enough to accept reincarnation as the truth* :" Indeed, reincarnation is humane, just, merciful.

NATURE'S PRISONS

The true teaching stresses two facts which are sometimes overlooked : (1) It is the doctrine of human progression and perfection ; the soul of the Cabinet Minister who is callous to slums will be born there, not so much to draw on himself merited punishment, as to get opportunities to learn through experience what slum life means, and presently, morally enriched and rendered more compassionate, he will once again be reborn and, pushing himself to rule in Downing Street, will then utilize his past experience, forgotten as far as brain memory goes, but not lost, existing in the depths of his consciousness. (2) It is the doctrine of self-reliance and therefore of responsibility. Each one of us is responsible for his own mistakes ; we are not at the mercy of some unknown and whimsical god, but we ourselves possess the capacity to acquire knowledge of the moral law in nature, and thus of harnessing it in our own service. This moral law is not something vague and shadowy like the picture of a god on a golden throne on the other side of the sky, but it is susceptible of being observed and understood, just like any law operating in physical nature. Once again, to quote the teaching of the Buddha :—

Pray not ! the Darkness will not brighten ! Ask
  Nought from the Silence, for it cannot speak !
Vex not your mournful minds with pious pains !
  Ah ! Brothers, Sisters ! seek

Nought from the helpless gods by gift and hymn,
  Nor bribe with blood, nor feed with fruit and cakes ;
Within yourselves deliverance must be sought ;
  Each man his prison makes.

Hitler is building his own prison : who dares say that he

will not be born as a Jew to suffer the persecution he has started, and to experience the ghastly suffering of a concentration camp ? He may not believe in reincarnation, but the law in nature will not stop because the Fuehrer does not believe in it ! Hitler acts indeed as if he were not going to die ; as if he could intimidate and conquer death itself ! But die he will.

Premier Chamberlain also is building his own prison : is it not likely—more, would it not be just—that he should be reborn in a position similar to that of Dr. Benes, loving his country yet rendered powerless to serve her ? Is not Mr. Chamberlain responsible for creating this situation for Dr. Benes, and, if so, must he not learn the lesson thereof ?

PRACTICAL APPLICATION

Each one of us is making his own prison ; but nature's prisons are not the gruesome institutions of modern states. Nature is ever compassionate, and her prisons are educative. One of the major instruments of nature's activities is suffering : "*Woe to those who live without suffering.*" But human beings are slow in learning, even through suffering, and that is why nature has to be so patient. Nature repeats the lesson until man learns. The suffering she imposes is but the just effect of our own actions, and hence always has real educative value, unlike that which man-made laws impose.

The most important point, however, in the quotation from *Time and Tide* infers the practical application of reincarnation for improving social conditions. Would not our social and political programmes undergo a tremendous change if reincarnation were accepted as a fact in nature ? What a transformation would take place in international affairs !

Take this very question of prisons and penitentiaries and their much needed reform. Who are the prisoners ? Human souls overpowered by the forces of passion, of lust, of anger, of greed—and what opportunities do our existing jails give them to purify those passions and to learn from their eradication the meaning of real living ?

Or take education. In every country people are talking about a better system of education. Infants, boys and girls, are human souls who have returned to *continue* the work begun in past lives ; much attention is paid to their new bodies, but who bothers about their old souls ?

We could go on showing the great practical usefulness of reincarnation in other departments of public life. But our space is exhausted. In closing, let us once again state the necessity for all Indians, especially our youths, both boys and girls, to take note of the important fact that the truth of that which they are discarding as a superstition of their fossilized forefathers, can be ascertained and it can then be utilized to improve and to enhance our work of alleviating human misery and human suffering, and of bettering the lot of millions of our fellow men.

WORLD CONDITIONS AND INDIA

POLITICAL science teaches its votary the way of expediency and values the quality highly. It is an ingenious device and ranges from the necessary compromises on non-essentials to Machiavelian perfidy, which may save the skin but kills the soul.

There is some talk on the part of one class of Indian politicians about using the weapon of expediency, and taking advantage of the breaking out of a European war, which seems so likely, to wring from Britain India's political independence by embarrassing the Imperial power. To one who is not a politician and to whom moral and spiritual principles of life and of conduct appear superior and more valuable than rules of political strategy and tactics, such a plan is fraught with dangers to India herself. India's freedom should not depend on the arising of embarrassing situations for Britain. It should rest on the moral strength inherent in India herself.

Political bondage is but an outer sign of inner, shall we call it psychic, enslavement from which the Motherland has been suffering. Imperialistic Britain is but a Karmic agent and as such has been instrumental in forging the fetters of India's political slavery. That we, the sons and daughters of India, should aspire to break those fetters is not only natural but necessary. The method of freeing the country from her chains differs with different classes of Indians. All desire India's emancipation, and in this India is thoroughly united, but she is not united as to the way thereto. A large mass of people has agreed to the way of non-violence, but not all who have agreed to it have adopted it. To tread the path of non-violence is to work not only for India's political emancipation, but for complete emancipation. *Purna Swaraj*, complete self-rule, does not mean only political power which can be misused, just as the dictators are misusing it. Those who secure political power through any other means than non-violence are most likely to use that power to control the free will of the people instead of advancing their culture ; to mould the mind of the people after a particular pattern instead of educating them ; to impose upon the people ways of living which curb the very expression of their souls.

SELF RELIANCE NECESSARY

Therefore, to adopt the way of expediency is to be caught in the trap in which all Europe is already caught and from which it wants to escape. There is no *Purna Swaraj* in Europe ; even democracies are not self-governing dominions, though slavery is not so thoroughly developed in Britain, France and Scandinavia, as it is in Russia, Italy and Germany.

Did India's attitude and action during 1914-1918 bring her recompense ? No ; men gave their lives and money was poured out in the hope of arousing generosity in the mind of Britain—a wrong motive. Going to the other extreme and resolving that causing embarrassment will arouse fear in the mind of Britain must also fail ; and even if it succeeds India will not be really better off, but only superficially so.

Why should India bother about pleasing or embarrassing Britain ? This attitude itself is an expression of slave-mentality, and those who talk about adopting it not only go counter to the law of non-violence, but also show lack of confidence in India's moral strength, in the power of her immortal soul.

India has something to do with the tragedy now being enacted on the European stage. War may or may not engulf Europe, but chaos prevails there and sooner or later the clouds will burst and the storm will rage. After that ? Along what lines will reconstruction take place ? If India has not proven her own moral strength by following intelligently the plans of Gandhiji she will have nothing to offer to the world. Nay more—she will be tempted to try out some new panacea manufactured by those who survive the tragedy, the main ingredient in which panacea will be violence and hatred.

It is imperative and pressing that India should perceive more and more clearly that her political emancipation, to be real and in conformity with her own genius, must follow the main lines of Gandhiji's plans. The path of non-violence interferes with a speedy march, but once the strength of *satyagraha* is clearly recognized the nation can steadily and surely go ahead from success to glory. India must assimilate the lesson of self-reliance, dependence on nought else but her own moral strength. This line of ideation, let us hope, will prevail. Not on any external and extraneous factor, but on our own moral and soul-force should we learn to rely.

STUDY GANDHIJI'S PHILOSOPHY.

THE race of men is ever trying to resolve the great duality of nature represented by the words—*thought* and *action.* Conflict in the individual mind arises because man is not able to square his actions with his thoughts, his methods with his motives, his daily routine of life with the vision of his inner ideals, however vague and dim that vision. Philosophies are but means to cleanse his perceptions and to enable him to see his ideals a little less vaguely. Evolving man is ever seeking from nature a basis of thought which becomes his basis for speech and action. Great thinkers, in every field of life, have succeeded a little better than the average man in securing a basis for thought. To the record of their thoughts mankind in general looks for a basis for its own thinking, and each reader of the record adapts the thinker's findings tc his own mental urge. But many are the philosophies which are false, for their authors have misread the divine mind working in nature. On the other hand, some philosophies are only partially correct to the extent that their authors have read correctly the writing of and in nature, the great book. Only those sages who have read nature correctly and wholly are the most reliable friends of humanity, and they alone provide for us all the right basis of thought which enables us to act rightly, that is, righteously.

CONFLICT

There is a mighty conflict now going on in every country in the world : Britain cannot resolve her ideation on liberty and on justice with her actions, say, in India, or her recent letting down of Czechoslovakia. France and several American Republics are facing a similar conflict. Germany, enslaved by a handful of men, so barbaric in her cruelty and so conceited in her new-found strength, is also in the grip of that conflict, for the very orgy of cruelty and conceit is making the rise of an *Aryan,* that is, a noble, Germany an utter impossibility; while she ideates in terms of being noble, she acts ignobly. So also in Russia: great ideals of liberty and of peace on the one hand; the action of the killing of citizens for their opinions on the other. Here in our India the same conflict exists.

Recently, more than once, Gandhiji has complained about Congress politicians not acting out the ideas and the ideals which they have accepted as being true. This cannot be all due to rank hypocrisy. In a very great measure it must be due to the non-understanding (not even the misunderstanding) of the philosophy which is the soul of Gandhiji's actional programme. The programme is well known to all, but is it understood by all? Are its implications and its significance assimilated by a large number of minds among those which are directing public affairs? It looks as if a careful study of, followed by some reflection upon, Gandhiji's philosophy, which is the spiritual soul or *Buddhi* of his programme, is a pressing need of this hour.

Week by week people read what Gandhiji has to say in the columns of *Harijan,* but ere the next number comes out what has already been published and read is forgotten! *Harijan* is looked upon as an ordinary newspaper and in a busy life many an active politician and publicist misses the significance of many a column of that weekly. This is far more serious than it looks on the surface. Ideas rule the world; thoughts lead to actions. Unless by study and reflection the mind is made clear and its perceptions are freed from the influence of the day-to-day struggle for existence—in shop, court or secretariat—there is bound to be confusion, neglect and failure. Nourishment for the soul, the thinker who uses the mind, is as necessary, if not more so, than food for the body, which so many give to it even three and four times a day. Busy leaders and politicians make time to eat, and certainly it is possible for them to reserve a period also for the company of holy books and for deriving from them the nourishment necessary for the soul. Besides, knowing as they must the problems which are coming up before them during the day, they can and they should seek the views and the opinions of Gandhiji and give them the serious consideration that they deserve.

AN UNFAIR DEMAND

But there is another pressing need which has to be fulfilled ; a need not of the busy political leaders but of the mass of political followers, especially the young. It seems imperative that young men and young women who aspire to serve their country by enlisting themselves under the banner of Gandhiji be given an opportunity to learn his philosophy *ere* they are made active in carrying out his programme. To ask them to act thus and so because Gandhiji says so is not a fair position to place them in—not fair to the leader, or to the follower. To act because mental and moral assent has been gained from conscience *after* study, reflection and understanding, is not only a fair stand ; it is also one which will endure.

As one who is not actively engaged in the political struggle the writer has a slight advantage in judging the situation over those who are very likely to be befogged by the dust of the battlefield on which they are engaged. It seems that in carrying out Gandhiji's programme our educated cities and towns are likely to occasion most concern to the leader and to his faithful and devoted helpers ; the villages will be found more ready to adopt his views, for they have little to unlearn. The unlearning process of towns and cities is very slow and some effort needs to be made to organize small study groups to acquire a knowledge of Gandhiji's philosophy—his ideas and his ideals, his views and his opinions on a hundred topics. These study groups should not be for mere debate and discussion, but primarily for the understanding and the grasping of Gandhiji's thoughts.

WHICH WAY ?

The present offers a very suitable opportunity and this article is prompted by it. We have received a publication entitled *The Gandhi Sutras,* composed by Professor D. S. Sarma, Principal of Pachaiyappa's College of Madras. Professor

Sarma is well known for his translations of the *Gita* and the *Kathopanishad* and for his writing of a very useful *Primer of Hinduism.* He has composed 108 *sutras* in Sanskrit and an English translation of each is followed by well-selected extracts from the writings of Gandhiji. The *sutras* are divided into three chapters on : (1) "The General Dharma" ; (2) "The Dharma of Satyagraha" ; and (3) "The Dharma of the Varieties of Satyagraha." This small book of 150 pages contains a wealth of material brought together in compact form. The *sutras* are according to subjects and cover a large portion of the wide field of Gandhiji's philosophy. We hope that the next edition will contain a good index to facilitate the work of publicists, educators and teachers if, by any chance, any of them adopt the plan suggested above and organise study groups in our towns and cities.

We understand that a new edition of Gandhiji's *Hind Swaraj* is to be published soon. That little book with a great message can also well be made a text-book of such study-groups.

It may not be very long before India will have to face a great decision ; which way to go ? Shall we who love the Motherland choose the path which is destroying the Occident or shall we carve out for ourselves, and for the future benefit of the world a path of our own, build out of the ancient material a new road and proclaim to the world :—

> "The World is indeed the family of God."
> "Love is the only remedy for hate."
> "India points the way."

COLONEL ARTHUR OLVER

O. B., C. M. G., F. R. C. V. S.,

Expert Adviser in Animal Husbandry, Imperial Council of Agricultural Research, India. was born 1875 and educated at Godolphin School and Royal Veterinary College, London, Joined Army Veterinary Dept., 1899; Served in the South African War, 1901-02 (Queen's Medal, 5 clasps); Egyptian Army, 1906; P. V. O., Egyptian Army, and Sudan Civil Veterinary Service, 1907; Asst. D. G., Army Veterinary Service, War Office, 1908; Great War, 1914-18, (Despatches three times. Bt. Lt.-Col.); Canada and U. S. A., 1917; A. D. V. S., Egypt Command, 1922-27; A. D. V. S., S. Command, 1928; D. D. V. S., N. 1929-30.

We are indebted to the Animal Husbandry Commissioner with the Government of India for permission to reproduce the following note which was prepared by Sir Arthur, before he left India.

THE SYSTEMATIC IMPROVEMENT OF LIVE-STOCK IN INDIA

As I am shortly vacating my appointment of Animal Husbandry Expert, I feel that I ought to place on record, for the information of those who have not had the same opportunities, the conclusions which I have formed after eight years of close study of the problem of live-stock improvement in India.

SYSTEMATIC BREEDING CONTROL

For improvement on the vast scale which is needed, it is obvious that few Governments can afford to undertake the actual breeding, on Government farms, of sufficient numbers of suitable sires. Nor can they afford to maintain the large numbers of special staff which would be required for systematic live-stock improvement throughout the country, in addition to the extensive provincial Veterinary Departments which, owing to the lack of veterinary practitioners in India, Provincial and State administrations are compelled to maintain for the control of disease.

Experience has, moreover, shown that it is generally more effective and cheaper to help and encourage village breeders to improve their own stock, by systematic breeding and disease control in the villages, than to attempt to breed the very large numbers of sires required, but this can only be done where adequate and suitably trained staff exists, in close touch with the live-stock of the country. Such staff, suitably distributed at veterinary hospitals or other centres is therefore essential and as it is not possible to deal with the whole country at once, it follows that control should first be concentrated in the areas where the best recognized breeds are at present found and where the breeding of improved live-stock is economically feasible. Before deciding on a plan of campaign, it is thus necessary to make a rough survey to determine broadly the areas in which definite types at present exist and to choose suitable breeding centres, for each breed, at which suitably trained personnel is likely always to be available to carry on the systematic control, which is necessary for lasting progress.

PEDIGREE REGISTRATION NECESSARY

It is true that some improvement, particularly in the first generation, can be achieved by buying non-pedigree bulls and issuing them to villages where the cattle are poor, even where strict breeding control does not exist. But lasting progress cannot be expected unless arrangements are made to provide an adequate supply of sires whose genetic origin is known and to carry on systematic registration, not only of bulls and their progeny but also of selected cows whose approved progeny could in course of time be registered as pedigree stock. This seems to me the only way in which it will be possible to provide, throughout the country, for the gradual breeding up of a cadre of pedigree stock, which could eventually be drawn upon to provide the great numbers of pedigree animals which are needed for systematic live-stock improvement.

It will probably be found that the areas in which the best cattle are bred, and which should be developed first, are areas in which free grazing is scanty and where attention is paid to the production of fodder crops to supplement such free grazing as is available. Under fodder crops, I include cultivated or properly managed grazing, the most valuable of all fodder crops, and grain crop residues of good feeding value such as *kadbi*.

It has in fact been found in India, as in other countries, that if full advantage is taken of the manurial effect of their urine and dung, the gross return from the land and profit per acre can be greatly increased by well-fed live-stock under a balanced system of mixed farming. Moreover, properly managed live-stock, besides increasing the return from the land, has the effect of equalizing the income over a series of years, while in mixed farming a large proportion of the return is obtained from animal products, such as dairy products, without which it is not, as a rule, practicable to provide a satisfactory diet for the people, and at the same time comparatively high priced work-cattle can be bred. For these reasons, I have for years past advocated that mixed farming with reasonably high yielding cows should be adopted wherever possible as likely to be the only way of enabling agriculture in India to meet the ever-increasing pressure on the land.

FOREIGN BREEDS UNNECESSARY

The improvement of live-stock, and of the cattle in particular, is indeed a matter of great social as well as economic importance and urgency in India and it is necessary to emphasise that it has now been amply shown that it is unnecessary, and unsound as a general policy, to attempt to introduce European breeds of cattle into India. Systematic investigation, carried out by the Animal Husbandry Bureau of the Imperial Council of Agricultural Research, has shown that, by careful selection and proper feeding and management, herds of pure Indian dairy cattle have already been produced within twenty-five years, which can more than hold their own in India, with European cattle and with the best Indian buffaloes, in economy of milk and butter-fat production [Kartha, 1934]. Already they exceed the average milk yield of commerical dairy herds in Europe and America and there is every evidence that these results are likely to be steadily improved upon for years to come, while it has clearly been demonstrated that, even with the best of care and under the best possible conditions, cattle of European origin always tend to degenerate in India.

Nor should it be forgotten that, if a policy of using imported cattle were adopted, it would be necessary to keep up, year after year, a huge supply of pedigree sires, purchased abroad at very high prices, the cost of which would generally be prohibitive. Without most careful and expert breeding control the use of foreign cattle for stud purposes is moreover very dangerous. Indeed, it has already done incalculable harm by destroying valuable pure-bred herds of Indian cattle by unscientific mating.

It is far sounder, therefore, to effect systematic improvement by means of selective breeding and better feeding and management of indigenous stock than to attempt to grade them up by the importation of stock of European origin. Systematic breeding control by a suitably trained Government Department, devoted solely to the interests of live-stock, thus appears to be the only sound policy and it is now clear that the most far-reaching result so far obtained in India have been secured under some system of providing approved sires; purchased as far as possible from breeders in the best breeding areas and issued under subsidy or on concession terms under the supervision and control of such a department.

PART PAYMENT SYSTEM

Probably the cheapest, most effective and lasting method of all appears to be to purchase suitable sires in the best breeding areas and to issue them under some system of part payment ; the animals becoming the property of their allottees as soon as their total cost has been repaid to Government, in annual instalments. Some such system has been extensively adopted in various parts of India and the following terms are suggested as likely to prove suitable :—

(*a*) When a village in a cattle-breeding tract requires a new bull, the local representative of the department responsible for cattle-breeding should arrange, in collaboration with the principal breeders of the area concerned, to purchase a suitable bull, either in the same area or from an area where a better class of animal of the same breed can be obtained.

(*b*) The bull should be issued to a selected custodian, on payment of 25 per cent of the cost price, and a register kept by the department of his services and progency, the allottee being permitted to charge a reasonable service fee on the condition that the bull is always well-fed and exercised and preference given to registered females.

(*c*) At the end of the first year and each following year, the allottee should pay a further 25 per cent of the cost price, until the whole has been repaid to Government.

(*d*) The bull would then become the property of the allottee who would be at liberty to sell or otherwise dispose of it but not to retain it for service in the same area beyond the 4th year, by which time a fresh bull should be available, supplied by Government on the same terms, so as to obviate a bull covering his own daughters.

(*e*) Normally provided that he had proved a satisfactory custodian, a new bull would be issued to the same allottee as before, who would thus continue to pay to Government each year, 25 per cent of the cost of a new bull.

In this way, the bulk of the funds provided by Government for the supply of suitable bulls could be recovered and a great deal done for the systematic improvement of cattle at comparatively small cost. Should the bull die or prove unsatisfactory, the loss should, however, be borne by Government as a part of their contribution to departmentally controlled live-stock improvement.

Such a system has the advantages that it provides a remunerative market for well-developed young males from registered parents and, as the bull eventually becomes his own property, it would be in the custodian's interest to look after it properly.

It may be necessary to pay a small subsidy to ensure proper maintenance but experience has generally shown that there is not much difficulty in finding suitable custodians willing to take bulls from breeders, under some such system, a great stimulus is given to better breeding and proper care and management of stock.

COWS TO BE REGISTERED

To get the best out of such a system, it is necessary that a few of the very best cows in the areas served by approved bulls should also be registered and they and their approved progeny tattooed as selected stock. Where good cows do not exist, it may be necessary to buy a few and issue them on similar terms to selected ryots, on their undertaking to feed them properly and mate them regularly with approved bulls. Such cows should obviously be of the same breed as the approved bulls working in the district and should be good milkers. Registers of all such stock should be maintained at veterinary hospitals or other suitable centres, and annual cattle shows should be held at suitable fairs at which prizes and *sanads* would be given and suitable young bulls selected, annually, for purchase by Government.

To ensure proper development of these and to carry on systematic breeding of the very best strains available, particularly of dairy breeds, it will generally be found advisable for each Government to maintain at least one central breeding and rearing farm, within easy distance of a city where some experimental breeding can be carried on and a dairy maintained at moderate cost, and where elementary provincial instruction could be given in dairying and animal husbandry.

In order to build up an adequate cadre of pedigree animals within a reasonable space of time, it might be advisable also, for the first few years, to select, at local shows, a small percentage of the best heifers by approved bulls, but not out of registered dams, and to mark them as selected females whose progeny would become eligible for registration as pedigree stock, if found suitable in following generations.

Any stock produced from these females, by a pedigree bull, would in any case be considerably enhanced in value but to ensure proper care and supervision of all registered females and their progeny, it would be necessary to refuse to register any young stock not up to standard ; in size as well as conformation and type.

Registration should in fact be withdrawn if pedigree females or their progeny are not maintained in good condition or if a cow has proved an unsatisfactory breeder.

YOUNG BULLS MUST BE REMUNERATIVE

It is essential that the prices paid by Government for sires should be sufficient to encourage local breeders to feed their breeding females and young stock well and, before issuing a bull to a village, Government should insist that all other bulls, in the areas to be served by approved bulls, are castrated or otherwise disposed of.

SYSTEMATIC CASTRATION ESSENTIAL

In any policy of live-stock improvement, one of the most important items must be the vigorous prosecution of systematic castration to eliminate all scrub bulls before they are old enough to commence service. Unfortunately the very degenerate scrub bulls commonly seen are very active servers and unless this side of the problem is successfully dealt with, little permanent progress can be expected. This work could under veterinary supervision be carried out by suitably trained stockmen along with other animal husbandry work.

ANIMAL HUSBANDRY DEPARTMENT ESSENTIAL

The above are the general lines but pedigree breeding is expert animal husbandry work which can be satisfactorily controlled only by suitably trained staff devoted solely to live-stock. It cannot be done by men, however trained, whose interest in live-stock is only subsidiary. In every province or state there should therefore be an expert department capable of undertaking systematic breeding control along these lines ; particularly in the best breeding centres for each important breed.

In addition to exercising systematic control of breeding operations and carrying on systematic castration and inoculation against disease, the animal husbandry department should maintain registers of all pedigree stock and should be responsible for the periodical inspection of all animals which are the property of Government or under subsidy, and should also keep in touch with their progeny.

TRAINED STOCKMEN NEEDED

To carry out this class of work, on the very big scale which is needed, some cheaper staff than qualified veterinarians will probably be found necessary and, if adequate progress is to be made, it seems certain that, as recommended by the Animal Husbandry Wing of the Board of Agriculture, it will be necessary to supplement provincial or state veterinary departments by employing suitable stockmen who, after six months veterinary training, could assist veterinary assistant surgeons in carrying out systematic castration and inoculation against disease and in the tattooing, registration and inspection of pedigree stock.

While carrying out this work in the villages, stockmen would be brought in close contact with village live-stock, of all kinds, and should be of great assistance to provincial veterinary departments in obtaining early information of disease. For this reason and to ensure proper supervision of castration and inoculation, it is clear that all stockmen should be under veterinary control.

By these means the whole of the provincial veterinary staff could be made full use of for systematic live-stock improvement and it should certainly be cheaper to strengthen existing veterinary departments by providing specially trained men in special lines such as dairying, sheep and goats and poultry than to attempt to provide the very large numbers of special staff which would be required if veterinary staff were not employed for live-stock improvement. Such specially trained men are necessary to form properly constituted animal husbandry departments capable of dealing authoritatively with every branch of animal husbandry work and should in any case be provided.

CLASS OF CATTLE TO BE BRED

Obviously the decision as to the class and breed of cattle to be used for breeding purposes is a matter of the first importance. As a general rule, it can be taken that where reasonably well-developed and efficient cattle already exist,. it .is sound policy to endeavour to raise them to higher standards, by selective breeding combined with better feeding and management and effective disease control. For such work the method of issuing bulls on part payment and registration suggested above should prove the most satisfactory.

FAULTY FEEDING

In areas where cattle are hopelessly degenerate and inefficient, it may be taken that the main cause is improper feeding due, as, for example, is commonly the case throughout the rice-breeding tracts, to feeding mainly on defective fodder or to some mineral or other deficiency in the food stuffs available in the locality. For example, it has recently been shown that there are large areas in India where mineral deficiencies are so marked a feature that the breeding of good cattle is impracticable without special feeding. Other observations have shown that vitamin deficiencies are liable to be of great importance to stock-breeders in areas where there is a long dry period, unless adequate provision is made for the growing of fodder or semi-fodder crops which can be fed green in sufficient quantity to maintain health throughout the year. On the other hand, my own observations, supported by data obtained from farms under Government control in different parts of India, show that, with proper feeding and management, well-developed, efficient cattle can be produced and maintained except in areas, such as certain parts where the whole country is badly waterlogged during a great part of the year or where cattle are so infested with biting flies, ticks and other parasites that it is difficult for them even to maintain life.

DRIER TRACTS

As a general rule, it can be taken that throughout India the best cattle are bred in the drier tracts where free grazing is scanty and the grass grown is not coarse and the fact may be taken as a sure indication that the coarse grass produced in forest areas, under heavy rainfall conditions, is not sufficiently nutritious to produce good stock. In wet areas it is unlikely therefore that much improvement can be effected by the mere introduction of stock accustomed to drier conditions and more highly nutritious food stuffs. The policy should therefore be to endeavour to improve the local breeds by careful selection and systematic animal husbandry work designed particularly to provide better fodder and to control parasites which, in such areas, are nearly always a serious cause of degeneracy and ill-health.

In the rice tracts the degeneration of cattle which occurs appears to be largely due to the fact that the people are not cattle-minded and take no steps to provide nutritious and health-giving fodder or semi-fodder crops such as the legumes and grasses or *juar kadbi* which are extensively grown by cattle-breeders in districts where the best stock are bred and reared. It seems, however, that crops of this kind could usually by produced in the rice tracts if suitable seed were thrown in on the last watering of the paddy fields.

WELL-FED MILCH CATTLE

In areas where the cattle are hopelessly poor and inefficient, it may even be necessary to introduce better stock from other parts of India to demonstrate to the ryot that good cattle, and in particular milch cattle are very profitable if properly fed and maintained on the holding in such a way as to ensure that as little as possible of the manurial value of their urine and droppings is wasted. With a view to making rice growers more cattle-minded, I have recommended to provinces and states within easy reach of Calcutta that they should take advantage of the opportunity of obtaining good Hariana cows there, at moderate prices, and hand them over to selected ryots, on part payment terms, on the condition that the allottees undertake to introduce a sufficient proportion of suitable legumes or grasses into their rotation to supplement the usual rice straw ration. Such a system should make economical milk production possible and should enable the stock to be maintained in better condition all the year round. I have also suggested that a sufficient quantity of silage should be made for each of these cows from young grass or a leguminous or other suitable crop, quantities of which could be grown during the monsoon in such areas and cut at an early stage of growth, to ensure that sufficient succulent fodder would be available during the dry season. Under departmental supervision such cows should prove a valuable source of additional income besides producing useful young bulls or bullocks and should be useful as an object lesson not only to the allottees but to their neighbours as to the value of superior stock if properly fed. For rice tracts within easy reach of Calcutta, I have therefore recommended small type compact Hariana bulls and they are doing well and proving highly popular. In similar areas, not within easy reach of Calcutta, I have in the past recommended Tharparkar cattle and I consider that they or, even better, good Rath cattle should prove the most suitable. Both are very compact and hardy and good milkers and Rath cattle in particular are quick, active workers.

FODDER-CROPS ESSENTIAL

It is a truism that no good stock can be bred without proper feeding and management and that the best blood in the world is useless unless it can be given the best opportunity to express itself in development. I have already mentioned that through-

BEN MISRA
WRITER & JOURNALIST

out India the best cattle are to be found in areas where free-grazing is scanty and where in consequence stock-owners are compelled to grow sufficient nutritious fodder-crops or semi-fodder crops to supplement such free grazing as may be available. Throughout vast tracts of India these facts are however either not known or ignored and attempts are made to provide for the want of really efficient cattle by maintaining large numbers of poor stock, on free grazing, which are incapable of producing useful work bullocks and are of little value either as milk producers, or as soil fertilizers, since their droppings are mostly deposited on land not under cultivation. To emphasize this point it may be mentioned that while a good pair of well-developed oxen may easily fetch from three to four hundred rupees it is possible to obtain large numbers of the poor type of bullock bred in forest areas, where coarse grass is produced in large quantities, at an average of Rs. 10 a head.

MILK AND DAIRY PRODUCTS

We have recently had well authenticated figures from a large number of cattle-breeders which show that though the breeding of work bullocks is regarded as their main business, the profit derived from the sale of moderate priced bullocks bred mainly on free grazing is small compared with what is derived from the milk or other dairy produce obtained from their mothers. The truth of this has been verified in other parts of India, where conditions are quite different, and if full benefit is to be derived from Indian agriculture, it is, I believe, essential that more should be made of the milk which, by proper feeding and management, under a proper system of mixed farming, could be derived from the mother of the working ox. As a side line of mixed farming milk can in fact be very cheaply produced and, provided that arrangements can be made to provide a steady market, might well prove the most profitable of all cottage industries and one which the women-folk of the family could usually undertake. Indeed to increase fertility and the return from crops every cultivator should devote a sufficient proportion of his land to the production of fodder or suitable leguminous crops, so that the whole area would come under such crops and be grazed by stock at least one year in every five or six.

CULTIVATION OF FODDER-CROPS

The cultivation of leguminous and other fodder-crops such as lucerne, berseem, *senji*, *guara*, Sudan and Guinea grass and crested wheat grass and semi-fodder crops such as *juar*, should therefore be encouraged and the great value of a reserve of ensilage for use in the dry season should be explained. Reasonable concessions to cultivators to grow such crops should be given and every effort should be made to popularize silos for conserving grass or green crops cut at an early stage of growth. Experience has in fact shown that valuable working cattle can be satisfactorily bred and maintained on the holding, by growing legumes and fodder-crops in the rotation, and that their owners, in addition to producing useful work bullocks can thereby obtain a most valuable addition to their income, from suitable cows.

Such a system, however, postulates the breeding of a reasonable amount of milk into the recognized working breeds and I am sure, from my own observations and from the observations of experienced breeders of Indian cattle that, up to milk yields considerably beyond what would be necessary, this can be done without damage to the stock as work animals.

PRODUCTION OF CHEAP MILK

Probably the greatest boon which any philanthrophist could confer on India to-day would be to at least double the total output of milk. To do so is, however, no easy matter. Milk production on special dairy farms is only profitable where there is an easily accessible market for liquid milk, at prices much higher than the poor can pay, and it seems that reliance will have to be placed on the production of milk as a side line of mixed farming if cheap milk is to be made available in adequate amounts throughout the country. The production of milk, at the same time as useful bullocks, as a cottage industry, supplementary but subsidiary to the main activities of the cultivator, in fact appears to be the only solution.

Government and wealthy philanthrophists ought therefore to do everything possible to encourage this by investigating the problems involved in the handling, processing and transportation of milk under Indian conditions and in the manufacture of ghee, *khoa*, etc., and by establishing collecting centres at suitable points, all over the country, at which a steady market would be made available, all the year round for milk, cream, ghee and other cottage produce such as eggs and honey. They should also assist poor cultivators to secure good cows as well as reliable seed from which to produce the succulent fodder-crops which are necessary to make even the best cows really profitable.

The prices given at such centres need not be high. Indeed it would be a mistake to make them so because the main purpose should be to bring milk and dairy produce in India to price levels at which poor people would be able to buy them in reasonable quantities. At present milk, even at the rates at which it is obtainable in rural areas, is much more costly than in countries where dairying is a well-organized rural industry and, for years past, I have emphasized that until steady markets are provided in rural areas, at which small producers can be assured of a steady outlet for their produce, very little can be done.

On the other hand there is ample experience to show that wherever such centres have been established, in various parts of India, the supply of milk has rapidly increased and the villagers have become more prosperous.

The usual system is to obtain cows through the milk-buyer and to pay for them in milk so that the cows eventually become the sole property of the milk producer.

CALVES SHOULD BE WEANED

In this connection, it is of the greatest importance that village producers should be taught that it is easily practicable and profitable to wean the calves of Indian cows at birth and rear them by hand, in the same way as has become the universal practice in all progressive dairy countries. Until it is, little general progress can be hoped for in improving the average yields of Indian breeds of dairy cattle but the general adoption of this practice would have a very beneficial and far reaching effect on the development of dairying in India.

LACK OF GREEN FODDER

The need for fresh green fodder to keep animals in health is well recognized all the world over but in many parts of India there is difficulty in obtaining any fresh growth for several months each year and during the past few years we have obtained definite evidence that a great deal of harm is done to breeding stock owing to the lack of essential vitamins which this lack of fresh green food entails. For example, on a certain farm where the lack of fresh green food was extreme, as many as 40 per cent of otherwise well-fed and managed cows, which did not receive any green food for several months each year, produced blind or otherwise badly developed calves which usually did not survive and if they survived were of no value. A careful study of their feeding and investigations, carried out at the Mukteswar Research Institute, has shown that this condition was due entirely to lack of green food and since an adequate supply of locally grown green fodder has been made available the cows have produced normal calves, thus making it possible again to carry on breeding satisfactorily in this herd. This was an extreme case but it is clear that a great deal of harm is done, each year, to cows which have an inadequate supply of freshly grown green fodder and that every effort should be made to provide a sufficient supply of such fodder, or silage prepared from young grass or other immature fodder crop, all the year round.

OTHER CLASSES OF STOCK

Sheep, goats, poultry and horse breeding could be dealt with from veterinary hospitals or other suitable centres along similar general lines ; by providing suitable sires or breeding units on an instalment system of payment. In this way pedigree breeding could be carried on under the supervision of the department concerned, and this department, besides obtaining suitable breeding stock and arranging for the necessary exchanges of males, should be responsible for giving advice as to the proper care and treatment of stock, in health as well as in disease.

BEN MISRA

WRITER & JOURNALIST

The eldest son of the late Pandit Rameshvar Prasad Misra and Braj Rani Misra an ancient aristrocratic family of Lucknow was born in February, 1930. He was educated at Canning College, Lucknow and the University of Washington. He won the All-College Prize in Public Speaking in open contest while a second year student at Canning College, and made his debut in the magazine world of America with an article in "*Current History*" while a sophomore at Washington. He graduated from the School of Journalism, University of Washington, after five years' intensive study of all the varied phases and features of American journalism, fetching a first in Journalism and English Literature.

Ben Misra practised journalism in America for twelve years, and attended five Annual Sessions of the Washington Press Conference. In recognition of his work as a writer and journalist he was made a member of *Sigma Delta Chi* (American Society of Professional Journalists) and of *Sigma Upsilon* (American Society of Professional Writers). Membership of these exclusive American societies signifies the hallmark of literary and journalistic excellence. This was followed by an invitation, by the Uuiversity of Washington, to offer courses in Indian literature and English literature in India and he offered similar courses at various university centres. He also lectured on Indian literature, culture, civilization, religion, philosophy and politics before distinguished clubs, forums, churches, synagogues, college assemblies and inter-university gatherings. During the storm of controversy that followed the publication of Miss Mayo's *Mother India* he carried on a vigorous campaign of enlightenment from the press, pulpit, platform and radio.

Ben Misra writes articles, short stories, serials, features, book reviews, plays and photoplays ; edits books of popular interest, both fiction and non-fiction and is an adept at almost every type of writing.

He is keenly interested in the progress of Indian journalism along American lines, prevention of cruelty to animals, Hindu-Muslim unity, the abolition of war, and social reform.

In the article which follows, Ben Misra, asks us to bear in mind that Chirraappoonnjee, Dhurandharam, Rangammayyah and Bhayankaram are fictitious and have no reference to any particular place or person. The article is offered by the author to fellow newspapermen in India in the humble hope that it may prove instrumental in giving a new orientation to Indian jouralism along modern American lines.

JOURNALISM IN INDIA AND AMERICA

AS I stepped off the deck of a pleasure boat in Bombay one warm summer evening and entered the Gateway to India, a young newspaper reporter approached me and asked : "What do you think of journalism in this country ?"

The question was in order. I had just returned after twelve years' journalistic work in the United States, and was trying to negotiate the formidable stone wall that the Indian newspapers presented, and feeling rather lost and baffled. "There are no snakes in Iceland," I replied.

"You mean—you don't mean—you can't, of course—do you really—er—" the young man stuttered in surprise.

"I do," I answered.

"Indian journalism boasts of some of the greatest names in the world," he reminded me with enthusiasm. "Rudyard Kipling, Mahatma Gandhi, Lokemanya Tilak, Pandit Madan Mohan Malaviya, Sir Phiroz Shah Mehta, Sir Surendra Nath Banerji—these are the torch-bearers of Indian journalism."

"No doubt. But we don't think of Kipling and Gandhi and Malaviya as journalists. Gandhi, Malaviya, Tilak and others you mentioned shine as great Congress leaders. They saw what the Fourth Estate could do for them, employed it to advance the cause, and in their hands it became a tremendous power in the land. But these men do not stand out as journalists, as Lord Northcliffe in England, and Joseph Pulitzer, William Randolph Hearst, Arthur Brisbane, and Ochs do in America."

"Then you mean we have not produced any real journalists in India ?"

"We have. Sisir Kumar Ghosh and Mati Lal Ghosh and their successors. Ghosh Brothers were the fathers of Indian journalism, and the *Amrit Bazar Patrika* to day is a monument to their journalistic genius. Mr. Robert Knight, who was first the Editor of the *Times of India* and later went to Calcutta and founded the *Statesman*, would have made a great journalist anywhere."

"And others ? Mr. Chirraappoonjee ? Mr. Rangamayyah ? Mr. Dhurandharam ?"

"Sacred cows of Indian journalism ! But sacred cows are not necessarily milch cows. Chirraappoonjee and Dhurandharam ! Mountains have been in labour and produced a mouse !"

"Will you elucidate that ?"

"Gladly. Nothing more pleasant than to talk shop." And here is, in effect, what I told him. He was a clever chap, and having got the interviewee started, he held his peace.

Journalism as an art and a craft, as a science and a trade has not developed its peculiar technique in India, as it has in America and to a certain extent in England. Our newspapers are carbon copies and smudgy caricatures and third and fourth hand imitations of English newspapers. No, it would be wrong to judge of English newspapers from the Indian product.

We in India have been content to let things drag and drift and shift and slide much as they would. Let well enough alone, has been our motto in journalism, as in everything else. We have not rolled up our sleeves and gone to the copy desk and the press room with will and determination to manufacture a really first class newspaper. Our newspapers are views papers and propaganda sheets, self-opinionated, smugly self-satisfied, gazing spell-bound at the miracle of their greatness and crowing in conceit. News is at a discount, editorial opinion is at a premium, and dullness and boredom hold unrelenting sway.

Once in a while some one groans : "Let us teach journalism in our universities." Instantly the sacred cows in their sheds and the chanticleers in their coops set up a howl of protest.

We never learned anything. And look at us now! Uncrowned kings, laying down the law for everything, criticizing everybody at will. There is nothing to teach in journalism. Journalism can't be taught."

COMPARISON

Certainly not, if the idea is to teach what passes for journalism in India. Print the Reuter, A. P. and U. P. telegrams, print dispatches from your sleepy correspondents, write three editorials, labored and long if not exactly learned, and you have your Indian newspapers, crude and stale as the first newspaper published in China two thousand years ago. Nothing to teach in that. But if you would produce a newspaper, as newspapers are produced in America and, from example and precept, in the neighboring countries of Canada, Hawaii, the Phillipine Islands and Japan, then the whole works will have to be streamlined. And you can't achieve that unless journalistic progress is not merely a means but an end in itself, and you go after it in dead earnest and impart instruction in journalism along scientific and systematic lines.

When in America journalists gather in conferences, they talk of the technique of editorial writing and news display, of intelligible headlines, front-page editorials, popular features, law of libel, linotype machines, display and billboard advertising, and other cognate matters and details. When Indian journalists foregather, they grow loud and vehement against the Press Act and indulge in their favorite pastime of venting their spleen against the foreign government.

"Let us teach journalism," a reed shaken by the wind suggests. "Let us not!" someone else comes down on him like a ton of bricks. "Why?" someone enquires. "Why not?" somebody else informs him. And they wipe the perspiration off their high brows, decide to call it a day, and disperse with a self-satisfied yawn. One thing that Indian journalists never, never discuss—why, I do not profess to know—is the niceties of journalistic technique. The result? Indian newspapers are what they were fifty years ago: dull and heavy and boring—dull as ditch water, heavy as lead and heavier, and boring to tears.

Compared with journalism in America, Indian journalism is primitive and prehistoric. It is not aggressive and progressive. It is stale and mildewy. There is a rich odour of ancientry about it.

I pick up an Indian newspaper and read :

PUNJAB MAIL
MURDER ECHO

NEVER SAW DECEASED

ACCUSED'S STORY
IN BHOPAL COURT

What in the blank is this all about ? The first bank tells me nothing. The second is equally meaningless, and the third, as if to make up for the puerility of the first two, is ambiguous. It may mean that the accused has told some story in the court, or someone has told a story about the accused. There is nothing in the three banks to induce me to read the item.

A second heading announces :

BOSE AND NEHRU
DECLINE

That looks serious. Bose has been declining. But Nehru, too ? I read :

"Babu Rajendra Prasad (???) in announcing the personnel—" What in the name of jumping Jehosophat have Prasad and his personnel got to do with Bose's and Nehru's decline ? Let me find out. "......of the working committee stated that it was a matter of—" Yes, but what about Bose and Nehru and their decline ? "......deep regret that he could not persuade Mr. Subhas Chandra Bose (at last !) to serve on the committee." Gosh ! "So also Pandit Jawaharlal Nehru had declined to be on the committee."

Gosh almighty! It was the membership of the working committee they had declined. But why in the name of clarity and commonsense didn't you say so in the headline?

Another heading reads:

LURKING DANGER

NEHRU EXPLAINS IMPLICATIONS

I am getting wise to the tricks. The heading does not say what the danger is that lurks. And, with all due respect to Pandit Nehru I let it lurk and pass on.

WRONG PROCEDURE

NARIMAN LEADS MEMORIALISTS

Why is it a wrong procedure for Nariman to lead memorialists? Because of the recent unpleasantness in which he was involved? Let us see.

> With the permission of the President, Mr. K. F. Nariman read a memorandum signed by 30 members of the A. I. C. C. protesting against the procedure adopted by the chairman, etc.

Entirely different from what the headings would lead one to believe. But this is the usual newspaper procedure: for ever wrong and misleading.

Nothing interesting seems to happen to an Indian newspaper. And when it does happen, once in a blue moon, the paper does not know what to do with it. If it is *risque*, the paper wallows in unrestrained obscenity, calling a spade a spade. If it is clean fun, the paper indulges in its traditional dullness.

U. P. SOLONS

HAVE THEIR FUN

PANDIT ASKS; MISSUS BALKS.

PREMIER ANSWERS QUERY,

would make an attractive two-bank headline for the following, reproduced unedited from a quasi-Indian daily.

In the U. P. Assembly yesterday Sir J. P. Srivastava asked whether having regard to the communal tension in the province Government intended to postpone the elections to local bodies which were due to take place this year.

Mr. A. G. Kher Parliamentary Secretary, replied that the matter was under consideration. Government would, however, like to add that the reference to communal tension had no bearing on this question..

It was further asked whether Government would state if they had any idea of introducing joint electorates in local bodies.

Mr. A. G. Kher replied that the matter was under consideration.

Lt. Sultan Alam: "How long will Government take to come to a decision?"

Mr. A. G. Kher: "Probably within a month."

Mr. Tahir Husain: "Is it the intention of Government to hold elections under the old Municipal act?"

Mrs. V. L. Pandit: "The whole matter is under consideration."

Mr. Mahabir Tyagi: "Have Government issued instructions for the preparation of new electoral rolls for local bodies?"

Mrs. Pandit: "No."

Mr. R. S. Pandit asked if there was any alternative to joint electorates which was also under consideration.."

The Premier: "Of course, so long as joint electorates are not accepted all other alternatives will remain under consideration."

Kunwar Sir Maharaj Singh: "Could not Mr. Pandit's question be answered domestically?" (Laughter.)

But the paper topped the story with the following uninspired heads:

COMMUNAL
TENSION
IN U. P.

PLEA FOR PUTTING OFF
ELECTIONS

Sir Jwala, it may be added in parenthesis, is not the feature, but the Big Boss. So he must be kept in the limelight like a glorified circus clown, feature or no.

Let us turn from the unmitigated boredom of the Indian newspapers to the clean and clever writing done on American newspapers.

'BRUTE FORCE' WORLD POLICY
DENOUNCED BY ROOSEVELT

Crystal clear, isn't it ? And space-saving.

LAD POSES
SIX YEARS
AS 'WIFE'

FOOLS HIS HUSBAND ;
WORKS AS CUTIE
IN BURLESQUE

You'd want to read that, wouldn't you ?

WATCH 'TO WEAR SWIMMING'
ROOSEVELT GIFT TO WIFE, 53

Complete information in a few words, and no fooling.

JAPS DEFY POWERS;
CALL MORE TROOPS

is a banner headline set up in one-inch type.

The second bank, set in half-inch type across two columns announces :-

WAR TO BITTER END'
THREATENED ; PEACE
OFFER SPURNED

And the third bank reads :

AGGRESSOR WILL TURN DOWN ANY
BID TO PARTICIPATE IN
PARLEY ON CHINA CONFLICT

Then follow news flashes from the nerve centres of the world :

TOKIO—Japan defies indictment as aggressor by League powers and United States ; decides to spurn nine-power peace parley ; calls new recruits and plans to carry air war in China to bitter end.

ROME—Italy decides to boycott nine-power conference and hints at boycott of American goods.

LONDON—Britain wants Roosevelt to call peace conference in Washington instead of London.

> WASHINGTON—Discarding 17-year isolationist policy, the United States waits invitation to join other signatories of Nine-Power Treaty in attempt to stop Sino-Japanese war.

This is news display and news ending *a la mode.* You know at a glance what epochal events are stirring in the world, and you are thrilled.

BEATEN WOMAN DISCOVERED UNDER BLAZING MATTRESS

> Beaten into unconsciousness by a blunt instrument, a 30-year-old mother of an unborn child was found sprawled today beneath a burning bed in a furnished room at 330 W. 56 st.

Who? What? When? Where? Why? and How?—all answered in the lead with proper emphasis on the feature. Having given you basic information, the story continues in climactic order.

> The victim, identified only as a Mrs. Anna Steigel was discovered when other residents in the five-storey rooming house smelled smoke.
>
> Tracing the fire to the third-floor front, police broke into Mr. Steigel's room and found the bed and mattress blazing.
>
> Not until the fire had been extinguished was the moaning victim discovered. She had a possible fracture of the skull, severe cuts about the face and an injured right eye, which surgeons despaired of saving.
>
> She was treated by Dr. McCarthy, of City Hospital, who removed her to Roosevelt Hospital. Police said the victim was an expectant mother. She had occupied the room since Monday.

This is how news ought to be written, and is written every day in every paper in America and in the neighboring countries of Canada, Japan, Hawaii, Alaska, and the Phillipine Islands. This is how news could be written in Indian newspapers if for once we ceased posing as Drs. Know-All and took pains to learn our trade. But we are mighty pleased with ourselves and things as they are. That puts a period to further progress and development, and mildew and stagnation overtake us.

News in Indian newspapers is written not in climactic order, but in chronological order—once there was a king—or in any old order the cub, sub, or correspondent takes it into his head to write. The feature is teetotally missing from the lead, where it ought to be played up in the first ten words to catch and keep the reader's interest. It is sometimes in the middle of the column, sometimes in the last paragraph, and sometimes, more often than one would imagine, nowhere at all, leaving the busy businessman to wonder where lay the point and purpose of the story.

A city editor once sent a cub to cover a society wedding. As the paper was being put to bed, all dressed up, the editor, coming upon the cub, inquired : "You got your story all right, Bill ?" "No Mr. Gruber, the bridegroom didn't show up," Bill replied, pleased as Punch at having got off the assignment so easily. And the city editor swore and cursed and pretty nearly kicked the cub down the garbage chute.

A CLASSIC EXAMPLE

The feature, conspicuously absent from news items in Indian newspapers, invariably calls to mind the story Al Jolson narrates with such telling effect. A farmer, returning home after a brief absence, is met at the depot by his negro servant and inquires : "What's the news, Jim ?"

"There ain't no noos," Jim Crow replies.

"No news ?"

"No noos at all, massa"—then as a concession to something of little account—"except that the dog's not too well."

"Oh ! How's that ?"

"Well, he nebba quite got over them burns wot he got."

"Burns ? How did he get burned ?"

"Oh—oh—that—that was in the fire wot we had in the garage."

"What ! The garage has been on fire ?"

"Ye-yes. Din't you know ? The garage burned down."

"But, how in hell did that happen ?"

"From the sparks from the house, massa."

"Sparks from the house ! Why, was the house on fire, too ?"

"Oh, yes. The h-house was on fire."

"But, how—how—?"

"Oh, the house ? Oh, that was from one of the candles fallin' over from around your mother-in-law's coffin."

"You don't mean to say my mother-in-law is dead !"

"Yes, yes. Didn't you know ? She died through shock."

"Shock ?"

"Yes, the shock o' hearin' that your wife ran off with the chauffeur. Apart from that their ain't no noos, massa."

WOOD AND TREES

Indian newspapermen from Herr Editor down are like the darky servitor. They don't sense news when all the time it is crying out loud to be put on the front page and boxed. The headings rarely shed a ray of light. More often than not, they are a meaningless jumble of words, written, not to arrest the roving eye and focus attention on the story, but because it is conventional to have them. Sometimes a story has so many heads that it looks positively hydra-headed, guaranteed to give one a headache if perused.

The lead is equally esoteric. To wade through a solid column of bad print to find out what it is all about doesn't seem worth while. But one must read or become a Rip Van Winkle. An Indian newspaper in a clumsy editorial called Sir Tej Bahadur Sapru, of all the men in the world, a Rip Van Winkle. That was a brainstorm. But the Indian newspapers being what they are, there is every reason for anybody to deteriorate into one.

From the emphasis placed on editorials in Indian news papers, one expects them to be the salt of the earth. As a matter of fact, they are neither hot nor salt. Once in a while there is a clap of thunder ; once in a great while a gleam of lightning. Mostly it is all quiet on the editorial front.

An Indian editor writing an editorial is like an Italian eating spaghetti : there are no half-way measures. When an Indian editor gets excited, it is nothing unusual for him to perpetrate an editorial three solid columns long. Here length passes for learning, and dullness for erudition. The readers, having never known anything better, are duly impressed. "My ! what a giant Mr. Bhayankaram is !" It does take a giant to sling gigantic editorials. The average editor being made of more human clay, prefers to keep his editorials down to negotiable proportions.

Anglo-Indian dailies like the *Times of India* are distinguished for a clear exposition of the currents, cross-currents, and under-currents of European politics. In dealing with Indian affairs, too, they are usually progressively liberal. On the whole, an Anglo-Indian daily is a far better journalistic achievement than its Indian or quasi-Indian prototype.

POLITICS—PLAIN AND FANCY

Indian newspapers are pretty heavy metal. It is politics, all politics, and nothing but politics, politics in and out, politics through and through, politics straight and honorable, politics warped and crooked, politics dished out in a most unappetizing manner, *sans* salt, *sans* pepper, *sans* gravy, *sans* dressing, *sans* sauce, *sans* sense, and sometimes, *sans* politics. If the reader is interested in aught besides, he must apply at some other shop. Features have not yet come into their own in India because Indian editors and publishers are too unimaginative and introverted to realize their importance and pulling power. To many it is a new world of which they have vaguely heard, but know little about.

An Indian newspaper was famous for two features : its editorial chat and the daily cartoon. Both the editor and the cartoonist left, the feature stopped, but the circulation did not decline. "What fools we were to employ those high-priced gents," the manager ruminated. "Our circulation hasn't suffered a bit. We are better off without them."

FEATURES

This way of thinking does not make for progressive journalism. Circulation did not fall because there was only one nationalist daily in the territory. If the manager had taken the trouble to send out a questionnaire to its readers, he would have found out how the public missed both the features. And the same editor on the basis of his column is today drawing more than twice his former salary on another newspaper, while the first paper is plodding along its unilluminated way, blindly self-content.

Every newspaper is bound by the very nature of things to publish news and editorials. It is features that make for popularity and enable the paper to serve an ever-increasing clientele. If you are strong on features, you can hold your own and make rapid headway, no matter what your political creed or religious complexion—provided you do not cook, color, or suppress news, as a certain quasi-Indian daily is doing all the time.

The *Christian Science Monitor* is, by its very name, a denominational newspaper. But the *Monitor* is a great newspaper in America and everywhere else in the world. It devotes just one page to the propagation of its religious doctrines. For the rest it is like any other first class daily, interested in everything that interests humanity, and therefore interesting. Its news is served not only promptly, but impartially. What it does not like it lambastes in the editorial columns. But its news columns are pure of editorial bias.

THE UNKNOWN QUANTITY

I have met editors sighing and crying to high heaven that their advertising revenue would go up, blissfully unaware of how and why it does. Advertisements come from circulation. Circulation depends on features, all other things, news, editorials, make-up and get-up being what they ought to be.

Advertisements in Indian newspapers are shamefully blatant and shamelessly sexual. The paper doesn't draw the line anywhere. It will publish any ad., no matter how tall its claims, how hollow and absurd its pretensions. Quacks, astrologers, miracle-mongers and mountebanks, all pass muster. To look at our ad. columns, one would imagine we were a race of sexomaniacs, syphilized, sexless, sexful, sex-starved, having all the ailments and appetites that sex is heir to. We are not. But an open shop policy in advertising, come one, come all, gives one the impression.

The art of advertising is unknown in India. The advertisements are plain, boastful, and brazen to obscenity. There is never a catch nor cunning in them. No persuasion, artistic or aesthetic appeal, or educative value. It is like the town crier crying from the house top. It is more like

> A child crying in the night,
> A child crying for the light,
> With no language but a cry !

There is a number of English weeklies and monthlies in India. Among the weeklies three are notewothy : the *Illustrated Weekly of India*, the *Indian Social Reformer*, and the *Bombay Chronicle Sunday Magazine*. The disappearance of the *Hindu Illustrated Weekly* is a distinct loss to Indian journalism. The *Orient Illustrated Weekly* is frankly and frantically trying to become another *Illustrated Weekly of India*. There is room for a first class English weekly in the country, for many for the matter of that, and the *Orient's* sad imitation of the Bombay *Illustrated* betrays a sad lack of imagination, initiative, and journalistic acumen.

The *Sunday Standard* of Bombay is broad-based on the never failing appeal of human interest stories. But it is content to use canned stuff from the continent. It would take the country by storm if it dug up Indian stories and wrote them up as *Hearst's American Weekly* does. But *Hearst's American Weekly* is not everybody's money. You just cannot wish and produce one. No flying carpet formula can turn the trick. What one needs and cannot do without is trained and experienced writers and journalists. Hearst hunts them up, pays them, and it pays Hearst to pay them.

Among the monthlies two stand out : the *Modern Review* and the *Indian Review*. The *Indian Review* offers several short articles, once in a while a short story, and a heaping plateful of *rechauffe*, hash, and hodgepodge. The *Modern Review* functions on a higher plane. It is the magazine of the cultured class and its greatest contribution to Indian journalism lies in making available to its readers the work of Rabindranath Tagore. But its contributions do not maintain the same peak of literary excellence. Its serials have a beginning, body, but no end. It pays its contributors, but in name only.

SUICIDAL FOLLY

Free lancing is a precarious proposition anywhere, taken up only by the most brilliant of journalists. In India it is tantamount to an act of suicidal folly. Anglo-Indian publications pay fairly well. But what the Indian papers and periodicals pay their contributors, in regal disregard of the literary and journalistic merits of their contributions, is a disgrace to themselves and an insult to their contributors. And when, on top of it all, they start red pencilling a really first class contribution, often the height of editorial enormity is reached. At times it is not editing, it is not butchery, it is savage vivisection. The free lance in India may well exclaim with the Urdu poet :

> I wrote an article,
> Dawson made a boot ;
> The article made no headway in the land,
> And the boot DID !

The future in Indian journalism unquestionably belongs to provincial languages. But the world language will for a long time continue to occupy the leading position it does today. And that is as it should be.

Indian newspapers, with all their sins of omission and commission, have their commendable points. Among these may be mentioned the *National Herald's* foreign correspondence and Pandit Jawaharlal Nehru's articles in it, the *Amrit Bazar Patrika's* foreign correspondence and editorials and notes with their lively sense of humor, B. G. Horniman's *Tete-a Tete,* Joseph Pothan's editorial chat *Over a Cup of Tea,* editorials in Anglo-Indian dailies, specially those on foreign affairs and also their foreign correspondence, Shanker's cartoons, the *Hindustan Times*' get-up, make-up and matrimonial ads, the *Leader's* English correspondence and weekly edition, *Advance's* popular price and make-up, the *Bombay Chronicle's* foreign correspondence and *Weekly*

Magazine, and above all, the *Modern Review's* ability in giving its readers contributions from the pen of Gurudeva Rabindranath Tagore. This list notes the high lights and does not pretend to be exhaustive.

What India needs today is journalists who will tuck up their sleeves and go out and strive to produce a journalistically first class daily. But that must remain a pious hope until some far-seeing philanthropist like Birla will endow an American School of Journalism at some central institution like the Benares Hindu University. The U. P., of all the Provinces in India, is so backward and barren of journalistic talent, I am informed, that all its editors are recruited from England, Madras and other Provinces, Babu Ganga Prasad Verma having been the last U. P.-ean to occupy the editorial chair. This is another reason why the Universities of the United Provinces should seriously consider starting a really progressive department of journalism. The suggestion is commended to the attention of Sir Harry Haig and the Vice-Chancellors concerned.

With grateful acknowledgements to the *Toledo Times*, I wish to close this article with a tribute to American newspapermen, with whom I passed the happiest years of my life as a humble co-worker.

I see a man pushing his way through the lines
Where the work of the terrible fire fiend shines,
"The Chief?" I inquire, and a policeman replies,
"Why no; he's one of them newspaper guys."

I see a man walk through the door of a show
Where the great throngs are blocked by the sign "S. R. O."
"Is this man a star that no ticket he buys?"
"Star nothing: he's one of those newspaper guys."

I see a man start on the trail of a crook
While he scorns the police and brings him to book,
"Sherlock Holmes?" I exclaim, and some one replies,
"Sherlock Holmes! he's one of those newspaper guys."

And some day I'll pass by the great gates of gold
And see a man pass through unquestioned and bold,
"A Saint?" and Saint Peter will surely reply:
"He carries a pass. That's a newspaper guy."

DR. HENRY HERAS

S. J., M. A.,

Is a Professor of Indian History and Director of Indian History of the Research Institute, St. Xavier 's College, Bombay and a Corresponding Member of the Indian Historical Records Commission. Professor of History and Ancient Indian Culture, University of Bombay. Member of the International Committee of Historical Sciences. Corresponding Member of the Royal Anthropological Institute, London and of Academia Espanola de la Historia, Madrid, corresponding Member, Institute Italian Per il medio Ed. Estremo Oriente, Rome. He was awarded the Gold Cross of Merit by the Republic of Poland.

Born 11 September 1888 he was educated at Barcelona and at Cleveland, Ohio. He has been Professor of the Sacred Heart College (Barcelona) and the Principal of Our Saviour College (Saragossa).

An imposing list of contributions and publications stand to the credit of Dr. Heras among which may be mentioned "History of the Manchu Dynasty of China", 3 Vols (in Spanish); "The Aravidu Dynasty;" "The writing of History."

Most of Dr. Heras' articles are published by the learned societies and institution of the world, among which are the "Journal of the Bombay Historical Society" "Journal of the Royal Asiatic Society", "Journal of the Carnatic Historical Society", "Journal of the Bihar and Orissa Research Society", "Journal of Oriental Research", Madras. "Indian Culture", Calcutta. "Journal of Indian History", Madras. Revista Asiatica, Rome. The New Review, Calcutta and etc.

In his contribbtion to "*What India Thinks*" Dr. Heras gives us an insight in the vast field offered by ancient Indian history.

NEW VISTAS IN THE FIELD OF ANCIENT INDIAN HISTORY

FOR a very long time the study of Indian history has been based upon two principles which did not require any proof; they were two postulates. These principles were: *first,* Northern India is inhabited by Aryans, and Southern India by Dravidians. *Second,* whatever is great and noble in ancient Indian culture is the inheritance of the Aryan race; the Dravidians were an uncultured race whose destiny was to be the slaves of the Aryans.

These two principles are clearly read through the lines of the following narrative of the Aryan invasion and its immediate consequences. They come from the pen of Mr. Romesh Chandra Dutt:

> "There was a continuous war between the Indo-Aryan and the dark-skinned aborigines during this age. The aborigines retreated before the more civilized organization of the Aryans, but hung around in fastnesses and forests, plundered the peaceful villages of the Aryans and stabled their cattle. With that tenacity which is peculiar to barbarians, they fought for centuries as they retreated; they interrupted the religious sacrifices of the conquerors, despised their "bright gods", and plundered their wealth. But the Aryans conquered in the end; the area of civilization widened, waste and jungle lands were reclaimed and dotted with villages and towns, and the barbarians either submitted to the conquerors or retreated to the mountains where their descendants still live."

Modern criticism and sound impartiality cannot approve of these two principles. Let us examine them carefully.

The idea that North India is inhabited by Aryans and that South India is inhabited by Dravidians is so deeply rooted in the minds of the people of India that the so-called Dravidians themselves are of opinion that South India is their original homeland. Yet this opinion is not founded upon any historical, anthropological, or ethnological truth. This principle is the fruit of a confusion between race and language. Language is not the same as race.

A FALLACY.

This confusion for practical purposes exists in Europe as well as in India. Because the Germans speak an Aryan language, the idea has been spread that the Germans are Aryans. Since the Italian language is also an Aryan language, the Italians are likewise supposed to be Aryans. The confusion is so widely spread that it has unfortunately been accepted even by scientific people, as if it were a dogma. Last September I attended a Congress promoted by the Spanish Association for the Progress of Science at Santander. At the opening session a great scholar read a well-thought out and wonderfully documented address on the synthesis of the Spanish race. The paper was as interesting as it was well written and magnificently read. Yet a flaw blurred its wonderful lucidity. Without any proof, the lecturer asserted that the Spanish race was a branch of the great Aryan race. As if the *substratum* of the Spanish race were not the Iberian race. As if Latin, with all its beauties and classical character—from which all* modern languages spoken in Spain proceed—was not imposed upon the people of Spain by the conquering Roman Empire, which in itself was more Etruscan than Latin-Aryan.

A few days later I also attended the 20th Congress of Orientalists at Brussels. I was specially interested in some communications about the latest archæological discoveries in Phœnicia, read in the section of Biblical studies. One day a lively discussion ensued after the reading of one of

* I do not speak of the Basque language, which is the oldest language of Spain.

the papers. At the end of the session I approached one of the scholars who had shown in his remarks great erudition and learning. I daringly proposed the following straight question to him: "What race did the Phœnicians belong to?" Astonished at my question he replied without delay: "They were Semites." "Why?" My newly made friend showed still more astonishment and answered not without showing some impatience: "But they spoke a Semitic language." I suppose I showed more astonishment still when I heard such a statement. All Biblical, historical, anthropological, and cultural evidence against the Semitic origin of the Phœnicians was thrown overboard in favour of the linguistic evidence, upon which nothing but a fallacy could be built. The Phœnicians spoke a Semitic language, therefore they belonged to the Semitic race.*

This is also the reasoning in connection with India. The people of North India speak Aryan languages. Therefore they are Aryans. On the contrary, the people of the South, who speak Dravidian language, must certainly be Dravidians. The consequence is not logically drawn, and must be acknowledged as false unless we know of their race through other sources. Let us examine them.

The great Italian anthropologist Sergi has been rightly entitled "The father of the Mediterranean race", for he scientifically studied the Mediterranean nations from the anthropologist's point of view, and he could finally formulate well-defined principles as regards the characteristic features of this race and its spread. The Mediterraneans are dolichocephalic, totally defferent from the Aryans who are brachycephalic. † Now it is acknowledged that the majority of the Indians are dolichocephalic and therefore belong to the Mediterranean race. Archæology has confirmed this view, for the same terracotta bath-tub shaped sarcophagi

* The author of these lines studied this very interesting question after the conversation held at Brussels and expects to be able to publish the results of his research soon. The Phœnicians were Hamites and formed a branch of the Mediterraneo-Dravidian family originally hailing from India.

† Cf. Sergi, *The Mediterranean Race*. pp. 5,215-220

have been discovered at Pallavaram and Perumber in the Chingleput District, in the Salem District and at Dadampatti in the Madura District, as at Brahmanabad and Mohenjo Daro in Sindh and in several places in Mesopotamia.

EXAMPLES

The languages of Northern India still offer us some relics of the ancient languages spoken by the Dravidian population. Brahui, Uraon and Kui are Dravidian languages, forming islands in the middle of people speaking Aryan languages. But even in these Aryan or Sanskrit languages numerous words of Dravidian origin reveal the ancient Dravidian *substratum.* The average northerner who does not like to have anything in common with the Dravidians will bluntly affirm that those are words borrowed from Sanskrit by Dravidian languages, in spite of the fact that philology and history argue against it. Let us take two words only. *Min*, "fish" and *moti* "pearl". *Min* means fish both in Sanskrit and in many of the northern Indian vernaculars. Thousands of times I have heard that this is "a Sanskrit word borrowed by the beggar Dravidians from the wonderfully rich sacred language of India." Let us go slowly in order not to fall into a pit, and examine this word carefully. *Min* in Sanskrit means generally "fish", and sometimes also "constellation". Now, in Dravidian languages *Min* originally means "to shine", and because the fishes shine under the water they are called *Min* ; and because the stars shine in the sky they are also called *Min.* The original meaning of this word "to shine" is not found in Sanskrit. Moreover the second meaning of this word in Sanskrit is a derived meaning. It is but natural that the primary meaning in connections with the sky would be star : constellation is evidently a secondary meaning. This is, therefore, a word that Sanskrit and the modern Sanskrit vernaculars borrowed from Dravidian languages. (1)

---

(1) Cf. Caldwell, *A Comparative Grammar of the Dravidian or South Indian Family of Languages*, pp. 578-4 (London, 1913)

Let us consider the other word, *Moti.* This word means "pearl" in Aryan languages. In Dravidian languages *Muttu* also means "pearl". Now what was the origin of the pearl trade in India from very ancient times ? All the pearls came from the Coromandel coast, the most famous pearl fisheries in the world. The Aryan invaders of North India received the first pearls from the southern shores, and enchanted at their sight, they demanded of the traders what was the name of that little snowy ball. "*Muttu*", they replied. Then they started calling them *Muttu,* which finally became *moti.* Another word that found its way into the Aryan languages, hailing from the Dravidian stock.

THE VERB

Now if we consider the construction of all modern Aryan languages spoken in India, we shall be struck once more at finding the Dravidian imprint upon all of them. Non-Indian languages belonging to the Aryan family are totally different in this respect. In some of these languages the verb may be placed in the middle of the sentence after the subject, or perhaps at the end of it. Such is Latin. Others, like English, do not admit the verb but between the subject and predicate. But there is no language in this group that requires the verb at the end of the sentence. Yet Aryan languages spoken in India forcibly demand this construction : subject, predicate and verb, without exception. This is precisely the Dravidian construction. This shows that modern Aryan languages in India were first spoken in the Prakrit period of formation by persons accustomed to the old Dravidian construction. They spoke Sanskrit—Prakrit languages without forgetting the old Dravidian grammar.

It could not be otherwise, for the Aryan invaders were very few. The Rgveda mentions five tribes only : the Yadus and Turvasas, who probably landed in Kathiawar (1), and the Purus, Anus and Druhyus who entered through

---

(1) Cf. Banerji : *Prehistoric Ancient and Hindu India, p 25 ;* Chanda, *Indo-Aryan Races,* Pt. 1, pp. 24-5 ; Heras, "*The Origin of the Round Proto-Indian Seals discovered in Sumer*", *B. B. & C. I. Annual* 1938, p. 4.

the Khyber Pass. The latter opened their way through the thickly populated land of the five rivers (Panjab) and after effecting a union with the other two tribes, they settled in what they called *Madhya-desa,* the Middle Country, roughly speaking what is now the administrative division called the United Provinces. Once settled there, their aim at conquering new lands stopped. From Benares eastwards they never marched an army. South of the Vindhyas they never conquered an inch of land.

DRAVIDIAN INFLUENCE

Consequently, Magadha and Bengal in the East, Panjab, North-Western frontier, Sindh and part of Afghanistan in the West and the whole of Dakshina-patha, from the Vindhyas and the Narbada river down to Ceylon, remained as Dravidian as they were before. In the late Vedic period, when Viśvamitra led ten tribes against the Bhāratas, whose king Sudās was the patron of his rival Vaśishtha, he gathered round him Aryan and Dravidian tribes. The Alinas and the Śivas were certainly Dravidians, and there are strong reasons to suspect that the Bhāratas themselves belonged to the same race. Sudās had also to fight with the Yakshus, Ajas, and Thigrus, whose Dravidian origin is also acknowledged.

When the *Brāhmanas* were being written, Magadha was still an unexplored country to the Aryans. From time to time minstrels from the Magadha kingdom entered the Aryan villages and towns, singing the praises of their kings to the accompaniment of the *yāl,* the ancient Dravidian harp. They spoke a Dravidian language. Their *lingo* could not be understood by the Aryans. They were Mlechchhas. The Aryans called them "Māgadhas".

Meanwhile the Aryans of Madhya-dēśa were getting Dravidianized. They mixed freely with their ancient enemies the Dasius, even by family ties. One of their tribes very soon accepted the ancient Dravidian god in their own pantheon. This was the god An or Ándivanan, and for this reason they were soon called the Anus. (1). This god was finally worshipped by all the Aryans, but they called him Śiva for he was worshipped by the tribe of the Śivas. They became acquainted with the ancient Dravidian script, they learnt the philosophical systems and ideas of their neighbours, they tried to imitate the latter's asceticism by insituting a new *asharam*, where even married men could practice it performing at the same time vedic sacrifices; they even raised a number of sages of pure Dravidian stock to the state of Brahmans (2). Prof. Weller of the University of Bonn, Germany, has satisfactorily proved that Bhrigu, one of the four *rishis* from whom, according to the *Mahābhārata*, the earliest priests of the Indo-Aryans descended, was Dravidian. (3). The late Prof. R. D. Banerji writes about this amalgamation as follows :

> "The Indo-Aryans came to India in very small numbers, and they did not make any attempt at preserving the purity of their stock. From the very beginning they admitted tribes of foreign or mixed origin into their communities, and the statements of the present day Brahmanical writers about the racial purity of the Indo-Aryans and rigidity of their marriage regulations are inaccurate." (4). And again : "The Vedic literature contains no reference to any female deity to which the Durga or the Devi of the present day might even approximate. Even Śiva and Vishnu as they are represented in worship at the present day, contain certain elements of non-Aryan origin. Śiva, with his emblem, the *phallus*, is evidently a non-Aryan deity whose admission into the Indo-Aryan pantheon caused bitter strife."

---

(1) "The name Anu, of the tribe whose seven cities were conquered by the Aryan chief Purukutsa, also appears to be of non-Aryan origin." Banerji, *op.cit.* p. 19.

(2) Cf. Chanda, *op. cit.*, pp. 24-5.

(3) Weller, "*Who were the Bhriguids,*" *A. B. O. R. I.*, XVIII, pp. 296-302.

(4) Banerji, *op. cit.*, p. 24.

The new mixed religious creed and code of social customs had to be spread throughout the length and breadth of India. From Kurukshetra, the centre of the original Aryan possessions, bands of missionaries, some of them Aryan Brahmans, others Aryanized Brahmans of the original Dravidian stock, entered the Dravidian kingdoms not conquered by power of arms. They were to be reduced to the new religious theocracy of Brahmanhood. Those who would not accept would remain outside the fold of the new religious society. They would be the outcasts.

MISSIONARY WORK

One of these missionaries was the famous Agastyaswamy, the teacher of Aryan civilization to the natives of South India. But the Aryan civilization had a very small percentage of Aryan blood. It was practically the old Dravidian civilization presented as Aryan and preached through the medium of an Aryan tongue, Sanskrit. An image of Śiva, found in most of the temples of Southern India, and which undoubtedly was the product of the missionary efforts of those days, is symbolical of this monstrous travesty of facts which has been called "the Aryanization of India." This represents a four armed Śiva, just as the Dravidian Āndivanan was represented centuries before. The Aryans misnamed him as Śiva. In one of his hands he holds a manuscript of the Vedas, which nevertheless had never been written because the Aryans did not know how to write. His right foot tramples over an *asura*, the demon of Dravidian ignorance. Next to him on either side there are two *rishis*, squatting in raptured attention at the lessons given by the lord. They are Agastya and Bhrigu ; the latter emaciated to an extreme, is the Dravidian ancestor of a Brahmanic clan ; the former, parading an ocean-containing pot-belly, is the accredited messenger of the Aryans amongst the people of the South, whose racial origin nevertheless is not yet fixed beyond dispute. The image is styled "Dakshināmurti". It is the Southern image *par excellence*, Śiva teaching the Vedas to the people of the South. They, poor Dravidians, were barbarians, uncivilized, not

DR. HENRY HERAS
S.J., M.A.

knowing the Vedas. But was Śiva acquainted with the Vedas? Was not he himself the god of the Dravidians, in his original denomination Āndivanan? True, but Brahma and Vishnu were unknown to the southerners. Śiva was their own god, well known to them. He could not know much of the Vedas considering his origin. Since his name was not even once found in the Vedas he was identified with Rudra. Yet he would be the best to make the southerners realize their inferiority complex. After that they would be ready to receive back all the treasures of their own ancient wisdom and lore put in Sanskrit language, the sacred language of the gods, by Brahmans of their very race who had been exalted to the supreme rank in the social hierarchy created by the circumstances and emphasized by the ambition of the Aryan priestly clan.

LANGUAGE DIFFICULTIES

This intercourse by the people of the two races is of great importance to understand the Aryan craze of later ages. Speech naturally was the only means for this social intercourse. Yet the Aryans always claimed that the language of the Dasyus was not understandable. Their ears could not get accustomed to those "funny sounds". Contrariwise, Dravidian speaking people, perhaps on account of the difficulty and complexity of their own language and especially of its construction, have always shown great facility in learning foreign languages. From the early times of the East India Company servants, who were bound for Madras and its neighbourhood, were not in need of studying any Indian languages for the Indians whom they had to deal with spoke English; while those whose destination was North India always had to learn Hindi, Bengali, or any other language of the countries of the North. The Aryan speaking people of North India did not speak English so much, nor learnt it with the same facility as the people of the South. This is also experienced in our own days. While travelling through South India, all servants, travellers' bungalow cooks, *ghari-*

wallas, and *rickshaw-drawers*, speak in English. But go to Bombay, travel through Rajputana, visit Delhi, Agra, Benares or Calcutta and you will meet with very interesting and at times, difficult experiences if you do not speak Hindi or know at least a few Hindustani words ; no uneducated person will speak to you in English.

So it happened in those early days. Since the Aryans did not learn a *mridharavak* (hostile) language, the Dravidians, who were living amongst them, learnt Sanskrit or the corresponding Prakrit. The Dravidians inhabiting the neighbouring kingdoms did the same for social, commercial, and cultural purposes. Thus the modern North Indian vernaculars, Aryan in their origin but having indisputable relics of Dravidian influence, naturally grew, while the old Dravidian languages were little by little forgotten. It was then that a very interesting and not uncommon psychological phenomenon took place ; a phenomenon which explains many important later facts which are otherwise inexplicable.

The true study of a language undertaken either for mere pleasure or for real need at the first instance creates a sort of enthusiasm for the new tongue. This enthusiasm is reflected in a kind of respect for the people who speak that language as their natural tongue, followed by a natural depreciation of one's own language and people according to the laws of the scale : the higher the one pan rises the lower the other pan sinks. If to this high esteem of the new language and of the nation that speaks it, endless praises of the culture of that nation are added, one will finally begin wishing to be a member of that nation or race. At first he will state so in whispers but finally he will consider himself persuaded of it and proclaim it to the four winds. The last stage of this metamorphosis will include the fabrication of fanciful pedigrees. If all this is true in regard to a person, it becomes much easier in the case of a community, whose origin is less certain and whose characteristics lack in that note of individuality which is the inheritance of family and education.

This is precisely what happened to the Dravidian communities of Northern India who came in contact with the Aryans.

Even South Indian dynasties, like the Kadambas of Banavasi and the Chalukyas of Badami, whose native language had always been Kannada, and ancient Dravidian tribes whose tongue was never changed, as for instance the Paravas of the Tamil-nādu, intoxicated by the Aryan craze, either claimed descendency from Vedic *rishis* or declared that their present denomination "*Paravas*" or "*Paravar*" was a corruption of the ancient Sanskrit name "*Bharatas,*" or "*Bharatar*" the denomination of the famous sō called Aryan tribe of Brahmanic and Puranic reputation.

LEGALISED THEFT

Yet in the case of this Dravido-Aryan transformation an element is to be considered that makes it unique. While the great culture of ancient India was being styled Aryan and was being taught to the Dravidian peoples as if it were the inheritance of the Aryan invaders, a practical theft was being legalized ; a theft which exalted the vanity of a few Aryans and of a number of Dravidians persuaded to be "Aryan born". For that culture with practically all its treasures of administration, religion, philosophy, asceticism, architecture, sculpture, history, poetry, navigation, agriculture, and trade, originally belonged to the Dravidian race, which generously made a present of it to the Aryan invaders and, not satisfied with it, spread it through the Mediterranean basin in the west and through the nations of Greater India in the East. This colossal theft, than which the annals of history have not seen a greater, seems to have prescribed, when the original meaning of the word "Āryan" that was a "ploughman" was changed in favour of the meaning of the Dravidian word "arīan" that is a "nobleman"—a meaning which has found its way into the Oxford Dictionary of the English language.

Where are now the original representatives of the Aryan race in the great Indian continent ?—some readers may ask. If there are any, they may perhaps be found in the United Provinces or their neighbourhood ; but we sincerely think that the search will not be very fruitful. In the case of the

Indian branch of the great Aryan family it happened in ancient times what every day happens in the case of botanical specimens shifted from the cold regions that were their natural *habitat* to warm zones or really hot climates. The plant thus imported to lands where the sky looks brighter and warmer winds blow, has an extraordinary growth in one or two generations ; luxuriant leaves cover its branches ; its flowers multiply their variegated petals ; its fruits reach a size never imagined in its pristine land. Yet after this extraordinary expansion and show of life, the plant cannot grow in its new climate any longer and one day, alas ! the leaves appear yellowish, the stem bends mournfully to the soil that gave it that new influx of life, and the whole plant fades away forever. So it happened with the Aryan race in India.

CONCLUSION

Before its arrival in the land watered by the streams that the snow-clad Himalayas feed, this branch of the Aryan family had not a single achievement to its credit. In the cold regions along the southern course of the Volga river, (1), they led a peaceful pastoral or agricultural life, as eventless as the monotonous flow of those waters that witnessed their growth. After reaching the new land of their destination their clash with new peoples, the novelty of the surroundings, the fomenting caresses of the breezes of their new home, caused also an extraordinary efflorescence never dreamt of before. They became the authors of the most beautiful religious poetry, the Vedas, which placed them among the first nations of mankind. At the same time they converted the rude, matter-of-course speech of shepherds and agriculturists into a classical language of wonderful elasticity, that may rightly be classified as one of the most developed and intellectual languages ever spoken. But that was the swan song of the Aryans. After a few generations they vanished, leaving their inheritance to the powerful nation whom they fought but whom they admired.

---

(1) Cfr. Heras, "*The Cradle of the Aryans,*" *The New Review*, V, pp. 473—476.

PROFESSOR DIWAN CHAND SHARMA

M. A.,

Head of the Department of English, Dayanand Anglo Vedic College, Lahore was born on March 9, 1896 and was educated at the D. A. V. College, Lahore, and the Presidency College, Calcutta. He married Shrimati Durga Devi the daughter of Gosain Bhagat Ram in 1910 ; Convener, Board of Studies in English, Punjab University ; Part-time Lecturer in English to the University of Punjab ; Secretary, Punjab Provincial Hindu Maha Sabha, Lahore ; Member, Working Committee, All-India Hindu Maha Sabha ; Member, Indian Centre of P. E. N., Bombay ; Contributor to several well known journals of India ; Chairman, Reception Committee, 2nd Session of the All India Hindu Youth Conference. His publications include "The Prophets of the East" "Ideals and Realities" "Tales of Friendship" "Hindu Heroes and Heroines" "Makers of the Arya Samaj". In the following article Professor Sharma deals in an authoritative manner with a very vital problem.

EDUCATION FOR DEMOCRACY IN INDIA

THE reconstruction of education is everywhere in the air. It seems as if in his present plight man is again coming to believe in the beneficent nature of education which can humanise and ennoble and which can strengthen the forces of civilization as against the forces of barbarism. It is, therefore, no wonder that the objectives of education are being re-defined everywhere and syllabuses are being modified. As everyone knows we are living in a fast moving world and education must keep pace with changing conditions.

TOTAL CONDEMNATION

What is true of the rest of the world is also true of India. During the last twenty years or so the face of India has been changed almost beyond recognition, yet the educational system in India has remained mostly static. It is true that it has been modified here and there but mainly it has remained unchanged. This has given rise to a great deal of dissatisfaction, and the result is that our educational system has become a kind of scapegoat and the teacher a target for all sorts of attacks. If the national wealth of India is not on the increase, it is the teacher who is to blame. If our villages are not little paradises of cleanliness and comfort, it is because the village teacher takes no interest in his environment. If the health of the people does not compare favourably with that of the inhabitants of other countries, it is because the present system of education stunts our growth. If there is unemployment in the country, it is the schools and colleges in India that are responsible for it. If India suffers from communal bickerings and provincial jealousies, it is because the system of education is not national in the true sense of the word.

In short, our education system has been denounced quite often as bookish, abstract, out-of-date, and examination-ridden. All this condemnation is unfortunate in many ways, but it is fortunate at least in one ; it shows indirectly what importance people attach to education and what they expect from it.

A SLENDER THREAD

Yet one thing is very conveniently forgotten by these critics of education, and it is this ; that education in itself is not bad but educational methods and programmes must be revised from time to time. It would therefore only be idle to expect, from a system which is rooted in the traditions of the middle of the nineteenth century, something that is vital today. What India needs today is a training in democracy and surely this cannot be obtained from the present system which is semi-feudal and semi-autocratic. What India needs most at the present moment is education for democracy, because of all the different forms of governments in the world democracy needs education most of all. An autocracy or dictatorship can function properly even if the masses are not educated along the right lines, but a democracy comes to nothing if the average citizen is not well-educated, intelligent and adequately interested in the welfare of his country. Said John Galsworthy, *We think too much of politics and too little of education. We treat it almost as cavalierly as the undergraduate treated the Master of Balliol.* "*Yes*", he said, showing his people round the quadrangle, "*thats' the Master's window ;*" then, picking up a pebble, he threw it against the windowpane. "*And that,*" he said, as a face appeared, "*is the Master !*" Democracy has come, and on education democracy hangs ; the thread as yet is slender. If this is true of Europe and America, surely it is much more valid in the case of India, where democracy in its modern form has been transplanted only recently from the west.

AN ANCIENT DEMOCRACY

To say this is not to deny that democracy in some of its forms has been known and practised in India throughout the ages. Those of us who have studied *Hindu Polity* by the late Mr. K. P. Jayaswal know that democracy, in theory as well as in practice, was not unknown to the Hindus of a bygone age. The learned author after delving into the records of Hindu literature—*Vedic,* classical and *Prakrit* has shown that popular assemblies and institutions existed in ancient India, and exercised legislative, judicial and administrative functions. He has further shown that a republican form of government existed in the country of the Buddha and his neighbours. Some republics existed even when the Greeks invaded India, so that we find many references to these in the writings of the Greek travellers. Even under the Mauryas several republics continued to flourish and these became extinct only when the imperial power of the Hindus began to disintegrate. Still even in the days of political anarchy and misrule some vestiges of democracy continued to exist. It was no wonder that village *panchayats* continued to flourish in India for some years even after the introduction of the British rule, and the villages in India remained in a way autonomous units for purposes of internal administration. This goes to show that the spirit of democracy is not utterly alien to Hindus who form the majority of the population in India. As regards Islam, it is a vital part of it and even the followers of the other faiths in India, for example the Sikhs, are not totally unaware of its machinery, methods, principles and implications. Democracy, however, in its modern western form has been introduced in India by the British. It is true that self-government has been granted to India slowly and in small measure, but now, after years of political struggle, India has come to enjoy quite an adequate measure of self-rule. All the various instalments of reforms in India have made the people democratically minded and have introduced them to the methods and procedures of democratic government. But the pity is that no attempt has been made to inculcate in the minds of the coming generations a faith and belief in democracy. It seems that though politically and socially India has been undergoing tremendous and far-reaching changes, educationally it has remained practically backward.

UNITY OF AIM

This seems rather deplorable, 'because in every progressive country of the world the structure of education has been based upon some dominant political and social theories. When Mussolini took over the reins of government in Italy, he overhauled the educational system there to a great extent with the result that the schools, seminaries, universities and educational establishments in that country became the nurseries of Fascists. In other words, he made the educational system of his country subserve his political philosophy. Hitler, too, reorganised education in Germany with a view to inculcate in the minds of the rising generation the principles of National Socialism. To mention these two instances is not to approve of them, but to show that education in a country should be in conformity with the dominant political and social philosophy of that country. To be sure, no one would deny that the salvation of India, in spite of everything, lies in democracy. It is the only form of government which can promote within its borders internal peace and harmony and which can make it an ally of peace in the comity of nations. It is true that India has a heterogeneous mixture of communities, languages, races and faiths. But it is also equally true that no fiat of a dictator can obliterate them. The destiny of India lies in securing unity through these diversities, in attaining to a sense of oneness in spite of many varieties of types, and this can happen only through democracy which, in spite of diversities of purpose, leads towards a unity of aim. In this matter India has to possess the same faith which E. M. Foster has embodied in one of his recent essays, ***What I believe*** :

> "This brings me along to Democracy, "even Love, the Beloved Republic, which feeds upon Freedom and lives". Democracy is not a beloved republic really, and never will be. But it is less hateful than other contemporary forms of government, and to that extent it deserves our support. It does start from the assumption that the individual is important, and that all types are needed to make a civilization. It does not divide its citizens into the bossers and the bossed—as an efficiency regime tends to do.
>
> The people I admire most are those who are sensitive and want to create something or discover something, and do not see life in terms of power, and such people get more of a chance under a democracy than elsewhere, They found religions, great or small, or they produce literature and art, or they do disinterested scientific research, or they may be what is called "ordinary people", who are creative in their private lives, bring up their children decently, for instance, or help their neighbours. All these people need to express themselves ; they cannot do so unless society allows them liberty to do so, and the society which allows them most liberty is a democracy.
>
> Democracy has another merit. It allows criticism, and if there is not public criticism there are bound to be hushed-up scandals. That is why I believe in the press, despite all its lies and vulgarity, and why I believe in parliament. Parliament is often sneered at because it is a talking shop. I believe in it because it is a talking shop. I believe in the private member who makes himself a nuisance. He gets snubbed and is told that he is cranky or ill-informed, but he does expose abuses which would otherwise never have been mentioned, and very often an abuse gets put right just by being mentioned. Occasionally, too, a well-meaning public official starts losing his head in the cause of efficiency, and thinks himself God Almighty. Such officials are particularly frequent in the Home Office. Well, there will be questions about them in Parliament sooner or later, and then they will have to mind their steps. Whether Parliament is either a re-

presentative body or an efficient one is questionable, but I value it because it criticizes and talks, and because its chatter gets widely reported.

So two cheers for democracy: one because it admits variety and two because it permits criticism. Two cheers are quite enough: there is no occasion to give three. "Only Love, the Beloved Republic, deserves that".

ORDINARY PEOPLE

I have singled this quotation out simply because it expresses so beautifully what is relevant to the conditions in India. Indian philosophical thought has always laid stress on the importance of the individual and democracy also postulates a belief in the individual. India has always aimed at the consolidation of civilization and so does democracy. Indians had seldom interpreted life in terms of power but always in terms of service, and democracy has also similar aims. Again, India's genius has been mainly creative and democracy also puts a premium on creativeness whether in literature or art, religion or science. The end of all religions in India has been aptly defined as self-expression or self-realization, and democracy also allows people freedom to express themselves. Moreover, democracy brings a message of hope to ordinary people, and India is nothing but a land inhabited by very ordinary people. At the same time, India needs a great deal of self-criticism and even censorious criticism at the hands of others, because it has to eradicate so many social abuses, political disabilities and economic iniquities and nothing gives a country a greater measure of this kind of wholesome but occasionally blunt criticism than democracy. From all these things we cannot but conclude that democracy can alone save India and that education for democracy can alone safeguard in India.

We therefore need a real training in democracy in India; a training not only in democratic institutions and methods and procedures but also a training in the principles of democracy. First of all, therefore, every citizen of India, the citizen of today as well as of tomorrow, has to understand the underlying principles of democracy. I believe these were very aptly defined by Pericles in the palmy days of Athenian democracy. The great sage and statesman said, "*Our constitution is named democracy because it is in the hands of not a few but many......our laws secure equal justice for all in their private disputes......we have no black looks or angry words for our neighbour if he enjoys himself in his own way.*"

This statement of his gives us the three fundamental principles of democracy. In the first place, democracy is the government of the many ; in the second place, it aims at justice for all, and in the third place it secures liberty and tolerance for all. Nor have these principles been bettered or improved upon, though democracy has been tried in several countries in several forms. This goes to show that the corner-stone of democracy is the common man, and a democrat believes that the average citizen by practice would acquire all those virtues which are needed for the success of democracy. These, as we know, come from two things :—from practical experience in handling small affairs and from the free and frank discussions of public questions. In other words, democracy gives every citizen a sense of public responsibility and makes him as tolerant of the views of others as he is enthusiastic about his own.

A BASIC PRINCIPLE

In a way democracy is the school of tolerance, kindliness, wisdom and sympathy. This does not mean that in democracy everyone is free to act as he likes while in a totalitarian state everyone has to carry out the behests of the leader. This idea has been, with much shrewdness and humour and practical sense, expounded by Mr. A. G. Gardiner in one of his essays, *The Rule of the Road.* A democracy has to frame laws for its guidance but these laws are such as secure the maximum amount of freedom of thought and action for every individual. These are some of the political concepts which underlie democracy and which every citizen has to master. How different they are from the principles underlying Nazism or Fascism will be clear from these two pronouncements of Mussolini and Hitler.

Mussolini once asserted "*that the State is an absolute in comparison with which all individuals or groups are relative only to be conceived of in their relation to the State.*" Similarly it has been said "*That justice and Hitler's will are one and the same.* Democracy, however, reverses this. While in totalitarian countries the individual exists for the state; in democracies the state exists for the individual. The grasp of this basic principle is necessary because without it the democratic procedure seems to be a farce. In India, it is sad to relate, the people know all about the right to vote, but they do not know the responsiblilities which go with this right. So it is necessary that Indians be taught the basic principles of democracy. Has not Plato said, "*We call man a gentle animal; and, if nature has been kind to him and his education has been right, he is the most gentle and God-like of creatures. But if his education is inadequate or bad, he becomes the most savage of all the products of the earth.*" We find from this that even Plato makes a plea for the right kind of education for democracy.

ECONOMIC EQUALITY

It is, however, wrong to suppose that democracy is merely political; true democracy is effective also in the economic field. A political thinker of recent times has put the whole problem in a nutshell by saying that effective political democracy is unobtainable without economic equality. "*What good is freedom to a starving man? He cannot eat freedom or drink it.*" It is very difficult to define clearly what economic equality means. But all political theorists would agree that in a democratic country a citizen should be able to lead a life of reasonable security and comfort. That he should be able to bring up his family without the fear of starvation and that he should have a reasonable amount of leisure and the means to enjoy it.

In other words, the faith of a democrat requires that he should work for the eradication of poverty in all its forms, and so conduct the affairs of his country that the drudgery of life is minimised and the economic welfare of all secured.

Democracy, however, does not mean merely good government through representative institutions and economic security; it also connotes a way of life. It gives us, so to say, a working philosophy of life, which has been admirably summed up in the Biblical precept, "*Love thy neighbour as thyself*'. This means that a democrat does not lead the life of a hermit in a cloister who shuts himself away from human contacts and is afraid of tackling the problems of life. Nor is he an intellectual escapist who pursues the ends of truth or dreams noble dreams of beauty without soiling his hands with the affairs of the world. A democrat is essentially a practical man, whose faith implies practical usefulness and whose religion consists in serving others. He cannot be indifferent while others starve, nor can he go to sleep while things are going wrong. He believes in putting his shoulder to the wheel and in trying to set things right. He is a missionary of goodwill and a crusader against hatred and other thing. He believes in sharing life with others and not isolating himself from mankind.

FAITH IN CITIZENSHIP

This all-embracing concept of democracy has to be brought home to the minds of the people of India, if this ancient country of ours is to be rid of poverty, communal troubles, religious extremism and political separatism. But this can happen only if democrats preach a new faith in citizenship—citizenship which can rise above economic greed, partisan passions and sectional welfare—citizenship which knows that group interests, must be sacrificed to higher interests and that an active interest in the country's welfare is the only guarantee for peace, happiness and prosperity. But this faith in citizenship is not an occult or mystic faith. It has to be acquired by disciplining one's emotions, by training one's intelligence and by cultivating certain virtues. In a way it means intellectual and moral training.

Sir Ernest Simon who has done much hard thinking on this subject has described some of the qualities which a citizen of democracy must possess. Among the moral qualities he thinks that a sense of social responsibility is the most vital. A citizen of democracy must work not only for his own welfare but for the common good. But he should not do so as a blind ignorant person. "*He must be a man of independent judgment ; he must respect the individualities of others and therefore be tolerant of opinions in conflict with his own ; he must prefer methods of discussion and persuasion to methods of force.*" In addition to these moral qualities he must have some intellectual fitness, and this means that he must have knowledge and the ability to think clearly. He should know not only about those problems which concern him directly but also about the others which the world is facing. Above all he should have the capacity "*to choose a good representative and trust him when chosen.*" This means that he should not be at the mercy of tub-thumpers and spellbinders, but he should honour those men who possess honesty and ability, fearlessness and patience. These qualities, however, cannot be acquired through any religious formula or mystic incantation. They can come to us only through education. But, if we study the system of education prevalent in India at present, we shall find that its framers had conspired to rule such considerations out of it altogether. Our schools and universities have produced eminent scientists and men of letters, distinguished business men and educationists, competent clerks and artists, but they have never given any training to their students in the art of citizenship. The result is that students in India are very often at the mercy of demagogues, who appeal to their passions and prejudices and never try to train their intelligence or enlighten their conscience. The books that are taught at these institutions and the syllabuses that are framed for them are such as would enable the students to do everything but discharge their duties as responsible citizens. The teacher also thinks more of examination results than of anything else, and the student looks upon education merely as an avenue to a career.

FINDING A REMEDY

If such is the state of affairs, it would not be wrong if we try to find out the remedies for this kind of apathy.

The first remedy is that illiteracy should be liquidated in India. In spite of so many years of enterprise in the field of education at the hands of officials and non-officials India has only eight per cent of literates. No one would deny that this kind of rudimentary literacy is not conducive to the growth of democracy in India. Therefore the first requisite is a nation wide campaign for literacy. I think from this point of view the various adult education schemes sponsored by the provincial governments in India must be supported by every right thinking citizen, though it should be borne in mind that adult education does not merely mean an adult school but also a library and perhaps also a radio set which imparts instruction in a very delightful and digestible form. It is only by means of adult education that we can train those who have grown up illiterate. In addition to these agencies there should be institutes of citizenship in every village and town of India, where a citizen can learn to understand the questions that are awaiting solution in this country. If adult education is essential for grown up persons, education for democracy is required in our schools and colleges. For this purpose the content of our education, especially of primary and secondary education must be changed. Mr. Spencer Leeson has suggested that all boys and girls should receive instruction in the following subjects in England :—

(*i*) Modern English and European History—modern in the sense that it merges into current events ; the latter to be treated as an organic part of the course, not an occasional frill for a dull period.

(*ii*) Political and Economic Geography.

(*iii*) Modern Languages ; or to put it in a fairer way, a study of two modern European countries, based on a knowledge of their languages, spoken as well as written ; no doubt in most cases the countries would be France and Germany.

(*iv*) Elementary Constitutional Law ; or to put it in a simpler way, How we are Governed ; this should have reference to the Dominions and Colonies, as well as to this country. It will explain what Democracy means and what Liberty and Equality before the law mean; and special pains should be taken to describe the machinery which has been devised, by the reform of local government and in other ways, to cope with social problems, and so to bring into view the wide field of service that lies before the citizen in his own town as well as at Westminster.

(*v*) Economics. Pretty well every political question to-day is at root an economic question. I do not yet feel sure what place should be given in the schools to the teaching of economic theory—as a teaching subject it is in its infancy and we have not yet the experience to guide us; but modern economic history, and what may be called descriptive economics do not present the same difficulty. How many boys know what a trade union is, or what a bank does, or have ever analysed the Budget?

(*vi*) We should ask teachers of science to include among their aims the task of explaining what science has already done and may shortly be expected to do in reducing the demands made on human labour of all kinds. The next age must be prepared for its new leisure before it arrives, else when it does arrive, it will overtake an empty mind. Here is the immense importance of education for leisure. If the prophets of technocracy are right in predicting that at some not far distant time the working day will not exceed four hours, either it is to be leisure filled with satisfying employment or an ennui that will destroy us all.

I believe that this scheme of studies is admirable and it can be adapted to the needs of India.

From all this it is clear that education for democracy can alone save India, and that our educational system should be overhauled. It should have a major objective which is education for democratic citizenship and its content should be changed. Perhaps the Wardha Scheme of Education which aims at the widest possible literacy, education through activity and which aims at combining the liberal and practical aspects of education, would be helpful if the necessary modifications and changes are introduced in it.

GOVIND MAHADEO JOSHI

B. A.,

Mr. Joshi who is a lecturer and writer on social topics was born on 24th March 1899 and educated at Nutan Marathi Vidyalaya and Fergusson College, Poona. He took his B. A., with Honours in Mathematics 1918, was a college scholar throughout and started his public career in 1925 writing articles in *Kesari* and various papers on social subjects. Made a brilliant defence of the caste system in Hinduism and is a great champion of *Varnahram Swarajya Sangh* defending Indian culture on the principles of western science.

His work "Hindooche Samaj Rachana Shastra" (A structure of Hindu Society) was recently published. In this book the author first examines the structure of all civilizations, past and present, and concludes that there are two types of society with the two types of ethical systems corresponding to them. The first type is based on the classification of mankind on the basis of birth and leads to the structure based on castes. The second type is based on the principle of equality of man and leads to individualistic society. Between these two societies the author, from the standpoint of survival values, thinks that the caste form of society is far superior to any individualistic form, and is, according to Mr. Joshi, the only form which takes into consideration the aspects of mankind, nature and nurture.

Mr. Joshi's contribution to this volume deals trenchantly with the various problems and ramifications of population.

THE POPULATION PROBLEM

WHATEVER may be the type of economic theory that we may accept, it is evident that all sociological problems *e. g.* the problems of human culture and civilization, that of war and peace, of human happiness and misery, of nationalism and inter-nationalism, of stagnation and progress are fundamentally the population problem in its various ramifications. In their quantitative aspects populations may be expanding, may be tending to be stable, may be contracting. In their qualitative aspects populations may be expanding in number and contracting in quality or they may be contracting in number and growing richer in quality.

The term "quality" introduces another question "*What are those qualities and to what are they mainly due ?*" It is now universally acknowledged that man in society is a function of two variables—heredity and environment, or, nature and nurture according to Prof. Julian Huxley or heredity and selection as I prefer to call them. Though it be granted that these two variables, one of which is subjective and the other objective, one inherent and the other extraneous, interact in producing a personality. it is high time that the relative importance of these be examined in an unbiased spirit. The policy to be enunciated with reference to the structure of population, economic distribution and the sex code must necessarily follow the conclusions arrived at in such an impartial investigation. If it be decided that improvement in environment will ultimately lead to the improvement of race or *vice-versa,* the line of action of social legislation cannot be identical.

THE REAL QUESTION

The next point to investigate will be the causes or circumstances which primarily influence the numerical fluctuations in a given population assuming that the given group is not affected by emigration and immigration. If the population grows, irrespective of human volition as suggested by some influential scientists like Prof. Raymond Pearl of Baltimore, all talk of population control and the amelioration of temporal conditions is simply moonshine. If populations can be adjusted as we wish, all talk of revolution for equitable economic distribution is meaningless. In either case these fluctuations indicate physical vitality of a population. Again, fluctuations in a population may directly be affected by the variations in birth-rate and death-rate. The real question, therefore, deciding the vitality of race, is "*Which of the hypotheses, an increasing birth-rate or decreasing death-rate decides the vitality of races, is true*". As the death-rate is the function of birth to my mind a higher birth-rate shows the superior vitality of a people.

Before proceeding further let us try to ascertain the exact connotation of the phrase "*victorious in the struggle for existence*" so often used in these days of power-thinking. Really speaking the phrase is ambiguous. In the biological sense, those races and classes whose progeny, in the ultimate analysis, will populate the greater portion of the habitable space may be said to be victorious in the struggle for existence. In the social sense those classes which win a place for themselves near the apex of the social pyramid, may be said to be victorious in the struggle for existence. If there is a kind of parallelism betweeen the two senses *i.e.* if the class that dominates the apex of the society is identical with the class that populates the greater and the greater portion of the habitable earth, we can say that society is following the right path to betterment and evolution. If on the other hand the class that populates the earth is defeated in the social and temporal struggle, while the class which dominates the society numerically vanishes, we shall have to conclude that there is something fundamentally wrong in the social structure and tenets of such a society.

A SURVEY

Now if any one cares superficially to survey the classes and nations dominated by what is known as scientific or western civilization it will be clear that the phenomenon presented by that civilization falls exactly under the second category. Impartial writers warn these nations, that whoever may want to introduce that structure in their homes, will have to share the same fate. Mr. Bertrand Russel says that "the most intelligent classes in the most scientific nations are dying out, and western nations as a whole do not do much more than reproduce their numbers. Unless very radical measures are adopted, the white population of the globe will soon begin to diminish. The French have already been led to depend upon African troops, and if the white population dwindles, there will be an increasing tendency to leave the rough work to men of other races. In the long run this will lead to mutinies and reduce Europe to the condition of Haiti. In such circumstances it would be left to China and Japan to carry on our scientific civilization, but in proportion as they acquire it they, too, will acquire a lower birth rate." It is very puzzling to a plain layman. Why should it be so and what will be the effect of such a phenomenon on the destinies of the human race ?

ETHICAL VALUES

We intend to point out that the real cause of this strange phenomenon of recent occurrence lies in the ethical values that are introduced by the so-called rationalistic and scientific civilization. Any civilization which implicitly makes wealth the only criterion of social worth and social differentiation cannot escape this fact. Firstly, the civilization enunciates that a man is free to leave the category in which he finds himself, for any other category or form within a given group or nation. Secondly, the status of an individual may be ascertained by the wealth a person possesses. Any society naturally divides itself into classes and categories and thus forms the physical structure, the categories near the apex being supposed to be the superior ones. Russians proposed to invert this pyramid ; but we must wait for some time till we are able to assess the effects of their labours. In a classical pyramidal society in accordance with the first value, conventional currents start from above to below and *vice versa.* If we try to examine the currents we can easily realise that the whole categories or classes never leave their places (see—*Task of Social Hygiene* by Havelock Ellis).

A few individuals from lower categories may aspire to rise higher and achieve their ambition. A few others, who may not have got vitality enough to maintain their position in the class to which they belong to, go downwards. Notwithstanding these currents, as I have stated above, the classes are not very much disturbed and thus a class on the whole remains an endogamous group. It is also a truth, accepted by reformers, that parties to marriage must be of equal status. But the term status is not co-extensive with economic status only. In short, the status of the parties to marriage is judged according as the other members of that status approve or disapprove of such a a marriage. "*By reason of influence of class on mate-selection distinctions of social classes are distinctions of relatively permanent biological entities*" R. A. Fisher.

THE REWARD OF STERILITY

When ambitious members of lower categories want to rise to higher rank there is a possibility of accomplishing their aims only if they are not burdened by economic responsibilities. Let us take the case of two persons, one of whom is more fertile than the other. The individual who is more sterile and less encumbered by children has a greater chance of rising to the higher class than the other one. Sterility, therefore, becomes the means of social advancement. If the sterility is not inherent then an ambitious man will naturally turn into other channels and induce it in himself. Thus in every upward movement of individuals fertility is bound to fall.

The unfortunates, who have to leave an upper category for a lower one, bring their own sterility to the lower class and thus reduce the fertility of that class. A sociological difficulty that crops up in the case of individuals and families on the downward march is that there is no place left for these on, the lowest rung in the social scale. If they are hard hit they have no place to go down and have to rely on alms as a means of subsistence.

Thus we are forced to the conclusion that the society which lacks the solidarity necessary to impress upon each social category the limits within which the aspirations of its members may be considered legitimate—having regard to the general level attended by social evolution—is on the road to destruction. I pointed out this effect 15 years ago and I am glad to see that it is now being endorsed about Northern and Western Europe by nearly all noted statisticans.

This phenomena "*fertility varies inversely as the social status and economic remuneration*" leads to other very far-reaching socially destructive effects. The burden of bearing, rearing and educating future generations falls most heavily exactly on those who are the least capable of bearing the same. The wealth remains concentrated as there are no partners to share, while smaller quantities of wealth became smaller and smaller on account of divisions among the claimants. The natural consequence of this is that smaller and smaller percentages of population know very little of comfort and become prone to Marxian revolution. In short, we can summarise the effects of so-called scientific civilization as follows :—

(1) Social classes thus become gentically differentiated local varieties of species. R. A. Fisher.

(2) Differential fertility directly sets in. Survival varies inversely as social status and economic remuneration.

(3) Greater percentage of population is produced and bred by those who are least capable of doing it. This leads to the propagation of dissatisfied population prone to revolutions.

(4) A great chasm is created between the cultures of the higher and lower categories.

(5) Incessant shifting of individuals from class to class creates no loyalties and therefore no culture worth mentioning.

It will be clear to the reader that the present policies of the western world, who are themselves groping in the dark, cannot guide other nations to the correct solution of population questions.

Any population to be scientifically treated must be examined from the standpoint of four cardinal principles—composition, constitution, economic distribution and sex-code.

INVESTIGATION

To my mind it is now high time that administrations, leaders of the public and others who possess any influence in the social legislations recognize the value of regular and comprehensive surveys of the nation's resources both in material wealth and in personnel. Before tampering with an existing structure and introducing substitutes the first necessity is to assess the distribution of intelligence and unintelligence ; capacity and incapacity in a given group, society or nation. The rule of untutored intuition and prejudice must give place to scientific investigation.

The elements in population, which is to be constructed into smoothly working living organism, must be evaluated as far it is humanly possible. Such a survey will indicate the form into which all these elements can be integrated. The same principle of classification must be used to form the limbs of the organism to be created. Then, by the method of the survival of the complementaries, the groups are to be so arranged as to form a smoothly working organism. Such groups (of every conceivable kind) may or may not be organic, may tend to be social, anti-social and unsocial. The Indian caste system is largely organic, the groups of western society are dangerously tending towards the anti-social.

PRIMARY PRINCIPLES

What then are the principles used by the Hindoo in forming the structure of their society and what are the principles used in western culture ? So far as one can see the westerners have deliberately and intelligently used no principle of classification at all. The Hindoos have used birth as the primary principle of classification and have built up the system of endogamous caste. We have to examine that system from the standpoint of the complicated question of population. The moral values ennunciated by this system are exact contradictories of those enunciated in the western world.

(1) No individual, on account of his intellectual superiority or economic affluence, can change the category to which he belongs without reference to the general level attained by the social-evolution of the whole class. He must remain in his place as a centre of vitality for that class. If there is to be any rise the whole class must rise or must fall. In short, in this system, there is the method of selection by groups not by individuals.

(2) Status of an individual is decided not by any intellectual brilliance or economic affluence, but by the performance of *varna* work, which is individualistic in action and socialistic in effect.

In this type of organism the numerical strength of a caste is the function of total organisation. If the rules of the caste are rigidly followed the growth or otherwise of a caste in its quantitative aspect depends on the growth or otherwise of the total population. The growth or otherwise of the total population will increase or decrease the demand for a particular service or a particular commodity which in a caste society is the monopoly of a particular group. In this way all the castes in their quantitative aspects being controlled, no individual can be produced who may become indigestible in the social metabolism. If the total population suddenly contracted (which, by the way, very rarely happens) the numerical strength of the caste gives an opportunity for the action of natural selection thus selecting the superior individuals for the propagation of future generations. In this system, the profession of an individual being inherent in his very birth he does not find himself a helpless unit, without any profession or future in the social economy. A member of the caste society is always free from economic competition, which is the curse of the present day European structure. These thoughts are slowly being grasped by the western experts. Thus says Prof. Carr-Saunders "*competition can only be avoided in so far as the structure of the society becomes segmentary, that is, divided into hereditary castes and it is away from and not towards, social structure of this kind that those who attack capitalism wish to move*" WORLD POPULATION' page 250.

AUTOMATIC CONTROL

In caste society the control of population in its quantitative aspect is automatic. For the control of the population in its qualitative aspect the social structure must be so created as to eliminate the inferior stocks and select the superior automatically without the help of any volitional agency. The fundamental necessity for any such permanent arrangement is to ascertain the distribution of intelligence and non-intelligence ; ability and incapacity in a given population. The present arrangement of the western society forces the centres of ability to gravitate towards a common point and leave the remaining mass sapped of all the vitality. In the system governed by caste no such skimming process occurs and the centres of ability are evenly distributed throughout the population. The status in a caste society, being based on the functional manifestations which are complementary and exclusive, interdependant and interlaced to form a complete whole, is horizontal and, naturally, there is in essence no higher or lower caste. Historically (that is, in practice) some castes are supposed to be higher and others supposed to be lower; but these differences were deliberately intensified after the advent of British rule for the political purposes of the British rulers. In the pre-British period Dr. Ghurye of the Bombay University, tells us all the castes supposed themselves to be equal in status on account of their functional equality. "*Ideas of status were quietly accepted and did not prevent healthy co-operation and neighbourly feelings amongst various caste groups represented in ihe vigorous village communities of Southern India.*" 'CASTE AND RACE IN INDIA' page 25. The author further remarks "*A quarrel between cousins in respect of some hereditary rights was referred for settlement to to the whole village. The assembly that was to give decision included Marathas, Dhangars, Gurav, Sutar, Lohar, Kumbhar, Koli, Barbar, Chamar, Mahar and Mang.*"

Partisans of individual selection may raise a question that, assuming ability breeds ability, is it not better that able individuals at various centres be collected in one group and mated amongst themselves? In the present state of eugenic knowledge we cannot definitely ascertain but whatever proof exists is decidedly against such assumption. Prof. Julian Huxley remarks "*But usually the distinction will be quantitative. The characters or genes which are present will be in different proportions in different groups; their most frequent combinations will also differ from one group to the other. It is only by means of quantitative differences in representation that in the main we can hope to define the differences between one group and the other.*" 'WE EUROPEANS' page 108. But fundamentally the selection by individuals is wide of the mark in the process of social evolution by natural selection. If we closely observe nature the process of evolution is most effective when the selection proceeds by the method of selection by groups.

The test of vitality of the population and civilization is that the population must be able to expand in any direction whenever demanded by pressure of circumstances. Hindoo population has shown this capacity so many times in the history of that people that to question it is nothing less than exposing our own ignorance. Second test is the capacity of the population to preserve itself under any circumstances and under the pressure of any hardships. One author remarks "*The real danger is not that of immediate military aggression from Japan or other oriental countries, but the gradual, peaceable, passive extension of the oriental races who have developed and adapted themselves to a kind of existence that enables then to undermine and destroy other forms of civilizations and destroy or absorb other races*".

AUTHORITIES

The word "progress" (whatever that may mean) presupposes some level in the hereditary and traditional evolution that any people or races may have achieved. If the races or nations are not to regress, they must accomplish stable equilibrium at a certain level in respect of both their cultural achievements and biological evolution. The deplorable fate of a number of civilizations (causes of their rise and fall I have discussed in detail in my Marathi work "*The Structure of the Hindoo Society*") warns us to infer that they had not taken this necessary precaution to create such stable equilibrium necessary for future progress is possible only in a society governed by a system developed by Hindoo castes. Prof. R. A. Fisher, the famous mathematical geneticist of the London University remarks "*A rigid system of occupational castes, each compelled to bear the burden of its own necessary reproduction, would ensure biological permanence, much as the permanence of the society of genes is ensured in the cell-division*". "GENETICAL THEORY OF NATURAL SELECTION" by R. A. Fisher. A member of generations of a. caste practically makes a caste biological sub-species. Inside a community of different types, originated from a cross which do not further intercross, we will get, as calculated above, after a large number of generations a large number of species and but a few heterozygotes" *Evolution by Hybridization* by G. P. Loisy. The biological stability and traditional or cultured standardization are necessary conditions for future progress. Prof. E. M. East remarks "*Special progress requires better breeding in the first instance in order to raise the racial potentiality for accomplishment, it requires the voluntarily standardized population in the second instance in order to retain the environment in which the potentialities can be realised*" "MANKIND AT THE CROSS ROADS" by E. M. East.

We have discussed up to now without entering any statistical details, the effects of the structures of society on the populations in their quantitative and qualitative aspects. All the difficulties of the political economist of the west are easily solved by the arrangement of population in such a structure as developed by the Hindoos.

From the standpoint of sociological classification of the population Prof. Giddings distinguishes three fundamental or primary orders of population classes—Social classes, vitality classes and personality classes. These different types of classes do not occur in the caste society as the classes in that are differentiated by the criterion of the degree of their sociability. As pointed out above by me, Hindoo society in its economy does not form any personality classes (1) geniuses and talented (2) normally endowed and (3) defective. This society does not collect all the geniuses and talented together and form them into a class. As every caste is responsible for its own reproduction it never happens that any one section of the society, say geniuses or morons, reproduce the next generation. In this sense every caste is in itself a vitality class. If any particular class is reduced in vitality it does not affect the whole structure.

There are four patterns of social classes—social, non-social, pseudo-social and anti-social. Social classes are represented by natural aristocracy; non-social classess are strongly individualistic; pseudo-social classes are those classes which are unable to hold their own in the social metabolism and at the same time have not vitality enough to harm the social organism such as congenital and habitual paupers, anti-social classes are those who have vitality enough to attempt to harm an organism such as congenital and habitual criminals.

The last two classes are parasitical and must be fed by social organisms under one guise or other. What methods are used by the western peoples to reduce their incidence? These classes are two fold:—1. Who comes as a guest, the beggar, the prostitute. 2. Who comes as an enemy, the thief, the forger, the speculator and so on.

Really speaking the non-social is fundamentally the basis of all the other three. Social class—the professional and intellectual classes must be so evolved, that the tendencies of the last two must be eliminated from them. It is exactly this that Europe has never been able to achieve. Let us hear what Ruskin has to say about the matter. "*The first reason for all wars and for the necessity of national defence, is that the majority of persons, high and low, in all European nations are thieves and their hearts greedy of their neighbours' land, goods and fame.*"

I have according to my lights discussed the merits and de-merits of the Eastern and Western structures of society from the standpoint of composition and constitution. The caste society is superior to non-caste for the following reasons:—

1. From the standpoint of survival value caste society has superior vitality.

2. The segregation of the fit at one end and unfit at the other, found so desirable by the influential school of eugenists, is easily accomplished in this system.

3. This type of society does not produce disinherited class ready to destroy the social structure itself.

4. This system automatically controls the population both in its qualitative and quantitative aspects.

MAULAVI ABDUL KARIM

B.A., M.L.C.,

Is a government pensioner, a Member of the Council of State and has been a Member of the Bengal Legislative Council since 1926. He was born on 29th August 1863 and was educated at Sylhet and Calcutta. The Maulavi started life as a teacher in the Calcutta Madrasah afterwards becoming Assistant Inspector of Schools, for Mahomedan Education for about 15 years and Inspector of Schools, Chittagong Division, for about 5 years.

His published works include "History of India for Beginners," (in English, Bengali, Hindi and Urdu) ; "Hints on Class Management and Method of Teaching" (English) ; "Mahomedan Education in Bengal" (English).

ISLAM'S CONTRIBUTION TO SCIENCE

ISLAM laid the foundation of modern science and inaugurated a scientific era in the history of the world. The impression, prevalent in western countries, that Islam is an unprogressive religion, antagonistic to science and civilization, is absolutely incorrect. When the whole world was immersed in ignorance and barbarism, Islam gave an unprecedented impetus to the intellectual development of mankind and made the Muslims the precursors of modern scientists and pioneers of modern civilization. For about one thousand years the followers of Islam held high the torch of light and learning to the uninitiated world. The subsequent intellectual sterility and stagnation that came upon the Muslim world, giving rise to a false impression regarding Islamic influence, was due to certain historical circumstances similar to those that prevailed in Europe during the Middle Ages, before the Renaissance and

PROFESSOR DIWAN CHAND SARMA
M.A.

the Reformation. The Islamic faith and its teachings were in no way responsible for this regrettable deterioration.

DISSEMINATION OF KNOWLEDGE

The world was enveloped in ignorance and illiteracy when Islam was promulgated. No messenger of God, before the Prophet of Islam, had done anything for the dissemination of knowledge. As the great attributes of the Almighty God could not be adequately realised by the ignorant, Prophet Muhammed made the acquisition of knowledge essential for his followers. He laid down "*Talabul-Ilme Farizatum Ala Kulle Muslimin Wa Muslimatin*". "Seeking of knowledge is imperative for all Muslims, males or females". The Muslims were enjoined to "study from the cradle to the grave", "the ink of the scholar being holier than the blood of the martyr", and "an hour's contemplation and study of God's creation being better than a year's adoration".

Before the promulgation of Islam, religion had to be blindly accepted without the use of intellect or judgment. Freedom of thought and enquiry were strictly prohibited. Religion and science were supposed to be irreconcilable to each other. Any one expressing any opinion contrary to the prevailing sacredotal belief was branded as a heretic and was relentlessly persecuted and inhumanly tortured.

EARLY MARTYRS

Vamini was horribly persecuted for his belief in the theory of evolution ; his tongue was torn out of his mouth and he was burnt alive. Hypatia, the renowned commentator on Plato, had to pay the penalty for her intellectual audacity with her life.

Copernicus, who tried to demonstrate that the earth revolves and not the heavens, was denounced by Calvin and Martin Luther as "as upstart astrologer" and he had to end his life in disgrace. Bruno, who dared to advance the Copernican theory, was imprisoned and then put to death by a "fire made slow to increase the torture".

Galileo, who supported the Copernican theory, was thrown into a dungeon, horribly tortured and compelled to recant as follows :—I, Galileo, in my seventieth year, being a prisoner on my kness before your eminences, having before my eyes the Holy Gospel, abjure, curse and detest the error and the heresy of the movements of the earth". Not content with mere recantation, the Holy Inquisition sent him into exile for the rest of his life.

Thus some of the most inhuman atrocities committed on men in search of truth, were perpetrated in Europe, during the Middle Ages, in the name of religion. Besides, some of the famous libraries, containing accumulated treasures of ages, were consigned to the flames for the destruction of what were regarded as heretical writings.

REASON—THE TEST OF FAITH

When such fanatacism and barbarity prevailed throughout the world, Islam made reason the test of faith and discountenanced all dogmatic teachings. "The first thing created" says the Prophet of Islam "was reason. God has not created anything better than reason". According to the *Quran* "there is no piety in turning the face towards the East or the West and there is no reward for performing prayers, fast, charity, pilgrimage and other good deeds save in proportion to the sense employed". In Islam faith means knowledge of a truth or principle up to which one can live. It does not signify belief that cannot be translated into action. All this unmistakably demonstrates that Islam does not regard mere rituals and ceremonies as essentials of religion. A Muslim may indulge in free thought and enquiry concerning everything that man's intelligence is capable of apprehending. To him science, the aim of which is truth, is the greatest ally of true religion. "Islam stands almost alone" says Guizot in his *History of European Civilizatian* "among the religions in discountenancing the reliance on tradition without argument. It demands that its votaries should undertake the investigation of the great work of their faith". By thus putting an end to all conflicts between religion and science and by making the subservice of nature to man an article of faith, Islam revolutionised the human mind and impelled it to investigate the marvels of creation. Every branch of learning conductive to human weal and progress was thus brought within the purview of Islam.

THE FOUNDATION OF MODERN SCIENCE

In early age the bulk of mankind could not think in the abstract and they did not realise the utility of the elements of nature. These were looked upon as sacred objects, possessing supernatural powers, and were worshipped as gods and goddesses. It was Islam that brought them down from the pedestal of divinity to the position of servants of mankind. For the first time the holy *Quran* declared that the main purpose for which different objects, from the mightiest sun to the insignificant atom, were created, was to administer to the needs of mankind, who were commanded to investigate their properties and to harness them for the service of humanity—in other words, to cultivate every branch of science for the good of mankind.

The *Quran* clearly indicated how to reduce nature to human service by contemplation and observation and thus placed in the hands of man the key with which the treasure-house of nature could be opened. Everything in the universe having being intended for the use of man, it was a virtuous act for him to make researches in the realms of nature in order to discover the utility of its various components. Thus the first principle of progress, the utilisation of the forces of nature for the needs of man, became an article of faith with Muslims and impelled them to engage in scientific research.

Muslims were also enjoined to look upon the universe as an expression of God's attributes and to glorify Him not by mere expression of lip-gratitude, but by discovering and utilising the properties and potentialities of the things he has created for supplying the needs of His creatures. Realisation of the bounties of God is the realisation of God Himself. A Muslim has to spiritualize, as it were, his material surroundings by seeing and feeling the evidence of God's power and love in every blade of grass and in every breath of air. In fact man knows nothing of God except through his work in nature. "Verily in the creation of heavens and earth and in the alternation of night and day, there are signs for men of understanding, who remember Allah ; standing, sitting and while lying on their sides and ponder over the creation of heaven and earth" and say "Our Lord Thou has not created (all) this in vain. Glory be to Thee". *Al-Quran.*

SCIENTIFIC DISCOVERIES

Thus in that dark age Islam created an insatiable thirst for knowledge and gave to scientific research a religious aspect unknown and unthought of before. It was this religious stimulus that particularly impelled the early Muslims zealously to exert themselves for the advancement of science and thus caused a tremendous upheaval of science in realms hitherto altogether unexplored. Such an extraordinary outburst of intellectual activity was unknown in human history. In a wonderfully short time the Muslims made phenomenal progress in science. Thirteen centuries ago they visualised many things which are being discovered today. They explored and exploited the potentialities of objects which were unknown and unthought of since the creation of the world. In fact there was hardly any conceivable subject to which they did not give serious thought. They created modern chemistry, made important discoveries in astronomy and valuable researches in botany, geology and zoology. They unearthed alchemy and algebra. They initiated and developed the study of political economy and sociology which were unknown sciences till then. They added much to the knowledge of mathematics and medicine.

Muslims also investigated and wrote on various other subjects, as navigation, irrigation, agriculture, gardening, statistics, chronology and topography. Even aviation, the latest achievement of Europe and an early wonder of the twentieth century, was not left untried. Abul Qasim Ben Firnas, invented a flying machine in the ninth century and succeeded in flying great distances at considerable speed.

In the eight century, the Abbaside Khalifas established the famous academy of Baghdad, where the famous works of the renowned mathematicians Euclid, Archimedes and Applonius, of the astronomer Ptolemy, and of the naturalists, Hippocrates and Diomedes, were translated into Arabic. In this and other Muslim centres of learning Greek culture was kept alive at a time when, outside Byzantium, it had no abiding place anywhere in the non-Muslim world. Many were the libraries, observatories and laboratories that were established by Muslim kings. In the library attached to Baitul-Hikmat, the abode of learning, a remarkable university founded by Khalifa Harun-ur-Rashid, there were many hundred thousand Sanskrit, Greek, Coptic, Chaldean and Persian books besides those in Arabic. Khalifa-Al-Hakim's library was so very extensive that its catalogue had to be prepared in forty very large volumes.

CHEMISTRY

As Humboldt truly says "Modern chemistry was admittedly the invention of the Muslims", whose achievements in this sphere were of unique interest. They conclusively proved the worthlessness of ancient chemistry. They found out the chemical affinities of mercury, lead, copper, silver and gold and knew the chemical process of oxidation and calcination. Jabir-ben-Hyyan, known as Feber in the western world, wrote some five huudred treatises on chemistry. He discovered, for the first time, nitric acid, sulphuric acid, aqua regia, silver nitrate and several compounds. The Muslims were the first to teach the world distillation, filtration, crystallisation etc., They knew how to change a liquid into vapour. It was in Muslim Spain that chemistry was first established in Europe, and would have reached its zenith there had not the Muslims suffered the disastrous defeat at Poitiers.

ASTRONOMY

The Muslims made wonderful discoveries concerning the movements of the solar system and other astral bodies. They identified and classified a large number of stars in their observatories. They ascertained the size of the earth, the variation of the earth, the variation of the lunar latitudes and the procession of the equinoxes ; Ibni Rushid, known as Averroes. discovered the sun-spot ; Abul Hasan discovered atmospheric reflection, Al-Maimun determined the obliquity of ecliptic ; Ibni-Junus, Nasiruddin Fusi and Albani constructed astronomical tables of great value. Albani's tables were translated into Latin and formed the basis of astronomical study in Europe. It was the Muslims who first built observatories in Europe and invented the telescope, the compass, the pendulum and many other useful astronomical instruments.

MEDICINE

The father of the present day European medical science was Ibni-Sina, known as Avicenna, whose *Materia-Medica* is still in vogue. Ibni Zoar, known as Aven Zoor, was a great authority on pharmacy, which was an institution of Muslim invention. He and some others carefully studied the effect on the body of drugs obtained from various parts of the world and discovered many remedies. The Muslim doctors were the first to use anasthetics. Al-Bucasis of Cordova was an expert surgeon of world-wide reputation. The science of optics owes much to Muslim research. Al-Hazan, who understood the weight of air, corrected the misconception of the Greeks as to the nature of vision and demonstrated for the first time that the rays of light come from the external object to the eye and not from the eye itself, inpinging on external objects. It was he who showed that the retina is the seat of vision and proved that the impressions made upon it were conveyed along the nerves to the brain. He discovered that the refraction of light varied with the density of the atmosphere and *vice versa.*

In Baghdad there were no less than 860 doctors of different classes, each class of whom made one particular branch of medicine their special study. Doctors as well as chemists had to pass an examination in order to obtain a license to practise. There were innumerable hospitals throughout the wide Muslim empire. All classes of people, irrespective of their creed, caste, colour and country, were freely admitted to these hospitals.

MATHEMATICS

Almost every branch of higher mrthematics bears the impress of Muslim genius. Many were the improvements effected by the Muslims in this important subject. The Arabic numerals, the decimal system and art of figures, which Europe got from the Muslims led the world in astronomy, mechanics and mathematics. The Muslims were the first of all nations to translate Euclid and to use it. It was not properly translated in any European language till the sixteenth century. The Muslims for the first time applied algebra to geometry. They discovered equations of the second degree, and developed the theory of quadratic equations and the binomial theorem. They invented spherical trigonometry and, by introducing the use of sine and cosine, made great contributions to the science of surveying and astronomy. The Muslims were the first to use instruments of precision for the measurement of time by the use of the pendulum and the measurement of heavenly bodies by the use of the astrolabe.

GEOGRAPHY AND HISTORY

In Arabic there are many immortal works on geography. The sperical shape of the globe was demonstrated by the Muslims at a time when the scientists of priest-ridden Europe emphatically asserted that it was flat. The historical achievements of the Muslims are too well-known to require detailed mention. They produced several thousand books on history ranging in magnitude from one to eighty volumes.

Thus for about one thousand years the Muslims made history and spread knowledge and culture throughout the world. But for the great intellectual heritage bequeathed by them to the people of the west, it would not have been possible for them to make the immense progress they have made. It is to be noted that the Muslims were in the vanguard of the world's advancement as long as they were true to Islam and faithfully followed the injunctions of the 'holy *Quran*. Their downfall commenced when they became remiss in their loyalty to the lofty ideals of Islam. With the western people the reverse seems to have happened. They were unable to make any appreciable progress as long as they were orthodox Christians. It was only when they shook off the grip of their religion that they could make sufficient progress in science and civilisation. In this connection it should be noted that the outstanding achievements of people, over whom religion has little influence and who seem to be guided more by the fear of man than by the fear of God, have been in the domain of arms, ammunition, explosives, poisons and of death and destruction rather than of peace and construction.

AN AWAKENING

The height of scientific progress forecast by the *Quran* has not yet been fully attained. The world is full of materials that await man's exertion and ingenuity for their development and utilisation. There are are millions of things in the bowels of the earth and the ocean that have been created for man's use. All these have to be harnessed in order to meet the ever increasing requirements of human society. The *Quran* repeatedly speaks of the subservience of the physical world to man whose duty it is to explore it for his use.

The Muslims themselves, and not their religion are to blame for the intellectual sterility and spiritual stagnation that have been prevailing at present in the Muslim world. A glance at the condition of the world before and after the promulgation of Islam would show what Islam is capable of accomplishing. The decadence of the Muslims must not be attributed to any shortcoming of their religion. It is a matter of satisfaction to note that some of the master minds of western countries, such as the great poet Goethe, the great historian Gibbon, the great philosopher Carlyle, the great orator Ingersoll, the great socialist Bernard Shaw, among others, have been profoundly impressed by the message of Islam and think that it can absorb every progress made by philosophy and science. I have reason to believe that Islam will again assert itself before long.

G. G. RAO.

B.A., LL. B. (LONDON) BAR-AT-LAW

Is the son of G. Rameswara Rao, B. A., B. L., and was born on the 1st June 1912 at Patakottacheru, Gooty Taluk, Anantapur District. He concluded his studies in the Municipal High School, Anantapur (1919-1929) by passing the S. S. L. C. Examination and then joined the Ceded Districts College, Anantapur in July 1929 taking his B. A. degree in 1933 with physics as his optional subject. While at college he was awarded prizes in debating competitions.

Mr. Rao left for England in Nov. 1933 joining the Hon. Society of Lincoln's Inn in January 1937 and the University College, London for LL. B. course in October 1935. He received his LL, B. degree from London University in May 1938 in which year he passed the Bar Final and was called in London on the 30th of June of the same year,

Returning to India he was an Advocate of the Madras High Court in August 1938 and has been practising in Cuddapah since 1st January of this year. He was also in charge of his father's office in Cuddapah. An article on Public Health and Homeopathy written by Mr. Rao's father also appears in this volume.

FASCISM

EUROPE today is menaced by the fire and force of this new political philosophy called Fascism and Spain, Austria, Czechoslovakia, Albania and other countries have all been the unfortntate victims of Fascist aggression. Abyssinia fell to the first mighty stroke of Italy and in the East, Japan is engaged in a gigantic plan to devour China. Fascism has thus been following an aggressive militant policy and we cannot predict what the next move of Fascist leaders is going to be. Sooner or later India may come into the picture and it is, therefore, necessary that we should make a careful study of this new political theory which is becoming increasingly popular.

Fascist philosophy (if philosophy it is) originated in Italy after the Great War, (which, by the way, was called a war to end wars !) and is the outcome of disillusionment and disgust arising out of defeat. This is a paradox as most striking things in life are. Italy was no doubt on the side of the victors but she felt humiliation rather than elation at the Treaty of Versailles. She felt, perhaps justifiably, that Great Britain and France got all the plums and Italy none. The reward for sacrifice was disappointment.

Mussolini, who is the author of Fascism, started his political career as a Socialist as Hitler also did, but today neither of them can be called a Socialist for their theories are opposed completely to everything that the Socialists hold sacred. The growth of the Fascist party to power and the meteoric rise of Mussolini to the position that he now occupies need not be discussed in detail beyond stating that the movement, supported by able propaganda, soon became popular and received immense public support.

What is striking and significant about Fascism is its extreme Nationalism. The Duce, whose ambition it is to resurrect the great Roman Empire of the past, is attempting to build up a vast empire by marshalling around him forces that are trained and taught to obey. There is but one voice that can dictate. You follow the leader or you face the firing squad. *'Their's not to reason why. Their's but to do and die'*. Contrary and conflicting opinions are suppressed with a heartless tyranny that renders the autocrats of the past mere monarchs of mercy. "*Today*" says Sir Radhakrishnan "*a state sacrifices millions of its citizens with a clean conscience in the name of war. Life has become one continuous ritual*".

"*Fascism*"says Ivor Brown, correspondent of the '*Manchester Guardian*', "*is the deification of the State and the Hero who is its champion. It has sought to inflame instead of healing, and has astutely mobilised hatred against foreigners, against political opponents or against Jews. It has used all the arts of execration and persecution*". Thus the individual is reduced to a state of non-entity and is a mere tool in the hands of the government.

Such an explanation of the function of the state sounds strange to us who are trained to think in terms of democratic ideas where the individual liberty is held loftier than the interests of the state. *Magna Charta* and the *Bill of Rights* proclaim these well established principles in unmistakable terms. The motto of the French Revolution was 'Liberty, Equality, Fraternity'. Thus those who still believe in the sanctity of ballot boxes cannot reconcile themselves to the idea that a single individual, or a single party even, can determine the destinies of a nation, however distinguished the individual may be or however popular the party is. "*The best index to the quality of a state*" writes Harold Laski "*is the degree in which it is able to permit free criticism of itself*'. The very existence of opposition benches in England, France and U.S.A. is ample evidence to show that discordant voices are not only not permitted but positively encouraged. Major Attlee and M. Blum are not rotting in concentration camps or condemned cells but are held to be personalities of great asset to their country. They remain to challenge the government when the government errs.

Another striking feature of Fascism is that it is opposed to the idea of peace and thrives on fermenting hatred and war. Pacifism then is, for Fascists, a symptom of weakness.

Machine guns are preferred to olive branches and Hitler told us recently that Germany preferred guns to butter! Mussolini says that "*Fascism does not believe either in the possibility or utility of universal peace. It therefore rejects Pacifism which masks surrender and cowardice. Imperialism is the enternal and immutable law of life ; peace is hence absurd or rather it is a pause in war.*" In "*My Struggle*" Hitler strikes the same note when he says that "*an alliance whose object does not include the intention of war is worthless nonsense.*" Herr Von Papen declares that Germany, on 30th January 1933 struck out the word "Pacifism" from its vocabulary. Goering declares that "*the woman's place is in the home and her duty, the recreation of the tired warrior.*" "*There is no higher or finer privilege for a woman than that of sending her children to war*" is what is contained in the declaration of the Women's Order of the Red Swastika.

In these paragraphs we have treated Italian Fascism and German National Socialism as being identical. Indeed they are alike except for a few minor differences which will be considered later. Primarily they are alike in their disregard and contempt for peace and in their glorification of war. It consequently follows that Fascist countries do not believe either in the utility or in the advantage of the League of Nations. An institution which has, as its avowed object, the permanent establishment of world peace has no use for political theorists who believe firmly in the necessity and usefulness of war. True, Germany, Italy and Japan were members of the League but they were members only so long as their interests were not affected. The moment they found that the League was an impediment and an obstruction, they withdrew their membership and have now begun to spurn it. After the war in Manchuria, Japan was out of it; the application of sanctions during the Abyssinian War drove Italy away from the League and Germany has not forgiven either the League or the Treaty of Versailles. The Treaty of Versailles and the Kellogg Pact will interest only future historians.

It would be idle to suggest that a whole populace would be roused to a pitch of enthusiasm by the mere promise of war. No sane man would court war any more than he would court hell. It is here that the might of the Ministry of Propaganda becomes apparent. The ministry, with its unerring instinct for judging the weakness in the emotional make-up of man, manœuvres things in such a way as to make him believe and feel convinced in the usefulness and inevitability of war. The finer chords are touched and his hidden wrath is roused. His patriotism becomes also his fanaticism. Let us quote Ivor Brown again: "*Romantic appeals shout down the rational; resonant slogans seem more substantial than practical programmes. Symbols acquire a mystical potency......Voting papers are less romantic than swrods as doves are less imposing than eagles*".

Fascism thus purports to succeed where, apparently, democracy has failed. It promises tempting rewards without disclosing the sacrifices it demands. It throws the blame on the democracies for the horrors of the Great War. To a bewildered, war-weary man-in-the-street come offers of security and stability and in his simplicity he clings to them steadfastly. Fascists tell the workers that they will be given employment; they tell the shopkeepers that they will bring them customers; they promise the capitalists huge profits and they assure the agriculturists their lands. In short Fascism opens out to all people a new vista of hope and gives them a glimpse of a Utopia. The promises are attractive for they are cloaked in such sweet, tempting language.

But how could these dreams be realised? By war, declare the Fascist prophets. The rich gifts of God are for the brave and the strong and not for the weak and effeminate. Success depends upon sacrifice and sacrifice means strength. In the light of this, the colonial demands of Hitler and Mussolini are explained (though not justified). Colonies are demanded to solve their over-population problem, and at the same time, the Dictators are encouraging increase of population and condemning birth-control methods. Men get a proportionate reduction in their taxation as their families increase for every child is a potential soldier of the state. This is inconsistent, for a country cannot, on the one hand, increase her population and on the other, claim colonies to populate them. The truth is that these Fascist countries are always seeking for some excuse to fight, as war forms an intergal part of their politics. They are continually preparing for war and there is conscription all the year round. Compulsory military education has become the fashion in Europe. Even democratic England has had to follow suit, and Mr. Chamberlain was forced to falsify Baldwin's assertion that there would be no conscription in England during peace-time.

Again, a country that is always preparing for war might wish to try its strength against others. She might even wish to experiment on some small countries and find out how far their destructive weapons of warfare have improved. Thus, Germany and Italy were able to covert Spain into a playing field where elaborate tests were made of their latest planes and machine-guns. Loss of life was of no concern to them, especially when the victims were not either Italians or Germans. Further, there is always the possibility of the army revolting against the dictators themselves unless it is shown some work to do. Does that not explain Hitler's invasion twice a year and is that not the reason why Japan is engaged in China ?

A political philosophy depends for its success, primarily, upon the economic theories it advances and the way it is able to meet the exigencies of the money market. In one sense, a Stock Exchange, a Bourse or a Wall Street can paralyse, and even extinguish a state, if any of them care to. No state can afford to live in a sort of self-made vacuum for there are very few countries in this world that are self-sufficient. The Four Year Plan of Germany is only a fantastic experiment of Goering.

In Fascist economy, private property and private profits are preserved but under severe state control. The state directs economy for its exclusive benefit. At the same time, the Duce has more than once proclaimed that there would be no capitalism, as such, in Italy. While the financier is given his share of the dividends, he cannot organise labour or enlarge industry except under the direction and patronage of the state. Now, this is somewhat of an anomoly. For, state control of industry means socialism while the existence of capitalism points the other way. They cannot coexist ; yet they are made to coexist in Fascist countries. They worship God and mammon at the same time.

In Fascist countries, while the capitalist suffers only an inconvenience, the unfortunate worker suffers a positive disadvantage. His Trade Unions are abolished and he may neither bargain for higher wages nor take the extreme step of bringing about a strike. His poverty is his misery and he is reduced to mere slavery. The capitalist usually works in league with the state for he requires representation in parliament ; he is also assured of his share of profits though they may not be as large as he would wish them to be.

Prices and profits of commodities are determined by three factors, namely, what is to be produced, who shall produce it and how much of it shall be produced. So long as the means of production are left in the hands of private enterprise, the owners of capital are the sole arbiters in the matter and they cease to advance capital when they do not see any profit emanating from their enterprise. If the state imposes its mighty will upon them and tells them what to produce and how much of it, and also regulates the prices thereof, then, the capitalist must either become bankrupt or refuse to obey. No sane man will work his industry at a loss. To this charge the answer is that the state would never order the capitalist to produce unless it foresees a huge return by way of profits. Well, if that be the case, the financier would undertake the enterprise of his own accord. He does not want the state to be his broker in the business.

The truth is that while the Fascists are unable to disturb the gigantic firms of repute controlling capital and commanding credit, they are able to disturb the petty shopkeepers and the proprietors of small stores. Woolworths and Selfridges (or the like) are above Fascist mischief; it is only Mr. Brown or Mrs. Bundle who suffer. The big stores, with their branches spread all round, flourish ; the small ones perish. In Germany, the attack is concentrated against the calculating Jew, in particular.

The Fascists are fundamentally opportunists. Their policy changes as situations alter. They soon adapt themselves to the new situation and are not slow to invent a philosophy or theory that would exalt them in the eyes of their admirers. Their philosophy is essentially dynamic and ever-changing.

At the bottom of this glorified nationalist philosophy is the conception of the totalitarian state whereby the state becomes the organ in which is concentrated the national life, both private and public. The state is supreme and man is its component, having no independent existence and deprived of his fundamental liberty. The state thus symbolises the sum total of its subjects. If the individual displays any tendency to nonconformity, then force is used to bring him to the path of righteousness. By a process of psychological jugglery, the state becomes identified with the individual who is at its head and whom we call the Dictator. Hitler is Germany, Mussolini can do no wrong—these and other similar slogans immediately come into being and soon get popular. "*The dictator*" writes Prof. Naidu in '*Prabuddha Bharata*' (May, 1939) *is believed to confer real liberty on the individual when he terrorises the citizen into subordination. The Dictator's atrocities are justified on the ground that he alone possesses the peculiar gifts of intuiting the good which the vulgar masses desire and grope after blindly, but never succeed in grasping*'.

Fascism differs from Socialism and Marxism in that it does not believe in the existence of a class struggle and is not opposed to capitalism. German Fascism is called National Socialism which is, as Chesterton crisply says, neither socialism nor nationalism. Germany differs from Italy in three main respects. Firstly, she has no monarchy co-existing with her dictator ; secondly her attitude towards religion has been far more revolutionary than in Italy, and lastly racial persecution is practised with a thoroughness that is not practised elsewhere. Of late, the Duce too is imitating his worthy partner of the axis in his dislike and contempt for the Jews but his measures have not been half so severe.

Of all the totalitarian states (including the U. S. S. R.). Italy is the only one that has reconciled its theories to the existence of monarchy and religion. John Gunther says "*The Duce is the only modern dictator who has come to terms with religion*". In private life, the Italian Dictator is reputed to be very religious and that may be one reason why he established contact with the Pope. The Lateran Treaty with the Pope was signed in 1929. We now begin to wonder if Mussolini is religious after all when we remember that he invaded Albania on a Good Friday. It would be idle, however, to suggest that the Vatican is independent of Fascist influence. In the very nature of things it cannot be. No European religion has ever been able successfully to divorce itself from the materialistic activities of the state. We have not yet forgotten the severe shock which the civilised world felt when the Pope, during the Abyssinian War, coolly characterised it as a just war and justified the invasion. We have thus reached a stage in civilisation when even the pulpit is being used for political propaganda.

The Fascist march on Rome in 1922 was préceded by an assurance by Mussolini that he would not interfere either with the existence or with the security of the monarchy. Thus his followers encountered no opposition even though the army could quite easily have crushed them. The King of Italy (now Emperor as well !) was gained over and was primarily responsible for there being no opposition to Mussolini. The existence of a monarchy, did not, however, prevent the assumption of dictatorial powers of the leader and parliament merely ratifies the laws pronounced by him.

Religious persecution takes a very virulent shape in Germany and is practised with unabashed severity. Hitler does not pretend to be religious and indeed his greatest grievance is that Christ was a Jew ! The persecution of Pastor Niemoller, even after he was pronounced "not guilty" by the highest judicial tribunal is a glaring instance to show how far he can go and how deep is his contempt for religion. Again and again the question arises whether religion can be above or at least independent of the state and the Fuhrer insists that it is only a subordinate factor in the well-being of the state. The Fuhrer himself is God and indeed German marriages are solemnised in the name of God and the Fuhrer The Dictator is thus not only the political head but the religious head as well.

Another important feature of Fascist government is the important and inevitable part played by the Secret Police on the political arena. The Gestapo in Germany, the Ogpu in Russia and a similar institution in Italy are the institutions by which the government is able to carry on with success and with scarcely any opposition. Their researches and investigations are directed towards the detection of forces that are alien to their political philosophy and severe measures are taken to annihilate immediately those forces. It would be no exaggeration to say that in totalitarian states, the Secret Police service is above the judiciary and it remains unaffected by fetters that legal interpretation of existing laws might impose. A man may not be a criminal and so he may be found "not guilty" by the courts; but he may be a traitor and so he may be rotting in concentration camps all his lifetime unless he has faced the firing squad or met the axe. There are no *Habeas Corpus* writs available in Fascist countries but only prison cells. A patriot may often be proclaimed a traitor if he does not follow the leader and the rest of his lifetime may have to be spent in prison. Pastor Niemoller, Dr. Schusnigg and a host of others are guilty of no other crime save that of being patriotic. The Ogpu in Russia takes it a step further and stages elaborate trials wherein the prisoners know long before what their fate is going to be. The trial is often a mere farce. Trotsky escaped the ordeal but his colleagues didn't. Patriotism may thus sometimes mean treachery and treachery means legalised murder.

We shall now examine the effect of Fascism on the press. The press under Fascism tends to be nothing but a mouthpiece of the state and it may not voice any opinion that is prejudicial to the avowed objects and policy of the state. Under Fascism there is no freedom of thought or speech; consequently there can be no freedom of the press. Wickham Steed, the celebrated journalist and former editor of the '*Times*' says "*Dictatorial systems which muzzle or control the press and do away with freedom of speech and of public and private criticism are claiming for themselves a degree of political and social efficiency superior to that of democracies.*" Whether this claim be justified or not, the fact remains that the press exists not so much to voice the views of the public as to voice those of the powers that be. The press is thus one branch of the Ministry of Propaganda just as a broadcasting house is another. Men are not taught that they should think; they are told what they should think. Dr. Geobbells and Senor Gayda know how best to use the press for propaganda. News is often censored and views are generally dictated. People remain in absolute ignorance of what is happening in the outside world, nay, even in their own countries sometimes. We are told that the German people knew nothing about the Austrian *anschluss* until 48 hours had elapsed after the German troops had marched into Austria! The result is that journalism has lost its spark of genius and there appears a drab monotony in the views expressed. The words may be different but the views are alike. In Rome or Berlin we do not find such divergent expression of views on the same topic as we do when we read for example the '*Daily Mail*' and the '*Manchester Guardian.*'

Another noticeable feature is that dictators have a fascination for show and glamour. Everything they do is calculated to attract the eye and impress the mind. Spectacle and pageantry are relied upon to impress and attract. Thus when the Duce speaks or when the Fuhrer makes a pronouncement, there are to be found hundreds of thousands of admiring people who cheer and applaud with mad enthusiasm. Coloured shirts and dazzling flags help to add to the spectacle, and indeed the whole Army, Navy and the Air Force, complete with tanks and cavalry appear on the scene. Sometimes we wonder whether these dictators are not like shopkeepers who exhibit all their goods in the window and have nothing behind. The show thus fills the people's hearts with pride and delight and their patriotism gains an additional impetus. The utterances of the leader, therefore, carry more conviction and weight. In democracies, such shows are significantly absent.

We shall now briefly examine what Fascism has done to Europe and the rest of the world. Events that have happened are still green in our memory and detailed accounts of them are necessary. The last ten or twelve years have seen Fascists shatter the dreams of President Wilson who was responsible for the League of Nations. The League had no sanction behind it except the strength of moral law and Fascists have no moral law but the law of the mailed fist. Thus the Disarmament Conference ended in a fiasco and the League has failed in its objective. It is even alleged by some that Great Britain and France wrote the epitaph to it when they winked at the war in Spain and felt helpless when Abyssinia and some central European countries sighed for relief.

So Italy has conquered Abyssinia by the use of poison gas

and by bombing harmless citizens. Japan, encouraged by the weakness of Geneva when she occupied Manchuria, is now engaged in a gigantic war to crush China. Hitler has scored a series of *coups* and has been scoring triumphs with mechanical and monotonnous regularity. The Rhineland was occupied; Austria has become part of the Greater Reich; Czechoslovakia has lost her independence and Memel flies the swastika. All these victories have been achieved, strangely enough, not by the use of force but by the show of arms, by blackmail rather than by war. No wonder, Hitler recently declared, addressing the Reichstag on the 21st of April in these terms: "*I have repeatedly asserted that I and the German people have no desire for war and that if this be true, there need be no war. I wish to point out; Firstly, that I have not conducted any war; secondly, that for years past I have expressed abhorrence of war; and thirdly, I am not aware for what purpose I should wage war at all.*" Of course, he need not wage a war if he can conquer without firing a single shot.

And what is more, Spain is conquered by the rebel Franco aided by Italian soldiers and German engineers even as the farcical Non-Intervention Committee was sitting in London. The latest victim of Fascism is Albania, and Poland and Rumania have never been so uncertain of their independence as they are today.

Dictators have no regard for treaties any more than they have love for the League. The Anglo-Italian Agreement and the Munich Pact have gone the same way as the Anglo-German Naval Treaty has gone. Treaties may ease international tension but they cannot prevent aggression. Duff Cooper has called Hitler '*the thrice-perjured traitor*'; Dean Inge wittily remarks that the letters in A Hitler may be arranged into '*the liar.*' Mussolini seems to say '*The tongue hath sworn, but the mind is not on oath*'. Agreements therefore are denuded of their sanctity.

In this connection it is pertinent to observe that Russia has come out of it all with a clean slate. True, the U. S. S. R. is a totalitarian state but Stalin has not adopted the destructive tactics of the other dictators. Litvinoff has been a faithful friend of the League and his outspoken utterances on numerous occasions have shown that Russia is a firm and unfailing believer in the maintenance of world peace. In her unrivalled might, she remains calm. She is unflurried even in the face of anti-Comintern pacts (which are in effect directed towards the Soviet Government) and the so called Rome-Berlin-Tokyo axes. Fascism, and not Bolshevism, is the menace to civilisation, for now-a-days wars are fought (or threatened) not for territories but for ideologies. They are commenced without a warning ; no longer are ambassadors dramatically withdrawn or zero-hours proclaimed. Disturbances, previously manipulated, take place and the aggressor marches in to save the suffering minority and to restore peace. Recently it was argued (unsuccessfully) in the Court of Appeal in London that there was no state of war exisiting between China and Japan !

The key to world peace, therefore, remains in the hands of the democracies. If the world has to be saved from this huge deluge of Fascism, the democratic powers have to take a firm stand. The combined might of all the Fascist countries cannot stand up against the mountain strength of France, Great Britain, the U. S. A, and the U. S. S. R. This aggression, this law that might is right, this blackmail, this law of the jungle can be, and must be, promptly stopped. Nothing succeeds like success and the Fascists have been allowed to score many successes already. We are happy to note that Chamberlain has at last opened his eyes to the seriousness of the situation. In his speech at Birmingham, he has warned the Fascist countries in unmistakeable terms. Daladier and Roosevelt have stood by the British Premier and Russia will soon join hands with the peace-loving democracies. The dictators will hereafter begin to walk warily.

Finally, we must ask, will India succeeed against the forces of Fascism ? Is not Fascism closely allied to Imperialism ? Not very long ago, Pandit Jawaharlal said. "*A certain seeming contradiction arises in regard to our policy towards war. On the one hand, we are anti-Fascists and we think that a Fascist world victory will be not only disastrous for the world as a whole but bad for our own freedom. Therefore, inevitably we do not want a Fascist victory. On the other hand, supporting British Imperialism is obviously a wrong policy for a country dominated by that Imperialism."* And he adds : *"If we think of the question in terms of a free India, obviously we are led to the conclusion that we should support the forces of democracy as opposed to Fascism. If we think in terms of a subject India we are led to the conclusion that we cannot support dominating Imperialism."*

We cannot therefore tolerate either Imperialism or Fascism. The Nationalist view is that the British Government is guilty of Fascist tendencies in her administration of our great country. The acts of violence during the Civil Disobedience Movement, the severe press censorship during that period, the imposing of laws restricting civil liberties (especially in Bengal)—all these bear witness to that charge. India cannot afford to ignore it because the aggressor is one who upholds democratic principles (in her own land) or because persecution is not as severe as it is in Italy or Germany. The backbone of Imperialism is exploitation and exploitation means poverty and suffering.

We are given legislatures and to a certain extent we are given also freedom of action and expression. But we are not given full control of the finances and what is more, we are dependent upon Great Britain for military assistance. We have thus democratic institutions in form and Fascist control in practice. We are asked to be generous to our people without being given the wherewithal to be generous with.

"*Where thy treasure is, there thy heart will be also.*" This quotation from the Bible sums up the British attitude towards India. Britain clings to India not because she wants to civilise us (for we were building the Taj when European civilisation was only primitive) but because the immense economic resources of our country help to keep the British workers alive and the capitalists to draw their huge dividends. The Britisher is fundamentally a business man ; indeed, he came to our country as a merchant and eventually settled down as a monarch. We cannot get away from the fact that it is economics and not ethics that is keeping the Englishman in our country. "*India's struggle today*" says Jawaharlal "*is part of the great struggle which is going on over the world for the emancipation of the oppressed. Essentially, this is an economic struggle, with hunger and want as its driving forces".* Britain cannot clothe the masses in India nor feed them all.

But to fight the menace of Fascism, we have no better friend than Great Britain. We have a common enemy in Fascism to fight which we should all unite. The enormous man power of India will be a great asset to any country that invokes our confidence and demands in return our co-operation. "*It will be a stroke of statesmanship*" writers Prof. Saha "*on the part of our rulers if they can overcome their present policy of distrust and if they can take India into their confidence regarding defence measures about which they are clearly and unmistakably very nervous......*". The threat of Japan is very real and not illusory and unless we get ready soon, our fate will be to surrender meekly. Sir Sikandar Hyat Khan, Premier of the Punjab says : "*A vacillating policy will be suicidal to India because it may tempt aggression from other powers against India, which cannot defend itself alone. ......Previously we fought the battles of others. Now we may have to fight for the defence of liberty and of our Motherland. We shall not hesitate to do so*".

A free and an independent India will be a greater asset to the British Commonwealth than an India that is dominated by Imperialism. As a partner and participant in the British Commonwealth of Nations India is bound to play a very vital and useful part in the shaping of Europe's destinies in the event of war. The co-operation of a fettered India cannot be relied upon. Prof. Adarkar writes : "*Without a strong and sympathetic India, England will be fighting a losing battle in Asia. Lacking timely assistance and co-operation from Britain, India will fall an early prey to gangster nations prowling in search of easy game...... Britain is likely to be our best ally dictated by the necessity of the situation as by the danger of handing over our destinies to the tender mercies of our predatory enemies whose intentions are too clear to be misinterpreted*".

This then is the opportunity for Great Britain to enlist India's services and be assured of her continued support.

Great empires and little minds go ill together, we are told. Will Whitehall respond to this call ? We quote Prof. Adarkar again : *"A noble word, a friendly gesture, a generous concession, will throw India into the arms of Britain, if only the latter would realise that hope deferred maketh the heart sick, and that a delicious gift, long delayed in the giving, turns into a Dead-Sea fruit"*.

But what about Gandhiji's doctrine of non-violence, the reader might ask us. We humbly submit that that doctrine, cannot work in a world that is denuded of moral or spiritual considerations. As an ideal, it is perfect ; as a political shield, it is dangerous. We may show the right cheek when slapped on the left but we shall have to be prepared to have our ears boxed as well. The forces of Fascism are stronger than the forces of spiritualism, particularly in a world that is getting increasingly materialistic and where international justice and morality are scarcely to be found. Albania, Austria and other countries did meet arms with arms and they are now vassal states. There is nothing to show that India will be treated any better by the Fascist powers.

H. G. Wells recently declared, in an interview in Bombay that "*Non-violence is the policy of the vegetable kingdom and I cannot agree that it is a panacea for the World's present troubles*". If we want to retain the liberty that we have, we must fight with arms the Fascist forces. Even the *Bhagavad Gita* insists that wars are necessary and should be fought in the name of justice. The gospel of Shree Krishna will be our message.

SIR PRAFULLA CHANDRA RAY

KT., C.I.E., D.SC. (EDIN.), PH.D. (CAL.) ETC.

Onetime Professor of Chemistry, University College of Science, Calcutta was born in 1861 and is unmarried. He was educated at Calcutta and at Edinburgh University. Graduated at Edinburgh, D.Sc., Honourable Ph.D., Calcutta University, 1908; Honourable D.Sc., Durham University, 1912; Dean of the Faculty of Science, University of Calcutta 1915. Sir Prafulla who has been Professor, Presidency College, Calcutta, since the beginning of his career in 1916 is a Fellow of the Chemical Society, London, and of the Asiatic Society of Bengal. He was the first President of the Indian Chemical Society, 1924-26 and is the Founder-Director of the Bengal Chemical and Pharmaceutical Works, Limited. His publications include "History of Hindu Chemistry;" Life and Experience of a Bengali Chemist; Contributions; Mercurous Nitrate and its numerous derivatives; Nitrates of the Alkaly-ammonium Series; Nitrates of the Mercurialky and Mercurialky-Larylammonium Series; Determination of Conductivity of Nitrites and numerous other original Papers on allied subjects.

THE FOUNDATION OF KEY INDUSTRIES IN INDIA

ONE great difficulty in India of starting big industries is that she is called upon all of a sudden to face fierce competition from the long established, highly developed industrial organisations of Europe, America and Japan. Foreign products are dumped into the country at rates which defy competition and thereby indigenous industries are throttled out of existence. Needless to say, prices are again enhanced after the local enterprise has been crushed to make good the temporary losses of the foreigner. The difficulty is now further increased, when England herself, under the new constitution, in the name of Imperial preference or some other euphemistic epithet, is entering the field by jumping over the tariff wall.

Just now this is our unfortunate position. Gigantic British industries incorporated in England, are opening branches in India. But if unhappy India is to exist at all she must be prepared, dwarf as she is, to fight with the colossal giant.

Hitherto in India only a single attempt has been made by Indians to start a big key industry, the Tata Iron and Steel Works Ltd. It has outlived its infancy and has come to adolescence. At the outset it had the financial backing of the late J. N. Tata and latterly of the Bombay capitalists. When the Great War broke out and the supply of foreign steel was cut off, our government realised the supreme importance of an indigenous industry and of making India self-contained as far as possible in her needs. But the Tatas at that time behaved like spoilt children. Once, while presiding over an industrial conference, Sir Dorab Tata boasted that his expert was drawing a pay higher than that commanded by the Viceroy of India. The criterion of efficiency had thus been judged by the concern by the salary of its expert. Things went on merrily for a time, but a crisis arose when peace was concluded and the efficiency of the experts was tested in the fire of foreign competition. German and Belgian steel produced from a much lower grade iron ore began to pour into the market at a much reduced rate. A cry was raised for the support of an infant industry and national backing was secured for the concern for its protection and subsidy.

It is needless to proceed further. Suffice it to say that Tata Iron and Steel Works got something like a crore a year from the Imperial coffers and latterly under the Imperial preference somewhere near about eighty lakhs a year. In other words the poor peasantry of India were taxed for their commodities, such as corrugated sheets and implements of husbandry, and the country had to pay seven or eight crores of rupees to cover the losses of inefficient running of this concern. Still the cost is not too high if the concern thereby becomes efficient and completely Indianised.

These preliminary remarks may seem irrelevant to many but they have an important bearing on the subject proper which I now introduce.

India is yet in her infancy in industrial progress and capital is naturally very shy and she lacks organising power. Hence undertakings of colossal scale as obtain in highly developed industrial countries do not appeal to her and are at present beyond her means. Therefore the example set by an Asiatic country naturally appeals to her.

AN EXAMPLE

Japan has developed to a remarkable extent during the last decade in her industrial activities in diverse fields, following the example of European countries. In the metallurgical industries, such as copper mining and refining, she started from a very small beginning; now she occupies practically second place in world production. In an article published in *The Electrical World*, Dugald Jackson, Emeritus Professor of Electrical Engineering of the Massachusetts Institute of Technology, gave a survey of Japanese electrical plants. He stated that practically all the power stations, both hydro-electric and thermal are now run by Japanese generators. The sizes of these generators and their efficiency are quite on a par with those of other nations. Electric locomotives in Japan have all been manufactured in Japanese factories. A number of Japanese lamp factories have been started and the productive capacity of one of them could be compared favourably with some of the biggest factories in the world, having a daily output of three lakhs of lamps.

In electric-chemical industries her development has been remarkable. By the electrolysis of common salt she not only supplies her need for alkali, bleaching powder and liquid chlorine but manages to export large quantities abroad at a price much lower than that produced by other nations. She produces the artificial fertilisers needed for her agriculture by the atmospheric fixation of nitrogen and even exports considerable quantities. Though she lacks in aluminous ore, which is imported mainly from our country, she has within the last six years developed a big aluminium industry. Her texile, silk, rayon, and rubber industries have developed within the last decade to such an extent that they excite the envy of people who had been pioneers in these and have considerable experience.

SELF SUPPORTING

The secret of these undertakings in their inception and growth may be attributed to many causes, but it may be pointed out that she is now almost independent of foreign manufacturers regarding the equipment of her industrial concerns. Japan now is in a position to equip almost all her factories with machinery and equipments developed in Japan and a considerable number of them are of higher efficiencies than those developed abroad. This is the finding of an eminent foreign engineer, a teacher of a renowned engineering institution and no mean observer in world progress in the engineering line.

Japan has to import pig and scrap iron from India ; she readily converts them into steel and now her mercantile marine and naval equipment including battleships, cruisers and submarines, aeroplanes for commercial navigation and warlike operations and all the ingredients for war purposes are secured from steel of her own making. The textile machinery is entirely of her own production. The development of the rubber trade and of the rubber products both in variety and in price has been remarkable. One really looks for the basic factors which have led to this astounding progress and one finds that a spirit of self-determination and self-confidence to produce the elements of her industrial equipments independent of foreign countries form the foundations of her industries.

Things are different here in India. One can cite the case of the sugar industry. Thanks to the prohibitive duty on Java sugar we have had a rapid growing up of an indigenous sugar industry. Already there is over-production and rate cutting and loud complaint against the excise duty on home-grown sugar.

Here is an example of the effects of ill considered excessive protective duty. But the important fact must not be overlooked. Any one who examines the customs duty on imported machineries will be surprised at the enormous quantity of machinery worth several crores introduced into our country from abroad, from England, the continent of Europe and the States.

THE WAGE SCALE

This comparison would surely indicate the secret of Japan in a nutshell. As soon as her period of probationership was over she, with commendable foresight, turned a new leaf in her chapter of industry. She realised that she must manufacture on the spot her own requirements and has managed the same on an economic basis. She is no longer dependent on foreign countries. She charges wages for labour from a coolie to an expert in a scale which would puzzle us. She is a rice-eating nation like ourselves and her cost of living is not of the standard of European countries. An expert technician or a college professor serves on a pay which appears to us ridiculously small. But unlike us she takes advantage of her asset of brain and brawn for her own benefit. There is no tendency for job hunting and service securing in Japanese youths. While we are frittering our energies in securing paper qualifications without any definite end in view, thus running to waste our potential brain wealth, Japan has been utilising to the fullest extent her intellectual elements for the development of her industries, her commerce and other avocations of modern national life. Though in the beginning she, like other oriental countries, had been stunned by the force of impact of science on society, she rallied quickly and set up an organisation to equip herself to meet the altered conditions. And, further, her government gave well-planned and highly efficient financial and technical backing to her enterprises during their infancy.

In explaining the industrial growth of Japan we have diverged from our main theme regarding the difficulties of initiating new industries in our country. It is well known that there are a number of industries which are essential for the development and growth of other industries. Of these key industries one finds alkali manufacture has an unique position. Soap has been stated by Liebig to be an index of modern civilized society and though India, situated in the

SHANTARAM GANPAT WARTY
M.A., PUBLICIST & JOURNALIST

tropics, abounds in vegetable oil and has within the last twenty five years grown an indigenous soap industry it may be pointed out that she is entirely dependent on imported alkali for the same. The quality and price of soap are naturally found to be affected by the fluctuations in the price of this imported alkali.

AN ANCIENT INDUSTRY

Within the last forty years India has been growing a textile industry mainly for her home consumption and it is not realised how far the industry is dependent on the imported alkali. The growth of an Indian paper industry, apart from other causes is handicapped not to an inconsiderable extent due to cheap alkali. In a modern paper mill established in the neighbourhood of Calcutta we have the information that the annual consumption of alkali runs up to about 3,000 tons a year. These are only a few examples to illustrate the nature of this key industry.

Alkali manufacture can be traced to very olden times, but modern methods can be said to originate from the processes well known to students of chemistry—the Leblanc and Solvay processes,—about the beginning of the last century. With the development of electrical energy the electro-chemical decomposition of sodium chloride to produce caustic soda, chlorine and hydrogen has been evolved and within a short period of twenty years the long established older processes have received a check. In America specially, the electro-chemical process soon supplanted to a considerable extent the older industries. More particularly, since then its bye-product chlorine, transformed either into bleaching powder or into liquid chlorine, is finding considerable use for disinfection and other sanitary purposes.

As we discussed the industrial development of Japan we found that her secret lay in devising means to build up her own equipments without external aid. For some time there has been an attempt to design a suitable electro-chemical plant for the production of alkali and bleaching powder locally and it may now be said that there is every chance of installing a successful plant for the purpose. For more than a couple of years the untiring efforts of a band of workers, who, for reasons best known to them, do not like to give their names to the public, have been engaged in the problem and they feel that the successful establishment of this important key industry may not be very far off. The experimental plant is a very modest one with a small output but it shows signs that it is capable of expansion. It has as its competitor one of the biggest organisations but there is reason to believe that India has a scope, not only for such big organisations, but also for small ones.

A NEW ERA

If the spirit of selfconfidence, self-sacrifice and efficiency in organisation can be combined such small concerns may not lose heart to face competition. In these days of motor lorries and quick transport, even in the streets of big metropolis hand carts have not ceased to ply their trade. But apart from plain and honest competition, there are other methods of killing an infant industry practised here, chiefly by foreign concerns, or "Indian" concerns that are "Indian" only in the location of their industrial machinery. Zonal price cutting, threats to purchasers or wholesalers of non-supply by the European concerns, if they purchase from Indian concerns, and similar octopus methods of strangling infant Indian industries are practised here with impunity. Such practices must be regarded as criminal and penalised. The foreigners have stipulated and obtained their safeguards. It is up to us to agitate for and secure anti-trust laws and other safeguards against the destroyers of Indian enterprise.

The dawn of a new era in the industrial development of India would certainly begin when this and other important key industries take their footing in the indigenous soil and be entirely developed by us unaided by extraneous help.

GULESTAN RUSTOM BILLIMORIA

M. A.,

(nee Miss Gulestan J. Bahaduvji) is a Licentiate, of Trinity College of Music, London and has for several years been the principal of the Alexandria Girls' English Institution, one of the premier schools in Bombay for imparting instruction to girls on modern lines.

Educated at Girton High School and St, Xavier's College she obtained several college and university prizes and scholarships. Fellow of the University of Bombay, elected by the Registered Graduates in 1930 and again in 1936 on the expiration of the term. Twice elected member of the Academic Council of the Bombay University and in 1939 she was elected to the Syndicate. Examiner, Moderator and Chairman of the board of paper setters and moderators at the matriculation for several years. She is Honorary Treasurer and Acting Honorary General Secretary of the all India Women's Conference and serves on the Managing Committee of several Associations doing educational or social work, either as president or treasurer or secretary.

Mrs. Billimoria was invited to give evidence before the Government Commission on Education before the University Commission and before the Lothian Committee. One of her paintings has been bought by, and is exhibited in, the Prince of Wales Museum, Bombay.

Since her marriage, has been helping her husband Dr. R. B. Billimoria (founder of the Bel-Air Sanatorium for consumptives at Panchgani) in his humanitarian work for the suffering poor.

THE PERSONALITY OF THE CHILD

TO those of us who are interested in the growth and development of the child, its personality and the conscious cultivation thereof afford material for a very serious yet fascinating study.

When I speak of the personality of the child, I am using the term in no mysterious sense but simply as indicating his individuality. That does not signify the presence in the child of any marvellous or extraordinary qualities which would mark him as a genius or as something abnormal. Ordinary powers, normal faculties, simple, common, average attributes, these make often the richest field for study in the child to those interested in a conscious, deliberate and well thought out system of cultivating and developing that personality; bringing out some of its most agreeable traits; curing its weaknesses; explaining, and so rendering innocuous, any peculiarities which may have untoward consequences.

Unless one studies carefully the individuality of the child, there is every danger of waste of human energy and dissipation of the powers and faculties that lie dormant and untreated in the child. Social misfits are thus often created. I am indeed not unaware of the relatively recent origin of the scientific study of personality—psychology of the child, and the still more or less experimental nature of many of the lines of treatment being practised in advanced countries to attain the objective. But recent as this study may be, there can be no question of the grave social interest bound up with it. The individual does not indeed, cease to be the object of interest, because the scientific educationist emphasises the social viewpoint in inviting attention to this problem. But the proper attention to the growth of the individual has, besides the personal justification to the individual itself, the much greater justification of the individuals social possibilities—in which the entire organized machinery of society—represented by its educational section is interested.

MASS RESULTS

Notwithstanding the grave importance of cultivating the personality of the child, in every modern community, the conditions of social organization are such that those looking after the education of the young are not always able to attend to such root problems of their professian. We live in an age of intense industrialism, the outstanding characteristics of which are standardisation of the product and mass production. Those particularities of our present day social activity are even invading the field of education. Our schools and seminaries have to be large scale institutions which differ very little from the factories of the machine age. The outlook of those in charge is insensibly coloured by their environment, and so the directors of our educational system tend, almost unconsciously, to think in terms of standard patterns and mass results.

I am not blaming them for this feature of our educational system for many of them, perhaps, are as ardent critics as the most blatant tub-thumper against the social order of the day. But the conditions of the society in which they have to work, the financial and other limitations, naturally prevent a more wholesome outlook being adopted. So long as education is open to the private entrepreneur to make a profit for himself, so long as the state does not assume the entire obligation to provide education at all stages to the entire community, there will be the complication and distortion caused by the invisible working of the system of mass production and uniform patterns. We may thunder as much as we like against the regimentation of human life ; but while the institutions concerned with the bringing up of the human child function on the model of a factory, the human mind will become regimented, drilled, patterned and standardised into a copy of its neighbour in all essential particulars and make our outcry against the regimentation of human life a cruel mockery of the whole social system.

While, however, educational institutions function as mass producing factories, they have little chance to indulge in the luxury of carefully attending to the personality of each human being entrusted to their care in the most impressionable period of life. Much as they might dislike the cruel necessity imposed upon them to ignore the individual and think of the class, the educationists of to-day must confess their inability, under existing social conditions, to tackle the problem of attending to the personality of each child in their charge. Their regret is the greater because they have now-a-days begun to realize the utility of a task they cannot even attempt. We find, too, that at the age at which an ordinary school takes charge of a child, it is ready also to attend to the more subtle aspects of the problem. The personality of the child, if not formed in all material particulars by the time it reaches school-going age, is already set in a mould and it may not be easy to undo or modify the lines already cast by influences at work long before that of the teacher could come into play. Besides, modern educationists are opposed to isolation or individual training. It is much better for the growing child if it is in the midst of its fellows and equals while it is receiving instruction or training. So many faculties develop without any special effort of observation, reasoning or self-discipline when a child is at school and with its equals.

CO-OPERATION VITAL

Since it is not possible, for reasons enumerated above, for the teacher to attend to the personality of each child, the need becomes imperative for the closest co-operation between parents and teachers. For what the teachers cannot do in their ordinary course of work, might easily be attended to by the parents, with guidance from the teachers. The teacher is, presumably, acquainted with the more salient features of the problem of attending to child psychology but is unable to devote himself to each individual child. The parent, on the other hand, might be ignorant of the peculiarities of his children's cases. Between the two, therefore, there is an obvious division of labour, and some machinery should be devised to overcome such division and obtain the best results. The teacher would point out the child's peculiar characteristics and indicate, if possible, the treatment needed to foster, or modify, these. The parent might follow the instruction or seek professional advice from the rapidly growing number of nerve specialists or psychoanalysts who make a speciality of this business. Home conditions may have to be altered and the parents' own behaviour before children may have to be studied if the child's personality is to be promptly treated. Reports of progress may have to be submitted to the teacher or to the specialist advising on the matter. But none of these would be possible unless some kind of a regularly functioning machinery is devised to obtain such co-operation between parents and teachers and give effect to its suggestions.

Before probing further into the problem created by the personality of the child, I may answer one or two questions which might well be thought to be the central theme of this article. What is personality in a child? How is it to be discovered?

A CHANGING ENTITY

As already stated, personality is nothing but the sum total of the characteristics inherited by a child, or developed in him by environment, which have a bearing upon others around him, besides having their reaction upon his own individual happiness. This of course is, at any given moment of time, not fixed, absolute and unchanging, but is a constantly changing state, reacting to new suggestions, new influences, new environment and conditions, though, perhaps not apparent to those who are watching over the changing entity. The human child is, at the moment of its birth not a fully developed personality, and remains undeveloped, but constantly developing for many years to come. Of all the living animals, the young of the human being are the most helpless and dependent at birth, not only for their physical welfare but for the growth in them of all that constitutes man. At birth and perhaps all through the period commonly called infancy, the human young is little more than a bundle of instincts and impulses, which those in charge should understand and train according to the proper nature of such extremely subtle forces. Why, in the course of mere attention to the physical wants of the child, the careful parent will discover traces and symptoms of repression (or the sub-conscious in the child) functioning, which will give food for thought. At this stage may commence a proper study of the personality of the child ; and if rightly handled from the beginning, may produce the happiest result. Both instinct and impulse play important parts in the development of the child and as such need special attention.

CAUSE & EFFECT

Beginning all its activities by instinct, the human young, however, soon develops a sort of rudimentary thinking, whereby he unconsciously connects cause with effect and whenever, thereafter, he needs to have the effect repeated, he sets in motion the causal force residing in him. Does he cry and attract the attention of his elders ? Why, every time thereafter that he vaguely senses the need of some attention, he just cries. His very helplessness, his inability to express himself, becomes an exquisite sort of tyranny that the child wields over its elders and gets served and waited upon and coddled and cosseted in innumerable ways that may not always be good for it. Again, every child has a "Will to Power" which it exerts in its own ways, playing upon the affections of its parents. The process which helps the child to discover the effect it produces through its crying or refusing to eat food, or otherwise making itself a nuisance, are difficult to explain ; but they are there all the same, and it would not do to thwart the child in this, its unconscious, sub-conscious, groping after an expression of personality. But at the same time, it must be remembered that the unthinking parent, who responds as an automaton to such childish pranks, lays up a store of misery for himself as well as for the child, in after years. The child very soon becomes aware of the power of the love its parents bear for it. Through this power it can work upon a lever that can turn upside down the whole world. But the love of the child is a double-edged weapon as indeed every primal emotion is. Psychologists call it by the big-sounding expression "Bipolarity" but its essence consists in a sort of inconsistency, whereby one and the same object that a child loves it also, at times, hates. Hence come to develop those innumerable complexes, repressions and fixations that modern psychologists revel in flinging at unsophisticated heads and all of which end in materially affecting the personality of the child, its character and its life.

It is in moulding gently and imperceptibly these activities due to instinct or impulse that the careful parent would best serve the long-term interests of the child. The child is, from the start, endowed with the instinct of possession, of seeking pleasure for itself, of imitating those around it, which eventually end in developing its power of movement, speech, thought and the rest of the active life that follows. Its motive force, the impulse, is also derived from these same primary urges. The parent who finds a child refractory self-willed, undisciplined, worries himself almost to death, without realizing perhaps that most of these manifestations of childishness are really traceable to the carelessness of the parent himself, when a little gentle but firm handling would have ended once for all the growth of these traits.

IMPULSE

Take for example the common childish phenomenon of crying for no apparent reason. The child knows that the parent will discover its need and satisfy it and this familiar chain of cause and effect being established, the child pulls it at all times to stop the entire mail train of the whole household. If a child cries wantonly, however much your heart may ache to see him cry, let him cry himself to sleep through sheer exhaustion. In this way, you will cure him of this childish trick of howling for no apparent reason, except that it pleases His Majesty the Baby to do so.

Parents may find such counsel difficult to follow. But their love for the child must certainly not take the form of indulging its slightest whims. They must check the growth of unhealthy instincts without distorting or suppressing the child's legitimate development of personality. I may give one more illustration of a childish impulse, which, unless corrected in time, can be the source of grave mischief in later life. By its imitative instinct, a child soon learns to reproduce, on its own scale, the life of the elders around it. If it sees them bickering or if it discovers special affection for one of the parents, it would be on the high road to developing into an individual with some horrible repressions which may effect his whole future life. The germ of the Oedipus complex —as the Freudians call the boy's hatred for the father and partiality for the mother or the Electra complex in the converse case of the girl's aversion to the mother and affection for the father is to be found in most children. But it rests with the parents to see that no ground is afforded to the growing child to develop that unfortunate tendency to the degree of morbidity.

A FEW DON'TS

Never exhibit your differences before your children ; never call upon them to take sides in your quarrels ; never show them the skeletons in your cupboard. And, if you notice any tendency with the remotest bearing upon such incipient fixations, take the necessary measures, including expert advice if necessary, to dam the tide of such unfortunate developments. Above all, do not openly show partiality for one particular child. Leave the children always to fight out their own differences among themselves. Do not also let your children be too much in the company of elders ; let them be among people of their own age. But I would not therefore, suggest condemning the tender child to institutional treatment from its earliest years, thus abolishing the personal contact between parent and child. Plato is said to have advocated in his Republic, what might be termed, in modern phraseology, the nationalization of the child. But I think a closer study of Plato's own remarks will not support the utter monotony and machine-like regularity of institutional life for the tiny tots of to-day who are to be the props and pillars of our society tomorrow.

Apart from the conscious moulding by its parents and teachers, child personality is affected in other ways. In the first place, the size and nature of the family has a great deal to do with the formation and shaping of a child's personality. An only child is almost certain to be spoilt by its doting parents, since all the wealth of their love and longings has to be showered upon this victim of excessive love and over indulgence. Little better is the fate of the solitary boy in a family of girls or of the only daughter in a family of boys. The still persistent undercurrent, whereby a male child is preferred to a female, becomes doubly dangerous, when the male child happens to be the only representative of its sex and of its age in a given family. All unconsciously, the very attentions showered upon him and the needless and unjustifiable partiality shown to him are so many fatal poisons to the growth of a healthy personality, free from repressions or complexes. The position of a solitary daughter may not be quite so enviable but the danger is there as well. Thus every child's personality is shaped by family conditions ; and ways and means should be devised whereby children could be redeemed from such environment as would materially affect their future.

Again, there may be parents who are utterly undesirable as guardians of children. Habitual criminals and dipsomaniacs are, for example, unsuited to bring up children or to influence their personality ; and yet the most advanced societies have so far failed to devise means to take away these innocents from their parents.

OTHER FACTORS

A second factor affecting child personality lies in the relations of parents *inter se.* It is indeed too high an ideal always to be attained that all parents should be utterly devoted to and in love with one another ; for, after all, we live in an imperfect world. Hence, whenever it happens that two married people cannot hit it off well among themselves, the future of the children demands that they should be redeemed from the deleterious influence of a discordant household.

Every thoughtful parent, who boasts of the least rudiments of a civilized consciousness, should endeavour, of course, to keep from the children the sordid aspect of broken and shattered ideals as far as it is possible to avoid such tragedies from manifesting themselves in the daily life of the actors in such tragedies. But when the absolute breaking point has been reached, and where for social or economic reasons, divorce is not possible, there must be found means to save the children of such unions from the sight of parental dissension, deception or distrust.

In India, the problem is at once more difficult and yet a little easier than in countries where the family has become wholly individualistic. With us, the institution of the joint family, wherein several generations live together, is still a living reality. There is, therefore, with us the common complication caused by grandparents taking a hand in the bringing up of the children and influencing their personality in ways which are remote from a scientific outlook on such matters. But the grandparents may also prove the unconscious saviours of children at moments when the parents are at breaking points between themselves. I am not suggesting that we must reinforce the institution of the joint family ; but a ready safety valve must be devised for the offsping of unions which have proved failures.

ENVIRONMENT

The last of the factors that influence the personality of a child is to be found in the general environment made up of all the friends and relations of the parents, their ways and habits, their ideals and upbringing, as also the servants, the neighbours and the like. The economic and spiritual atmosphere round about has also a say in colouring this environment and in its reaction upon the child. This is obviously far more complex and difficult to treat because its influence is indirect, imperceptible and, therefore, elusive. None the less that influence is there. We cannot always control our economic position, for example, and so are not always able to afford our children the advantage which a safe or prospérous position might afford. But we can arrange so as to prevent any marriages; or any children, at least, being born to people who are unable to provide a stated minimum of living and growing conditions for the children. This is, of course, more easily said than achieved. But still it is a point worth emphasising, if only to draw attention to the reaction such questions have upon the growth of our children and the future of the race. Then again, the influence of servants is incalculable and the only counsel one can give if the child's personality is not to be perverted by the ignorance, incompetence or unworthiness of servants, is to avoid giving ones children unnecessarily in charge of servants. In our country, this is a serious matter, in view of the appalling ignorance in the masses of the people and, therefore, in the average servant one might find for such tasks.

Given such factors which influence the personality of the child in its earliest years (apart altogether from the influence of heredity) we may next consider how we must train this personality in the desired direction. The influence of "example" of those around the child is too obvious to need emphasising, though the ability of those concerned, always to make that example a model and a pattern, is more easy to insist upon than to achieve. Parents, particularly, must make their own example as salutary as they possibly can. There is nothing superhuman expected of parents in this direction. Already we find, in advanced countries, that a conscious endeavour to do their best is marking the new generation of parents in every strata of society that claims to be cultured and thoughtful. In this country, we may not yet be so happily situated, so far as the large bulk of our people is concerned. And they have other handicaps in the economic poverty and social customs from which others may be free. Still, even here, it is not too early to emphasise such facts as bear upon the education of the children; for the more widely this knowledge spreads, the more fully will the actual approach the ideal in course of time.

Apart from the influence of example and precept, there are other ways of shaping a child's personality. The occupation of children, with toys for instance, will take them from other habits, complexes or repressions; and every parent should provide these. The personality of the growing child is manifest in the toys it likes to play with, in the manner of its playing, and in the moods shown at different times in the play. A careful and observant parent can gather a lot of useful hints from such unconscious exhibitions of the inner personality of every child, and may help to temper and direct and mould it in ways unsuspected by the object of such solicitude. All games of child life should also have the same end. It has been said of no less a person than Mr. H. G. Wells that his wonderful games for his children may have been the source of great happiness for them, but they would have been of still greater value had the children been left to shape those games for themselves and derive their own joys of creation, their own amusement at the successful working of the idea embodied in each game. The influence of toys and games in shaping and developing, in expressing and fulfilling the personallty of the child, remains yet to be carefully and scientifically studied, but so far as the matter has advanced today, it is evident that these instruments of influencing the child have an immense and yet incalculable value.

QUESTIONING

At the stage when the child is old enough to go to school, a new element enters. The teacher now comes on the stage though the lessons with which he is primarily concerned are not all designed to develop personality. Yet the need for co-operation between the parent and the teacher, the school and home, is more than ever apparent to-day, when every country is in the throes of intensive industrialism and old units, old ideals, old methods are everywhere in disintegration or discredit. Finality may not have been reached in the science of education, but such progress as we have already made shows quite clearly that the one great need of a healthy and effective system of education of the young is a constant and intelligent co-operation between the school and the home.

PROFESSOR MOHINI MOHON MUKHERJEE

M. A.,

M. M. Mukherjee, who is a Professor of English at the Asutosh College at Calcutta, was born in Behala on the 2nd of January 1899. He was educated at the Presidency College, Calcutta between 1912 and 1918, in the latter year standing first in English language and literature among his college students in the M. A. examination. After attaining his degree he was appointed temporary Professor of English in the Presidency College, Calcutta (1919) and this was followed by an appointment as Senior Professor of English in Midnapore College from 1920 to 1923. Professor Mukherjee is an examiner in English to the University of Calcutta.

In 1930 Professor Mukherjee started and edited a children's monthly magazine in Bengali known as *Pat-Tari* and also wrote a children's *Ramayana* in English which was published by the Oxford University Press, London. A prolific writer, Professor Mukherjee has contributed articles in English to the *Calcutta Review* on the history and origin of the Bengali stage and has contributed many articles and short stories to leading journals written in English. He is also the author of various books for school and college students written in English. Among his Bengali works is a novel, *Chira Kumar*, and a collection of short stories which include translations from the French and Italian. While Professor Mukherjee takes a great interest in aviation and photography he is also engaged in research work in Bengali literature.

For his contribution to *What India Thinks* Professor Mukherjee has selected a monograph on Bengali poetry of to-day which originally made its appearance in *Triveni*, Madras to whom due acknowledgement is hereby made.

BENGALI POETRY OF TODAY

THE striking note of modernity in Bengali poetry owes its inspiration and origin to the many-sided poetic activities of Rabindranath Tagore. The evolution of his poetic genius may be traced back to the seventies of the last century and still it goes on blazing forth in undiminished glory. In spite of its rapid growth in manifold forms, the poetic genius of Tagore is deeply conservative through its happy fusion with Sanskrit learning. We read in his *Autobiography* how he was brought up in an atmosphere of Sanskrit culture even when he was a bright-looking shy boy in his teens. The vogue which Rabindranath created among the younger generation of writers was almost well established before the end of the last European War, which unsettled the established order of society all over the world. A new intellectual outlook was manifest in our country which changed the values of things in every aspect of life, political, social, economic and literary.

Bengal always shows a wonderful power of receptivity in assimilating and utilising western ideals when they easily fit in with national ideals and requirements. There were happenings in various aspects of European life which dazzled the imagination of young Bengal. There have been easier modes of transport curtailing the distance between the East and the West. Broadcasting has contributed a good deal to wearing out incompatibilities in inter-provincial relations. The new Government of India Act has transferred at least some power to popular control. The barrier to inter-caste marriage is being slowly but surely pushed aside by those cherishing advanced views on social problems.

Literacy is rapidly advancing and the circulation of books among the masses has been fairly brisk because of a more insistent demand among them to know things at first-hand. The network of talkie houses all over India has been a powerful instrument in disseminating foreign ideas among the more cultured section of the people. The establishment in many metropolitan cities of schools and colleges adopting co-education has changed the relation of the sexes. The demand of national government, the propagation of new political ideas through Indian political sufferers in Russia, Germany and Japan along with the overthrow of monarchy in the first two countries have contributed not a little to breeding new ideas and stirring new aspirations among thinkers at large. Even the *Harijan* movement initiated by Mahatma Gandhi has sent a wave of change to the hitherto unexplored corners of our society. The unemployment problem, so long confined among able-bodied men, has now to be grappled with by young women as well. Young men and women with some amount of higher education fight shy of entering into wedlock, though in some cases they do not disapprove extra-marital relations. The facts set forth above do not apply to Bengal alone but to all other provinces in a greater or less degree.

Rabindranath, wonderfully plastic as his literary powers are, has been fully alive to these changes. Many of his fine poems, narrative, dramatic and pure lyric, describe in impassioned language the element of conflict raging in our society. The essential difference between Rabindranath and the new generation of writers is not one of themes but of ideals of poetry. Poetry with Rabindranath is the breath and finer spirit of all knowledge : it is an attempt to reach the eternal verities of life. But to the younger writers of Bengal it is an exploration of the possibilities of language. To them it does not aim directly at consolation or moral exhortation, as it is with Wordsworth, or at the expression of the eternal problems of life, as it is with Browning. They do not paint on a big canvas with a mighty sweep, as Rabindranath has done in many of his sustained works. They do not probe, like a master analyst, into those passions of the human soul which have been swaying it since the days of Homer. Neither can they experience that magnificent and sublime *elan,* which Tagore does with instinctive ease.

Coleridge, in his celebrated *Biographia Literaria,* describes in highly metaphorical language, the various elements which constitute poetic genius : "*Good sense is the body of poetic genius, fancy its drapery, motion its life, and imagination the soul that is everywhere and in each, and forms all into one graceful intelligent whole*". These aspects of poetic genius, however real and convincing they may be, have been outworn with the poets of the new generation. They aim at an extension of significance and probing into the subconscious. They are adept hands at manipulating evocative rhythms and image-sequences. They practise the motto that elegance of writing keeps a poem alive. In this respect they are at one with the famous dictum of Wordsworth that all good poems are "*a spontaneous overflow of powerful feelings*". They have cut themselves adrift from the old moorings of orthodox canons in criticism, paying homage to that ideal of the eastern rhetoricians *kavyam rasatmakam vakyam* (mellifluity of word-sequences constitutes poetry). Mallarmé, the protagonist of the symbolist movement in French poetry, means the same thing when he says, "*Poetry is written with words, not ideas*".

In their attempt to absorb all poetic knowledge of the west these Bengal neo-romantics have borrowed, sometimes quite successfully, the poetic ideals of the Imagist and Surrealist (as represented by its English admirer David Gascoyne). They lay under contribution such English, American and continental poets as Masefield, Blunden, Auden, Spender, Davies, Edith Sitwell, de la Mare, Eliot, Pound, Mallarmé, Baudelaire and even some Communist poets. The most curious feature in this connection is that the difference in language, thought and mode of life as represented by these foreign writers has not stood in the way of their transformation in Bengali style, though this has been a ludicrous misfit at times. This is obviously due to the fact that the rich and varied experiences of life lived by the foreign writers do not and cannot come within the zone of Bengali life, though the vaulting ambition which overleaps itself is there.

To mention only a few representative publications in Bengali poetry of recent times, we may refer to *Prántik* by Rabindranath (composed just after his last serious illness) ; *Bandir Bandaná* and *Kankábati* by Buddhadeb Bose ; *Bisma-*

rani and *Smara-Garal* by Mohitlal Mazumdar; *Anámi* and *Suryyamukhi* by Dilipkumar Roy of Pondicherry; *Urbasi-o-Artemis* and *Chorábali* by Bishnu Dey. There are some other poets of the younger generation who have made their mark in Bengali poetry, e. g. Premen Mitra, Achinta Sen Gupta, Sajanikanto Das, Dr. Bolaichand Mukherjee and Sudhindra Dutt. In fact their number is legion. All these writers, with the exception of Rabindranath, have carved out a name in the pages of Bengali periodicals in the course of the last decade or so.

In this brief article it is not possible to give a survey of the poetic output of each of these writers, though for a proper understanding of modern Bengali poetry we shall refer to the poetic tendencies and currents represented by some of them. For instance, Dilipkumar's longer poems deal with the deep and yearning passion of the soul for spiritual regeneration. His practical knowledge of the Indian and European styles of music has been an asset, as it is with Rabindranath, to experiment in foreign verse and stanza-forms with eminent success. His translations into graceful Bengali of some famous German and Russian songs, which he sang last winter before an admiring and cultured audience in Calcutta, elicited unstinted praise. The most curious fact about these translations is that they retained intact the original musical notation. Dilipkumar's lyricism is spontaneous, vital and passionate.

Sudhindranath Dutt, often accused as a difficult poet, writes with brilliant effect. The virile passion of his verses is well balanced by an effective use of happy compounds showing his wonderful range of study in Sanskrit and foreign literature. Some of his lines are marvellously chiselled and produce a scintillating effect. He is cumbrous, yet graceful beyond measure. His singular technique stands unrivalled among the poets of the new generation. There is a statuesque mould to his rhymed fourteenliners. As a technician, he is a diligent student of the effect of words. His sheaf of Bengali lyrics, which he fittingly calls *Orchestra,* makes a warm and fervent appeal to an appreciative spirit through the strange diapason of its verses. They create a rushing tide and one cannot but wonder at the exuberant spate of his vocabulary. Unfortunately enough, he has been much maligned by his critics. His treatment of love has nothing elusive about it ; but his description of it in gorgeous verses has the grace and dignity of Kalidas and other Sanskrit poets of the romantic type. Undoubtedly he has enriched the stock of our ever-growing vocabulary.

Buddhadeb Bose's *Bandir Bandana* contains many lyrics which reach the highwater mark of literary finish. His recent cadenced verses have, however, not much of substance. He is a clever psychologist, but needlessly verbose at times. His knowledge of European literature enables him to translate many fine lyrics from it into his mother-tongue. He has been responsible for creating a poets' coterie, most members of which are grotesquely artificial and full of mannerisms. Their stock-in-trade is to indulge in quixotic figures, drawn from a young girl's fleshly charms, and hold up to ridicule all our cherished ideas of womanly chastity and orderliness in society. They are no better than "*idle singers of an empty day*". But Bose, in spite of his vulgarisms and conscious striving after effect, is a poet of some eminence, who writes on psychological and, at times, pathological moods in a happy way.

Premen Mitra is another powerful poet, who is more an imagist than a mere narrator of moods. He also satirises conventional forms and ideas in a merciless way: but the pungency or bitterness of his criticism never offends. In a poem entitled *Sasya-Jataka* he traces the evolution of man's harvesting of corn from the prehistoric to the capitalist age. Mitra is an uncompromising critic of capitalism like some of his brother poets, who want to make art an instrument in the class struggle. The adequacy or otherwise of this poetic creed need not be discussed here.

Bishnu Dey writes fine verse and out of his jugglery of words emerges many a well-drawn pen-picture. But his image sequences are projected so rapidly on the canvas of our mind that hardly any impression of abiding interest is left there. One image wipes out another, and the poet's efforts, sometimes really magnificent, are rendered infructuous. Like Mitra, Dey also writes in a satirical vein with a sly smile on his lips to expose the hypocrisy reigning rampant in high society. The centre-piece in many of Dey's longer lyrics is a city bred society girl, whose cruel caprices and amorous whims he describes with gusto. Some of his lyrics deal with pure whim-whams and fantasies, their materials being drawn from the rich storehouse of our nursery tales and rhymes. He makes good use of the pun on words like *Birbal* (pen-name of Mr. Pramatha Choudhury, an eminent barrister-poet and critic) and Rabindranath. But Dey is often lured by the catholic mysticism of Eliot, and such mythological names as Artemis, Diana and Proserpine, with a liquid and melting sound are needlessly dragged in his placid Bengali lines.

Smritisekhar Upádhyáy (pen-name of Principal Surendranath Maitra, an ex-professor of Physics and a Cambridge man) writes excellent lyrics. His recent translations into Bengali of some of the difficult and well-known lyrics and dramatic monologues of Robert Browning and some well-known lyrics of Shelley are valuable contributions to our rapidly expanding language. He has a striking facility in writing powerful Bengali, full of vigour and effect. One of the outstanding features in his Bengali poems, as it is with Sudhindra Dutt, is the happy use of the *vox liva.*

There are other poets who write on themes taken from rustic life. Their verses are unadorned and unpretentious. You feel in their lines the sweet smell of new-blown flowers and paddy-fields,. the touch of an "*everlasting wash of air*", as Browning puts it, and the depth and passion of unsophisticated love. Their language is the language of common men : folk-lore and folk-songs give them themes and music and diction. Some of their poems have been given musical notations, and like the popular songs of Rabindranath, have been recorded on the gramophone. Such poems are best written by the poets hailing from the riverine tracts of East Bengal, where the habitable places are in a perpetual flux and where the tragedies of life are elemental at one with the grim hunger of rivers and wild waste of their banks waxing and waning with the change of their mighty course.

Sajani Das, a very successful journalist, is another powerful poet. He has a lyric and a satiric mood and the satiric mood is more effective than the lyric. He has also been carrying on extensive research work in the field of old Bengali literature. He possesses the right perspective of a versatile writer and edits a Bengali monthly, which acts as a brake on the mushroom poets of Bengal.

No estimate of modern Bengali poets is complete without some remarks on the form and technique of their poetry. Much hostile criticism has been levelled at these modern poets, much like what was done in the case of Rabindranath in the early eighties and nineties. Any innovation, especially in literature and arrangement of society, is opposed by those who cling fast to a conservative outlook. The charge against Rabindranath was that his poetry was generally unintelligible and contained nothing but a concatenation of sweet words. But the long passage of time has given its considered verdict, and Rabindranath is a world figure today. The greatest misfortune of a poet is that he is hardly appreciated in his own age. When the *Times Literary Supplement* published a highly appreciative criticism on modern Bengali poetry, this batch of young poets was not only heartened but also assured a patient hearing, at least among a certain section of readers, however microscopic it might be. But the uproar of hostile criticism continues unabated even today, and much leeway is to be made up before the more successful of them can secure a sure footing.

Unintelligibility often reveals impatience and betrays our alliance with age-old traditional conceptions. Bengal, or, for the matter of that, India has nothing to show, as Europe has, of political, economic and literary movements. The Reformation, the Renaissance, the French Revolution, the Industrial Revolution, the Chartist and Oxford movements, the pre-Raphaelite movement, the evolution of the U. S. S. R. —all these movements have left their impress upon the life, culture and tradition of the European races. Have we anything like these in India ? The slow-footed East, looking in deep disdain on the conquering West, is again plunged in philosophical thought, as Arnold says. Someone has very aptly observed that the introduction of the democratic form of government in India is a Rolls-Royce system of administration in a country of bullock-carts. But in spite of the absence of many things so essential to a leavening in literature and politics, Bengal has been silently forging ahead, overcoming many a handicap set up by those literary Philistines who cannot brook any innovation. Inability to understand is often a convenient plea to undermine and discredit real excellence. Of course there is much of tinsel, cheap verbiage and vulgarity but this should not blind us to what is really valuable in modern Bengali poetry.

The second charge adduced refers to the peculiar verse-form used by many of these poets. Cadenced verse which they use was employed long ago by the translators of the Bible and by Walt Whitman. Rabindranath first made use of it in many of his narrative poems with great success. The Philistines may call the new poetic form *vinum daenoum* with St. Augustine ; but the vogue has already established itself. The *verse libre,* used as it is in French and English poetry of today, possesses singular facility not attainable in rhymed verses. The poets of the new school write forthwith about any impression in straightforward unrhymed lines : sometimes only the trained ear can detect the music arising out of accented words, of happy compounds or of caesural effect, which is an entirely new thing in Bengali prosodic arrangement. Rabindranath's recent poem *Africa* may be cited as an example .

Africa has a striking, swinging flow like the organ-voice of Milton's blank verse ; the original Bengali lines possess the additional beauty of long and short vowels, not available in Milton. Here the use of rhyme with the sequence of the same number of words would have spoilt the effect of the poem altogether.

Another noticeable feature in the verses of modern Bengali poets is the clever use of condensed metaphor and simile. In this respect, too, they follow in the wake of their European confréres.

An English poet describes a beautiful girl, who "*was slim*

as Ramzan's young moon". Some stray examples from modern Bengali poems will illustrate the point :

"Let your eyes be more blue than the dark sea,
Let your hair be like the bud of grey flowers."

"Her hair was dark like the old, old night of Bidisa :
Her face was moulded like the antique art of Srabasti."

"This strange earth, this lonely hush,
And the mock of the dying moon in the horizon."

"The moon from the broken clouds in the rains ;
A pencil of greyish light was percolating through the mossy roof
Like wet foam.
In that chiaroscuro, in your greyish *sari*
You appeared, and looked like
Well, I cannot make you know."

"Inclines towards the *kasa* bush the seventh digit of the moon
Like the brand-new scarf purchased on a festive day
Washed bright in the rains" (Tagore : *Translated*)

Bengali verses of today abound in surprising imagery and comparisons. There are improvisations at every step, switching off to allied imagery, harnessing into use every subject and object bound by a subtle association of ideas. We feel sheer joy, however fleeting it may be, arising out of life, passion and suffering itself.

The most notable contributions of the modern Bengali poets (at least those who habitually write cadenced verses, as distinguished from those of the major group of the old school who use rhymed verses) are their severance from the old school as a result of which they are in a position to experiment in various fields and forms ; their insistence on the moment and their attempt to "pluck the soul" of a subject ; their admiring recognition of the gripping beauty and interest which detached lines and passages call up ; their studied cultivation of the art of probing into the subconscious, and their popularisation of foreign ideas and images. Time alone will show their worth, but the appeal in cadenced verses continues.

S. K. SARMA

B. A., B. L.,

Was born on 4 April 1880, educated in the S. P. G. College, Trichinopoly and, while a student, developed a taste for journalism and contributed to "*The Kayastha Samachar*" (afterwards called "*Hindustan Review*"), "*The Indian Social Reformer*", "*The Oriental Review*" and other popular journals.

When the "*Bengalee*" became a daily newspaper he was one of its correspondents in the South. In 1905 he founded the "*Wednesday Review*". From 1906 to 1908 he edited the English pages of the "*Indu Prakash*", Bombay. He was also a leader-writer to "*The Madras Standard*". At the time he contributed freely to "*The Commonweal*".

In 1911 he published his "*Indian Monetary Problems*" which gave him a recognised place among the economic writers and thinkers of the time. His criticism of the Prices Enquiry Committee's Report was held to be one of the best made and he was invited to give evidence before the Royal Commission on Indian Finance and Currency in 1919. He was also invited to give evidence before the Indian Taxation Enquiry Committee and his memorandum is a valuable survey and criticism of the taxation system of British India.

In 1928 he published his "*Towards Swaraj*" in which he put in a plea for a unitary type of government. When the Reserve Bank Bill was under discussion, he wrote a series of articles to the "*Hindu*" and other journals, which he later published under the title of "*Papers on Currency and the Reserve Bank for India*".

THE FUTURE GOVERNMENT OF INDIA

NOTHING is more symptomatic of the spirit of the age than the rapidity and ceaselessness of change in our political convictions. A decade ago when the Statutory Commission reported, they could only envisage a federation of a greater India as a gradual process in evolution. But the ink was hardly dry before a full fledged federation became an Act of Parliament. No doubt there were forces in operation that egged the constitutional smithy on to work with furious activity.

The hasty declaration of the princes at the first flush of enthusiasm to respond to the call of the Simon Commission was the fatal step ; next came succumbence of the solitary representative of the Congress at the Round Table Conference to the lure of what he perhaps thought was a well-tried experiment. Both have now begun to regret at leisure what they blessed in haste, though for different reasons. The princes have begun to feel that once they get into its tentacles, there is no escape from the domination of the demagogue and the party caucus which may even encroach upon their sovereign power : it is with them a question of self-preservation. Mr. Gandhi is opposed to it because it is imposed by a foreign agency and not framed by the native rabble gathered in a constituent assembly. And when we know that it is prepared to acclaim him as a dictator supported in state by Mr. Patel's Prætorian guards, we know his opposition is purely personal—in that it did not emanate from him.

And yet there is a vague misgiving in the country which has not crystallised into effective shape that federation is no good either intrinsically or for our peculiar circumstances. It is not so much a closer study of the working of federal constitutions elsewhere, as the practical result of the working of the first part of the Government of India Act that has caused the murmuring distrust. The wielders of political power have fully justified, by their blatant acts of aggression, the fears of those who expressed prudent fears as to their developing the conscious virtues of democracy.

It is well-known that a federal democracy requires for its successful working qualities and virtues of a different and superior order to what can be developed by the adherents of a unitary democracy. For one thing, the representative democrats have to disclose a bias for impartiality in the conflicting claims of state, inter-state and federal problems. The representative is not merely the mouthpiece of the state-unit but of the federal whole. Where their interests conflict he has to be a disinterested judge. Has the working of provincial autonomy revealed the latent talents of the democratic leaders testifying to the capacity for the germination of those ennobling virtues ? Is the approach made by the democratic holders of power to the solution of the problems facing them laid on truly national or merely parochial lines ? Or, to put it differently, have they at least revealed the moral qualities of democratic leadership requisite for the safe piloting of representative institutions for which we have fought for well-nigh half a century ?

To put these questions is to provoke an answer which cannot be complimentary to those who have now snatched the reins of political leadership. The country has swung back, for all the talk of forcing down the throats of unwilling princes and their subjects their own craving for representative government into a system of oligarchical dictatorship, a more than Carlylean hero-worship, a form of impersonated god-worship. Everywhere the responsibility of the so-called representatives in the assemblies and councils to the voters is removed and an allegiance to a party clique which takes invariably the clue from a solitary avater of power is enforced under the cloak of party discipline.

It is stated and defended with unabashed violence that once the ignorant voters, who hardly know the distinction between various colours of the ballot-paper, have crammed particular boxes, then they should be deemed to have voted for the party they connote, whose invisible wire-pullers must thereafter control the policies of the governments. It is significant that the lonely monitor, who has usurped this unchecked and uncontrolled power, has no safer guide than the occasional promptings of an inner voice and it is still more significant that the confidential advisers, who sometimes dictate to that voice what it shall prompt, are no more in touch with the wider public issues that govern the political organisation of the state than the monitor himself. If Mr. Gandhi had put himself as a high-priest of a social reform organisation, it would all have been for the good of the country ; but his entry into politics in an anxiety to keep its reins entirely in his hands has unfortunately created a situation as bad for democracy as it would be for the Pope or the Archbishop of Canterbury to lead a political party. The suppression instead of the stimulation of individual conscience is the price of that incongruity.

The drift towards a totalitarian state under the unveiled dictatorship of a fanatic whose moral fervour is concentrated against supposed social injustice, is sapping the foundations of democracy to the dismay of all who had expected something totally different. How far this reaction is due to the sudden renovation of two western powers under two able men we cannot guess ; but their example is out of tune with the high moral purpose which Mr. Gandhi assumes for every deed of his. Western dictators, whatever their faults, are at least men with a keen political sense. They are not social reformers or moral censors : their sole anxiety has been to raise their states from the mire of economic and financial serfdom into which they had drifted. It was a forceful drive on an unprecedented scale for a determined reconstruction in all fields of state and individual activity. Who can deny that the Italian and the German empires are stronger, sounder and better-equipped in all that make for modern civilisation than they were soon after Versailles ?

The material advancement might have been at the expense of the individual soul whose freedom or what they enjoyed during the pre-war regime, the people seem to be willing to surrender in exchange. Indian dictatorship can show no greater comfort than the economics of the loin-cloth and the glorification of hobbies into handicrafts as the basis for the education of the future. It is cold comfort that the successor may take a more realistic view of the state organism, while the deification of the present one continues. The relapse from the clamour for democracy to acquiescence in personal dictatorship of a "naked fakir" is the most disquieting outlook for the feature.

This has naturally had its repercussion in the politics of the native states. If the princes are alarmed at the onslaught on their prerogative power, their subjects are afraid of the hornets nest where, in place of their autocratic ruler, they would have transferred their allegiance to an oligarchical tyranny of outsiders masquerading under a form of seemingly responsible government. Is this transfer of allegiance, they ask, in their interest ? The hereditary autocracy has at least the tie of paternal association for years in weal or woe to commend it ; the transitory affection of the Indian politicians for a form of government, which in their own territories is held in discount, has generated a suspicion whether, after all, it is wise to cut asunder the dynastic bond between them and their rulers. The repercussions may possibly be even worse.

The growth of fiscal, economic and social institutions hallowed by custom and developed in native simplicity, may have to be made subservient to the more complicated system in British India to their lasting detriment. The distinctive individuality of life and progress may have to be absorbed in complexities of life abroad. To be drawn into the vortex of party strife, communal misunderstandings and economic and fiscal experiments, aye, even to attune their coherent policies to what obtain in British India, may be too costly a price to pay for the privilege of federal partnership. The genuine fear of the more thinking among the subjects of the Native States who are anxious to preserve their independence and escape enslavement to the dominant partner is maturing into a real block to their association with any scheme of federation which

DIWAN BAHADUR HIRALAL L. KAJI
PRINCIPAL
GUJERAT COLLEGE, AHMEDABAD

promises no balancing advantage to the assured loss of their status and importance. From every point of view, they are beginning to suspect that nothing is to be gained which cannot be had by the preservation of their distinctive type in splendid exclusiveness. And who can gainsay that there is much to be said for this view ?

If we remove the Native States then from the picture of a federation of a Greater India, we are yet faced with problems in British India equally destructive of the growth of the democratic spirit. The communal tension has assumed proportions which are daily growing in magnitude. Eighty millions of Mahomedans, a population as large as that of the German state and twice nearly that of Italy or France or the United Kingdom, are getting sore, distrustful and resentful of the majority community. The bridge is widening from year's end to year's end. They do not present problems more acute than what presented themselves before the patriots of Canada, having lived as peaceful neighbours during the course of centuries; but the spirit to solve them is nowhere. They have a fear that the majority community wants to absorb them if their sheer numbers cannot allow of annihilation and call for guarantees to allay it. Democracy means the responsibility of every one ; and it cannot thrive in an atmosphere of mutual suspicion and hatred which divides millions in two armed camps.

The failure of the ambassador of the Congress at the Round Table Conference who was armed with plenary powers, which precipitated the Macdonald Award is perhaps the darkest blot in the escutcheon of congress diplomacy; and since then there have been fasts to remove minor difficulties. The Harijans were re-absorbed into the Hindu fold as distinct political entities; but the Moslems remain as far apart politically as they are in their religious outlook. The canker has so eaten into the vitals of society that the country is sought to be cut into Hindu provinces and Mahomedan provinces where each must give hostage to the other for their good behaviour to run a federated Hindu-*cum*-Moslem India. A divided responsibility on a socio-religious basis is the weakest link that can enchain the parts of a federation to the whole.

As if this is not enough to damp the ardour of national democracy, whose expression is sought to be symbolised in a federation, the separatist tendencies are taking deeper root every day. To communal separatism has now to be added linguistic separatism. If a constitutional pandit had been asked to make an incision into a strong unitary state to carve out scientific units of a federation, he might perhaps have hesitated to do so in the manner of the Government of India Act ; but it is questionable whether he would have cared to segregate mankind into various linguistic areas. But the patriotisim of the tongue is eclipsing the fervour of nationalism. The Congress in its attempt to avoid the confusion of Babel by enforcing Hindi as the *lingua franca* of India, the State language of the future, has opened out a vista of racial animosity in parts of South India.

Compulsory Hindi is said to be a token of the conquest of the Aryan over the Tamilian civilisation which, as the excavations of Mahendra Daro prove, was the civilisation of all India six thousand years ago. The Aryan *Vs.* Tamilian conflict is degenerating as fast as the anti-Jew Nazism of neo-Germany, with consequences as fatal. The Tamil Nad for the Tamilians, the Telugu land for the Andharas, the west coast for the Karnataks and so forth may conserve linguistic patriotism, but cannot solve the problem of minorities in a land where settlements have not been made on a linguistic basis. A truer nationalism which sought to erase the barriers of dialects with English as the *lingua franca*, as it is the language of wordly commerce, is to be subdued by the parochialism of Indian democracy. The agitation of the Andharas for a separate province is only a precursor of similar claims by other clans for the disruption of the state, though it ill-accords with the logic of commonsense that two movements, one for administrative segregation of the population in water-tight compartments in accordance with their mother-tongue should be fostered at the same time Hindi is whipped into service to do duty as the universal language of India. But then it is only evidence of the general confusion of ideas and the policy of time-serving the democratic leaders seem to pursue.

With keener political vision and a higher sense of patriotic duty, it might be possible to approach a solution of these difficulties in the larger interests of democracy, but one does not know where to look for them. Man in the mass is an unthinking animal, and the leaders of thought do not seem to have cultivated anything superior to the mass mentality. Where the average of general education is higher, there the level of public spirit is equally higher. The phenomenal growth of illiteracy accounts for the meagreness in the numerical strength of popular leaders, the more efficient of whom keep aloof from the enchantments of the hustings. The Congress cannot truthfully escape the charge that in its representatives to the legislatures, it is not learning, ability or resourcefulness that have counted, but mere figure-head voting-power.

It is not surprising therefore that the reins of administration have fallen into the hands of seventh-rate celebrities drawn from the lieutenants of the higher coterie. If even industrious research of "Who's Who" does not enlighten us as to the qualifications of the vociferous spokesmen of the Congress or even the Ministers advising the executive heads in the provinces, it is a situation full of peril. That there is a dearth of really capable, informed and cultivated minds imbued with the true democratic spirit in charge of popular governments, instead of mere tools in the hands of a scheming clique irresponsible to the general body of voters, is the most pathetic scene in the tragedy of our political life.

The assertion may appear sweeping, but a record of the achievements of the provincial governments during practically two years of their tenure is as blank in the constructive side as it has been disruptive of the social economic ordering of society. Acting under an unwarranted hallucination that Congress democrats meant business the present writer submitted a proposal for the immediate rehabilitation of the agricultural population in the form of a letter to the Viceroy, which would besides lifting the heavy load of debt on the agricultural industry, have at the same time placed an annual fund of forty crores for the capital expenditure of the state. Whereas the scheme evoked sympathetic consideration from non-congressmen and administrators of experience, Congressmen kept silent over it : they were apparently not educated up to the realisation of its usefulness.

We have had, on the other hand, insolent attacks on the rights of property. In every province under the cloak of improving the lot of the peasants, measures have been adopted or are incubating to cut at the root of large land-holding. Under the cloak again of relieving their indebtedness stringent acts have been passed which do not regulate but strangle money-lending. Measures of taxation have been undertaken which are likely to upset trade and commerce, jeopardise all business activities, enhance the price of commodities and the cost of living of the poor and at the same time reduce the price for the primary products. It is needless to catalogue them here. Such a sedate politician as Dr. Sapru had openly warned that the taxation measures in his province would lead to a catastrophe ; but they are in no way more aggressive than those adopted elsewhere. Sir James Gregg had to admonish the provincial Ministers against the policy of so regulating their tax system as to attenuate imperial revenues.

Indeed, it is upon the rock of finance that the ship of federation will be wrecked. There is a touching irony in the determination of the Congress to wreck the constitution by working it. Even under ordinary circumstances the conflict between the units and the federation in their attempt to lay the most rapacious hand upon the taxpayer is bound to be keen and bitter (and Australia is giving a vivid example of it) ; but when Congress governments have begun deliberately to forego a prime source of their income and in its place substitute every available tax they are sedulously exploring, which can hamper trade, unsettle business, thwart enterprise, worsen agriculture and smother all industrial activities,—that suıely is the quickest route to the sepulchre of federation.

Between provincial taxation and federal taxation, each vieing with the other not only in the municipality of the sources and severity of incidence, but even the one levying a surcharge over the other, the general taxpayer will be bled white.

Provincial financiers at all events do not conceal their glee in their drive against the "drones" of society. Not that they are content with applying the lancet to those parts of the body where, if anywhere, the blood is most conjested. They want to propitiate the new god they have set up in the pantheon, the People, but little care they how the deity is going to be famished by laying violent hands on every offering in the form of ingenious taxation. And the worst of it all is, there is no clear vision as to what these measures are likely to yield and on whom the incidence will fall. The cup of humiliation will have been reached when after exhausting all new sources they can tap, the surcharges come to be levied up to twenty-five per cent of what are now regarded as the most oppressive forms of taxation to satisfy the experimental craze of Congress idiologists.

In every democratic country the people who take an intelligent interest in public questions and are willing to sacrifice their health and leisure in political work are few, and in India they are very limited. They can hardly be dispersed over provincial and federal activities. It is more economical to conserve them to one administration where, whether in power or in opposition, they can make a dispassionate survey of public events, study public questions and harness public monies to the best possible use. A unitary government can take a larger and a more appropriate view of the needs of the country and the resources to meet them ; and can evolve measures of universal application without affecting the parts. A strong central government as the sole custodian of public revenues and regulator of public expenditure can lay its fiscal policies on sounder lines than a number of petty tyrannies scrambling for power. A common educational policy to eradicate ignorance, a planned scheme of industrial organisation applicable to the whole country, central institutes of research for the improvement and resuscitation of the prime industry of the country, a generous scheme of universal relief of indebtedness are all as essential as a single policy of internal transport, common tarriffs or even a central reserve Bank.

If a unitary government is essential for the concentration

of economic power and the reconstruction of society, it is no less essential for the preservation of our national existence. Defence is as important as opulence ; perhaps more important. And the organisation of the defensive strength of the country can only be done effectively by a single authority. It is recognised to be so even by the Government who have given us this unwanted federation. The amending bill to the Government of India Act recently introduced by Lord Zetland and defended as a war measure, is indicative of the realisation of a single-minded policy in emergent times. But preparation for war is perhaps a more vital concern with a people situated as we are as a dependency, to whose defence in times of world conflagration not a single soldier will be sent by Great Britain. A self-governing India must be self-sufficient in her organisation of military strength ; the enemy cannot be kept at bay by chanting the manthram of non-violence.

Indeed the problem of defence was the one block to constitutional advance to full dominion status as the Simon Commission reported. If a dominion army is to be created, the funds for it will have to be raised from the annual savings of the country. A unitary government would certainly be in a better position to distribute the burden of taxation equitably and raise the revenue with as little dislocation of the productive efforts of the country than a federal government whose purpose may be frustrated by the activities of a dozen provincial governments sponging the people of their earnings in competition with the federal tax-gatherer.

It is not possible then to say whether a reversion to a type of government which imperial powers have found most desirable and stable, is within the range of practical politics and whether federation is likely to be torpedoed by Congress activities. That certain settled facts have by force of circumstances been unsettled need not raise any hope that the Government of India Act may meet a similar fate. If it is going to be, it may not be because of the half-hearted agitation against it, but when the people begin to realise that ground down by rigorous systems of federal and provincial taxation, they have nothing left to subsist upon and rise in revolt against the dual oppression. But that is not yet. The accumulated injuries will take some time to be felt. There have not been statesmen who did not see the ills of a complicated system of government which federation involves. When the Statutory Commission was touring India I raised my humble voice against the federal type of government in a book I published then. That acute observer and critic of Asiatic problems, the late Sir Valentine Chirol, wrote to me to say that he concurred in the views expressed in "*Towards Swaraj*" and said that he was opposed to any form of loose federation. The question was not disposed of on its merits; and federation appeared to be the only practicable way of roping in the Native States. If they are going to back out; and wisdom points it out to be the safest thing for them to do the problem that will confront statesmen will be whether to continue with a federation of provincial units or revert to a unitary type. In which event, the best solution will be had by perhaps cutting the units into any number of linguistic areas if need be to placate parochial patriotism, but render them innocuous by taking all powers of taxation from them by reducing them to the position of administrative agencies of the central government.

If responsibility is introduced in the central government without any form of dyarchy—and I have pointed out in my letter to Lord Chatfield how the problem of defence can be solved in a manner which will remove the block to constitutional advance—we shall have harnessed to public service the best type of Indian intellectuals who will be willing to give the cause of democracy all they can. The administration will then be run on the cheapest, most efficient and up-to-date lines without communal or sectional rancour. The bitterness and rivalries of narrow communalism will have disappeared and a larger nationalism beyond the approach and reproach of petty provincialism will have taken its place. May God give the forces of anti-federation the strength to revert to a genuine type of unitary government!

SRI BHARATAN KUMARAPPA

M. A. HONOURS (MADRAS), B. D. (HARTFORD, U. S. A), PH.D. (EDINBURGH), PH. D. (LONDON)

Received his early school and college education in Madras and then abroad. His training and research were primarily in European and Indian Philosophy, and he taught as Professor of Philosophy in the Hislop College, Nagpur, the Madras Christian College, Madras, and the Theosophical College, Madanapalle. Not content with professorial work, at a time when the country was fighting imperialism, he joined in the Second Civil Disobedience Movement early in 1932, when he was arrested and jailed for a period of 18 months. After release he resumed his scholastic work, but when the All India Village Industries Association was established by the Congress for improving the lot of the masses of this country he offered his services to the Association and has been its Assistant Secretary since 1935.

He is the author of "*The Hindu conception of the Deity as Culminating in Ramanuja*", and "*Village Industries and Reconstruction*". He has contributed articles on village industries, education, religion and philosophy, to various periodicals.

THE MACHINE AGE VERSUS CIVILISATION

THE tendency today is to mistake civilisation for a greater and greater use of machinery and the west is thought to have made great strides in civilisation since the industrial revolution. Similarly, Japan has obtained rank among the 'Civilised' nations of the world since she, following the methods of the west, industrialised herself.

Nor is this surprising. For what, after all it may be said, distinguishes us from the other animals but our capacity to invent tools to help us accomplish our purpose ? The animal has to have natural protection such as a covering of fur or hair, or teeth and claws, if it is to survive in the struggle for existence. Civilised man does not require these. He can afford to shave his beard off every day and have all his teeth removed. Why ? because he has invented devices which make it unnecessary for him to depend, like the animal, on natural methods of protection.

WHAT IS CIVILISATION ?

To cover himself he needs no hair. He uses cloth, silk, rugs, blankets, shawls, quilts and what not. He lives in houses which he can artificially heat to maintain an even temperature through the severest winter or cool with ice or electric fans through the hottest summer. Nor does he need teeth and claws to protect himself from his enemy. He uses submarines, bombs and poison gas whereby he can take lives without exposing himself to danger. With the weapon that nature gives, one animal can but attack another, but man has so improved on nature that with his weapons he can wipe out whole cities. Well, is this not civilisation ? It should be, if civilisation is but the capacity to accomplish our purposes through devices born out of our ingenuity. The more effective the weapon the more civilised the man using it. This sounds logical, but not quite convincing. We feel instinctively that there is a flaw in the argument somewhere, for it cannot be that the logical outcome of civilisation is the wholesale massacre of mankind.

If we are to detect the flaw, we must define our terms. We cannot speak loosely of "Civilisation" as we have done. Civilisation cannot consist merely in effectively accomplishing our purposes whatever they may be. Then a clever pickpocket or a skilful robber will have to be classified as civilised (which is perhaps what he is actually thought to be in some circles when the culprit works on a national scale) as in Europe today. But the unprejudiced opinion of mankind will be opposed to equating civilisation with such skilful plunder.

A CONSCIOUS QUEST

If we would gain a true idea of what civilisation is we must ask ourselves what are the purposes which are peculiar to man ; longings and aspirations which distinguish him from the rest of creation and make him superior to them, for it is in the realisation of these that civilisation must consist. The answer is obvious. The aims peculiar to man are those that relate to knowledge, morality, art and religion. It is in his conscious quest for the true, the good, the beautiful, and the infinite that man distinguishes himself from, and rises above, the level of the other creatures. These others may move towards the same end in an unconscious instinctive way, but in man these purposes attain self-consciousness, and if he pursues them he does so deliberately and by choice. Civilisation then, on the subjective side, will mean that quality of character and conduct which makes a man alert to matters pertaining to knowledge, morality, art and religion resulting in a greater and greater realisation of these in his own life. And, on the objective side, civilisation will mean progress in science and philosophy, and the application of these to make life easier and more comfortable. It will mean social and economic organisation which will promote the greatest happiness of the greatest number. It will mean development of literature, music, dancing painting, sculpture, architecture, crafts, beauty of speech, movement, manner and such like. Finally, it will mean a form of religion which seeks, through knowledge, morality and art to find that, the only real, the imperishable, the eternal, the home of the true, is God and the beautiful.

CIVILISATION OR—?

If civilisation is all this it is obvious that mere ingenuity in devising machinery does not make a man civilised. Much will depend on the purpose for which the machine has been invented. If it is in order to satisfy the lust of the owner of the machine for power and wealth, even at the cost of enslaving and exploiting the helplessness of others, then the use of such machines, far from bespeaking civilisation, proclaims the lack of it. Viewed thus the so-called advanced nations of the world, who are at each others' throats for colonies and dependencies and ultimately recognise no law other than physical might, belong more properly to the jungle. The machine instead of aiding civilisation has in their case hindered it. It is easier, it would seem, for a camel to pass through the eye of a needle than for these machine owners to be susceptible to human values. Contrary then to the common assumption, that the use of complicated machinery spells civilisation, we appear to be driven to the conclusion, made clearer from day to day and amply vindicated by events in Europe and Japan, that the machine age is, if anything, an age of barbarism.

The machine admirer is, however, unconvinced. He replies that it is not the machine which is responsible for this sorry state of affairs but the greed of the capitalist, and even as the machine has served the greed of the capitalist it can serve the needs of the community if only the community could have possession of the machine. The mammoth machines which science has made possible will then bring in a new heaven and a new earth. Wealth will be obtained in abundance and distributed amongst the workers, who will have plenty of leisure and ample opportunities provided in the way of schools, colleges, libraries, institutes of music and fine art, drama, and public parks for their all round mental and physical development. The scheme is alluring especially as it promises much for little. The only snag is that civilisation such as we have described being impossible, as we shall see, with the use of large machines, is sought to be acquired in moments of leisure. But this raises the crucial question whether the damage done to one's mental, moral and physical make-up by factory labour can be made good by recreational activities during leisure.

For what does factory labour involve beyond attending to the machine as it performs the same movement hour after hour, day after day? For this nothing is required on the part of the factory hand except a pair of eyes and hands; no intelligence; no initiative; no character; no artistic sense; no religion, nothing that makes a man a human being. What can a person who spends the best part of his life thus amount to but a walking machine devoid of soul? As there is no outlet for the human side of his nature in his occupation he is a nervous wreck and is driven to indulging in drink, gambling and vice or, at the best, in frequenting cinemas, dance halls and vaudeville shows, or reading novels or walking the streets. These have come with industrialisation and, perhaps, form an indispensable adjunct to it.

A PLAUSIBLE ARGUMENT

But, it may be replied, though factory labour may have a bad effect on the worker, still, under communism, there will be ample opportunities provided for developing oneself in leisure in accordance with one's own inborn capacity and inclination so that the evil will be more than counterbalanced by the good and lead to a great civilisation broad-based on the life of the workers who in the end constitute the people. Plausible as this may sound in theory it is worthless unless it stands the test of practice. Fortunately the test is within the reach of all of us. We need only ask ourselves how we actually spend our leisure from day to day: we the educated and the so-called privileged class who ought to know how to spend leisure. Do we not waste most of it, if not all of it, in idle talk, light reading or some other form of amusement? Leisure is for most of us a time for relaxation or for frivolity, where we go from one thing to another as suits our fancy. If we are to develop ourselves our activities must be controlled by a seriousness of purpose which will keep us at our task in spite of obstacles and hardships, and that is provided for the bulk of mankind in work. Work calls for thought, perseverance, patience, steadiness of purpose, initiative, industry, application to detail, exactness, precision, a sense of proportion and finish, skill, self-reliance and artistic ability; all valuable traits of character which cannot be acquired by most people except in and through their occupation. Leisure is too easy going and frivolous to evoke these qualities. If this be true, then to hope to achieve through leisure what work under factory conditions makes impossible is a counsel of despair.

Whether under capitalistic or under communistic methods of production, the civilisation of mankind seems to be endangered through the use of large scale machinery. A multitude of goods is no doubt assured, to some, under capitalism and to all, as it is claimed, under socialism ; but at what cost ? At the cost of dehumanising the masses. A generation of factory hands is to be produced which in the process of work is to have no scope for intelligence, initiative or artistic sense. What is produced, and how, is to be determined not by themselves but by a few who plan production and by the nature of the machine. Theirs is not to reason why ; theirs is but to do and die. They are but cogs in the wheel. The most sacred thing a person possesses, *viz* : individuality, is to find no expression in work. The nation is thus to be reduced to a regiment of men, devoid of personality. Can anything be more terrible for the future of humanity ?

DEHUMANISING THE MASSES

If this great evil is to be averted and civilisation saved, the only way is to see that the work of the world is not carried on by means of huge machines, but that as far as possible it is left in the hands of small producers who will plan and determine for themselves what they will produce and how. It is only thus that there can be a healthy development of individuality, and with individuality, civilisation.

But, it may be replied, if we revert thus to cottage production, sooner or later we shall find ourselves again under capitalism where the more efficient producer gradually swallows up the less efficient and, enlarging his machinery, monopolises to himself all the production and centralises it in a factory under his ownership and direction. To this, our answer is :—an enlightened state cannot allow greed and selfishness to play havoc with its people. It exists to protect them and safeguard their interests. It will therefore put an end to such a development immediately. Further, under a well planned economic system, people will be educated to see how they cause injury to themselves and others by encouraging factory production, how they deprive themselves and their neighbours of employment, and upset the whole economic stability of the community by increasing production without relation to demand. They will be taught the virtue of putting into practice the ideal of swadeshi according to which consumption is restricted as far as possible to articles produced in the immediate neighbourhood. Consequently there will be little incentive on the part of producers elsewhere to expand their business in order to capture other markets. The economic order (or is it chaos) that prevails today in capitalistic countries has no philosophy or plan behind it. The only consideration that has brought it into being and controls it is greed for more and more wealth. In an economic system which can claim to be civilized, on the other hand, human values, *i.e.*, considerations as to whether the economic system promotes the development of intelligence, character, artistic and spiritual sense of the masses will have supreme control.

GOD OR MAMMON ?

In our country wealth was never given supreme place. On the other hand poverty and renunciation for the attainment of spiritual ends was well nigh worshipped. The highest caste was the priest who was expected to look after the spiritual needs of the people and was maintained by them, while the merchant, who lived for amassing wealth, was classified as one of the lower castes. If we are then to be true to our cultural traditions we shall have to set the lead in establishing an economic order where it is not gold that is worshipped, but spiritual values. We may not in that case be able to turn out an abundance of goods like the industrialised nations are doing but we shall be able to preserve and develop what is of incomparably greater value ; the personality of the individuals that constitute our people. Only thus should we be able to save our nation from the demoralisation and barbarism into which the countries which have taken to large scale centralised production are plunged, and only thus can we help to lead mankind from war to peace, from darkness and misery to light and joy, from savagery to civilisation.

SARDUL SINGH CAVEESHAR

MANAGING DIRECTOR, PEOPLE'S INSURANCE COMPANY LTD., LAHORE. AND MANAGING GOVERNOR, THE NEW HINDUSTAN BANK LTD., LAHORE,

Was born in 1886 at Amritsar, and graduated in 1909 from the Punjub University afterwards taking post graduate studies in the Government College, Lahore. In his younger days he was a first-class footballer and has been captain of his college cricket team.

The Sardar began his career at Delhi and started the *"Sikh Review"*. Is a Congress leader and the Founder of the New National Movement among the Sikhs. He took a leading part in the non-co-operation movement. He was elected a Fellow of the Hindu University in 1917 and in 1918 went to Lahore where he started the "*New Herald*". He has been Secretary to the Provincial Congress Committee and all India Central Sikh League and has presided over the Punjab Provincial Conference. In 1928 he was elected a Member of the Congress Working Committee holding the position for six years when he resigned membership on the Office Acceptance Question. He also acted as Congress President in 1932 and 1933.

His publications include "*The successful Life Insurance Agent*", "*Non-Violent Non-Co-operation*", "*The Sikh Studies*", "*India's Fight for Freedom*" and many other religious and political tracts.

THE AKALIS AND SWARAJ

"Ye good people, remember that I was born,
To spread the truth, to help the righteous,
And to destroy those who practise evil and tyranny."

IN these words Guru Govinda Singh expressed the mission of his life. To spread this mission he created the Khalsa in his own image. The Khalsa could best serve its purpose by supporting right against might, truth against falsehood, the weak and the innocent against the strong and the tyrannical.

The world has always needed the Sikh spirit ; but it never needed it so badly as it does to-day when greed and hatred envelope the whole world like a poisonous fog. In Europe, in Asia, everywhere you find people fighting against each other, the strong and the rich crushing the poor and the weak. The spectacle is indeed sad and sorrowful ; no true Sikh can see all this with hands idle and folded.

A NEW SECT

For a Sikh the best way to put this trouble to an end is to place himself at the service of humanity, to make every sacrifice for truth and justice. When Guru Govinda Singh baptised the first five Sikhs he baptised them with the water that dripped from a dagger. By this he meant that the Sikhs should unhesitatingly sacrifice all that was best in them for the cause of the Guru and God. They were given the life immortal and called Khalsa only when each had gladly offered his life as a sacrifice at the feet of the Guru.

"*We are yours, make a sacrifice of us at the altar raised by you to save humanity.*" Thus offering their lives, and their all, for the weak and the oppressed, the first five Akalis became the pioneers of the Sikh faith.

One could regard the Akalis* as a new sect, a sect different

*** The order of Akalis was founded in the days of Guru Govinda Singh. They were like Knights Templar of mediaeval Europe. Originally a sect of religious communists, there is not much difference between a Sikh and an Akali these days. Those in the vanguard of the Sikh struggle for freedom are now called Akalis.**

from others in the sense that it required its followers to make greater sacrifice than any other order or sect had done before. It required its followers to make these sacrifices, not for their personal or communal interests, but for the interests of others who most needed their help ; for the poor, the weak and the oppressed. An Akali could call himself by this name only when he worked in the spirit of the Guru : when he fought, not only his own battles, but also the battles of those of his brethren who needed his help. An Akali could have no idea of personal gain in his mind ; whatever he did he did for truth and righteousness, for God and his creatures.

A SACRIFICIAL SPIRIT

For the cause of truth and justice Guru Govinda Singh sacrificed his father, mother, four children and in the end, himself. Had he any personal ambition ? Did he require any riches or power for himself ? His ambition never lay in that direction. The supreme sacrifice he made, was made for us ; for those who were weak, for those who were in sorrow, for those who were oppressed.

The same was the case with his followers. In the middle of the eighteenth century, when some Durrani robbers attacked the Punjab, on their return march they took with them about a thousand young Hindu and Muhammadan girls as lawful booty. The whole country helplessly watched its shame, but could do nothing. The Sikhs were then holding a meeting at Amritsar. Hindus and Moslems, whose homes were devastated by the Durranis, approached the Sikhs and laid their complaint before them in pathetic terms. The Sikhs were moved ; their leaders said that it was useless for them to live if crimes of the kind could be perpetrated in the country. All those who were present promptly equipped themselves with arms, and at once started in the pursuit of the Durranis to rescue the girls. The Sikhs came in touch with the robbers near Gujrat. A hard battle was fought ; many were killed ; but in the end the Durranis were repulsed and the innocent girls rescued.

One can find many such stories in the history of the Akalis ; they were ever ready to lay down their lives for the honour of their country, for the honour of those amongst whom they lived. And why should they not have done so ? They were the Sikhs, the followers of the Guru and, as such, it was their first duty to make every sacrifice, for the weak, the poor, and the oppressed.

Now and then one hears interested people whispering : why should the Akalis come forward to make such sacrifices when most other Indians desire simply to watch the game ? Why should they suffer for others ? Why should they be made tools in the hands of other people when these people themselves are so cautious and half-hearted ? What shall the Sikhs get if Indians get Swaraj and become free ? An Akali's usual reply to all such objections is that freedom is its own reward ; if India becomes free Sikhs become free. Indian dependence to-day is as much to the shame of the Sikhs as to that of any other sect. If to-day Indians suffer from foreign domination, Sikhs do not suffer any the less.

SELF HELP

One could reply like this from the point of view of self-interest. But Akalis often rises to a higher plane, the plane where the spirit of the Sikh Guru leads them. When asked why the Sikhs should come forward to make more sacrifices than others, an Akali would simply reply, "As Akalis we cannot do otherwise ; the best traditions of our race and the example of the Gurus demand that we should make every sacrifice for the honour of the country. Did not Guru Tegh Bahadur seltlessly offer himself for the sake of others, for the sake of those who did not follow his religion ? In order that the world should be free, that India should be free, that the mist of evil and falsehood be cleared, it is necessary that every Sikh who calls himself the follower of the Guru Tegh Bahadur, should come forward and make a sacrifice of all that he possesses without caring what others say or do. He is an Akali, and his duty is clear. Akalis would not be Akalis if they served not the oppressed ; they were born for the purpose ; they were created to stand as saviours of humanity."

It gladdens a Sikh's heart to see that the Akalis have so

earnestly associated themselves with the new national movement. The new movement has done so much good to the country ; it has raised national consciousness to a point never before reached. It is true that the movement has so far failed in gaining for Indians the object of their heart ; it has not yet got them Swaraj. But the failure does not lie in the movement, it lies in the fact that a sufficient number of Indians have not yet come forward to carry things to their logical conclusion. It is now the considerd opinion of every true patriot, that leaving miracles aside, Indians can get Swaraj only through self-help and self-confidence, which is what the new national movement really means.

RESISTANCE

Indians have not yet come forward to make the required sacrifices which other countries had to make to win freedom. But one can maintain that whenever and wherever the Indians have made the required sacrifices they have come out successful. The efforts of the Akalis in connection with the Gurdwara Reform well illustrate the point. The Akalis have proved that even under provocation, Indians can remain non-violent, and that Indians, however hard others might try to oppose them, can achieve their object when they have recourse to civil resistance on a large scale. The honour belongs to the Akalis of demonstrating to the world for the first time the truth of Mahatma Gandhi's claims. They have put before the world practical proof of the assertion that a government can be defeated by non-violent means as surely as by bayonets and guns.

The Akalis have not achieved success for nothing. History shows few spectacles more touching than their sufferings. It was suffering that brought the Akalis success. The sufferings have not gone in vain ; the sons of Guru Govinda Singh to-day feel as victorious as any army in the world. With the sword of humility and self-sacrifice they have inflicted as crushing a defeat on their opponents as any saint could wish. All the Sikh Gurdwaras where Akalis were treated as pariahs are now in their possession, under their direct control and management.

The Gurdwara question has been settled to the satisfaction of the Sikhs. But the Akalis feel that their duty does not end there. As Akalis they feel they are the custodians of the liberties of the whole human race. As long as India does not become free no Akali can feel satisfied. "This world is the temple of the True Lord, He lives in it for ever and ever." So said the Gurus. Unless this world Gurdwara is free a true Akali shall have no rest.

A WORD OF CAUTION

The Akalis feel that they should impart life to the national movement by their own vitality. They have freed their Gurdwaras from the hands of unscrupulous priests and their allies ; they now desire to free their country from the clutches of grasping and unyielding people.

An Akali feels that the present state of affairs is intolerable ; he feels he should no more bear the shame of it silently. True that opponents of Indian freedom have power to persecute Indians in even more inhuman ways than they have employed ever before, but an Akali is prepared to meet boldly and bravely all such persecutions just as his ancestors did in old times. Those who threaten an Akali should remember that the Akalis of old could survive, and survive triumphantly, even those of their persecutors who vowed to exterminate them from the face of the earth. The Sikhs were declared outlaws and everybody could kill a Sikh and get a reward for his troubles. The result of these persecutions was that Sikhs became heroes and rulers of the Punjab. If history is to repeat itself, the persecution of the Akalis, when engaged in lawful activities, will certainly lead again to the freedom of the country and the defaat of those who persecute them unjustly.

But the Akalis need a word of caution. Success leads to pride and vanity, and they should take care of danger from this source more than from any other. They should work in an humble spirit, in the spirit of service and self-sacrifice. Their hearts should be free from selfishness, malice and hatred ; even their worst enemies should receive their good wishes because, as Akalis, they cannot but pray even for the welfare of their enemies. *"God's glory ever increases; in His will Nanak prays for the good of everyone."* This is how their daily prayer ends; as followers of Guru Nanak they cannot go against it.

THE AKALI SPIRIT

Imbued with the spirit of humility and non-violence, with the spirit of love and sacrifice, Akalis desire to rise like the companions of Guru Govind Singh to free their country from irresponsibility and unrighteousness. Sacrifices they shall have to make, sacrifices perhaps greater than they have ever made before, but the example of Guru Govind Singh will always lead them on and on, from success to success.

In the battle of Chamkaur, when Prince Ajit Singh fell fighting for truth, Guru Govind Singh sent forward his second son, Prince Jojhar Singh, to meet the agents of tyranny face to face. After fighting for some time, the Prince felt thirsty and turned his horse back asking the Guru to send him some water. The Guru replied, "No water here for you, my son; do not turn your back to the enemy. On the other side of the world your brother waits for you with a cup filled with the water of life immortal. Go back and quench your thirst there." The Prince promptly obeyed; he went back to the enemy and humbly laid down his life for the Khalsa, for you, and for me. This is the spirit in which an Akali works. He regards it as his duty to leave aside all personal wants and desires, and die fighting like a brave prince. Let us pray for such Akalis: "Brothers rise; do your duty and prove to the world that you are the true sons of the Motherland. Through you shall the reign of truth and freedom spread to all corners of the earth; through you shall the Lord's universe be filled for ever with peace and glory."

SUBHAS CHANDRA BOSE

Was born in 1897 and is the son of Janakinath Bose, Government Pleader, Cuttack. He was educated at Calcutta and at Cambridge entering the I. C. S. and resigning in 1921 when he joined the Non-Co-operation Movement.

From 1922 to 1924 he was Manager of "*Forward*" and became a Member of the Calcutta Corporation in 1924 being its Chief Executive Officer in 1924.

He was arrested under Regulation III of 1818 ; he was elected a Member of the Bengal Legislative Council in 1926 and was President, Bengal Provincial Congress Committee for several years. He was released in 1927 and took a prominent part in the boycott of the Simon Commission and the Civil Disobedience Movement 1930. He has been imprisoned several times and interned as a State prisoner during the Satyagraha Movement. After release he was asked to go to Europe (except Britain) for medical treatment being allowed to fly back to India in December 1934 on account of his father's precarious condition. On his father's demise he was ordered to go back to Europe (except Britain).

THE TRIPURI SPEECH

Comrade Chairman, sister and brother delegates, I thank you from the bottom of my heart for the great honour you have done me by re-electing me to the presidential chair of the Indian National Congress and also for the warm and cordial welcome you have given me here at Tripuri. It is true that at my request you have had to dispense with some of the pomp that is usual on this occasion.

Friends, before I proceed any further I shall voice your feeling by expressing our joy at the success of Mahatma Gandhi's mission to Rajkot and the termination of his fast in consequence therefor. The whole country now feels happy and tremendously relieved.

Friends, this year promises to be an abnormal or extraordinary one in many ways. The presidential election this time was not of a humdrum type. The election was followed by sensational developments culminating in the resignation of twelve out of the fifteen members of the Working Committee, headed by Sardar Patel, Maulana Azad and Dr. Rajendra Prasad. Another distinguished and eminent member of the Working Committee, Pandit Nehru, though he did not formally resign, issued a statement which led everybody to believe that he had also resigned.

AN ABNORMAL YEAR

On the eve of the Tripuri Congress, the events at Rajkot forced Mahatma Gandhi to undertake a vow of fast unto death. And then the President arrived at Tripuri a sick man. It will, therefore, be in the fitness of things, if the presidential address this year can claim to be a departure from precedent in the matter of its length.

WAFDIST DELEGATION

Friends, you are aware that the Wafdist delegation from Egypt has arrived in our midst as the guests of the Indian National Congress. You will join me in according the most hearty welcome to all of them. We are extremely happy that they found it possible to accept our invitation, and make the voyage to India. We are only sorry that political exigencies in Egypt did not permit the President of the Wafd, Mustapha El Nahas Pasha to personally lead this delegation. Having had the privilege of knowing personally the President and the leading members of the Wafdist party my job today is all the greater. Once again I offer them on behalf of our countrymen a most hearty and cordial welcome.

EUROPEAN CRISIS

Since we met at Haripura in February 1938 several significant events have taken place in the international sphere. The most important of these is the Munich Pact of September, 1938 which implied an abject surrender to Nazi Germany on the part of the western powers, France and Great Britain. As the result of this France ceased to be a dominant power in Europe and the hegemony passed into the hands of Germany without a shot being fired. In more recent times the gradual collapse of the Republican Government in Spain seems to have added to the strength and prestige of Fascist Italy and Nazi Germany. The so-called democratic powers, France and Great Britain have joined Italy and Germany in conspiring to eliminate Soviet Russia from European politics for the time being. But how long will that be possible and what have France and Great Britain gained by trying to humiliate Russia ? There is no doubt that as the result of the recent international developments in Europe as well as in Asia, British and French imperialism have received a considerable set-back in matters of strength and prestige.

Coming to home politics, in view of my ill health I shall content myself with referring to only a few important problems. In the first place, I must give a clear and unequivocal expression to what I have been feeling for some time past namely, that the time has come for us to raise the issue of swaraj and submit our national demand to the British Government in the form of an ultimatum. The time is long past when we could have adopted a passive attitude and waited for the Federal Scheme to be imposed on us. The problem no longer is as to when the Federal Scheme will be forced down our throats. The problem is as to what we should do if the Federal Scheme is conveniently shelved for a few years till peace is stabilised in Europe. There is no doubt that once there is stable peace in Europe whether through a Four-Power Pact or through some other means Great Britain will adopt a strong Empire policy. The fact that she is now showing some signs of trying to conciliate the Arabs as against the Jews in Palestine is because she is feeling herself weak in the international sphere. In my opinion, therefore, we should submit our national demand to the British Government in the form of an ultimatum and give a certain time limit within which a reply is to be expected. If no reply is received within the period or if an unsatisfactory reply is received we should resort to such sanctions as we possess in order to enforce our national demand.

The sanctions that we possess to-day are mass civil disobedience or satyagraha. And the British Government to-day are not in a position to face a major conflict like an all-India satyagraha for a long period. It grieves me to find that there are people in the Congress who are so pessimistic as to think that the time is not ripe for a major asault on British imperialism. But looking at the situation in a thoroughly realistic manner I do not see the slightest ground for pessimism. With the Congress in power in eight provinces the strength and prestige of our national organisation have gone up. The mass movement has made considerable headway throughout British India. And last but not the least there is an unprecedented awakening in the Indian States. What more opportune moment could be found in our national history for a final advance in the direction of swaraj, particularly when the international situation is favourable to us ? Speaking as a cold-blooded realist, I may say that all the facts of the present day situation are so much to our advantage that one should entertain the highest degree of optimism. If only we sink our differences, pool all our resources and pull our full weight in the national struggle we can make the most out of our present favourable position, or shall we miss this opportunity which is a rare opportunity in the lifetime of a nation ?

ATTITUDE TOWARDS STATES

I have already referred to the awakening in India and to the awakening in the Indian States. I am definitely of the view that we should revise our attitude towards the States as defined by the Haripura Congress resolution. That resolution, as you are aware, put a ban on certain forms of activity in the States being conducted in the name of the Congress. Under that resolution neither parliamentary work nor the struggle against the work should be carried on in the name of the Congress ; but since Haripura much has happened. To-day we find that the paramount power is in league with State authorities in most places. In such circumstances should we of the Congress not draw closer to the people of the States ? I have no doubt in my mind as to what our duty is to-day. Besides lifting the above ban the work of guiding the popular movement in the States for civil liberty and responsible government should be conducted by the Working Committee on a comprehensive and systematic basis.

CALL TO UNITY

I have referred earlier to the advisablity of our making the final advance in the direction of swaraj. That will need adequate preparation. In the first place we shall have to take steps to ruthlessly remove whatever corruption or weakness has entered in our ranks largely due to lure of power. Next we shall have to work in close co-operation with all anti-imperialist organisations in the country, particularly the kissan movement and the trade union movement. All the radical elements in the country must work in close harmony and the co-operation and efforts of all anti-imperialist organisations must converge in the direction of a final assault on British imperialism.

Friends, to-day the atmosphere within the Congress is clouded and dissentions have appeared. Many of our friends are consequently feeling depressed and dispirited. But I am an incorrigible optimist. The cloud that you see to-day is a passing one I have faith in the patriotism of my countrymen and I am sure that before long we shall be able to tide over the present difficulties and restore unity within our ranks. A somewhat similar situation arose at the time of the Gaya Congress in 1923 and thereafter when Deshbandhu Das and Pandit Motilal Nehru, of hallowed memory, started the swaraj party. May the spirit of my late Guru of the revered Motilal and of the other great sons of India inspire us in the present crisis, and may Mahatma Gandhi, who is still with us to guide and assist our nation, help the Congress out of the present tangle—is my earnest prayer.

Vande Mataram

DEWAN BAHADUR HIRALAL LALLUBHAI KAJI

M.A., B.SC., F.S.S., F.R.S.A., I.E.S., J.P.,

Professor of Geography and Statistics at the Sydenham College of Commerce and Economics, Bombay and Vice-President, All-India Co-operative Institutes' Association. He was born on 10 April 1886 at Surat and married Miss Vasant Gavri Brijlal Sheth of that City. He was educated at Gujrat College Ahmedabad, and was for some time a Professor of Mathematics at Gujrat College and of Science at Rajkumar College, Rajkot. He is a leading co-operator and has written several important works on the Co-operative Movement. He is an Ex-President of the Bombay Divisional Co-operative Institute; Chairman of the Bombay Provincial Co-operative Institute and Honorary Secretary to the All-India Co-operative Institutes' Association. He was Founder and first President of the Bombay Co-operative Insurance Society, and presided over the Dasha Lad Bania Conference in 1922; Maharastra Divisional Co-operative Conference in 1926; Madras Provincial Urban Banks Co-operative Conference in 1933 and the Mysore Provincial Co-operative Conference in 1934.

His publications include "Co-operation in Bombay"; "Co-operation in India"; "Primer of Co-operation"; "Life and Speeches of Sir Vithaldas Thakckersey"; "Atlas of the Indian Empire"; "Introduction of General Geography". He won the Telang Medal in 1904 and was awarded a Kaiser-i-Hind Medal (II Class) in 1930. J. P. in 1925 and Magistrate in 1926.

In the following pages may be read the Dewan Bahadur's specially written contributions to this volume. In the first he seeks to rescue geography from the limbo of neglect and to place it on the same, or a higher, plane than certain other educational subjects. His second article is a dissertation on the Co-operative Movement in which he shows that, while the movement has achieved much, it should, and can, be capable of doing much more.

GEOGRAPHY, THE BASIS FOR NATIONAL EDUCATION

TO speak to-day of the great importance of geography seems rather superfluous. And yet, when one sees a systematic neglect of the subject in schools, the ignoring of its claims by the university and the belittling of it by the general public, one cannot but feel that the true nature of geography does not seem to have been quite well realised and understood. The old conception that it is a description of the earth still clings and as the description boils down in the short compass of a school text book to an inventory, to a list of names of places which hardly a few can ever hope to visit or hear anything about in the course of their whole lives, it is no wonder that people look upon geography as an extremely dull subject, incapable of being made interesting or useful.

The absurdity of geographical teaching of this character became the more striking when we found that with the text books in use, written as these are by Englishmen from naturally the Englishmen's point of view, teachers used to teach in detail the rivers, ports, towns etc. of the forty counties of England, skipping comparatively hastily through similar information about India itself which, besides being the homeland of the learners, is in size, population and natural productivity as important as almost the whole of Europe. It was a common phenomenon quite recently to find, therefore, our people knowing a great deal, for example, of the charming Lake District of England and precious little of the still greater charms of that land of perennial spring—Kashmir; knowing a great deal more of Newcastle and the Tyne than of Jamshedpur and the Ganges basin. Things are not as bad now; the trend is, happily, to expect more from students about India than about other countries; attempts are being made at expecting from students not merely enumeration but interpretation and discussion.

The study of geography should lead us to two important aspects : facts as they are known and their application to the various activities of man. Geography thus can be regarded as Pure and Applied : the Pure having reference to the facts and laws of geographical science, mathematical, physical, biological, anthropological and human and the Applied having reference to the applications of these laws and facts to the affairs and activities of man. The first supplies the basis on which the latter can be built up. From another point of view geography can be regarded not as divided into Pure and Applied, but as a whole, built up like a pyramid, each successive layer being based on the preceding one and being itself the base for building up the next higher layer. Thus the study of the earth as a planet, as a member of the solar system, and as a spheroid with the parallels of latitude and the meridians of longitude forming the co-ordinates, with its motions and the inclination of the axis, forms the base-mathematical geography—more or less fixed and unchangeable on which the further superstructure is raised. On this base, we proceed to build up the layer of physical geography—the study of the lithosphere, the hydrosphere and atmosphere, of the configuration of the land masses, the currents of the oceans and the great wind systems, planetary, local and variable, more changeable than the preceding layer. From this we go higher to biogeography, where we study the distribution of plants and animals on the earth.

As we go higher and higher still, geographical facts become more and more complex and changeable and yet become increasingly important to us. We proceed thus to anthropo-geography and to human geography, which aspect of the science is now claiming the greatest attention. Human geography is itself not one compact group of facts and knowledge, but is capable of division into a large number of different groups, each emphasising and studying causal relationships and interpreting facts from the special point of view of one single activity of man. Thus there would be military geography, naval geography, engineering geography, political geography, commercial geography and economic geography. The same

G. G. RAO
B.A., LL.B., (LONDON) BAR-AT-LAW

mountain, river or town would be looked upon and viewed from very different points of view by each one according to his special needs. Thus a mountain range like the Suleimans would be studied by the army men from the point of view of defence, the passes, the valleys, little streams, all guiding him to the selection of vantage points for offence and defence.

The Navy would be more concerned with bathygeographical charts, ports and harbours, about key positions on sea-routes and Singapore has a very different meaning for it than to others. The engineer, the builder, the architect thinks about the building materials, clay for bricks, cement and limestone, granite and marble, studies the wind system for devising the proper system of ventilation and meets the problems of life by wind scoops as in Sind, or high domes in the north, or tapering *gopurams* in the south, by flat roofs in dry regions or sloping ones in wet zones. The merchant studies the products of different regions and the means of transport available or made available to him and the industrialist is concerned with the proper selection of sites for his factory, from the point of view of the raw materials, the special facilities that are essential, and the questions of markets and transport. The statesman is most concerned with almost all points of view together. He is the custodian of all interests for his country and he has to formulate his policies with other countries, so as to secure the essentials for the Army and the Navy, for the merchant and the industrialist, indeed for all concerned in the well-being of the country whose destiny he is guiding.

International policies are determined very largely on a close study of the place factor, which is indeed geography and relations between nations are governed largely by the knowledge of geographical facts from various standpoints concerned in the well-being of a nation. Indeed geographical knowledge supplies the key to the proper understanding of the main springs that move the lever of international relationships and geography controls very effectively the activities of men and the well being of a country. The study of the geographical pyramid is thus of prime importance to the citizens of any land and of fundamental importance to the student population, which forms the men of action of to-morrow. To ignore the far-reaching importance of geography—understood in this way as a study of the place factor in the affairs of men and countries—is the greatest indictment that can be brought against the present system of education in our country.

Languages give us vehicles for the expression of thought and open the doors of culture ; mathematics train the faculties of the young mind ; history, the story of the dead past, gives us analogies from the past to work our way in the future, supplies us with parallels to light up our paths, enthuses us with tales of past glory. But what is the use of all these, unless we know and realise our present facts, the great basis on which we can hope to build up our future progress. The African savage in the Congo, the Eskimo in the Tundras, the nomad in the deserts, might remain content with ignorance of the great geographical facts that rule the destiny of nations ; but for a wide-awake people such as we are, or like to think ourselves to be, who have cast off the slumber of ages, who are on the eve of great and far-reaching changes, political and otherwise, to misunderstand the basic importance of geographical studies in our educational system is a transgression of duty to the future generation of the first magnitude. The universities, as custodians of the educational interests of the country, should recognise the vital need for a more thorough knowledge of the earth as the home of mankind and of India as the homeland of its students and for a still more detailed study of the great natural regions of this homeland which, with knowledge of their resources and therefore of possibilities, could become as prosperous and powerful as any single European State, as indeed they used to be on various occasions in the history of the past. In the field of applied geography, in the realms of the study of correlations between geography and the progressive and ordered development of the country, in the intensive studies of natural regions of our vast land and in the extension of geographical knowledge, principles and facts, there is a vast scope indeed for Indian universities to arrange suitable syllabuses for undergraduate and post graduate work.

The knowledge of the earth has slowly been extended by exploration and to-day more precise knowledge has been accumulated about the various parts of the globe than the ancients had, whether of India or whether of Egypt. Adventurers braved the perils of uncharted seas, of deadly climates, of the frozen north and the south, and though several became food for fishes, or found their resting places in the intestines of the cannibals or had cold storage in the Arctic and the Antarctic, they were the instruments for enriching our knowledge of the world we live in. And yet, what has been our contribution to the opening up of the world ? Areas still remain imperfectly known and the chief of these are the Himalayan regions.

The English, the Germans and others are financing and fitting out expeditions for the conquest of Mt. Everest, Kinchinjunga or Nanga Parbat. Sir Aurel Stein, or Dr. Sven Hedin and many others try to fathom the mysteries of the intra-montane regions of Central Asia ; and we sit still and admire, perhaps fail even to admire. Is it not a disgrace that while distant nations should find men adventurous enough to come out all our way and explore the unknown regions at our very doors, we should not find men, except the coolies for the climbing parties, or institutions to feel the enthusiasm and energy or to realise the far-sighted wisdom of contributing our share such accretions to the stock of human knowledge and of assisting our own moral and material progress ?

For explorations often pave the way for a fuller knowledge of the position, physiology, population and products of other lands, so necessary for the progress and development of one's own. The explorer is followed soon by missionaries, who become cultural emissaries and useful correspondents. These are succeeded by traders and merchants, in whose wake come the soldier and the flag to protect the vested interests created by the commercial and economic penetration. Thus instead of the usual course of events, when trade follows the flag, we find a spirit of adventure and enterprise, leading to explorations and surveys resulting in the flag following the trade. For a full national life, such we are being steadily led up to, a proper appreciation of the place of geography, a proper geographical spirit, is very vital indeed, and it is the universities that can largely be looked up to achieve our purpose.

Geography is a study of environment—how environment controls human activities in all directons. It is being recognised how the character of people in different areas is very largely the result of environmental influences. The correlation between tropical heat and rains and impulsiveness, impatience, enthusiasm and precocity, between temperate conditions and doggedness, perseverance, hard work and tenacity of will and purpose, between polar conditions and backwardness and simplicity, between arid regions and thrift, loyalty, bravery and chivalry, between mountain regions and a love of liberty, sturdiness and clan-spirit, between river plain regions and general progressiveness and agricultural developments, between coastal plains accessible from the interior and commercial developments. All these and many others have long been recognised and point out that man is veritably a creature of circumstances and that he can only be what his environment will allow him to be. This is, however, too narrow an interpretation of geographical control. Environment is never quite the same in a large area like India, nor even quite the same in any one of its provinces which, in several cases, are made up of a jumble of more than one natural region and there is variety enough even within a natural region itself, so that within a region, sufficiently large, there is bound to be available persons with the characteristics associated with different environmental conditions.

In tropical India, we can thus doubtless find enough people with the habits and characteristics usually associated with temperate conditions ; improved transport robs plateaus and mountain valleys of their isolation and other features which gave them such sharply defined individuality and brings to them intercourse, which is the basis of all exchange operations and thus of trade and commerce. Vegetation and climate are similarly closely correlated and various deficiencies of ours in the quality and yield of agricultural and animal products are often attributed to our climate ; and we sit quietly under the implied rebuke, forgetting that in vast lands like ours, with a bewildering variety of climates and geographical features enough to entitle India to be regarded as a geographical laboratory of the world, it is with proper investigation possible to find areas enough with suitable climatic and soil conditions to suit any product, vegetable, animal or otherwise.

If geography can teach us one thing, it is this that we must have a proper sense of environmental control and seek to regulate our affairs within the bounds that nature sets to them and not try slavishly to imitate what other countries and peoples do. No model adopted wholesale would suit us and the phrase 'with suitable local modifications' must be adequately understood and acted upon. And, for this purpose a proper study of geography becomes essential for otherwise, saturated with notions imbibed from the culture and literature of other lands and divorced from the grim realities of the local situation from the lack of study of local geography in its highest sense, our intelligentsia would become, more often that not, pale copyists of foreign culture and methods based upon quite different environments.

In industrialisation is recognised the prosperity and economic well-being of a nation and the success of industrialisation is associated with the control, political and otherwise, of large and assured markets. It was this need that led to the continued growth of the British Empire and to economic safeguards and devices for the retention of the huge markets even when the political control has had to be weakened in the case of the Dominions. It is this need for a vast market in the millions of China that leads Japan to the policy which brings the Yellow Peril to the fore and the Pacific Problem as an issue of first rate importance and brings the clouds of war ominously close, for America and Russia, too, covet. Indeed, which country with fortunes linked to industrialism would not covet the 40 crores of the Chinese. Britain and Russia, far apart on the Continent of Europe, draw near enough to each other through Burma and Eastern Siberia, for neighbours of the same prize are in a sense neighbours of one another. The rapid development of Italy, the reconstruction of Germany and the progress of Japan explain their desire for a place under the sun and throw a sufficiently illuminating light on the policies of the partners of the Rome-Berlin-Tokyo Axis.

Time was when manufacturing industries depended upon coal; when steam power begotten of coal was the motive force for transport and the forces of war on land and sea. Countries with great resources in coal and iron came to the front in the machine age following the industrial revolution. Now coal has fallen to a secondary place and it is the reign of King Oil. The advent of the automobile and aircraft, the use of oil for ships as also as a source of industrial power, ushered in policies by prominent countries of obtaining control of oil resources by political possession, by establishing protectorates, and spheres of influence, by obtaining mandates or prospecting and working licenses and concessions. This geographical fact—the oil resources of different countries—acquires, in the present age, a tremendous significance, for it throws interesting side-lights on the Japanese drive against Manchukuo, Jehol and against China generally; the Italo-Abyssinian dispute; the British mandate in Iraq; the Anglo-Persian complications over the oil company and the important position that Burma occupies in the Empire.

Our country, so far we know at present, is poor in coal and oil resources, though we can never say what intensive geological surveys might reveal in the future. But we are rich in another source of industrial power—hydro-electric power—and no one can say what possibilities of its use for purposes other than industrial this power may or may not have, in the days to come. How many in this land, however, care to think along these lines; how many care to learn the facts as fully as they are known at present and how many care to carry on researches, investigation, and experiments to extend the scope of usefulness of this great source of power of the future? We worshipped coal when coal reigned; we bow to King Oil, when its rule is established; but we do not care to accelerate the full advent of hydro-electric power in which our resources are truly great.

All this is so, I fancy, because our educational system is defective, because we have cared for linguistic studies, we have delighted in abstruse mathematical calculations, we have revelled in philosophical dissertations and speculations, we have rejoiced in the romances of history which tells us of the splendour that *WAS* Ind, but we have systematically ignored the facts of the present, the basic facts of our great natural resources and shut our eyes to the fundamentals on which the splendour that can and will be Ind must necessarily depend. Till we understand the earth as the home of mankind, till we fully understand India as our own homeland, till we study the resources and possibilities in detail of our own smaller natural regions, be it Gujarat, Maharastra, Karnatak or Sind, and the possibilities of its development into a great and powerful country and protected from outside aggression under a Federated India as a component part of the great Empire to which we belong, till our universities to this end elevate geography from the abyss of neglect to an eminence of first rate importance and make it a subject of study for graduates as well as for undergraduates till, that is to say, geography comes into its own, the vision of an India, developing fast socially, economically and politically towards its ultimate destiny as one of the great powers of the world, which is bound to materialise with the co-ordination and co-operation of organised human effort with huge natural resources, will remain a mirage receding into the distance with all efforts at approach.

THE CO-OPERATIVE MOVEMENT

THE co-operative barque has been in troubled waters for the last few years and is being drawn perilously near the eddies of liquidation, overweighted with the overdues. The economic blizzard and the trade depression have disorganised international trade and the severest effects have been experienced by the agriculturists who, with decreasing demand, have been receiving lower prices.

Increasing industrialisation in India has further influenced the course of events and by helping to reduce imports has induced a corresponding fall in exports. The war storms in China, Abyssinia and Spain with the ever increasing reverberation of the thunder in an armed world, the devaluation of currencies and the new orientation of economic policies, surcharged with exchange controls, economic nationalism, bilateral trade agreements, quotas, preferences and favoured nations' clauses have dissolved economic equilibrium into the mists of uncertainty.

THE MAIN OBJECTIVE

The Co-operative Movement in India, so far indentified with short term agricultural finance has, therefore, received a rude shock under which it is staggering. Overdues, the unhappy accompaniments of co-operative rural finance, approach perilously the icebergs of frozen assets, and the war between co-operative finance and agricultural indebtedness is becoming a war of attrition, so that redemption, like the elusive mirage, recedes from our grasp, ever into dim distances. It speaks very highly of the inherent strength and vitality of the Co-operative Movement in India, however, that in spite of being thus tossed about on the storms of world forces, it has managed to go on, adjusting here and readjusting there and shows every indication of its emerging triumphant, perhaps chastened but strengthened, better informed and reformed, to fulfil its mission of rural economic reconstruction.

The main objective of the movement has been the redemption of old debts and it cannot be claimed that we have achieved any conspicuous measure of success in our attempts to storm the stronghold of usury, the village *sowcar*, and to hoist the multicoloured co-operative flag on the citadel of agricultural finance. Old debts have now been replaced by new debts which rather reinforce the old ones. The *sowcar* yet remains the bulwark ; co-operation has merely captured the outposts. Indebtedness has increased, not decreased. And why ?

FOGGING THE ISSUE

Repayment of debts depends upon the willingness of the borrower to repay and his ability to repay. The first is a psychological factor. Every one is willing to receive but who likes to pay, unless he must ? The *sowcar* has his own money at stake and by tactful insistence manages to cover his lendings in diverse ways. The co-operative society is the members' own society, it is true : but the money it distributes is outside money and when all members are borrowers, the insistence on recovery is naturally less intense and sentiment creeps in, when the borrower prays for putting off the day when he must repay. The very moral basis on which we seek to raise our co-operative edifice, the sense of brotherhood, helps to befog the business background and brethren in distress respond to one another's call for loan sanctions and extensions.

I feel that while we should certainly emphasise the moral basis of the Co-operative Movement, we should never forget nor allow others to forget that our co-operative village banks are primarily banks and, as such, business concerns, and should not allow them to become institutions financed by outside creditors, and managed by borrowers who display an unlimited ability to absorb loans. The inability to repay indeed weakens the willingness to repay. Ability to repay results from greater savings or from greater earnings, or from both. Economy gives us the one and industry the other. It is this negative aspect of. savings that has received emphasis from the Co-operative Movement so far. Co-operative credit tries to help the agriculturist by making funds available for his current needs at a reasonable rate of interest, and thus enables him to save more by reducing the burden of interest charges. We insist on thrift as a cardinal virtue; we exhort him to cut down all expenditure on ceremonial celebrations and funeral feasts; we try to din it in his ears that money saved is money gained. But we have so far not sufficiently embarked on the road where more money can be earned, for it is money earned that is primarily and directly money gained. Co-operation is but a method of collective action not limited to finance. It could, and should, be applied to all those avenues which yield a prospect of greater realisation and greater income. It should now be switched on to the tunes of co-operative marketing of agricultural produce and subsidiary occupations for agriculturists. It is these which hold forth prospects of increasing their earnings and consequently their repaying capacity.

A COMPLEX MATTER

But co-operative finance often fails in its purpose by very often being inadequate and tardy. The amounts sanctioned are small and inadequate for the agriculturists' purpose, being correlated to some artificial limits imposed by a Registrar or the central financing agencies and determined not by the character of the borrower, which really co-operation seeks to capitalise, but by a percentage relationship of the loan to his assets.

Agricultural finance is so complex that it has been left severely alone by the joint stock banks of the country and yet co-operative banking has rushed in where commercial banking fears to tread. It is not that the former is foolish or that the latter is an angel. It is rather the other way about, for co-operation recognises character as the chief factor of credit and indulges in high ideals. The high ideals are, however, unfortunately, so countered by weak action and sentiment that business gets so curiously mixed up as to deprive our institutions of the elasticity and softness of the co-operative ideology, without importing the rigidity and hardness of the business body. Inadequacy of loans, insufficiency of scrutiny of loan applications and frequency of defaults threaten to stamp them with inefficiency. Credit can fructify if it is turned to productive account and yet we depart from this business dictum when we sanction loans for marriages and funerals or for payment of revenue and rent, since this last, being an item of the cost of production, must needs be met from the profits of production of the previous year and not from the anticipations of the next. Consumers' credit, rarely justifiable on grounds other than the record of past savings, has got so mixed up with productive credit and produces such confusion that the issues really get confounded.

ORGANISED THRIFT

No one, of course, can refuse to recognise the importance of marriages and funerals and their claims upon a man's purse. But these claims must be met not from fresh borrowing but from past savings, husbanded by organised thrift institutions, the best of which are undoubtedly the life insurance societies. Life insurance removes one of the most common causes of indebtedness and not only provides funds for the funeral ceremonies of the deceased but leaves a surplus which comes handy to the heir. Insurance extends its service to marriages also and a marriage policy supplies one with the means to launch out a little on feasts and shows on one of the most joyful occasions in a person's life.

The great objection that has been held forth to the popularisation of co-operative insurance in villages has been the inability of the agriculturist to pay a premium. This may be so in the case of persons already steeped in debt; but surely others, few though these may be, can certainly save the small amounts needed as premia for small insurance policies; and insurance, while it may not be remedial, would certainly be a very potent preventive. In the case of those who cannot save enough to pay the premiums, it can further be said that if they are not good cases for insurance, they are certainly hopeless cases for loans, since it is manifestly impossible for them to pay in one year or more to the credit society what they could not build up in the course of several years with the insurance society to provide for the inevitable—the death of the parent or the wedding of the child. If they are outside the pale of insurance, surely they are outside the pale of co-operative credit also.

INSURANCE

Rural insurance is indeed a very powerful agent that the Co-operative Movement in India should harness to its aid. The habit of compulsory saving it inculcates, the utilisation of the savings of fellow members for the benefit of one of them in distress underlying insurance as well as co-operation—all for each, its elimination of occasions for borrowing, its extensive ramifications with possibilities beyond marriages and funerals to crop insurance against droughts and floods, frost and pests, the sure security it affords to the sureties, the societies and society, make insurance a prime lever to make the machinery of co-operative finance run smoothly.

Co-operative insurance is not a plant of recent growth; Bombay, Madras and Bengal have insurance societies; Travancore and Indore have also embarked upon them. I personally do not favour small organisations on a provincial basis, for that militates against efficiency. A strong All-India Co-operative Insurance Society with branches and local directorates would preserve the efficiency and leave room for local initiative and leadership. I am aware that even these societies have not been able to build up the basis of rural insurance. Insurance is being successfully tacked on to urban co-operation, but efforts at ruralising insurance have so far not been seriously made, and much requires to be done in that connection. But the first thing which co-operators can do is to recognise and realise how vital insurance is in the co-operative scheme of things in the rural areas, as a preventive, corrective and remedial agency for the great problem of rural indebtedness.

The problem of insurance assumes greater importance

and significance when long term finance is now being seriously taken in hand by the formation of land mortgage banks. Redemption of debts cannot be achieved by advances for current argricultural needs in one season or two and larger amounts repayable in instalments extending over a long term of years are now being made available through these banks. While I am certainly of opinion that land mortgage banking is essential to the proper organisation of rural finance, I feel strongly that advances made by such banks are not likely to result in redemption by themselves with or without schemes of voluntary or compulsory debt conciliation, unless these are utilised for land improvement or strengthened and fortified by development of co-operative marketing and other schemes intended to increase the earnings.

LAND MORTGAGE BANKS

In the absence of such measures, the creation of land mortgage banks might merely mean transference of the bad and doubtful debts of co-operative societies to them and the postponement of the tragedy of accumulated unrepaid borrowing to a later date. A complete structure of co-operative finance however does necessarily require organised long term finance and all provinces should, as early as possible, aim at having the village co-operative society ably managed, wisely directed and effectively controlled and supported by central financing agencies federated into an apex organisation, which may be linked up with the central banking system of India represented by the Reserve Bank. These short term institutions should be supported by long term agencies of the land mortgage banks and supplemented by the strong arm of insurance.

LIMITATIONS

While co-operation can and has achieved much, it cannot work miracles, and it is but proper that we should recognise the limitations of co-operation. Co-operation, like the physician, can cure ills and, better still, prevent social and economic sores from expanding; but it cannot redeem hopeless cases, and it is wise to recognise that in society there are such hopeless cases, where the surgeon's knife is the only possible remedy or where death only can give a welcome release, unless divine aid comes to the rescue. Schemes of debt conciliation, voluntary or otherwise, like the surgeon's knife would cut out the swollen cancer of indebtedness, failing which rural insolvency like death, is the only release unless, like divine aid, the nectar of charity heals the cancer and places the patient within reach of the physician co-operation.

While, therefore, one might very much like concentration on schemes of debt reduction by conciliation and, while one might recognise the higher morality underlying insolvency and, while one might welcome co-operative barrages diverting the flow of urban charity by nationalisation to irrigate dried up rural areas, one must must realise that, to be successful, co-operation must leave the hopeless cases and attend only to those whom self help, mutual aid and thrift can lead to better farming, better business and better living. To recognise our limitations and do good to a few is far better than, like the good natured man, to try to please all and to please none.

ROBUST OPTIMISM

So far perhaps, the darker side only of the Co-operative Movement has been presented. The weaknesses of execution do not, however, detract from the greatness of the conception : divorce of action from ideals does not take away from the nobleness of ideals themselves ; and co-operation remains, when all is said and done, perhaps the noblest effort at the economic reconstruction of rural areas in whose healthy growth lies the development of the nation. The history of co-operation has been a romance ; the number of co-operative institutions has very rapidly grown ; membership has swelled remarkably ; the working capital has wonderfully increased ; so that co-operation is a unique movement, more important than any other single socio-economic movement in the country, enrolling under its banner an army of workers, official and non-official, stipendiary and honorary, fired with robust optimism and urged on by unflinching faith, intent on giving their best to the sacred cause of service to weaker brethren.

The completion of the co-operative structure on the financial side cannot however yield success in our main objective—rural economic reconstruction unless co-operation makes earnest endeavours to increase the earnings of agriculturists. It is this positive aspect that is fraught with great possibilities of freeing them from the heavy load of the indebtedness which goad us sometimes to despair. The co-operative organisation of the sale of agricultural produce must now be actively undertaken. The desirability of this form of co-operative endeavour has been always admitted but numerous difficulties have been marshalled in serried array and very little work has been done. The cotton sale societies in the Bombay Presidency are a striking example of the good results that can be achieved and the commission shops of the Punjab, too, have achieved success. Lack of warehouses for storing, the difficulties of grading, pooling and standardisation of the produce are regarded as insuperable obstacles. The Government of India and the Provincial Governments in British India have, however, recently appointed marketing officers and these are bringing out careful studies and surveys of marketing of different important crops.

We should refuse to be daunted by difficulties ; difficulties are there to be surmounted ; if the task were easy, it would have been done by now. But difficulties disappear before earnestness and the greatest task before co-operators everywhere is to set up co-operative organisations or to mould existing ones in such a way that the agriculturist may receive a fair profit from his produce. It is only thus that we can attempt to assist in making agriculture an industry run for profits and not for subsistence, as it has unhappily degenerated in most cases at present. We cannot believe in having distinct societies for different purposes ; the multiplicity of societies is a factor that tends towards mismanagement and in efficiency and we should favour central financing agencies through their constituent societies undertaking the sale of agricultural produce of their members, at least to start with, than wait for well organised sale societies or purchase and sales unions to come into existence. Collective bargaining for better prices is any day better than individual bargaining and financing institutions would find it to their interest to organise the sale of agricultural produce, as it would considerably simplify their recovery.

OTHER OUTLETS

The development of village industries and processing work and subsidiary occupations for agriculturists is also a necessity of the first order. If agriculture does not occupy the farmer all the year round, it is obviously necessary that he should find out something remunerative to do during the time he remains unoccupied. What occupations to suggest, what organisation is necessary for the purpose are matters which the Departments of Industries in the various administrative areas might well look into carefully. But co-operators through their co-operative federation might well select individuals or appoint committees to work out suitable schemes in this direction in co-operation with the authorities, so that the income from agriculture may be supplemented and the additional income help to solve the problem of agricultural indebtedness.

To secure the fruits, the Co-operative Movement is expected to yield, it must tackle the whole situation, and attack on all fronts. The agriculturist's year is, as it were, made up of two parts, the period of activity and the period of enforced idleness, of hibernation. During the period of activity he arranges for finance, buys seed, manure, implements and cattle, sows and reaps, sells his produce and buys household requisites ; during the period of hibernation, he rests. In this round of activities —finance, purchase, production, sale and consumption—co-operation has only so far directed its attention to finance and that too, very inadequately. In the *sowcari* system, the creditor is also the merchant who buys the produce and the shopkeeper who sells household requisites. Under the co-operative system we have so far neglected all stages of the agricultural cycle excepting finance. Purchase and sale we have neglected ; production has not seriously occupied our attention and consumers' organisation—the village stores, have been left out of our programme.

Co-operative credit, unless accompained by co-operative supply, co-operative sale and co-operative stores, with co-operative conversion of the period of hibernation into one of subsidiary activity, cannot hope to succeed against the tremendous task of economic regeneration of the village population. Production, we might leave alone for the time being. The technique required for its improvement is for the Departments of Agriculture to supply and yet, in that connection, consolidation of holdings and irrigation, draining, fencing and so forth have been attempted with success by co-operation in various parts of India. Unless therefore co-operation makes up its mind to develop its offensive extensively on all fronts, there is not much hope for the prize that we seek.

FULL DEVELOPMENT

In the work before us, we must consolidate our position, seek to ease the unprecedented hard times through which agriculture is passing by suitable concessions and extensions and by prudent fresh finance keep the co-operative credit societies going, till times improve and enable the members to meet their obligations as they should. At the same time, we must diversify our efforts and explore fresh fields. We must start land mortgage banks and run them with all due safeguards, we must requisition the services of insurance; we must organise collective sales under the auspices of the central banks or special distinct institutions, we must organise supply of agricultural requisites and we must facilitate the undertaking by agriculturists of subsidiary occupations to supplement their slender income.

AN ABIDING FAITH

In this work, we must remember that the persons directly affected are the village people, whose ignorance and illiteracy have been serious obstacles to success. The task of rural economic reconstruction demands a mental reconstruction of the human material to work upon. In British India, the need for village uplift schemes under the wise encouragement of the Government have been recognised and the work is well under way on a mass scale. Individual experiments like those of Gurgaon have shown the value of well considered schemes of rural reconstruction which would rouse the villager from the torpor of ages, make him a ready and fit subject for co-operation to work upon and make village life healthy, pleasant and attractive. Co-operation is, perhaps, the strongest agent of such reconstruction and a co-operative credit society with a broader conception of its mission should be a force in village economy which would marshall the forces of the reconstruction movement and lead to substantial improvement in the man, his materials and methods. Co-operation may be facing hard times but we workers in the cause need in no way despair. An abiding faith in the creed, and greater energy and wider effort will bring us soon within sight of our goal.

Co-operation in India has been identified with the rural credit movement. The urban movement is a bye-product and does not perhaps receive the attention it deserves. The human material is much better, the conditions are much better, and the results are much better too. When we feel a little dejected at the absence of that success that we had expected in rural areas, we might turn to a dose of proved efficacy—a peep at the urban movement. The successful working of most of the urban credit societies heartens us up, refreshes us. Yet when contemplating the problems of the small man in town, be he a member of the salariat or the proletariat, be he employed in trade or industry or absorbed in an adminstration or profession one cannot but realise how much remains to be done. The credit movement should develop more vigorously on the savings and thrift side and one longs to see a number of such credit-*cum*-thrift societies working in co-ordination with the higher organisations, the insurance society and the investment trust, the natural culminating points in the schemes of saving.

CONTROL ESSENTIAL

The weaknesses of the co-operative credit movement have led to the tightening of official control and this has aroused among the non-official workers a feeling of dis-satisfaction, so that these put forward a plea for relaxation of official interference more particularly in the case of urban societies. Dispassionately examined, the situation is natural. Official control is necessary for efficiency ; non-official freedom is necessary for elasticity and initiative. Besides, with the growth in numbers, the task of the departments too is becoming unmanageable and the authorities are unwilling, or unable, to sanction larger staffs and heavier expenditure on the movement. One wonders why the departments do not, like wise parents, release from control, at least partly the children who have been functioning efficiently, for a long term of years. In urban societies particularly, where efficiency has been the rule for years, there would be no harm if the experiment of loosening the control is tried. Efficient autonomous audit by approved and licensed auditors may be prescribed and a biennial or triennial super audit could be maintained ; quarterly statements in prescribed forms may be obtained and the department may be content with general supervision. Of course, when a particular society is thus detached as it were form the joint family the concessions and privileges should likewise be withdrawn, excepting the facilities of arbitration under the co-operative law.

THE ACID TEST

The societies cannot grumble since if they feel grown up enough and want autonomy, they must go out of the nursery and give up the concessions, the fondlings and caresses, which they received so far. The State in launching this very remarkable socio-economic service of co-operation could never have meant to include in it the whole population at a time, but must have desired to teach the method to the people and rouse and train them up to stand on their own legs. While no general relaxation of official control is desireable, particularly at a time when overdues and stagnation threaten the very existence of the movement in rural areas, it certainly seems very desirable, if, in case of proved efficiency, individual societies were released by progressive stages from the leading strings of the department and the concessions withdrawn. The great test of success of the Co-operative Movement would be the increasing number of societies thus released, so as to demonstrate that, at least in those cases, the co-operative method had proved successful in bringing strength and organisation where disordered weakness prevailed.

AN APPEAL

On the non-credit side, the consumers' movement has not taken root excepting in very special areas and under very special conditions. Experiments have been made but these have failed ; but the reasons for the failure are to be found in faulty organisation, small capital and small scale of operations than in anything inherent in the movement in our urban conditions. In these stores, we pin our faith on the loyalty of members ; and when failure comes, we bewail the absence of this loyalty which led to the failure. Loyalty which spells custom and success does not attend preachings and exhortations and calls to sacrifice ; it should be automatic ; but for this purpose the stores should be distinguished by the facilities it gives to its customers, or the sentiment it evokes or the economic advantage or lower prices it confers.

Co-operation has achieved much and is capable of far greater achievements. With a provincial bank, central district banks or *taluq* banking unions, and rural primaries for short term rural credit ; with a provincial land mortgage bank and smaller organisations for districts or *taluqs* ; with a provincial co-operative wholesale society, to tackle the problems of supply and sale on behalf of agriculturists and on behalf of consumers and small producers ; with a co-operative insurance society to minimise the risks in rural and urban areas through a network of co-operative primaries as its agents ; with a co-operative investment trust to husband the savings of the co-operative community and make them productive by proper investment ; and with a co-operative federation as a central thinking and thought clearance office and as a centre for propagandist supervisory and educational activities of the movement, the edifice of co-operation would be fairly complete and the fruits, the strengthening of the small man in the village, town or city will be well within our grasp.

DR. B. V. NARAYANASWAMY NAIDU

M.A., B. COM., P.H.D., BAR-AT-LAW

Studied in England for seven years joining the Middle Temple in 1926 and being called to the Bar, 1929. He joined the Annamalai University in 1930 as Professor of Economics and was Dean, Faculty of Arts 1933-39. He has also been Member of the Syndicate, Senate and Academic Council and Chairman of the Board of Studies in Economics, Annamalai University and Editor of the *University Research Journal.*

Dr. Naidu has been Member, Board of Studies in Economics, Mysore University 1935-38; Member, Board of Studies in Economics, Andhra University; Member, S. S. L. C. Board, Madras; General Secretary, All India Economic Association; Associated Editor, *All India Journal of Economics* (1936-1938); Associated Editor, *Service*, Madras; Vice-President, South Indian Library Association; President, South Indian Badminton Association; President Nangambakkam Cricket Association; Member Executive Committee, South Indian Lawn Tennis Association and the Madras Cricket Association; President, Chidambaram Paddy Sales and Loans Society; Director, Chidambaram Land Mortgage Bank; Executive Committee Member, Madras Provincial Co-operative Union; Member, Chidambaram Taluk Deb conciliation Board; served as member of the Sub-Committee of the Madras Provincial Economic Council; he acted as Vice-Chancellor, Annamalai University (1939).

In the following article written specially for "*What India Thinks*" Dr. Naidu deals trenchantly with some aspects of economic planning for India and formulates a set of noble ideals which no nation need be ashamed of setting up before itself.

SOME ASPECTS OF ECONOMIC PLANNING FOR INDIA

WHAT with the unexampled post-war depression in almost all countries of the world and the various economic experiments in Russia the question of planning has become a live issue in all civilized countries of the world.

One of the most outstanding effects of the War has been to instil into the minds of politicians and people the necessity for national self-sufficiency, conservation and the utilization of national resources to the best advantage of the largest number of the country's nationals. In short, nationalism has ceased to be racial and territorial and has extended to the field of economics so that it has been realised that wisdom and forethought are essential in the ordering of the economic life of a people as much as in the organisation of their political and military life. The ordering of the economic life of a people on national lines has been, therefore, a post-war phenomenon.

In recent years Russia has attempted, by detailed planning, to outstrip in production even the most advanced capitalistic countries of the West; perhaps with the idea of a spectacular demonstration of the superiority of socialistic organisation to a capitalist ordering of society. Since March 1933 President Roosevelt, recognising the importance of comprehensive planning for curing the *malaise* from which the whole economic life of the country was suffering, has embarked upon an unexampled course of state initiative in the economic adjustment of the nation. The main aims of the Roosevelt Recovery Plan are to limit the motive of profit makings in industry, to effect a more aquitable adjustment of national income and, in general, to subordinate individual interests to the needs of the vast majority of the people. In 1933 an unparalleled national crisis, leaving in the hands of the state 14 million unemployed workers, cried aloud to the President to undertake immediate and drastic action. Besides this, short-time work was in existence, the banking system of the state was crumbling, currency was insecure, and national confidence in the system under which they lived was being rapidly undermined. Hence President Roosevelt found it necessary to introduce drastic changes in the organisation of the production and currency of the country.

The threatened shortage of food-stuffs in Britain during the War, the restriction of her foreign markets as a result of the increasing industrialization of the countries involved and the consequent disturbance to her industries and currency have induced Britain also to seek for new methods of ensuring national economic stability. Conservative as ever, she has not embarked on any scheme of comprehensive planning but has tried to patch up her economic fabric by state encouragement of industries, by concluding commercial pacts with other countries and by trying to retain for herself imperial markets by pacts like those signed at Ottawa. Plans for national economic improvement have been adopted in their own differing ways by Kemel Pasha in Turkey, Mussolini in Italy and Hitler in Germany.

Alone of civilized countries, India has not yet adopted any systematic economic planning. While socialistic Russia has resorted to planning in a spirit of competition with capitalism, while America was compelled to resort to it to avert a grave national crisis, while various countries coquette with the idea for the sake of new national aggrandisement or the preservatiou of old dominance, India has to resort to it in self-defence, so that she may keep pace with the extremely complex economic organisation of her foreign competitors, out of mere humanitarian consideration for the millions of her nationals whose income is insignificant and whose purchasing power is the lowest on record in any civilized country. It should be the primary duty of the state in India to conserve and utilize the economic resources of the country for saving the hungry millions of her population from starvation and misery.

Planning, therefore, which is so essential to the continued progress of nations of the present day, means simply an adjustment of means to ends. Just as the individual prepares clearly before himself a programme of work before he starts working for a definite goal, planning places before a nation a clear objective and a programme of activity suitable to the circumstances of her case and necessary for her progress. Instead of allowing chance and whim to govern the development of nations, reason and humanity must assume control and work the resources of the country to the best possible purpose.

PLANNING THE WORK

Accurate and extensive knowledge of the resources of the country, as far as that is humanly possible, is no doubt involved in all ideas of planning. Planning presupposes, therefore, a sound knowledge of economic conditions, a definite goal for economic activity, and a fixed period of time in which the goal is to be reached. At first sight it might appear that the third element is not essential ; but it is no exaggeration to say that only a definite and fixed period of time will induce men to put their best foot forward and help to raise production to as high a pitch as the country can possibly attain.

A PARADOX

Planning in India should be undertaken not with the intention of developing our export trade or for curbing excessive industrializaton but merely for national ultilization of available economic resources for the greatest happiness of the greatest number. Immensely rich in her natural and human resources, India remains a paradox in the economic field since the vast majority of her population is in the grip of indigence and starvation.

The appalling poverty of her rural population and its excessive dependence on agriculture has become a commonplace of economic thought in this country. In the face of such a problem of illiteracy, indigence, suffering and hunger of such a large mass of humanity combined with the extraordinary wealth of material and mineral resources in the country it seems to be astonishing why effective and comprehensive action is not taken to diminish the illiteracy, to satisfy the hunger and to improve the physique of the people by utilizing the abounding resources of the country in all possible ways to the utmost possible extent.

FAR-SIGHTED ACTION

Death and disease, ignorance and squalor, starvation and poverty must be blotted from the face of India and this can be done only by increased industrialization of the land. India must cease to be a provincial farm, growing raw materials for foreign industry and a dumping ground for the finished goods of alien enterprise. The dependence of India on foreign markets is neither indispensable nor beneficial. India is well adapted to grow whatever her children need for their sustenance. This land abounds in the pre-requisites of industrialization : men, money, materials and motive power. All that is wanted is concerted and patriotic action of a far-sighted nature. Industrialization will solve the problem of inadequate employment and relieve the strain on agriculture which itself stands in need of far-reaching readjustment. Increasing productive power must mean larger incomes, greater comfort and increased happiness.

But the word 'industrialization' is suspect in certain quarters. I believe this is due to the mistaken notion that organised industry must mean greater exploitation of the masses by the moneyed classes, the rich growing richer and the poor poorer. Neither concentration of wealth nor slum life are inevitable features of industry. Industrialization simply means organised and planned effort towards greater production ; but this production can be adjusted to the needs of Indian village life. The only thing that is pleaded for is that in the reorganisation and revitilisation of village life the door need not be banged in the face of modern mechanical advance or systematic production. Thanks to cheap electric power it is yet possible that India's vital life can continue to be centred in the village producing the utmost it is capable of by wise organisation and united endeavour. It is the task of wisdom to find out how modern progress can become a willing and useful servant to the millions of India.

DEMARCATION ESSENTIAL

Agriculture, irrigation, transport, education, industries, public health and other phases of national activity must come within the ambit of national planning. To map out in detail this vast area to be covered must be an achievement of the labour of years. All that is attempted here is to indicate lines of advance which will be most beneficial to the interests of the nation. For a successful working of any plan a clear demarcation of functions as between the Central and Provincial Governments is necessary. Subjects like currency, customs, railways, and tariff can best be tackled by the Central Government while the development of agriculture, irrigation and industries can be undertaken with advantage by Provincial Governments.

INDUSTRIES

That India's actual industrial development is entirely disproportionate to her potential resources, considering her size, population and material wealth, is admitted on all sides. This state of things is in no small measure due to the fact that her captains of industry and leaders of thought have not yet fully realised, much less utilized, the wealth lying at their very doors. The resources of the country have not been sufficiently harnessed to progressive activities by the enterprising and intelligent portion of the population. Deficiency in leadership and lack of technical labour are the two prime factors which must answer for India's industrial backwardness. Want of systematic financing and absence of adequate facilities must also bear some measure of the blame.

This unsatisfactory state of things can be changed by a national economic policy by which the Government should attempt to encourage Indian industries in every way it can. Machinery and other raw materials of production can be admitted to the country free of duties, the burden on semi-manufactured goods can be lightened, adequate finance can be provided and facilities given for general, technical and industrial training by establishing technical schools and industrial laboratories. But the greatest benefit that Government can confer on industry is by helping in the financing of industry. Capital is the backbone of modern industry which is organised on lines of large-scale enterprise, mass output, and standardised production. Government must pursue a liberal policy of loans and subsidies to industries and so shape the working of the banking system of the land as to compel the banks to keep in close touch with national industries.

Such a policy should involve the disappearance of the pernicious managing agency system and an extension of the activities of commercial banks. The needs of industry must be met in some measure by a re-orientation of policy on the part of the existing commercial banks by taking an increasingly active part in the issue of shares and debentures and by the establishment of a network of Industrial Banks throughout the important cities of India. Such banks not only provide funds for adequate industrial expansion but can also serve as connecting links between industries and investors by giving useful technical advice. These banks should be helped by Government, if need be, even by taking shares themselves, thus securing public confidence in them.

AGRICULTURE

Turning to agriculture, again, we find a similar disproportion between its importance to the country in view of the almost total dependence of the people upon it and the extremely inadequate attention paid to its development. When compared to other countries, the yield per acre in India is ludicrously low and little attention is paid to scientific manuring and improved methods of cultivation. The extreme fragmentation of the holdings and the indebtedness of the agriculturist have brought agriculture to a standstill where the cultivator follows exactly the methods which satisfied his forefathers centuries ago.

The problem of indebtedness has to be solved by provision

for debt conciliation, by a simplification of rural insolvency procedure, by an adequate supply of long-term credit and by the establishment of Land-Mortgage Banks. To improve the methods of agriculture an agricultural bureau must be established in each district to give advice about mechanical appliances, fertilisers and marketing and to arrange for agricultural demonstrations. The spread of co-operative buying and selling will also be of considerable importance in the development of agriculture. Subsidiary occupations like dairy farming, cattle breeding, bee-keeping and poultry farming should also be encouraged by helping the peasant by a liberal provision for grazing lands, by importation of superior breeds and by arranging for technical instruction in improved methods.

A SCANTY RETURN

The proper development of agriculture is closely bound up with the question of agricultural marketing. The recent phenomenal landslide in prices is in no small measure due to lack of proper marketing facilities and it cannot be denied that even in his most prosperous days the Indian agriculturist never got the maximum price his commodities *could* have fetched. It is a common phenomenon in this country to find the agriculturist trying to sell his produce as soon as the harvest is over even though the market is glutted with the same goods and prices have fallen. He undertakes to do this since he has often to meet the insistent demands of his creditors, to pay the *kist* or other seasonal obligations, or has no facilities for safe storage and hence he invariably sells at the lowest price and thus gets a scanty return for his labours.

He labours also under many other disadvantages that arise from lack of standardised weights and measures, absence of grading, want of proper inspection of goods, secret settlement of prices by agents and brokers and the use of false and incorrect weights and measures. While these are his difficulties in the internal market which accounts for more than a 1,000 crores out of 1,200 or 1,300 crores worth of agricultural produce his disabilities in the external market are none too light. The absence of a unified selling organisation has not only resulted in unsettlement in the quality and specifications of goods and consequent ignorance in foreign markets of the real quality and quantity of his merchandise but it has also resulted in lower prices for his wares, in deficiency in advertisement and in the creation of an impression in other countries that India cannot supply high-grade products.

CENTRAL MARKETING

These difficulties cannot be overcome without taking into account the essential functions of marketing *viz.*, collecting and assembling, transportation, wholesale distribution, retailing, risk-bearing and financing in all stages. To my mind the foremost remedy for this state of things is the establishment of Sellers' Co-operative Societies which will prevent seasonal dumping, help the ryot to get credit till his goods are sold and store his products and arrange to release them for sale at proper intervals. Such organisations can improve merchandizing practice, help in the careful grading of commodities, provide for improved methods of advertisement, regulate the quantity and quality of supplies to different markets, increase the bargaining power of the producer and eliminate trade abuses. This will tend to great economy in marketing and serve to restrict the activities of middlemen. Such associations may be formed for definite areas and linked together in a central organisation.

The problem of agricultural marketing cannot be solved without improved communications, increased transport facilities and lessening of freights. A chain of private or railway warehouses has also to be established to facilitate storage of goods ; and the vouchers of such storage can be given by law the validity of negotiable instruments. The grave handicap of of indebtedness and lack of credit must be removed by the formation of financing companies for the marketing of goods and by liberal provision for agricultural credit by the Government. Government must also adopt stringent and continuous measures to stamp out adulteration and enforce standardized weights and measures. In addition they should appoint

SUBHAS CHANDRA BOSE
POLITICAL LEADER

provincial marketing officers to collect and co-ordinate marketing information and make it available to the producers. Each province should also have regional marketing boards to assist marketing officers and regional agricultural chambers wherein producers can meet to discuss problems such as those connected with finance, production and marketing.

IRRIGATION

Any study of agricultural development must take into account the problem of irrigation. The Indian peasant depends for his cultivation entirely on the monsoon and any failure of it or excess means starvation and ruin to him. The over dependence of the agriculturist on the vicissitudes of the seasons will be realised when one notes that only 16 per cent of the cultivated land is irrigated from tanks, rivers or wells and the remaining 84 per cent is entirely dependent on seasonal rainfall. A comprehensive scheme of irrigation is urgently needed in each province and any well-conceived policy of irrigation should devote greater attention to minor works. Introducton of modern pumping plants, construction of tube-wells, digging of new tanks, wells and canals from rivers, building of reservoirs and the supply of cheap power for pumping and other purposes will go a long way to the solution of the problem.

TRANSPORT

Closely connected with the development of industries and agriculture is the question of a comprehensive scheme of transport. In any scheme of transport railways naturally occupy a very important place. Railway development in this country in the past has taken sufficient account of the markets and the centres of production. This defect has to be rectified by having a definite plan of railway development which will make easy, not merely the import of goods from outside, but also the export of goods from the centres where they are produced.

The increasing importance of motor transport at the present day has once again drawn attention to inland roads.

Though roads need not be developed to compete with the railway they can serve as feeders for railways and channels of distribution. Though railways, posts and telegraphs must continue as a central concern there is ample scope for provincial Ministers of Transport and Public Works who will take the improvement of the road system as one of their main concerns. One of the best means of improving transport is the development of inland waterways. Since the war a comprehensive programme for the development of inland waterways has been drawn up in France by the Minister of Public Works and schemes like those of the grand canal of Alsace and the Marseilles-Rhone canal have aroused international attention. The French Government have been making increased provision for ordinary upkeep and repair as well as for new construction and improvements and the budget for 1926 provided more than a hundred million francs for this purpose. Germany also has undertaken such works and given state encouragement. The Rhine-Maine-Danube works, the canalisation of Nackar and the linking up of Hamburg with Bremen and the Westphalian industrial districts by the Hansa Canal clearly reveal the fostering hand of the state in this development. America also has expended large sums for creating waterways. Careful planning for the future must provide for a system of inland waterways which should be developed, not in competition with other forms of transport, but as a means of supplementing them.

PISCICULTURE

Another direction in which the material wealth of the country can be exploited is the extension and improvement of fishing and pisciculture. India has a very extensive seaboard and fish forms a very wholesome article of diet. Attempts should, therefore, be made to introduce improved methods of fishing even, if need be, by Government taking the lead in importing fishing trawlers and conducting deep-sea fishing and resigning them to private ownership when they become commercially paying. Fish-curing has also to be made scientific and facilities for inland transport of fish should be increased.

Demonstrations of improved methods must be given in selected places and fishermen taught to adjust themselves to modern conditions.

COTTAGE INDUSTRIES

In a land of villages the supreme importance of the development of cottage industries can be easily realised. The task of providing remunerative work for the farmer during the off season is one worth attempting, having regard to the fact that an overwhelmingly large part of the population devotes itself to agriculture. The cottage industries of spinning and weaving need a good deal of improvement. Efficient hand-loom machines, and diversified patterns for weaving are badly needed as well as better advertisement of new methods by demonstrations and of the products of industry by improved methods of marketing.

There are many cottage industries in India like metal work, lace-making and ivory-carving which involve a good deal of skill. The machine threatens these with extinction, and lack of enterprise has left them in neglect and decay. The skill of centuries, handed down through generations, should be conserved and exploited, so that these industries might be brought back into growth and usefulness. A central selling organisation for the sale of such goods will be a step in the right direction.

INDUSTRIAL LABOUR

Comprehensive economic planning should include not merely organisation and enlargement of productive power but it should also provide for the amelioration of the conditions of labour. A high turnover of labour is the bane of efficiency and this should be minimised in this country by offering the industrial worker stable and comfortable conditions of work. Though the efficiency of industrial labour has yet to be increased by various methods it is not correct to say that the low efficiency of the Indian worker is due to any inherent inferiority. Often he is supplied only with obsolete machinery and the defects arising from insufficient enterprise and brainless leadership are laid at the door of the poor Indian worker.

Amelioration of labour conditions has often been opposed on the ground that industry cannot support increased expense; but very rarely is it proved that enhanced profit has ever gone to the benefit of the worker. It would be a bad thing for Indian labour if it is to be cooped up without air in the slums of large industrial cities. Thanks, however, to modern planning and improved transport industrial suburbs can be built where the worker is sure of healthy housing in country surroundings. Compulsory measures for insurance, workmen's compensation, shorter hours and welfare schemes have to be introduced by suitable factory legislation. Greater contact between capital and labour can be secured by the institution of workshop committees and industrial councils.

EDUCATION

Neither money nor legislation can make reforms effective, nor progress possible, unless they are helped by the united will of an educated nation. Universal education is the only sure solvent of all national ills; and progress, social and economic, is inevitably bound up with the spread of education. To improve the efficiency of industrial labour, to make our countrymen understand the social and economic problems of the complicated modern world, to enable them to observe the laws of health and sanitation, to rouse their civic conscience and to inspire them with a sense of civic responsibility and to give them strength to shoulder the greater and wider responsibilities of political life a concerted drive against ignorance and illiteracy must be immediately undertaken. A planned scheme of compulsory education must provide, in every province, for the eradication of the illiteracy not only of the children of school-going age but also of adult workers and peasants.

ECONOMIC SURVEY

All planning for economic expansion must be based on an accurate and extensive survey of existing economic conditions. Statistics on everything that illuminates the future of the people are essential for every nation that wishes to progress. Economic empiricism can at best secure only a hand-to-mouth existence. Since statistics not only record what has been but also point to what may be they form sure guides for the improvement of administrative machinery and for shaping national activity so as to meet new demands.

Statistics are, therefore, essential at all times for accurate and quantitative information about the facts of production and consumption, for wise intervention and guidance by the state and for the efficient functioning of individual enterprise. A survey of this kind should cover production, national income and national wealth, collective wealth, consumption, wages, cost of living, prices and indebtedness. Internal, foreign and coastal trade, transport and communication, condition of crops, yield, crop experiments and value of produce should all come within the purview of this survey. A double classification of the population based, one on occupation, and the other on income should also be effected. Intensive studies of classes, communities or families should be systematic and representative, extending throughout the revenue year. The wages and prices statistics have to be collected and intensive enquiries in typical areas, typical crops and typical industries undertaken.

To effect a comprehensive survey of the 422,000 villages of British India is a task of no mean difficulty or of inconsiderable cost. Professor Bowley and Dr. Robertson have recommended a somewhat expensive and inadequate scheme. A work of such magnitude must depend for its success on the willing and voluntary co-operation of thousands of men; but when once the grave national importance of the work is realised I am sure efficient voluntary work will be forthcoming if an advance of the right kind is made. It is inevitable that in such a scheme the services of village officers and Government officials have to be secured. Labour and trouble can be minimised if general lines of survey are first laid down after careful investigation. Educational institutions throughout the country can be of great help in the collection of these data if in every institution students are appointed to gather the material under competent guidance. Each province must have a statistician who is helped by a body of officers to co-ordinate this information and make it available to the public. Since a comprehensive economic survey has not been attempted before in this country the difficulties in the way seem to be formidable. Though the first survey may present some difficulty later ones will certainly be easier and more complete.

VILLAGE RECONSTRUCTION

Foremost among the advantages that flow from an adequate supply of figures and statistics is the help that they will render in the moulding and shaping of village life. The villages of India are the centres of her vital life and no improvement, economic or social, is worth the name which does not take into account the conditions of life and work in the villages. The chief aim of village reconstruction should not merely be to provide increased occupation for the villager, though even that is a very important step ; but it should also be in increasing measure the concern of economic and social policy to remove the disparity between the attractions of the town and those of the country and to provide for those amenities in the country like water-supply, schools, dispensaries and entertainments which have hitherto been the monopolies of towns. Better work and more of it, more leisure, and greater capacity and means of utilizing leisure are the very urgent problems of village life in India today.

FINANCE

Stern realists are not wanting in this country or abroad who would predict that such an ambitious scheme must be enevitably wrecked on the rock of finance. Such schemes are interesting when they are in the stage of speculation but where is the money to come from even if a tithe of these is to be attempted ? The contention has often been made that the taxes in India are as high as they possibly can be and the addition of a single straw will break the back of the poor Indian tax-payer. But it has to be remembered that the taxable capacity of a people increases with their economic development and prosperity and that if the taxes that are already collected are utilized in large part for constructive effort, the pockets of the very tax-payer will show unmistakable signs of his increased capacity to pay.

I firmly believe that the scope for improvement in taxation is very great in India ; but the tax-payer has first to be convinced that the taxes he pays are used for his benefit. An overhauling of the system of expenditure is an imperative necessity in this country. Even without taking into account the costly federal structure and second chamber envisaged in the Government of India Act the administration is extremely top-heavy. The high salaries of British officials were at first justified on grounds of distance, climate, lack of social amenities, etc., it being then contended that expenditure could be reduced by Indianisation and Provincialisation. But even though these were effected salaries continued to mount up till at last there is now a vast gulf between the incomes and standards of life of the people and of the members of the public services.

The country's financial stability demands a radical readjustment of salaries. If the framework of government continues to swallow up large amounts social services are bound to suffer. In 1929-30 the Central Government spent 711 million rupees on essential service as against 27 millions on social services. Out of a total federal expenditure of 801 millions the Percy Committee assigns 470 millions for military purposes and no great progress is possible either in economic or social matters unless there is a reduction of the military burden. The resources of the country can be husbanded not merely by a re-ordering of expenditure but they can also be increased by duties on properties above a certain value which devolve by death and on increment of land value due to betterment of the area by roads, canals or train or tram services. The Government can also exploit the easy money conditions in the money market by undertaking well-planned public works. Thus an ambitious capital programme must be inaugurated by both the Government of India and Provincial Governments.

ECONOMIC ORGANISATION

These extensive plans for development and amelioration have to be classified, initiated and carried out by a development commission in each province. They can also have the help of a smaller body of experts in economic counsel which will help them to foresee and tackle the complex economic problems of the modern world, which will engage itself in continuous study of current economic problems, of the development of trade and industry in each province, which will complete and co-ordinate the statistical and other information required by the Executive and the Legislature, which will invite the attention of both these to important economic changes and tendencies and which will suggest to the Government plans for solving fundamental economic difficulties as those connected with the stabilization of trade and the development of national resources. It is desirable that such a body has only the minimum of paid servants and that it should contain within itself leaders of industry and labour, experts in economics, popular leaders and the heads of departments of Government such as the Director of Agriculture and the Director of Industries.

The survey and speeding up of production, the improvement of agriculture, the extension of irrigation, the spread of education and the general amelioration of the conditions of the mass of the people in town and country, the eradication of idleness, ignorance and indigence are noble ideals which no nation need be ashamed of setting up before itself. But true statesmanship and patriotism lie not so much in envisaging the future as in taking effective steps to make the dreams of today the realities of tomorrow.

A. S. PANCHAPAKESA AYYAR

M. A., I. C. S., F. R. S. L., BAR-AT-LAW.

Was born on the 26th January 1899 in Aiylam village, Palghat Taluk, Malabar District. Son of Sri A. S. Subramanya Ayyar and Srimati Akhilandeswari Ammal. In May 1919 he married Srimati Vedanayaki Ammal and went to England in October of the same year. Passed the I. C. S. Open Competitive Examination in 1921 and took his M. A. degree at Oxford University. He returned to India in December 1922 and is now District and Sessions Judge, Vizagapatam, Waltair. He is a member of the Inner Temple ; took a Certificate of Honour at the Bar Examinations and is the holder of the Langdon Medal.

He was elected a Fellow of the Royal Society of Literature of the United Kingdom in 1933.

Mr. Ayyar is the author of several books in English which have been translated into all the south Indian languages among them being "Indian After-Dinner Stories", "In the Clutch of the Devil", "An Indian In Western Europe", "Baladitya" : A historical romance of Ancient India", "Sense In Sex and other stories of Indian Women", "The Finger of Destiny and other stories", "Panchatantra and Hitopadesa Stories", "Sita's Choice and other plays", "A Mother's Sacrifice", "Three Men of Destiny (Alexander, Chandragupta and Chanakya)."

In his special contribution to "What India Thinks" Mr. Ayyar enlarges on the theme that Mother India is on the march once more after a thousand years of stagnation and sleep.

THE FUTURE

THE problem before India for the next fifty years will be the rapid adjustment of her ancient institutions to the changed times. Caste, untouchability, early-marriage, enforced widowhood, spurious spiritualism, all will go. There will be no place for the hereditary priest, the hereditary soldier, the hereditary trader, the hereditary artisan, the hereditary cooly and the hereditary scavenger in the future democratic India.

Specialisation of some kind there is bound to be, but allotment by birth to a particular occupation for life is not likely to survive or be tolerated. All the special enclosures will be invaded by the future children of the motherland. Even the hereditary rulers and the hereditary landowners will not survive, unless they are willing to become figureheads whose personal equations will not matter ; in other words, unless they become titular rulers and lords as in some western constitutional countries. The people of future India cannot afford to gamble on heredity which has cost India so much and has been one of the main causes for the present degraded state of the country.

If it were not for the hereditary priesthood, based on birth alone, Hindu priest would not be so ignorant, so sunk in superstition, and so powerless for good as they are today. Were it not for the fact that only one cast manned our armies, the country would not have succumbed to any foreign invasion. Had it not been for the fact that the masses had no part or lot in the government of the country, they would not have remained apathetic and gloated in the horrible proverb "*What does it matter to us if Rama rules or Ravana rules ?*" So too, the fall in our trade, the stagnation in our arts, the dying of our inventive skill, the inefficiency of our coolies, and even the indifference of our scavengers, are mainly due to the inertia of caste. From the temples of our gods to the latrines of our houses the curse of hereditary occupations, so necessary, useful and beneficient in ancient times of difficult communications, great insecurity and general illiteracy, are only prolific sources of evil now.

If any nation is to survive, it must march with the Time Spirit: else, Time will march on and leave it far behind. That has been the fate of unfortunate India. Her spirituality has stagnated for lack of free flow, her army is not representative of the whole nation, her traders have become mere middlemen to other traders, her artisans have not the requisite knowledge, her coolies have not the requisite muscles, and her farmers are sunk in age-long despair.

But a new spirit is stirring the country. The Behar and Quetta earthquakes are but symbolical of the tremendous earthquakes which are taking place in our social, economic and religious systems, crumbling down the out-of-date structures and paving the way for a new Quetta of a reconstructed India. The very Himalayas is shaking its snow, like some divine elephant, before being harnessed. Her peaks will be desolate no more; her passes will be negotiated by trains, her innermost recesses will be explored by aeroplanes. The mighty Brahamaputra will supply electric power and light to millions of homes, the life-giving waters of the Ganges will no longer waste themselves in the bitter sea, and the proud Indus will be made to turn deserts into gardens. Our army will become national by the spread of a sense of duty. It will become national by the spread of interdining between all the children of the country. At present if conscription is enforced, our army will require ten thousand different kitchens for its different castes, and the enemy will capture all our positions while we are eating in a thousand hidden corners. Wars are not yet over; the predatory spirit of mankind is dead. It will take at least a hundred years more before real peace and good-will among nations can be counted upon. And it can, and should, come only when every nation has come into its own.

We need not attack others, but, surely, we should not allow others to attack us. Our mighty god-given frontiers must be well defended on land, sea, and air by our own sons and daughters. To this end at least we must enforce periodical compulsory vegetarian dinners of a nutritive kind among all our officials, professors and students, and especially the last as they will be the guardians of the future. The practice of noting down caste, tribe and religion in census and other official reports and documents should be stopped so that the communal seed may not be fostered. The laws which we enact should have no reference to communities but should apply to the whole nation. All customs which are not conducive to the good of the country or progress of the nation must be ruthlessly abandoned.

Quarrelling politicians and communalists should be forced to pass an advanced examination in theoretical and practical astronomy, so that they may realise their own pettiness by getting an idea of the infinity of the universe. All priests should be made to see the grandeur of our mountains, rivers and lakes by free passes on our railways, issued as soon as they have passed the precribed examinations in the selected scriptures of not only their own religion but of all the religions of mankind. Students must be made to go round on foot over as much country as possible during the vacations by their teachers. Public servants must be made real servants of the public. Expeditions of young and suitable Indians must be organised at state expense to the North and South Poles and to the mighty Himalayas to climb up its giant peaks. Our seas must be filled with our ships, our atmosphere with our aeroplanes and our land with industrious, happy, God-loving people devoted to their country and to the cause of mankind.

The process has begun. The Agriculturists' Relief Act, the Sarda Act and the Poona Pact, the Devadasi Bill and the Travancore Proclamation, and the frantic attempts of many Indian princes to give at least a semblance of democratic regime to the government of their states are all signs of the times. All of them show that the spirit of India is not dead and cannot die. The dying India of fifty years back is now found to have only indulged in a cataleptic sleep from which he has awakened, refreshed and ready to take his place in the sun whose favoured child he has been throughout the ages. He is seriously considering whether birth-control, the soya bean or swaraj is the true remedy for India's teeming millions, whether the League of Nations should not be invited to spend a few years in India, a real live centre for racial, linguistic and cultural problems, instead of dozing away its existence on the shores of the lake of Geneva with its unruffled waters ; whether Fascism, Socialism or Communism will suit Indian conditions, and whether thoughts about the other world cannot wait till we have got a firm hold on this one.

The people are waking up to the necessity of a common tongue, Hindustani, a language of their own in which they can all talk as they talked in Sanskrit and Prakrit in ancient days. Every caste and community is awake. The apparently evil communal movement is really a god-send, it is galvanising castes supposed to be sunk in age-long apathy. It is only the castor oil in the system, only a purification necessary for health. It will cause much uneasiness while it is acting, but what a relief, what a feeling of strength, joy and fitness it will bring when it has done its work and the waste matters accumulated during centuries are purged out ! No more will caste blame caste. No longer will people blame the Brahmin or Kshatriya or Vaishya for betraying the country as of yore. Hereafter all stand for all, and each for all, until we reach the journey's end.

Reaching our goal will, doubtless, take some time, but time should be of no account in this land of *Yugas*, *Manvantaras* and *Brahmakalpas*. The main thing is to fix our ideal. The children of this country have known in the past, and may be trusted to know in the future, how to march up to it. The one point to note is that Mother India is once more on the march after a thousand years of stagnation and sleep. There will be no re-tracing of our steps. He who falters will be left behind. Our maxim will be, "*The Pilot drops, but the ship goes on*".

NALINI RANJAN SARKER

FINANCE MINISTER, GOVERNMENT OF BENGAL.

Few people in India have by their individual endeavours contributed more towards the development of economic thought in India than the Hon. Mr. N. R. Sarker. He is among the few successful Indian businessmen who has proceeded to an intellectual analysis of the problems that confront this country. Realising as he does that the economic and social conditions of a country condition other types of progress, he has applied his energies towards an examination of the ways and means of ameliorating the economic condition of the people, and has emphasised the need of economic planning in this connection. While acknowledging the undoubted value of economic doctrine, he at the same time emphasises the necessity of a pragmatic attitude towards the pressing problems of the day. The Hon. Mr. N. R. Sarker has by his numerous articles and addresses stimulated economic research in various spheres to no small extent so as to get to the root of current economic problems and is primarily responsible for the recent awakening in Bengal to the need for serious study of the various economic problems that beset us, and also for imparting to our young men a wholesome bias in favour of commercial occupations. An idea of his manifold activities will be given by the following enumeration of some of the high positions he has occupied. Finance Minister, Government of Bengal, Ex-General Manager, Hindusthan Co-operative Insurance Society, Calcutta, Ex-President, Bengal National Chember of Commerce ; Ex-Commissioner, Calcutta Port Trust ; Ex-Mayor of Calcutta, Councillor, Calcutta Corporation ; Ex-Fellow, Calcutta University ; Ex-President. Indian Life Offices Association ; Ex-President, Federation of Indian Chambers of Commerce and Industry ; Member, Board of Economic Enquiry, Bengal ; Member, Central Jute Committee ; Ex-M. L. C. Bengal ; Formerly Chief Whip, Swaraj Party ; Member, Bengal Legislative Assembly ; Ex-Member Board of Industries, Bengal ; Ex-Member, Central Cotton Committee, Member, Executive Committee, Federation of Indian Chambers of Commerce & Industry ; Member, Executive Committee, Employer's Federation of India, Ex-Member, Indian Insurance Institute ; President, Indian Economic Institute, Ex-Member, Central Banking Enquiry Committee and Railway Retrenchment Committee ; Member, Consultative Committee, Government of India for the revision of Company Law, 1935 ; Member, Board of Income Tax Referees, Bengal ; One of the non-official Indian Delegates to the Indo-Japanese Trade Conference ; author of "*The Ottawa Agreement*", "*The Problem of Unemployment*", *India's External Obligations*", "*Indo-British Trade*", "*The Problim of Agricultual Indebtedness*", "*Economic Planning*" and many other valueable articles and many monographs.

In the following article which he contributes to "*What India Thinks*", the Hon'ble Mr. Sarker discusses the problems and prospects of industrialisation with his characteristic lucidity and deep insight. Coming, as the article does at a time when India is fast going ahead in the task of tackling the problem of National planning, it will be found of considerable interest to objective students of India's national economy.

INDUSTRIALIZATION & PLANNING

WITH the inauguration of provincial autonomy, considerable powers of initiative have been vested in the responsible Ministers in the Provinces, but at the same time greater responsibilities for improving the economic conditions of the masses have also devolved on them. Naturally, therefore, the problem of the rapid industrialization of a country so predominantly dependent on agriculture has come to engage the serious attention of the provincial governments as well as the public. It is felt that unless the industrial development of the country is planned on a scientific and diversified basis, the deplorably low standard of living of the masses can never be raised and the numerous economic ills which assail our national life today can never be eradicated. These facts are receiving the necessary recognition and emphasis today and serious discussions and deliberations are in progress as to how an accelerated industrialization of the country can be achieved along sound and healthy lines. The problem is of such stupendous magnitude and involves so many complicated issues that serious constructive thinking and co-ordinated endeavours are essential to the end that a satisfactory solution may be evolved. The formation of the Congress Planning Committee and an adequate appreciation of the growing importance of this problem are welcome indications on the part of responsible leaders of public opinion and many provincial governments.

Two things should here be borne in mind. In the first place, the success of any scheme or policy of industrialization will be vitally affected by our ability or otherwise to exercise control over such matters as currency, tariff, railways etc. These fall, however, within the ambit of the Central Government. Close co-operation between the Central and Provincial Governments is, therefore, essential to the success of any rational and planned scheme of industrialization. In the second place, although this scheme must be framed on an all-India basis, adequate and sympathetic consideration must be effered to the needs and aspirations of the various provinces. It is probably desirable that the All-India Planning Committee should be assisted by the labours of provincial enquiry committees. These provincial committees will not only survey the existing position and prospects of industrialization within their respective sphere but also contain indications of their aspirations. It would appear that the work of the Central Committee would be greatly facilitated by placing at its disposal reports submitted by provincial enquiry committees.

In recent months the problem of industrialization has come under a searching and critical examination in numerous well-informed circles. But these examinations have served more to reveal certain grave complications involved in the task than throwing any light on possible lines of solution. Some of the complications are found to impinge on very fundamental questions that must be settled one way or the other before any satisfactory suggestions on methods of planned action may be offered. These questions, taking only those that have so far been thrown into bold relief, relate to the necessary adjustment between the claims of large and cottage industries, territorial distribution of the industries to be developed and the adjustment of the developmental scheme to the existing economic framework. Each of these questions calls for most careful consideration.

LARGE SCALE INDUSTRIES VERSUS COTTAGE INDUSTRIES

The question regarding the adjusment of the claims of large and cottage industries arises from certain ideological differences that are associated with two distinct schools of economic thought in this country. One of these is wedded to the belief that the economic salvation of India is possible of accomplishment only through the establishment of a network of large mechanised industries on the model of the advanced countries of the West. It explains the disintegration of India's old industries in the light of her failure to adjust the internal economic structure to the changed environments brought about by the industrial revolution and considers technical efficiency to be the sole criterion of an abiding success, in the prevailing state of intense international competition. The standpoint of this school of thought postulates progressive urbanisation of the people and regards the same as a sign of prosperity.

The other school of thought, on the other hand, looks upon with disfavour the establishment of mechanised industries in concentrated areas and argues that India's salvation is bound up with the expansion of her cottage industries. The protagonists of this view put forward certain ethical and economic considerations in support of their preference. They refer to the soul-killing consequences of modern factory life as a potential danger against which India should effectively guard herself. And it is further strongly urged that even the most progressive scheme of mechanised industries could possibly provide employment for no more than a fraction of the people who sorely need occupation to learn their living. The existing factories, it is pointed out, employ only about 1·8 million people, despite the fact that many of the industries have reached the stage of over production. The figure represents a very small fraction of the total population and is regarded as a clear indication of the limited potentialities of mechanised factories as a means of providing employment.

There is an element of truth in both these conflicting schools of opinion ; and there has latterly been betrayed a readiness on the part of their respective advocates to arrive at a compromise. That the desirable line of action to be chosen by India lies in the golden mean between the two extremes was, however, quite evident to those who took a more realistic view of the situation. The conclusion reached at the recent meeting of the Congress Planning Committee as to the respective roles of cottage industries and large industries in national development virtually supports this middle viewpoint. In their view both the categories of industries have an important part to play and it is all a difference in emphasis which sustains the controversy.

COMPATIBILITY OF THE TWO STANDPOINTS

Even about a year ago when the controversy was probably more acute, I had occasion to give some thought to the problem and although the discussions have since proceeded far into details, I have no reason to revise the conclusions then arrived at by me. I took pains to make it clear that we could justify neither of the assumptions on which the too conflicting standpoints were based, namely, that large scale industrialisation of

India is detrimental to the reconstruction of Indian village life, or that in chalking out the line of our future progress we possess an entirely free choice.

"We have reached a stage" I observed, "where industrialization is not only necessary but is also inevitable. But it is too dogmatic to state that the evils of industrialization which have been evident in the West are also inevitable in India. Even to-day our factory labour is much better off than average agricultural labour, while in view of the adoption by India of labour laws designed to remove the evils of the earlier industrialization of the West, the apprehension of our factory labour being reduced to the position of mere slaves of machines would seem to be grossly exaggerated. At any rate, without much conscious effort or greater freedom of action or policy, we have still succeeded in keeping many of the evils of industrialization out of the country. With greater political power and greater co-operation between the provinces, I believe, it is quite possible to reduce the evils of industrialization to the minimum in India."

SUBSIDIARY LINES AND DECENTRALISATION

At the same time I emphatically urged the necessity of maintaining the balance of our national economic life as between agriculture and industry. I also referred to the interdependence between industry and agriculture and showed how the development of many of the large industries, like cotton and sugar, have given a valuable support to agriculture, far outweighing any losses that might be entailed by the decay of certain cottage industries. This is not, however, to suggest that the cottage industries do not require any special assistance. On the contrary there are certain cottage industries which may have to be given some measure of protection against the products of indigenous factories ; evidently, such a scheme would call for the most delicate adjustment having due regard to its possible reactions on the wider economic interests of the country.

Such an adjustment is no doubt difficult to accomplish, but on a closer examination it does not appear to be quite impracticable. We may evolve schemes to provide discriminating protection to selected cottage industries particularly in respect of such goods as are in constant local demand and for which the villages possess obvious advantages ; and also with a view to opening up subsidiary lines in connection with large industries for assisting the cottage industry workers. It would, however, be necessary to devise suitable schemes of decentralisation if the benefit of the measures has to be brought within the reach of the rural population. And here lies a good potential field for fruitful planning by the government. In order that effective inducements may be offered for attracting capital and enterprise to the undeveloped areas possessing good prospects of ultimate success, special measures may have to be enacted. A sound scheme of decentralisation will not only give a fillip to our cottage industries by opening up new subsidiary lines but also provide an effective check on the growing evils of the congestion of factories in concentrated areas.

TERRITORIAL DISTRIBUTION

Regarding the territorial distribution of industries in the scheme of the future industrial development of India, one is apt to feel that the issues involved in this question have not so far been boldly tackled and that its intimate connection with the question of planning on a national basis has not been adequately appraised. The merits of a plan have to be assessed in the light of its human values and a national economic planning connotes a scheme of controlled production and distribution that contributes to the economic welfare of the community as a whole according to certain pre-determined values. The formulation of such a plan is different in different countries and at different times. It is all the more so in India where the people do not constitute a homogenous economic group affected in an identical manner by the economic forces working in the country. The conditions prevalent in the different provinces are so divergent in character that they cannot react to the economic forces in the same way. And this provides an explanation to the pronounced inequality which shall have to be lessened not by levelling down the progressive provinces but by levelling up the backward ones.

THREATENED DISLOCATION

And here the problem of economic planning is confronted with certain grave problems that are inherent in the prevailing condition of economic resources and development of different provinces. The under-developed provinces in India fall into two distinct categories. There are some which are very poorly endowed with natural resources and cannot be expected to develop any of the major industries on any appreciable scale. Any forced development in these provinces by extra ordinary measures of state assistance would be of the nature of a hothouse growth. Yet, on the other hand, we could not expect these backward provinces to continue on a lower economic level and yet provide a market for the more fortunate provinces As a solution out of this *impasse* may be suggested, not a forced development of industries, but a well planned scheme of taxation on the profits of industries and the distribution thereof among the provinces in equitable proportions. How far such a policy would be desirable or practicable will have to be considered in all its aspects.

Then there is another class of provinces that has probably excellent potentialities both for new and some existing industries but being late comers in the field cannot possibly realise these to the fullest extent without prejudice to sister provinces. Needless to say, in these provinces the old lines of industry would attract capital and enterprise with greater facility than altogether new and untried lines. Regarding industries belonging to the former category we need not, for obvious reasons, feel concerned about those which still remain undeveloped as compared with the effective consumption demand of the people. But a serious dilemma would arise in connection with those of the existing industries which are found to have reached the stage of over-production. Should any check be imposed on the late coming provinces, despite the fact that some of these may possess richer potentialities than any of the provinces where for some reason or other an industry may have already been established? Which of the two would be a greater evil : a temporary dislocation in the existing scheme of things followed by maximum productive efficiency, or the sterilisation of the potentialities of the late coming provinces with a view to avoid the threatened dislocation? These are questions which are bound to confront the National Planning Committee as much as any serious student of Indian economics. I have devoted many moments of anxious thought to these intriguing questions and I am inclined to believe that it may be possible to effect a compromise between these two conflicting issues through a scheme of compensation to be paid to the inefficient units on the assumption that the latter would be gradually scrapped over a number of years to allow the necessary margin of expansion to the underdeveloped provinces that may now or hereafter be considered to have superior natural advantages. The working of such a scheme, of course, postulates organised action on the part of the industry and also governmental support, if necessary, by statutory sanction, to all plans of rational development. The determination of the exact methods by which such schemes are to be implemented is a matter for detailed investigation. The National Planning Committee will have to tackle this question with due care and consideration of the existing conditions and requirements of the various provinces.

ADJUSTMENT TO ECONOMIC FRAMEWORK

Coming lastly to the question of adjusting the future scheme of industrial development to the existing economic framework, it will be found, on a close scrutiny, to involve quite a number of complicated issues which ought to be thoroughly clarified at this stage. The suggestion of a scheme of intensive industrialisation puts all the emphasis on production of goods. In its broad significance such a scheme includes agriculture as well. In the absence of any immediate prospects of securing external markets, the sustenance of an impressive scheme of industrial production will necessarily depend on a commensurate growth of mass consumption of goods, which, again would call for a progressive rise in the general standard of living. Unfortunately, it is rarely fully realised that the question of a higher standard of living of the masses in its correlation with the problem of industrialization has a purely monetary significance. A higher standard of living can hardly react on the prospects of industrialization unless it is backed by a proportionately larger purchasing power available for a larger consumption of industrial goods. It is a truism to say that more intensive or extensive agriculture cannot by itself bring about an increase in the purchasing power of the masses except to the extent that it may help to dispense with our present imports of agricultural staples or augment our present exports of such goods. Our prospects in respect of either the replacements of such imports or the stimulation of exports are not very large. For, we do not import much of agricultural staples nor can we rely to any extent on export markets as providing necessary outlets for an increased volume of agricultural products. In such circumstances, any spectacular expansion of agriculture, either intensive or extensive, may bring about a fall in agricultural prices resulting in no net gain to the existing purchasing power of the agricultural masses. Even assuming that some increase in income would accrue on the score of replaceable imports and new exports of agricultural staples, the excess would seem to be far too small to sustain any ambitious plan of industrial expansion.

THE STANDARD OF LIVING AND INDUSTRIALIZATION

The crux of the problem, therefore, is this : how are we going to place the necessary additional purchasing power in the hands of the masses ? It is to be admitted that industrialization by itself will tend to raise the standard of living while a rising standard of living in its turn will favourably react on the pace of industrialization. But the immediate problem is to suggest how the initial push is to be imparted and things set afoot. For this purpose, a careful planning of means and measures is an essential requirement. Without going into details, the possible methods of achieving a gradual accretion of purchasing power in the hands of the people may here be summarised. In the first place, efforts ought to be initiated to rationalize Indian agriculture on such a basis that whatever improvements may possibly be introduced in the methods of farming, without placing any undue pressure on the resources of either the cultivator or the government, may ensure to the agriculturists a fair price for their products and hence an economic return from their labour. In the second place, the commercial policy of the Government of India should be so orientated that the replaceable imports which India's industries can produce without involving an undue economic burden on the consumers may be manufactured within the country. Suitable commercial agreements with foreign countries, a liberal protectionist policy, a favourable freight policy on railways etc., are some of the desiderata which would assist the realization of such an objective.

In the third place it should be possible to effect a substantial increase in the purchasing power of the masses by the resuscitation of cottage industries and the development of such industries on a more extended scale. Here, again, the maximum net gain will be measured by possible replacement of imported goods supplemented by a larger patronage of cottage industry products not only by the wealthier section of the community but also by the government, both central and provincial, in the purchases of their requirements.

In the fourth place, the purchasing power of the masses can very materially be augmented by the nation-building activities and taxation policy of the government, both central and provincial. There is no getting away from the fact that the need for a scientific system of taxation framed with the purpose of redistributing the wealth of the society on an equitable basis is steadily coming into recognition. It may not be possible to introduce far-reaching changes all at once, but it should be the policy of governments to shape their system of taxation in a manner which will enable them to make available to the masses increasing amenities of life in the shape of improved medical aid, more sanitary facilities and education etc., the combined effects of which will exercise a wholesome influence on the standard of living.

Thus it is evident that the problem of industrialization bristles with many complications of a socio-economic character, which wlll have to be resolved before we can implement a policy of planned industrialization with fair prospects of success. Since, however, the need for industrialization is urgent in the interest of the economic advancement of the country, it is the duty of the public as much as of the various governments to pool all their resources to the end that a satisfactory scheme may be evolved which will harmonise the different interests and adjust the complicated issues in our national economy,

RADHAKUMUD MOOKERJI

M.A., PH. D.

Dr. Mookerji was born in 1884 and educated at Krishna Nath School, Berhampur and at the Presidency College, Calcutta. In 1910 he married Anasuya Devi. A profound scholar, Dr. Mookerji includes the following among the many awards he has received. Premchand Roychand Studentship for Rs. 7000 ; Mouat Medal and Cobden Medal for Economics, Calcutta University ; Calcutta University Readership Lectures on "Harsha" for Rs. 2000 ; Manindra Lectures at Benares Hindu University for Rs. 500 ; extension Lectures at Mysore and Punjab Universities ; His Highness Sir Sayaji Rao Gaekwad Prize of Rs. 7000. During his career he has been University Professor of History, Mysore ; Manindra Professor, Benares Hindu University and the Professor and Head of the Department of Indian History at Lucknow University. He was the President of the Punjab Youth Conference held at Lahore in October 1936 and his many publications include, "History of Indian Shipping," "Fundamental Unity of India," with introduction by J. Ramsay MacDonald, "Local Government in Ancient India" with Foreword by Lord Crewe, Ex-Secretary of State for India ; "Harsha"; "Men and Thought in Ancient India"; "Asoka" (Gaekwad Lectures); "Nationalism in Hindu Culture"; "Hindu Civilization."

In the following monograph Dr. Mookerji uses the pages of this volume to promulgate a hope that in the present serious and comprehensive attempt to reconstruct self-goverment in India, proper attention will be paid to the rich historical material and heritage that can be utilised for the structure.

THE HISTORIC FITNESS OF INDIA FOR DEMOCRACY.

INDIAN polity through the ages has shown a distinct tendency towards democracy. There were democratic elements in kingships to limit their absolutisms, while there were also full-fledged democracies co-existing with kingships from very early times.

The Rigvedic kingship was, from the first, limited by the assemblies called the *Sabha* and the *Samiti* which were organic parts of that earliest Indian constitution. The Vedic king was further checked by a powerful entourage of ministers called *Rajakrits* or "king-makers" including such officials as the commander of the army (*Senani*), the finance minister (*Samgrahitri*) and so forth. Advantage was also taken of the necessary religious ceremony of the king's coronation to impose on him certain oaths to emphasise the limits to his autocracy. Violation of these oaths was punished by his expulsion. This practically made Vedic kingship *elective*. There are also declarations that taxes are voted to the king as the protector of his people.

The Vedic precedents fixed the plan and pattern for the subsequent development of Indian polity. The limitation to absolutism became more and more developed and defined in the epics and the *smritis*. The sovereign is described as *Danda*, the instrument (or the executive authority) to enforce *Dharma*, the law and constitution, the supreme consideration of the state. The sovereign is thus not the source of law but its sanction. The sources of law are enumerated as (1) *Sruti* (Veda) (2) *Smriti* (3) *Sishtachara* (approved customs) and (4) decisions on doubtful points of the *Parishad* (Judge-made law). Law or *Dharma* was, on principle, not centralised. It varied with groups and comunities which legislated for themselves. The state, whether monarchy or democracy, stood for the self-government of the group. The groups which were recognised for self-government by the state were known and arranged in an ascending order as follows :—*Kula* (class), Jati (caste), *Sreni* (guide), *Puga, Gana. Samgha,* or *Samuha* (corporation). These were self-governing as regards legislation, justice and executive functions. The state subserving the ends of *dharma* believed in the free and natural groupings of individuals and encouraged all kinds of association, voluntary, local or functional.

Thus, India became a land of groups and communities, and of local self-rule, limiting the absolutism of the central government. It was also physically impossible in those pre-mechanical ages to have much of centralised government over a large area. Government had to be multi-central. Local liberty and not over government was the rule. This feature of ancient Indian indigenous polity also belongs to some of the most modern democracies, especially Soviet Russia. As pointed out by Miss Follet in her work *"The New State : Group Organisation—the Solution of Popular Government"* :

> "One of the characteristics of present day political *theory* is its reaction against the State and a silent political *fact* to-day is the increasing amount and power of group-life. The study of the group-process shows us that politics cannot be founded on representative or electoral methods but must rest on vital modes of association".

But apart from the limited monarchies, and the latitude they gave to local liberty, there were in ancient India full-fledged democracies. Panini (seventh century B. C.) mentions as many as 80 republics called *Ganas* or *Samghas* some of which, like the Yaudheyas, the Malavas (Greek Malloi) or the Kshudrakas (Greek Oxydrakai), had survived for centuries, resisted Alexander's campaigns in the Punjab and issued their own coins and inscriptions. The U. P. (along with Behar) at the time of early Buddhism was the chosen home of republican peoples like the Sakyas, Mallas, Lichchhavis or Vrijis, details of whose constitutions are given in Pali canonical works and the Jatakas.

We have also in these Pali works remarkable details about the forms and methods of democratic procedure inseparable from a live democracy which is fundamentally a 'government by discussion'. As early as the 5th century B. C., democracies of ancient India had developed a complete set of regulations for the conduct of their business by their assemblies or parliaments (called

Samghas) touching such topics as (1) quorum (2) notice of meeting (3) notice of motion (*Jnapti*)(4) resolutions (*Pratijna*) to be proposed (5) arrangement of seats (under an officer called *Asanaprajnapaka*) (6) the whip (called the (*Gana-puraka*) (7) vote (called *Chhanda*) (8) methods of recording and correcting votes by issue of tickets (*Salaka*) (9) vote by ballot (10) decision by vote of the majority (Yad-bhuyasika-kriya), (11) teller of votes (Salaka-grahapaka), (12) reference to select committee called *Udvahika Sabha*, (13) representation and (14) referendum.

The principle of local self-government led to the growth of self-governing village communities, to a system of social self-government functioning apart from the state as distinct political entities within defined spheres. This has helped India through the ages to preserve her *soul*, the integrity and independence of her cultural life and civilisation, against political revolution and foreign domination, up to very recent times, until the British system of centralised government supplanted the indigenous local institutions all over the country. This fact was very well explained by Sir Charles Metcalf (Report of the Select Committee of House of Commons, 1832, Vol. III, App.84, p.33) :

> "The village Communities are little republics, having nearly everything they can want within themselves, and almost independent of any foreign relations. They seem to last where nothing else lasts. This union of the village communities, each one forming a separate little State by itself, has, I conceive, contributed more than any other cause to the preservation of the peoples of India through all the revolutions and changes which they have suffered."

It is thus that we can explain how the period of Moslem rule in India, not a thorough-going system of centralisation and over-government, was also the period of remarkable progress in Hindu literature, religion and culture. During this period flourished some of India's greatest religious leaders like Basava, Ramanuja and Madhva in the south ; Ramananda, Kabir, Chaitanya, Vallabhacharya and Nanak in the North ; men of letters like Bhavabhuti, Shri Harsha, Rajashekhara, Jayadeva, Kalhana, Sayanacharya or Vedantadesikachar of the South, Vidyapati, Chandidasa or Mirabai, Tulsidas and Dadu and Tukaram ; or legists like Kulluka, Jimutvahana, Vijnanesvara, Vachaspati Mishra and Raghunandana who tried to adopt to the new times old customs and regulations of Hindu society as a measure of its protection against alien influence. (See for fuller references my *Local Government in Ancient India*, Oxford, 1919.)

It is to be hoped that in the present serious and comprehensive attempt to reconstruct self-government in India, proper attention will be paid to the rich historical material and heritage that can be utilised for the structure. In the words of Lord Haldane (in his letter to me)

"The History of ancient India (*as indicated in my work cited above*) shows how organic growth solves questions that are not capable of treatment from any mechanical point of view alone. The life of a nation consists in growth and not external causation."

PANDIT SHANKAR SHASTRI NARASINHA SHASTRI

JYOTIRMARTAND DAIVAGNAMUKUTALANKAR

Has been the President of Sanatan Maha Mandal since 1934 and is an astronomer, astrologer and landlord. He was born on 19th December 1884 and married Annapurnabai, daughter of Vedmurti Chandram Dixit of Lakshameswar Miraj (Senior). He received his education at Hosritti, Taluka Haveri (Dharwar District) and is the compiler of the Annual Indian Almanac known as "*Hosritti Panchang*" and the publisher of the *Annual General Predictions.*

His publications include Annual Indian Almanac Bhamini Dipika in Sanskrit (a treatise on Astrology) ; Kalachandika iu Sanskrit, Sanhit Tajak-Sara (a treatise on Astrology) with a commentary in Marathi. Daivajna Ratnakara in Sanskrit (a treatise on Astrology) Griha Ratnamala in Sanskrit (a treatise on Astronomy) and booklets regarding the Administration of H. E. Lord Brabourne, then Governor of Bombay and the lives of Pant Balekundri, Maharaja of Belgaum : and Sreemat Paramhansa Vasudev and Saraswati (Tembe Maharaj) ; The History of Canopus (Agastya) in English. History of Ursa Major (Saptarshi Malika) ; Author of booklets "Vizayanagar Kingdom."

The Pandit has written for this volume a studious article on the necessity for reforming the method of compiling the Hindu almanac—a subject of vast importance in this sub-continent.

HINDU ALMANAC REFORM

THE various almanacs now in use in India may be classified under two heads; those prepared according to the time-honoured Indian method of reckoning time, and those prepared with the help of the *Nautical Almanac.*

There seems to be a popular impression that the *Nautical Almanac* is a correct and safe guide. But it will be made clear in the course of this article that there is not sufficient warrant for this belief.

Almost all the almanacs prepared by modern Indian astronomers rely upon the famous *Karana-Grantha* the *Grahalaghava.* Astronomical tables are being prepared to facilitate the easy and speedy preparation of almanacs. To save time and labour works like *Thiti Chintamani, Brahat Chintamani, Makaranda-sarini, Thiti-ratnavali* have been composed and are being freely made use of by astronomers. If calculations are made according to the method followed by the author of *Grahalaghava* the conclusions arrived at are found to be at little variance with those arrived at by actual observation in the observatory (*Drakpratyaya).*

It must be admitted, however, that this is due, to a certain extent, to the different longitudes and latitudes of different places. At the same time it must be noted that almanacs prepared according to the *Nautical Almanac* do not agree with those prepared according to the *Grahalaghava,* a fact which may be verified by a reference to the various almanacs now in use in India. This divergence between the almanacs prepared according to the old method and those prepared according to the revised method comes seriously in the way of the due performance of the various rites and ceremonies enjoined by the Hindu religion.

Almanacs prepared according to the revised method are very few in number and are followed by very few in India. The almanac prepared by the late Bapu Deva Shastri of Benares is a case in point. Among the almanacs published in *Maharastra* may be cited, the Tilak Panchang and the Ketaki

Panchang. Articles have appeared in newspapers discussing the errors to be found in these almanacs and it may be noted in passing that there is a wide divergence between the various nautical almanacs published in different countries in Europe as it would appear from a glance at the articles appearing in the newspapers in those countries.

There is a widespread belief among those who rely upon the *Nautical Almanac* that calculations made according to the *Surya Sidhanth* are erroneous; that our ancestors had no idea of trigonometry; that they were not acquainted with the method of verifying their calculations in the observatory, and that old works on astronomy should, therefore, be no longer consulted in the preparation of almanacs.

The ancient Rishis, our ancestors, believe that this universe was created by Brahma who composed the *Jyotisha Shastra* with a view to facilitate the due performance of religious rites and ceremonies.

At first the permanently moving zodiac with the different constellations and planets was created and then two fixed stars, the northern and southern pole stars, were created. This zodiac is ever moving westwards at a great velocity, while the various planets in their respective positions have been made to move eastwards. This zodiac, along with different constellations, stars and planets, is set forever in motion by the Pravaha Vayu. Though these planets are moving eastwards they appear to be moving westwards owing to the great velocity of the zodiac which is moving westwards like an insect moving on a potter's swiftly rotating wheel.

The sun and other planets move from the constellation Ashwini (Arietis) towards Bharani and from Bharani to Krittika and so on. The constellations Ashwini and Bharani and others, after they rise in the east, move westwards but they appear to be moving westwards for the reason already stated obove.

The reputed authors of *Jyotish Samhitha* are eighteen in number; Brahma, Acharya, Vasishtta, Atri, Poulasthya, Romesha, Marichi, Angira, Vyasa, Narada, Shounaka, Bhrigu, Chyavana, Yavana, Garga, Kashyapa, Parashara, and Manu, and works on astronomy were composed by ten famous authors who studied this *Jyotisha Samhitha*, Varaha, Narasinha,

Shripathi, Satya, Bhaskar, Brahma Gupta, Vaidyanatha, Lalla, Shridhara rnd Renuka.

Astronomy is regarded as one of the six Angas of Veda and is looked upon as the eye of the Veda Purusha. This science of astronmy is essential for fixing the time favourable for the performance of ceremonies like marriage ; the study of the Vedas, the observance of rites to propiciate gods and pitris ; for predicting the solar and lunar eclipses and the passage of the various planets from one sign of the zodiac to another. Astrology is helpful in determining the effects, good or bad, of action done in previous lives. For all these purposes almanacs are quite essential. The science of astronomy is said to be a pratyaksha shastra *i.e.*, a science whose conclusions are borne out by facts observed and the sun and the moon are said to be the two witnesses to bear testimony to the truth of the conclusions reached by it.

This Jyotisha Shastra falls into three main subdivisions *viz.*, Hora (Astrology), Ganitha (Astronomy) and Samhita (the science which helps the fixing of the auspicious time for the performance of various religious rites and ceremonies).

Of these astronomy, or Ganitha, is the most important as its conclusions can be verified by observation. At the beginning of the creation of this universe the sun was in the constellation Ashwini. That system of astronomy, according to which the positions of the planets at a particular time are determined by counting the number of days that have elapsed since the first sun-rise or birth of Brahma, is called the Sidhantha. These Sidhantas are eight in number :—Brahma, Surya, Soma, Vashistta, Pulasthya, Romaka, Arya, and Garga. That system of astronomy according to which the positions of the planets are determined by counting the number of days that have elapsed since the beginning of Kaliyuga is called the tantra. That system of astronomy according to which the position of planets is determined by counting the number of days that have elapsed since any event or epoch more recent than the beginning of the Kaliyuga is called the Karana.

To save the time and labour required to make calculations according to the Sidhanta system the average position of the planets is determined by counting the number of days that have elapsed since the beginning of a particular Shaka year. This is called Kshepaka. This Kshepaka is added to what is obtained by making similar average calculations about the position of the planets in a particular year for which the almanac is to be prepared. Ganesh Dainajnya, in his work *Graha Laghava*, has found the Kshepaka of the sun according to the Surya Sidhanta to be 11 Rashis 19 Amsha or degrees, 41 Kalas and O Vikala.

We arrive at similar results if we make calculations according to the Sidhanta system. If this Kshepaka is added to the figures obtained for the years for which the almanac is to be prepared we arrive at the average position of the planets since the beginning of the universe. Even this system of calculation is not totally free from error. Much labour and time is required to calculate the average positions of planets in this way.

In order to get over this difficulty the exact position of the planets is determined with the help of the Shighra Phala and Manda Phala of the different planets. The exact position of the planets or spashta graha is that which tallies exactly with their position ascertained by actual observation. If the position of the planets ascertained by actual observation is at variance with that obtained by astronomical calculations, the help of the Beeja Saunskara is to be taken and the position of the planets ascertained by calculation is to be made totally with that of the planets obtained by actual observation. According to this method the Graha Laghava was composed in the Shaka year 1442 (*i.e.*, 1520 A.D.). Almost all the almanacs now prepared in India rely upon this Graha Laghva.

As the calculations made according to the Graha Laghava are at variance with the position of the planets as observed in the observatory, reform in the system of preparing almanacs is urgently called for. Even if calculations are made according to the Sidhanta system errors are bound to arise after a lapse of a number of years. The motion of the planets is affected by this velocity of this Pravaha Vayu and the change in the velocity of this Pravaha Vayu necessitates the Bija Saunsakaras.

The *Surya Sidhanta* is one of the many important works of astronomy which are useful for the preparation of almanacs. It has been stated in the *Surya Sidhanta* that towards the close of the Kritha Yuga included the current Maha Yuga, the demon Mayasura performed penance to propitiate the sun who taught him the Graha Ganitha or astronomy. Since the close of the Krata yuga 21,65,005 years have elapsed. To these must be added 12,96,000 years of the Treta yuga, 8,64,000 years of the Dwapara yuga and finally the 5,040 years of the Kali yuga that have elapsed up to now. This serves to give us an idea of how old the Surya Sidhanta is.

The method of reckoning time mentioned in the Surya Sidhanta is as follows :—

The time required for six respirations of a healthy man is regarded as a Pala. Western doctors say that a healthy man respires fourteen to eighteen times in a minute (Kirk's *Handbook of Physiology*). On an average a healthy man may be regarded as respiring sixteen times in a minute. According to the Surya Sidhanta fifteen respirations will be completed by a healthy man in one minute or 2½ Palas. This shows that the Surya Sidhanta is not much at variance with what modern scientists have discovered.

Sixty Palas go to form one Ghatika and sixty ghatikas form one day. The time required by the sun to go over the Rashi Chakra or the zodiac once is called a Soura year. On an average 30 days go to form one month and a year means twelve months. 4,32,000 Soura years form one Kali yuga, 8,64,000 years make one Dwapara yuga, 12,96,000 years make one Treta yuga, and 17,28,000 years make one Krata yuga. If we add the figures we get 43,20,000 years which make a Maha yuga. 71 such Maha yugas make a Manvanthara ; 14 such Manvantras make one day of Brahma. 17,28,000 years of the beginning and close of such Manvantra are regarded as the Sandhi Kala or the intervening period between two Manvantras. The closing Sandhi of a Manvantra is the commencing Sandhi of the next. In this way fourteen Manvantras and fifteen Sandhis go to make one day (from sunrise to sunset) of Brahma. Thus 1,000 Maha yugas are included in one day of Brahma which means 432,00,00,000 years including the Sandhi Kala or intervening periods.

Similar is the case with one night of Brahma. 30 days and nights of Brahma form one month and twelve such months make one year and one hundred such years are said to make up the space of Brahma's life. Para is the name given to this space of Brahma's life and fifty years of Brahma's life are called Parardha. The Mahakalpa at the end of the first Parardha of Brahma was called Padma and the first Kalpa of the second Parardha of Brahma which is the current Kalpa is called Sweta Varaha Kalpa.

The names of the fourteen Manus included in one day of Brahma are as follows :—Swayambhuva ; Swarochisha ; Uttama ; Tapasa ; Raivatha ; Chakshasha ; Vaivaswata ; Savarni ; Daksha Savarni ; Brahma Savarni ; Dharma Savarni ; Rudra Savarni ; Ruchi and Bhuthi.

The position of the various planets at a particular time is to be ascertained by calculating the number of years that elapsed since the birth of Brahma up to the current sunrise or day in the life of Brahma. The Sankalpa usually repeated at the commencement of a religious rite helps us to understand the number of years that have elapsed since the birth of Brahma and consequently the position of planets. According to the Sankalpa now usually reapeated the second Parardha of Brahma is current. The present Kalpa is the Sweta Varaha and the present Manu is Vaivashwata and the present is the twenty-eighth Maha Yuga and the first Charana of Kali yuga is now current. Thus we see that this Sankalpa is in full accord with the *Surya Sidhanta.*

Vaivashwata is the seventh of the Manus mentioned above. That means six Manus have elapsed and seven Sandhis, or intervening periods, have also elapsed. Twenty-seven Maha yugas have elapsed and since the beginning of the twenty-eighth Maha yuga, Krata, Treta and Dwapara yugas have elapsed and since the beginning of the present Kali yuaga 5,040 years have elapsed.

In the *Surya Sidhanta* it has been stated that after the lapse of 1,70,64,000 years since the beginning of the current Kalpa this universe was created when the sun was in the constellation Ashwini.

According to Sir Edward Fry quoting Prof. Poulton's address at the British Association in 1896 at page 390 in the 1969th issue dated 19-12-1902 of the *Mechanic and World of Science* obtains a total of two thousand seven hundred million years as the age of the world since it was first inhabited by living organisms. This goes to prove that the *Surya Sidhanta* is not purely the result of guesswork.

The Roman calendar of the western astronomers seems to have been commenced 800 years B. C. Since then almanacs have been prepared by western astronomers and, whenever the conclusions were found to be at variance with the observed phenomena, the system of calculation has been revised. Observatories have been founded to verify the conclusions of astronomers.

The following account of western almanacs is taken from the *Times of India Directory* for the year 1904 :—

The first Roman calendar was made by Romulus, the founder of the city of Rome (B. C. 753) who divided the year of 304 days, commencing with March, into 10 months only of an equal number of days ; and when he found out that the year thus constituted was much shorter than the solar year, he added two months to every year without inserting or assigning any names to them in the calendar. These two were named by Numa Pompilious (B. C. 710) but the year then in use contained 12 lunar months, and its deficiency was made up by adding intercalary days and months. Julius Caesar (B. C. 45) was the first to attempt to adjust the length of the year with any degree of accuracy and fixed it at 365 days, six hours introducing a day every fourth year (called leap year) which accordingly consists of 366 days, while the three others have only 365 days each. To introduce this system the previous year B. C. 46 was made to contain 445 days and was thence called lakran the year of confusion.

From him it was called the Julian year, and it continued in general use till the year 1582 when Pope Gregory XIII undertook to rectify the error which then existed between the Julian year of 365 days and the solar tropical year (which is subject to very slow variation) of 365 days, 5 hours, 48 minutes, 47.819 seconds or 365.2422001 days, being its value at the beginning of this century or 801. At that time the difference amounted to ten days. He accordingly commended the ten days between the fourth and fifteenth October in the year to be struck off, so that the fifth day was called the fifteenth. This alteration has been introduced throughout Europe, except in Russia, and by the Greek church and the year was afterwards called the Gregorian year or new style. The new style was not adopted in England until after the second September 1752 when 11 days to which the error amounted to were struck out so that the third of that month was called the fourteenth and it was settled by Act of Parliament (*24 Geo 11. 1751*) that the years 1800, 1900, 2100, 2200, 2300 and every hundredth year of our Lord which shall happen from time to time, shall be computed as each consisting of 365 days only, excepting every four hundredth year, where of the year 2000 should be the first.

It is clear from the extract given above that the western astronomers adopted the solar year. It must be noted that the number of days going to make up a solar year or its two halves are not fixed but vary from time to time. Fortysix years B. C. (*i.e.*, 1985 years before the solar year of Julius Caesar) was made up of 445 days. Similarly 185 years before the almanac in England was revised by the addition of 11 days to the then current solar year. After lapse of a number of years the solar year of Julius Caesar, the solar year of the Hindu astronomers, and the solar year of the western astronomers are bound to be found at variance with one another and it may be necessary in England to alter the number of days in a particular month by special legislation to make necessary adjustments. The method of calculation adopted in the *Surya Sidhanta* will be always found to be correct and never lead to error of any sort. If we find by calculation according to the *Surya Sidhanta* that a particular Tithi will occur on a particular day, our calculation will be always found to be correct. The solar year of Hindu astronomers is fixed permanently and is made up of 365 days, 15 Ghatikas 31 Palas, 33 Vipalas and 24 Prati-vipalas.

We thus see that the solar year of the western astronomer is not fixed. It will be clear from what has been stated above that any almanac that adopts the solar year of the western astronomers will not give correct results.

With the help of improved scientific instruments the western astronomers have found out the time taken by various planets to go over the zodiac. We will try to show below which of the results arrived at by them agree with those arrived at by Hindu astronomers according to the *Surya Sidhanta*.

According to the western astronomers the earth takes 23 hours, 56 minutes, 4.09 seconds to go round itself once and this is called a sidereal day. In an issue of "*The English Mechanic and World of Science*" dated 26-9-1902 is published this question put by a correspondent, :—"*What is the exact mean solar time between two meridian passages of a star? Is it 23 hours, 56 minutes and 4·09 seconds?*" And the reply given is "*Yes, the time of one absolute rotation of the earth on its axis is 23 hours, 56 minutes and 4·09 seconds*". According to the *Surya Sidhanta* sidereal day is made up of 23 hours, 56 minutes and 4·1 seconds. It will thus be seen that the conclusions arrived at by the *Surya Sidhanta* can easily stand the test of observation. The following table will help any one who would like to take a comparative view of the *Surya Sidhanta* calculations & those of the western astronomers.

TIME TAKEN BY PLANETS TO GO OVER THE ZODIAC

Planets.	Time taken according to Surya Sidhanta calculations.			Time taken according to Western Astronomers & verified in the observatory.			Difference.		
	Days.	Ghatikas.	P.	Days.	G.	Palas.	Days.	Ghatikas.	Palas.
Sun	365.	15	31.	365	15	23	—	—	8
Moon	27	19	18	27	19	18	—	—	—
Mars	686	59	50	686	58	46	—	1	4
Mercury.	87	58	11	87	58	9	—	—	2
Jupiter.	4332.	19	14	4332.	35.	5	—	15	51.
Venus.	224	41	55.	224.	42	3.	—	—	8
Saturn	765.	46.	23.	10759.	13.	11	6	33	12
Dragons-head.	6794.	23.	59.	6793.	23.	27.	1	—	32
Chandrocha.	3232.	5.	37.	3233.	34.	31.	—	28.	54.

From the table given above, it will be seen that there is a difference of 6 days in Saturn and the sun. But in Hockton's "*Astronomy*" we find that 10,763 days are assigned for Saturn. In that case the difference will be only two days. Another thing made clear by the above table is that the greater the number of days taken for going over the zodiac, the greater is the difference between the results arrived at by the two methods of calculation. The difference in the case of all planets excepting Saturn and Dragon's Head is almost negligibly small.

As the sky is covered with clouds almost throughout the year the number of days in a year when planets can be observed in the observatory are exceedingly few in number. Moreover in certain countries of Europe for days together they have hardly any nights. In an issue of the *British Mechanic* dated 27-6-1902 it is stated that *"upto and including July 21 there will be no real night in any part of the United Kingdom."* On such days time is to be reckoned by having recourse to watches. How far watches may be relied upon will be clear from the following extract from the *British Mechanic* dated 19-9-1902 :—

"The necessity for complete reliability in the watch or clock used is, perhaps, best demonstrated by the following personal experience ;— The Author, some years since, was anxious to do some real work in astronomical science, and a predicted occultation of a first magnitude star seemed to offer a rare opportunity for the use of his powers in this direction. All was ready 15 minutes before the disappearance was timed to take place, when, five minutes before the occultation, the reliable (?) chronometer which had been keeping accurate time for a long period stopped dead, and thus frustrated any attempt at chronological calculations".

The following table gives a comparative view of the time taken by a planet which starts from the sun to go over the zodiac and return to its starting point according to *Surya Sidhanta* and western astronomers.

Planets.	Time taken according to Surya Sidhanta.			Time taken according to Western astronomers.			Difference		
	Days.	Ghatikas.	Palas.	Days.	Ghatikas.	Palas.	Days.	Ghatikas.	Palas.
Moon	29	31	48	29	31	48	—	—	—
Mars.	779	55	12	780	0	0	—	4	48
Mercury	115	52	12	115	52	48	—	—	36
Jupiter	398	52	48	398	48	0	—	4	48
Genus	583	54	0	583	30	0	—	24	—
Saturn	378	4	48	378	4	48	—	—	—

From this table it will be clear that the calculations of the *Surya Sidhanta* are in complete accord with those of the western astronomers.

The zodiac, made up of 27 constellations, has been created by Brahma to facilitate the work of ascertaining the position of the planets at a particular time. All the planets have been incessantly going round the zodiac since the creation of the universe. To help the work of computation the zodiac has been divided into Rashis, Amshas, Kalas and Vikalas. Every twelfth division of the zodiac is called a Rashi. The time taken by the sun to go over the zodiac once is called a year. The particular constellation with which the moon is in conjunction towards the close of a particular Pournima (15th day of the bright half of a month) gives its name to the Pournima and the month to which the Pournima belongs. For instance, the constellation Chitra gives its name to the Chitra Pournima and the Chitra month. In this way the names of the twelve months have been assigned. Besides this, names like Madhu and others have been assigned to the different months of the year according to the Sankranti or passing over of the sun from one sign or Rashi of the zodiac to another. Every month has 30 Tithis. The month beginning with the Pratipada (first day) of the Shukla Paksha (bright half) and ending with the Amavashya (fifteenth day of the dark half) is called a Chandra Masa or Lunar month. The time taken by the sun to pass from one sign or Rashi of the zodiac to another is called a Soura Masa or solar month. That month in which there is no transition of the sun from one sign of the zodiac to another is called an Adhika Masa or intercalary month. That month in which the sun goes over two Rashis or signs of the zodiac is called a Kshaya Masa.

If calculations are made according to the *Surya Sidhanta* the conclusions arrived at with respect to the occurance of a particular Tithi or a particular day are never found to be at variance with the phenomena as they are observed in the observatory. It has been found necessary by western astronomers to revise their almanac by the addition of a particular number of days in order to square the calculations with the phenomena observed in the observatory. A similar contingency has not occured in the history of the *Surya Sidhanta* up till now (*i.e.* these 200,00,00,000 years) this fact is worth pondering over.

Why are there 7 days and why do they begin with Sunday? Since the creation of this universe it is so said in Maha Bhagavat that the seven planets, the sun, the moon, etc, have been going round the earth. They are moving at various distances from the earth. Saturn is farthest from the earth; then come in order Jupiter, Mars, the Sun, Venus, Mercury and the Moon which is nearest to the earth. Every day is made up of 60 Ghatikas which when divided into 24 equal parts give us what are called Horas (equal to 2½ Ghatika). The first Hora after sunrise on a particular day gives to the name of the planet to which the Hora is assigned. Thus the first Hora on Sunday is assigned to the sun; that on Monday is assigned to the moon and so on. The order of Horas is as follows ;—The Sun, Venus, Mercury, The Moon, Saturn, Jupiter and Mars. This order will help us to understand that the first Hora after sunrise on Monday belongs to the moon after which the day has been named. The day on which the universe was created has been regarded to be a Sunday and that is why Sunday is taken to be the first day in a week. The respective position of the planets mentioned above have been also similarly ascertained by western astronomers with the help of observation in the observatory, the only difference being that the earth is made to take the place of the sun.

How many times do the respective planets go over the zodiac in a Maha yuga ? The following tables supplies the answer to the question :—

Sun	43,20,000
Moon	5,77,53,336
Mars	22,96,832
Mercury	179,37,060
Jupiter	3,64,220
Venus	70,22,376
Saturn	1,46,568
Dragon's head	2,32,238
Chandrocha	4,88,203

A Maha yuga is made up of 157,79,17,828 days. If this number is divided by the number of times that a particular planet goes over the zodiac in Maha yuga we get the number of days required for a particular planet to go over the zodiac once. This is called the Madhyama Gati or the average rate of travel of the respective planets for one day.

The average rate of travel of the respective planets for one day.

Time.	Sun.	Moon.	Mars.	Mercury,	Jupiter.	Venus.	Saturn.	Dragon's Head.
Ghatikas.	59	790	31	245	4	96	2	3
Palas.	8	34	26	32	59	7	—	11

The results arrived at by the western astronomers are exactly the same as those given in the foregoing table.

In these days we have at our disposal various improved instruments and astronomers of the highest order. With all that the conclusions arrived at by calculation are found not to be completely in accord with observations made in the observatory. If we take the case of the *Nautical Almanac* we find that many a time the calculations appearing have been revised later on. In this connection the following two observations of two western astronomers published by the *English Mechanic* are worth quoting :—

1. "I fear, however, that it will be a long time before we get exact agreement between observation and prediction."

2. "We shall have to improve either our eyes or our instruments materially before one can look for such a result."

But this is not the case with almanacs in India. The religious ceremonies to be performed on a particular day are observed on that particular day in accordance with the almanac and there can never be any revision of the conclusions given. According to the *Surya Sidhanta* a particular Tithi is predicated to fall on a particular day. This can be verified by the position of the moon on that particular day. For example : suppose that the Chaturthi or the fourth day of Shukla Paksha or the bright half of the month falls on a particular day. On that day the moon will be found to set 8 Ghatikas after sunset. If it is the Chaturthi of the dark half the moon will be found to rise 8 Ghatikas after sunset on that particular day. But we do not find any such means of ascertaining the date of a particular day in the western almanacs.

At present according to the *Nautical Almanac* calculations are made by measuring the longitude of a planet from the vernal equinoctial point. This is the method adopted by what are called Sayana Panchanga or almanacs in India. In this connection the following extract from the *English Mechanic* No. 1979 will be found to be interesting :—

On March 21st, at 7 hours 14 minutes and 36 seconds p. m. the sun is said technically "to enter Aries" and spring is supposed to commence. As a matter of fact he is at that instant in a barren region in Pisces more than 28' from the nearest point of the constellation Aries. This foolish use or misuse of the so called

Zodiacal signs must sooner or later be abandoned as it is not only valueless but positively misleading. This is the theoretical date of the equinox, but in London the Sun will be about 12 hours and 10 minutes above the horizon and of course only 11 hours and 50 minutes below it ; whilst on the 22nd it will be longer above the horizon still, and hence there will no absloute equality of day and night".

From this it will be clear how far the Sayana Panchanga or almanac deserves to be encouraged. The position of the moon ascertained by the calculations made with a Nirayana Almanac is found to agree with what it is observed to occupy in the observatory ; this is not the case with that ascertained by the Sayana Almanac. All this will go to prove that the Sayana Almanac is unreliable. That is why the Nirayana Almanac has been in vogue in India from times immemorial.

SUMMARY

It must be admitted that the *Surya Sidhanta* method leads to the most difficult multiplications and divisions. But the greater the number of calculations made the more reliable will be the results arrived at. We have already referred to the fact that our ancient Rishis were well-versed in trigonometry and could make the most minute calculations. The *Surya Sidhanta* and other works on astronomy fully bear out this fact. It is, therefore, our humble request, to those who would like to find fault with our ancestors, to read the works written by them, understand them thoroughly and then pass any remark they like.

The almanacs prepared in India rely upon the method adopted by the author of *Graha Laghava* as the calculations made by the author, Ganesh Daivajnya have been made without the help of trigonometry. They are being found to be at variance with the observations made in the observatory.

The Author of the *Graha Laghava* himself has said in his work that after the lapse of 400 years the method adopted by him will need reform or revision. With regard to the Vridhi (increase) and Kshaya (decrease) of Tithis, the principle adopted by the Author is Bana (5) Vridhi, Rasa (6) Kshaya and is thus in full accord with the *Surya Sidhanta*. Hence this almanac does not violate the injunctions of the Dharma Shastra but the Indian almanacs prepared according to the method adopted by western astronomers adopt the principle Sapta (7) Vridhi Dasha

(10) Kshaya which violates the injunctions of our Dharma Shastra. I am, therefore, definitaly of the opinion that the Tithi arrived at by calculations made according to the method or western astronomers should be abandoned and that arrived at by calculations made according to the *Surya Sidhanta* should be adopted.

In conclusion I propose that the following reforms should be effected in our almanacs which have been already made in the almanac (of Hosa Ritti Panchanga) prepared by me every year.

1. The solar year according to the *Surya Sidhanta* should be adopted.
2. The motions of all the planets excepting the sun should be determined with the help of the Beeja Samskara mentioned in the *Surya Sidhanta.*
3. Ujjayani should be regarded as the first meridian.
4. The Ayanamsha should be taken to be 23'.

If these reforms are effected there will be no violation of the injunctions of the Dharma Shastra and the almanac will fulfill one of its main functions *viz*, that of ascertaining the position of planets favourable for the performance of religious rites and ceremonies.

MR. SADGOPL

M SC. (TECH).

Is the eldest son of the late Diwanchand of Jullunder City and was born on the 26th August, 1908. He received his education at the University of the Punjab and at the Hindu University, Benares. Was awarded a special prize in chemistry standing first in B. Sc. (Tech) and gained the Raja Vijaychand Prize and Purse. First also in the M. Sc. (Tech) he was awarded the Chancellor's Gold Medal and Prize. Practised as a chemist to an oil and soap mill at Patiala in 1932. Was University Research Scholar at Benares Hindu University from 1933 to 1935 and has been Chief Chemist and Managing Director of the Hindusthan Aromatics Company of Benares since its origin.

He was awarded the Government of India's Industrial Research Prize for his thesis on *The Aromatic Resources of India* in 1936. He married Kumari Kamala, B. A., a daughter of Professor Shivdayal M. A., of Lahore in 1937. He was the originator of the "G. S. Lines" for testing adulteration in butterfat and discovered special methods for the manufacture of kewda, bela and chamlei essential oils and originated the latest theories of cracking and sweating toilet soaps. He has been a member of the Editorial Board of S. P. C. of London.

Mr. Sadgopal has published a large number of research papers and books on oils, soaps and perfumes and his special article for "*What India Thinks*" deals with the perfumery industry of India.

THE INDIAN PERFUMERY INDUSTRY.

"The land of aromatic flowers, fruits, woods, roots and grasses"

HUIN-T-SANG.

THE knowledge and practice of essential oils and perfumes derived from plants in India dates back to a prehistoric period. The use of these products was not confined to aesthetic purposes but also made use of in almost all medicinal preparations. Numerous references to the properties and uses of these naturally occuring aromatic raw materials are to be found in old books on Hindu medicine and science such as "*Sushruta*", "*Charak*", "*Bhavaprakasha-Nighantu*", "*Kamasutram*" and "*Nagarsavaswam*". The richness of the country in such raw materials can easily be judged from the observation of innumerable aromatic plants and their products which are to be met in every nook and corner of India.

In view of these manifold advantages, it was but natural that, in ancient times, perfumes in the form of attars were one of the main items of export from India to the civilised countries of the world at that time. Detailed and interesting accounts of these are mentioned in famous books of various nations.

The recent excavations of the Egyptian pyramids have prominently disclosed the fact that the ancient Egyptians used to consume extraordinary quantities of Indian aromatics for embalming their dead.

In the Bible, numerous references are made to the perfumes of the Orient : the Jews and Catholics burnt aromatic gums in their religious ceremonies and in the *Songs of Solomon*, Indian perfumes such as oils of cinnamon, spikenard, myrrh and aloes are prominently mentioned. In the Bible too, a protest is registered by Ezekiel and Isaiah against the restrictions laid down by certain governments against the use of perfumes for other than religious purposes. Moses is said to have prescribed the preparation of certain kinds of incense for use in the tabernacle.

The ancient Greeks were so fond of Indian perfumes that, at one time, Solon had to promulgate a law prohibiting the sale of perfumed oils to Athenian men; not, of course, restricting their use by women.

The Romans were equally fond of Indian perfumes which were prominent items of import from India. At the funeral of his wife Poppaea, Nero used such a quantity of aromatics that these exceeded the total supplies of the whole year imported through Arabia, the then distributing centre of Indian perfumes to European countries. Roman extravagance with perfumes was carried to such an excess that, under the consulate of Licinus Crassus, a law was passed restricting the use of perfumery, there being good reason to fear that there would not be enough for the ceremonies in the temples. In Arabia itself, the people were very fond of Indian attars. In the holy Koran, Mohammed the Prophet, extended a promise to the faithful that they would be rewarded in paradise with the possession of black-eyed houries whose bodies were composed of the purest musk of the land of the Orient. It is reported that the Arabian physician Avicenna, was well-versed in the art of making perfumes and Sultan Saladin, in 1157 on his triumphal entry, had the walls of the Mosque of Omar washed with *rose water specially brought from the East.*

The legend goes that Catherine de Medici, the wife of Henry II, made use of the fashion of perfuming the body for the purpose of ridding herself of objectionable persons, by giving them scented gloves prepared, and at the same time poisoned, by a Florentine. In the sixteenth century, especially at the Court of Queen Elizabeth, perfumes were used with great extravagance, and were in fact looked upon as one of the necessities of life. This luxury was carried still further at the courts of the sumptuous kings of France ; Louis XV going so far as to demand every day a different odour for his apartments. A lady's lover always used the same kind of perfume as his lady.

These are some of the historical facts which show the great popularity of perfumes among nations of all climes. It was the intercourse with the Orient brought about by the travellers and merchants that made Europeans appreciate the perfumes at that time mainly manufactured in Hindustan. In this connection,

NALINI RANJAN SARKER
FINANCE MINISTER, GOVERNMENT OF BENGAL

it is worth while mentioning the great popularity of Indian made shawls in Europe. These shawls used to be marketed after having been incensed for a long time with the leaves of Patchouli; a fact responsible for their very long life and consequent high prices.

All these facts combined made India very famous for her various perfumes and there sprang up big centres of this industry at places like Kanauj, Jaunpur and Ghazipur, a mention of which is to be found even in old books like "*Shah Nama*" of the great poet, Firdous. As a result of this the Indian perfumers made a fortune but because of an absolute lack of the use of the science of statistics, no export figures are available. An idea of the greatness of this industry can be had from the fact that some of the old houses of perfumery of Kanauj are even today masters of millions.

Gradually, India began losing her world markets and European nations began seriously entering the domain of perfumes. A time came when France and Germany captured all the markets for their aromatics and today we find India, the cradle of the perfume industry, one of the biggest consumer of foreign perfumes. While Europe made rapid advances with the help of modern scientific knowledge, India lost even that much which it treasured so successfully for centuries. Even within our own country, people have been offered foreign perfumes, adulterated with some bases, as Indian attars. This latter practice made the common people dislike the pure Indian attars and give preference to synthetic compounds. Consequently, the export trade of India in perfumery has completely vanished.

It is really a tragedy that, in spite of the great strides which all sciences, and especially chemistry, have made in India, very scanty attention has been paid to the study of the aromatics so abundant in our country. All that has been attempted by Indian scientists so far is only an incomplete theoretical study of certain raw materials and other processes concerned with their preparation on a test-tube scale in the laboratory. To give an idea of this indifference of the scientists and industrialists of India, a few extracts of the presidential address delivered by the late-lamented Hon'ble Raja Sir Motichand, Kt., C.I.E. on the occasion of the First All India Perfumers' Conference held at Benares in 1932 are given :—

"It is highly deplorable that the art of perfume-making should be so much neglected in India that we should be importing perfumes even from countries which are proverbially known to abound in *flowers without perfumes*... .... Taking the figures of the last five years, we find that on an average, our total imports of the synthetic perfumes and ready-made blends amount to a little over fifty lakhs of rupees annually. The largest imports are from Japan and from Germany..........This total export and import trade of over a crore of rupees is a great drain on this already impoverished country of ours. Like many of our exports in other lines we are exporting our raw materials only to re-import them at very much enhanced prices..........This export of aromatic oil seeds and raw essential oils should cease".

The above extract gives a very true picture of the present state of this industry of our country. Even after seven years (since this well thought-out address was delivered) the balance of trade in aromatics has been against India. While this shows a regular increase in our imports and a decrease in exports, it also points to the folly of importing finished aromatics made out of our own raw materials. India has been a double loser in this way. Referring to this most unhappy state of affairs, the late Raja Motichand rightly suggested :—

"......We should first of all improve our existing methods of essential oil distillation as carried on in centres like Ghazipur, Jaunpur and others ; we are still working wtth very crude methods handed down to us from generation to generation. We are forgetting that science is progressing by leaps and bounds. ....Secondly, we must immediately take up the work of essential oils out of which very valuable synthetic perfumes are being isolated elsewhere.

"......Before the war broke out, the Mysore Government used to sell, by annual auction, all its sandalwood for a few lakhs of rupees.........As soon as the war broke out, the annual auctions automatically stopped and the Mysore Government was compelled to find a market for its wood..........After a little preliminary investment of money in carrying out trials for the extraction of sandalwood oil, the Mysore Government has succeeded in establishing an industry which in the place of 3 or 4 lakhs of old brings now an annual income to the state of forty lakhs of rupees and more.... .....We have many other oils like this which, if properly worked up, are full of potentialities in *not only saving the drain of money from the country but also of creating new productive industries in the country*. As another instance of how in India cheap goods are being sold under a wrong name, I would invite your attention to the huge figure of thirteen lakhs of rupees which we pay for "safron" coming into India mainly from Spain."

The above quoted words apply still more correctly to the present state of affairs as a study of the import and export figures for aromatics shows a steadily rising balance against India.

For want of proper scientific methods and other causes, the distillation of essential oils in India is ever on the decrease, whereas our friends in Europe are bringing under cultivation increasing areas of land for the growth and cultivation of various aromatic raw materials.

Under these circumstances, the present writer undertook to make an exhaustive research into the possibilities of re-establishing the perfume industry of India, and collected a very large volume of original data and commercial information. The need for such systematic scientific work was long overdue, and the information has revealed the astonishing potency of our Motherland in the matter of the supply of aromatic raw materials of various types. Their proper utilisation becomes all the more imperative in view of the following facts.

The consumption of aromatics is bound to increase by leaps and bounds along with the increase in the number of Indian concerns engaged in the manufacture of soaps, hair oils, cosmetics and the like. During the last few years alone, the imports of perfumes have been going up at a very high speed. It is time, therefore, that a serious attempt should be made with the full co-operation of the governments concerned to utilise the already existing resources and also to increase the availability of many more neglected ones. This alone can combat the ever-increasing imports of aromatics.

It has been found by the author that the resources of certain fundamental essential raw materials in India are so abundant that we cannot only meet our entire home demand but also successfully capture the world-market. That means increasing exports which is another very great factor in the economic prosperity of any nation.

A very great industry can be established in India by starting the manufacture of synthetic derivatives from essential oils and from other sources. A few important examples are given below :—

(*a*) Isolation of citronellol from the oil of citronella and manufacture of various citronellyl esters which are so important in modern perfumery.

(*b*) Isolation of geraniol from palmarosa oil and its conversion into important geranyl esters.

(*c*) Isolation of linalol from rosewood oil and its conversion into linalyl esters.

(*d*) Isolation of eugenol from clove oil and its conversion into vanillin.

(*e*) Isolation of santalol from the oil of sandalwood and its conversion into santalyl esters.

(*f*) Isolation of vertiverol from the oil of khuskhus and its conversion into vetiveryl esters.

(*g*) Isolation of rhodinol from pelargonium oils and its conversion into rhodinyl esters.

(*h*) Isolation of anethol and aubepine from the oil of anise.

(*i*) Isolation of carvone, cineol and eucalyptol from the oils of caraway, cajuput and eucalyptus respectively.

(*j*) Isolation of citral from lemongrass oil and its conversion into various ionones.

(*k*) Manufacture of terpineol from the oil of turpentine.

(*l*) Manufacture of camphor from l-pinene.

(*m*) Isolation of thymol from ajowan and thyme oils.

(*n*) Blending of essential oils and aromatic chemicals into artificial floral compounds.

(*o*) Blending of aromatic chemicals and essential oils etc., to give fruit flavours and perfumes used for biscuits, chocolates, tobacco and cigarette industries etc.,

Most of these aromatics have extensive application in medicinal preparations and are adopted by various standard pharmacopoeia. This is another very big field for the commercial utilisation of various aromatics. In Europe, it is usually found that excellent sanatoriums are built in areas abounding in natural aromatics. The climate of such places is considered to be excellent for treatment of certain chronic cases. It is needless to emphasise this useful and most desirable aspect of the industry. Even now, at various places like Barmana and Jaunpur, beautiful health resorts can be built for the benefit of the nation. All these efforts naturally require good chemical control over different operations and necessitate the employment of a very large number of highly trained chemists and will help in eliminating the unemployment of a large number of educated young men.

The only scientific principle on which this industry can be rebuilt in India is to open distillation centres at a number of places within easy approach to the centres of the necessary raw materials. This will necessitate penetration of the industry into the interior of the country and offer a very great opening for the employment of a huge number of villagers.

Along with the re-organisation of the perfume industry on the above mentioned scientific lines, a very great encouragement will be received by other industries especially that of manufacturing the proper packing materials in the form of cardboard boxes, packing papers and wooden boxes etc. The glass industry of India, which is at present practically on its last legs, will also be immensely helped. By properly organising the industry under *experts having full knowledge of Indian aromatics*, the distillation of essential oils can be made a very big field of activity for the proposed village industries organisations now contemplated by the various governments and non-official bodies for the purpose of rural reconstruction. Refining and chemical utilisation of all these essential raw materials will further allow the employment of a large number of young men at manufacturing centres.

Another problem for the poor agriculturists in India at the present time is that they do not find themselves interested in cultivation as the commonly known crops do not give even marginal profits. Very large areas of agricultural land are lying idle with no cultivation whatsoever but by organising the industry of aromatics an opportunity will be available to all such agriculturists to grow the necessary aromatic plants and thus make reasonable profits by selling the same and be duly rewarded for their labours.

Besides the manifold advantages to the people of India, it is needless to say that the Government of India and various Provincial Governments are bound to gain immensely because of the general prosperity of the masses. Another very important point for the consideration of various goverments is that the production of these natural raw materials grown in the various forests under them will mean a great asset to the revenues of the forests.

In brief, the various claims of this, so far neglected, industry have been stated above. Under proper guidance and with the mutual co-operation of the people, the government and the universities in India, this industry can be made a great benefactor to millions now on the verge of starvation. Further, while this will mean a dead stop to most of the imports in the line, at the same time it will create new and potent markets in the different parts of world which consume crores and crores of rupees worth of aromatic annually.

India's past history shows that by leaving aside the Mysore Government sandalwood oil factory, no other attempt worth the name has been made in the proper direction so far Some reports are to be found of an extinct essential oil factory at Bangalore, another at Gwalior and a third at Cawnpore. None of them enjoyed more than a couple of years' life. After a pause of more than a decade, it is satisfying to note that recently a very systematic effort has been made at Benares. Within an interval of less than five years' work, it has fully justified all the hopes expected of Indian aromatics. The successful isolation of pure essential oils of some typical Indian flowers like kewda, bela, and chameli etc. by the present author has already put India on the map of world famous centres of aromatics.

The perfumery industry in India has to fight against a number of heavy odds. The various causes hindering its future rapid growth are as follows :—

a. Natural disadvantage of India being a tropical country for most part of the year renders the handling and transport of raw materials a very difficult problem.

b. The non-co-operation of Indian State Railways with the industries of the country in general, in respect of heavy and unscientific freight systems and unsuitable carriages for the transport of raw and finished materials.

c. The interior of the country altogether lacks roads worth the name. Unfortunately and, of course, naturally, aromatic raw materials abound only in parts which are hundreds of miles from the nearest road.

d. Non-existence of a national waterways system in the country.

e. Monopoly of the perfume trade in the hands of illiterate and selfish agents and traders who care only for their own interests.

f. Lack of scientific knowledge of perfumes, not only among the general public, but also among the so called soap and perfume chemists.

g. Lack of any interest on the part of almost all the soap makers and cosmetic manufacturers in India to incorporate Swadeshi raw materials of perfumery even if they are cheaper in price and in no way inferior to the imported articles.

One hangs his head in shame when he finds these enthusiasts crying for heavy tariff walls against imported soaps and cosmetics at one time and actively discouraging Indian made raw materials of perfumery at the same time. It is strange to find these manufacturers supporting the raising of tariffs against imported soaps and cosmetics and lowering of duty on essential oils and aromatic chemicals from the same platform. There is no wonder, under these circumstances, if Indian soaps and cosmetics are being swept out of the market. The public is unaware of the fact that the so-called Indian soaps and cosmetics available under any seal in the market are nothing but innocent vehicles of foreign lables, foreign alkalis, foreign perfumes, foreign wrappers and sometimes even foreign oil stocks, if not foreign soap bases also. These various factors put together cost nothing less than 50% and sometimes even 90% of foreign articles out of the total cost of production of soaps and cosmetics. These are the facts which are staring, not only at the perfume industry, but also at the soap and cosmetic industries of India whose interest are most closely interwoven.

In the interests of economic utilisation and prosperity of our land, in the name of giving employment to thousands of skilled labourers by establishing this unique village-*cum*-manufacturing industry and to give practical relief to rural indebtedness in India extending to an abnormal and unthinkable limit of Rs. 1000 crores, it is necessary that all the resources at the disposal of the people and the governments should be pooled properly to organise this industry demanding full co-operation of the agriculturist, forester and chemist in India.

SRIMATI VEDANAYAKI AMMAL

MRS A. S. P. AYYAR

Born in January 1908 at Mooneracode, South Malabar. She is the daughter of Sri Venkateswara Iyer and Srimati Kavery Ammal. Mrs Ayyar was privately educated and in 1919 she married Sri A. S. P. Ayyar. Went on a tour of western countries with her husband in 1935. Keenly interested in the woman's movement in India and wants all-round progress without leaving the ancient mooring in essentials. An article by Mrs. Ayyar's husband Mr. A. S. P. Ayyar M. A. (OXON) I. C. S., F. R. S. L. (ENG.) Bar-at-law appears elsewhere in this volume.

WHAT THE WOMEN OF INDIA WANT

WHAT do the women of India want? First and formost, they want to be economically independent. "*The whole world revolves on the belly*," said Chanakya. So, nobody living in the world can be really independent without the means to fill the belly unaided.

In my opinion, that is all that old Manu meant by saying that a woman could never be termed really independent since her father had to maintain her as a child, her husband as a young woman, and her son as an old woman. It seems to me to be absurd to inveigh against Manu's maxim, which is only an expression of an economic and social fact, without any attempt to make woman economically independent. It might have been all right in Manu's days to give the property to men and only maintenance and *stridhan* to women. The strong arms of men were required in those lawless days to protect property, and *stridhan* jewels were also many.

Now jewels are few, and law and order much more rigidly enforced. So, there is no reason to continue the old Hindu law of inheritance on intestacy. This law must be changed, and men and women put on an absolutely equal footing. Widows should get a share like the sons, to do what they like with; daughters must get a share like the sons. Till the laws are changed, wills to that effect should be made by Hindus as regards their self-acquired properties. It is amazing how few wills are really executed, not even one Hindu in a thousand caring to do so. Propaganda is required in this respect.

But, to achieve the object in view, something more is required than merely changing the law of inheritance. For, often, there is, in this poor country, nothing to inherit or divide. So every woman must try to earn something, either by some cottage industry, or by being a doctor or a school mistress or canvassing among women. Incidentally, every wife should try to induce her husband to insure his life for a modest sum in a reliable company and to assign the policy in her name. Of course, unmarried women and widows can also qualify for and become whole-time government servants or lawyers and earn an independent income. Once women become economically independent, they will automatically take their proper place in society. All well-wishers of India, and especially workers for the uplift of women, should keep this as the foremost plank in their programme.

I may here add that workers in the past knew this well. Vignaneswara, the great author of the *Mithakshara,* tried, at one stroke, to extend *stridhana* to all kinds of property then known whether acquired by partition, inheritance, gift, adverse possession or purchase, and to make woman the absolute owner of all those properties. But, unfortunately for women, the Privy Council, in days when women in England had not got full rights in property, curtailed this right, and held that *stridhana* would include only the ancient and insignificant kinds of property, and that the ownership would not be absolute but only a limited estate for life. Now the women of England have got full rights; and, yet, Hindu women suffer from the above ruling.

Marriage is now almost obligatory for every man and woman in our land. This rule is, on the whole, quite sound. To make life complete one must be married. Exceptions there may be for lifelong ascetics or the incurably diseased. Hinduism, therefore, gave each woman her innings, and asked her to stand by for the rest to have their chance. That, it seems to me, was the genesis of enforced widowhood. The thing became monstrous because there was no enforced widowerhood. Otherwise it would have been a just rule, though operating harshly on some.

Some marriage reforms are essential. Polygamy, which has been greatly extended by its interpretation in British Indian courts, has to be put down with an iron hand. The marriage of girls below 16 or of boys below 21 ought also to be made illegal and void. Half measures are no good. We ought to have the courage to imprison all polygamists and to declare all marriages of children absolutely void. The Sarda Act ought to be amended in that direction.

Divorce is a minor question. It will always be repugnant to Hindu women. In this land of *Sita* and *Savitri,* women will prefer to nurse back to health even their incurably sick husbands than rush to the courts to get a divorce for their own selfish satisfaction. Once child marriage is abolished, and polygamy wiped out, even the advocates of divorce may have little enthusiasm left to proceed with Bills for securing it.

Bride prices and bridegroom prices are terrible evils, but are more fit to be dealt with by public opinion than by legislation. There always will be people who marry for wealth or family or influential connections, just as there are people who marry for beauty. This is only natural, as some men love to look at the sky, some on the mud which grows the crops, and yet others at the flowers and fruits. No doubt, no court should enable anybody to recover bride or bridegroom prices. But that is the case even now. We must always remember that a land with too many laws unpleasant is to live in, and that laws should be enacted only where unavoidable.

Women should adopt a sane attitude to changing fashions. That time should bring about changes is only natural. Indeed, it is also desirable. The boring of noses and ears is not necessary for beauty. That ear-rings are worn in some western countries too is no proof of their necessity. While ear-rings come on the borderline, nose-rings must certainly go, and the sooner the better. Nobody will regret the disappearance of the heavy gold ornaments worn by our grandmothers, though they served to train them to carry weights, and also to have reasonably secure banks for their savings. But, let us not congratulate ourselves too soon. New fashions, like smoking, eyebrow plucking etc, have to be guarded against. Let us not exchange King Log for King Stork ! That some fashions are necessary and will persist, it is idle to dispute. Occasional changes, too, are welcome. A drab uniformity is unthinkable in this land of brilliant sunshine and rainbow and multi-coloured stars. Beauty and aesthetics require something beyond mere utility. The stars burn out valuable energy only to make the sky beautiful.

Children are the flowers in the garden of life. There is nothing which can compare with the love of the mother and the child. "*Heaven lies at the mother's feet*" says Sage Tiruvalluvar of the Tamil country. The great Napoleon and Mussolini were largely shaped by their mothers. Unfortunately, in modern India, many mothers are not able to leave any indelible impressions on their children. The reasons are obvious, namely, lack of education, economic dependence and growing bewilderment at the increasingly common western ideals. All this can and should be remedied. What availeth a Mother if she gains the whole world but loses the affection of her child ? Education must proceed apace, and the future mother enabled to understand and guide her children.

Women must also give up many meaningless rites and ceremonies. Even the Emperor Asoka said, more than three thousand years ago, "*The womankind perform many manifold trivial and worthless ceremonies*" (Rock Edict IX) and urged the abandonment of useless ceremonial and the performance of the really useful and noble ones like rites of charity and hospitality. A reasonable belief in the mysterious and the unknown may be natural, and belief in the supernatural and the divine is essential for peace of mind, harmonious development and salvation. But ceremonies to propitiate serpents, demons and the small-pox goddess must be dropped once and for all.

I think women should also take a keen interest in all kinds of social, municipal and rural reconstruction work. Purdah must go, and child welfare and maternity centres and sanitation leagues started everywhere. Women, in the mass, will never care to fight and kill, like men. The mother of the race has little interest in such human sacrifice to the demon of war which is a thousand times more odious than the goat sacrifices at the temples of village goddesses and at devil shrines.

Woman's role in the social polity is bound to be different from man's. Manu has said that a child gets from its father its bones, sinews and marrow, and from its mother its skin, flesh and blood. This symbolic distinction, in my opinion, represents a real distinction between the contribution, of the two sexes. All stern, violent and strenuous action needed for the upkeep of society, like defence, mining, mountain climbing and polar exploration,must depend on man ; all gentle, softening, harmonising action, like creating sweet homes, an enjoyable civilisation and palatable meals, must depend on women. In other words without woman, civilisation cannot exist, without man it cannot be defended and kept going. Woman cannot fight battles like man ; nor can man nurse the sick and heal mental and spiritual wounds like woman. Man represents *Siva*, woman *Sakti*, but in the benign aspect of *Parvati* instead of the militant aspect of *Durga*. The difference between the sexes is fundamental, and cannot be eradicated, so long as mankind continues to exist. Both are necessary and complementary, like two semi-circles facing different directions, or the concave and the convex in different aspects.

It follows that the same kind of education for both the sexes is not desirable, if we are to get the best results. In my opinion, the education of boys and girls till they are ten may be the same. Indeed, they should be educated together in the same schools, preferably by women teachers, as in advanced western countries. From the age of ten till the end of the matriculation or school final class, boys and girls should have different schools and courses. The girls should pay more attention to religion, ethics, music, cooking, household economy, hygiene, first aid, needlework, painting, and embroidery than to languages, mathematics, elementary science, geography and history, though these too should be compulsory. In the college courses, while there should be provision for allowing such girls as desire it to join men's colleges, there should be separate women's colleges after the model of the Lady Irwin College at New Delhi (but, thoroughly nationalised and culturised) to train our grown-up girls to be ideal wives and mothers and to run their own households. The ambition of every woman all over the world, and more so in our country, is to have her own house where she can reign like a queen, instead of hankering after ordinary jobs and being somebody's servant. To keep the home fires burning, to maintain a cultured atmosphere at home, to take an intelligent interest in social and welfare work, to form correct opinions on problems of national or international interest, to be able to shoulder the responsibilities of running the home economically, efficiently and cheerfully with the undying faith which comes from a living religion, these are the ideals to be kept in view for the women of this ancient land. A knowledge of poetry and drama, astronomy and mathematics, politics and law may add to the zest in life, if added to these, but will be like rains in the Sahara Desert without the above things. I would certainly advocate also that at least women's institutions in our hot country should work only in the mornings and evenings, and that music, cooking, needlework and hygiene should form the four pillars of the edifice of secondary education for women, the floor being ethics, and the roof religion. Then alone will India regain her lost soul.

SHANTARAM GANPAT WARTY

M. A.,

Has long been known as a thoughtful writer of western India whose contributions on cultural, educational and political topics are very highly appreciated by the reading public. After graduation he co-operated in starting and conducting a High School in his district and was Head Master until he took up writing as his chief occupation. In 1928 he wrote "*Sister India*" a reasoned reply to Miss Mayo's "*Mother India*" which sold largely in the United States of America.

Mr. Warty is also a public worker. He is Secretary of the Indian Institute of Political Science, Bombay, and is the Founder and President of the University Reform League, Bombay. He also takes great interest in labour welfare and did excellent work as General Secretary of the Bombay Provincial Postmen's Union for more than five years. It was through his continuous endeavours that certain grievances of the agriculturists in Bombay Province where finally redressed. Mr. Warty recently started a high class monthly "*The Indian World*" to which distinguished writers, thinkers and leaders in India contribute. Mr. Warty is a recognised authority on university problem and his present contribution has therefore a value of its own.

UNIVERSITY REFORM

IT is my sad experience that when we plead for urgent radical reform in university education in India, after examining the present position to which it has drifted, we find ourselves usually confronted with a misrepresentation that we are attacking the whole university fabric built by the labour of generations of our great men. The convocation addresses in the universities read like grand orations describing the achievements of our universities in the past and their contribution to the spread of light, learning and culture in the country. By taking stand on the achievements of our forefathers, they seek to convey the impression that practically all is well with the universities even at the present day and there is no need to worry about them.

Because university education had done India immense good in the past, it does not follow that it does the same good now. The point that is invariably lost sight of in these discussions is that the actual content of university education today is not the same that it was. It is a counterfeit that has replaced the genuine and, far from contributing to the strength and the moral tone of the country, it slowly saps the vitality, like adulterated and spurious medicines which find their way to consumption by the force of advertisement.

We need not here enter into a theoretical discussion of what a university ought to be. Let us note that when university education of the western type was first introduced into India, it was done with the best of intentions. That it enriched India in culture, in her outlook on life, in morals, none can doubt. Criticisms, it is true, have been levelled against it that it was meant to create clerks for service in British administrations, and that the education was exclusively imparted through a foreign language, etc. There was a certain amount of truth and justification for these criticisms but, barring them, the system offered a genuine quality of educational food.

The fact was that the essentials of university education were then served by a group of circumstances which have long ceased to exist. In those early days, only those entered the university who had a genuine enthusiasm for learning and who had also the intellectual capacity to pass through it. Thus the right type of material was there. Next, the number of such entrants was limited, with the result that the relation between students and professors were very close. Such close contact is the very essence of university education. Not the study of books, nor the lectures in the classes, contribute so much to the opening of the intellect as the impact of mind on mind by close personal discussions. Thus, much that was wanting in other respects in those days was made good by the influence of personality.

But, as the number of students seeking university education increased in subsequent years, the scope for contact between the professors and the students grew less and less, and the influence of personality materially waned. For years after the universities were founded, the chief aim that governed their policy was the spread of higher education, cheapening and popularising it so as to make it reach as large a population as possible. The object was a good one but in the zealous carrying out of this policy, quality was, in the very nature of things, sacrificed to quantity until by about 1900, a position was reached when Lord Curzon found it necessary to act. But his somewhat rough methods created more discontent then reform.

Since then many enquiries have been held among which the Sadler Committee's Report, though more than 20 years old, still occupies an important place. A few reforms have occasionally been carried out in minor detail, but the essentials of university education still remain unserved. The evils that have crept in have grown to such dimensions that all the inner vitality has been sapped,. and the cover being left untouched from outside gives the deceptive appearance of a genuine fruit. What is worse is that the fruit is often diseased from inside and by corrupting the university, poisons the moral wells of the country.

What are the chief evils that have crept into the universities ? The first is that we aim at mass production under the mistaken ideal of spreading knowledge broadcast. When professors have to lecture to classes, each of about 200 or more in strength, there is little scope for the impact of mind on mind. If it be merely through such lectures that knowledge is to be imparted, a much better arrangement would be to engage for all the universities and the colleges one able professor in each subject and tell him to broadcast through radio and in place of 200 in a class, he will be able to handle 20,000 students at a time. But would you call it education?

I should think that ordinarily no class should be more than 50 strong, so that every student may come in direct and close contact with the professor, and in admitting students to college, only such as are really capable of passing creditably through the university course should be accepted. At present, under the impression that it is the degree that counts, thousands seek and get admission irrespective of their capacity or otherwise. It is not the desire for learning so much as the desire for the degree that attracts them, and under the pressure of these circumstances the standard of university education itself is lowered.

When once this process has been in operation, it is difficult to get out of it, even when its evils are fairly well realised. The larger the numbers, the greater are the financial gains to the college and to the university, and this in turn dulls the educational conscience and commercialization sets in. All universities today are so steeped in commercialization that we can never hope for any essential reform being brought in without a surgical operation. When a casual remark was made at a meeting that there was too much commercialization in a university, the vice-chancellor of the university who happened to preside at the meeting neither denied the charge nor regretted it, but sought actively to justify it by a retort that similar commercialization existed among the secondary high schools of the province. So low have we fallen that we do not scruple to justify our fall by pointing to similar corruption, elsewhere.

It is our boast that the universitiies form the conscience of the country. It is their duty to lay down standards of morality for the country to adopt. Their measure of values, we are led to believe, differs materially from the measure of the market place. A university is "*a guide set on a hill ; a light for the whole nation.*" But when commercialization sets the tone to the university, every offence, every departure from the high standard, be it the most substantial, gets compoundable in practice.

There is even something worse that follows and has followed in the wake of commercialization. The university, it is well known, is ridden by the examination system which plays an all-important role. The larger the number of students appearing at the examinations, the more profitable the business is to the examining professors. There exists equally the temptation to produce notes, model questions and answers, and such other aids to examinations which serve effectively to replace the textbooks and are crammed by the candidates. This explains why the appointment of examiners in the university forms the subject of keen struggle among the candidates giving rise to cliques and groups, the only object of each such clique and group being to secure to itself as large a division of the spoils and the patronage of the university as possible. It is no wonder that certain universities have become hot-beds of intrigues of very low character.

Professors, as a class, may not deserve a sweeping condemnation, but when a fairly large number from among them are in the habit of adopting questionable methods, the whole atmosphere is vitiated and the contagion daily spreads. Morality comes from example more than from preaching. The students must have good, honest professors before them to serve as models ; professors who disdain low intrigues and who selflessly devote themselves to the pursuit of knowledge. Perfect men it may be rare to find, but to have professors whose example is positively bad is the surest way of spreading moral disease throughout an organisation and ultimately poisoning the moral wells of the country ; for the students of today are the leaders of society tomorrow.

We have seen about how one after another evils have crept in and the position seems almost hopeless. The whole trouble is to be traced to the mass production of graduates. These graduates get a degree by somehow getting through the examination, but their true educational equipment is nominal. The country is unable to absorb them in fruitful pursuits and unemployment has grown rapidly. Lastly there is the problem of the *failed B.A's.* the result of promiscuous admission to college classes.

We want, in the first place, only the best material to attain higher education and this can be done only by a re-organisation of the whole system of education in the country. The several stages in education should be recast and re-defined so that each stage shall have a clear objective. The primary stage should provide the means of attaining literacy and the rudiments of learning for the masses. The secondary stage should be freed from university domination and from merely urban requirements; its completion should be marked by an examination which would be a clearing house for those requiring further preparation for admission to a university in higher secondary schools as well as for those who would be diverted to vocational training. The collegiate stage should not be clogged by a large number of students ill-fitted for such education. Vocational training should cease to comprise a few additional classes in secondary schools, but should be a modicum of general education.

It has often been observed that to put restrictions on the spread of university education would not be in the real interest of the country. It is pointed out, that in India, the percentage of persons who have received higher education to the total population of the country is much lower than the percentage in other countries. This is granted but perhaps a more just estimate would take, not the total population for comparison, but the number of literates in the country. But let me make it perfectly clear that in my opinion there never can be enough of university education in our country *provided the graduates coming out of the universities are products of the right kind.* I do not hold the view that university education is a luxury. Nor do I agree with Mahatma Gandhi that government should withdraw all support from it. On the other hand, I feel that the government should make much larger grants than now to university education.

We have seen that what really counts in education is the impact of mind on mind, the close relation between the professor and the student, and this cannot be ensured so long as large classes on the present scale exist. It goes without saying that only such men should be kept as professors who are intellectually authorities in their subjects, selflessly devoting themselves to the provision of knowledge and who would disdain to stoop to intrigue or to aim at unworthy ends. We have to be specially careful about this in India, for the word 'Professor' is indiscriminately used in this country, and any Tom, Dick and Harry is called a professor, while, in the west, it is a highly prized designation which even bright men cannot hope to acquire unless they have demonstrated their learning by their own substantial contribution to the advancement of knowledge by patient, continuous research of high quality.

One great defect in Indian university education is the absence of the tutorial system. This should be enforced at any cost. Without it higher education is a misnomer. It is this, more than anything else, that insures the closest contact between the student's mind and the professor's mind and constitutes true education. In Cambridge, it was recently reported, the students asked for the greater extension of the tutorial system, even at the expense of the lectures, so greatly is it valued. In India we set too much store on lectures or, rather, rely completely on them, while of the tutorial system there is none whatsoever. Lectures are not to be discounted, but their wearisome sameness, the passive receptivity of students and their mental inertia, makes the system dull. They can be improved to some extent by inviting questions directly from the class, but even with such improvements they have a supplementary value and the tutorial system is essential and should remain an indispensable part of university education.

Another indispensable part of university education is the development of corporate life among the students themselves. A university is a community of students. The degree that a student obtains from the university may give a measure of his capacity for amassing information, but it does not indicate what use he made of the priceless opportunity presented to him when he was taken into a fellowship of students. It tells us nothing of his capacity for leadership or for organisation. All this is revealed in the part he plays in the building up of the university. "*The university is primarily a community of students ; primarily people.*" The hardest task imposed on the university today, says Sir Charles Grant Robertson, is to convince the nation as a whole that they are not laboratories of knowledge but a very different thing, laboratories of *life*.

The essential importance of corporate life among university students was thus described by Cardinal Newman in his classic *"The idea of a University"* :—

> "When a multitude of young men keen, open-hearted, sympathetic and observant as young men are, come together and freely mix with each other, they are sure to learn from one another even if there be no one to teach them. The conversation of all is a series of lectures to each and they gain for themselves new ideas and views, fresh matter of thought and distinct principles for judging and acting day by day. It is seeing the world on a small field with little trouble ; for the pupils or students come from very different places and with widely different notions, and there is much to generalise, much to adjust, much to eliminate, there are inter-relations to be defined, and conventional rules to be established in the process, by which the whole assemblage is moulded together and gains one tone and one character."

In India, little attention has hitherto been paid by universities to the development of corporate life among students and it is in India more than in any other country that the capacity for leadership and for organisation is in urgent demand, as we have already entered on a new phase of political development. The Hartog Committee which was an offshoot of the Simon Commission devoted considerable attention to this question in their report, as the students of today will be the leaders of tomorrow. The universities should learn to give more attention to students, and promote social life among them as a well-pursued policy, by encouraging Students' Societies, Unions, Brotherhoods, under their own guidance and making suitable grants to them. There should also be members on the senate representing the students' interests, to be nominated in the first instance if a suitably devised elective basis is lacking. Enquiries should also be made regarding the residence of day students and their requirements should be met to the best extent possible.

We have now discussed the essentials of the university system, and pointed out how mass production has been the besetting sin like *"man's first disobedience"*. We have seen why admission should ordinarily be limited to those who are fit to pursue a real university course, why classes should be small and why the introduction of the tutorial system is an urgent need.

We have also stressed the necessity for developing, on an intensive scale, the corporate life among students without which university education remains practically barren. We may now briefly refer to one another activity which universities in India have not yet thought fit to undertake. While it is the business of the university to prepare graduates within the university, there is every reason for it to broadcast its knowledge among the populace also by certain methods which are available to it. Indeed this seems to be one of its principle functions, apart from the graduate courses within its precincts. The Royal Commission on Cambridge and Oxford Universities reported in 1922 that extra-mural lectures should be regarded in all universities as an established and essential part of the normal work of a university. Accordingly in the United Kingdom and the United States, such extra-mural activities, sometimes known as university extension lectures, have attained great importance.

There are large classes of the adult population who for one reason or other have had no opportunities of higher education, to whom early employment in some occupation was a necessity following their completion of secondary education, but who are yet eager for higher knowledge of some sort. For them, classes, seasonal or permanent, can be systematically arranged for an hour or two a day so as to suit their time, with a view to impart to them a modicum of higher knowledge. There need, or need not be, any examinations or diplomas attached to these courses. In the United States, such studies are encouraged by postal tuition. In India no university has yet undertaken anything of this kind. Here is an opportunity for bringing higher knowledge to the homes of the people, and fulfilling the great function of spreading it far and wide among the adult population of the country.

Before concluding, let me make it perfectly clear that I am not unmindful of many material developments in universities during recent years, especially on the scientific and technical sides. Nor has it been my intention to tar all the universities with the same brush as the phrase goes. My observations necessarily have to be of a general character when I write of university reform in India as a whole. Differences must naturally exist, but I am perfectly certain they are more of degree than of kind. My object has been to stress the essentials of university education and to show how they are lost sight of and how ultimately the country stands to lose. One can only heal the ills from which it suffers by speaking openly about them. Our universities, radically reformed and rightly directed, have a great part to play in the future. As Sir Charles Grant Robertson, the distinguished British authority on universities has well observed, there is indeed a real need for the universities severally and as a whole to remember that they can be the starting point of a new renaissance, the purpose of which is to raise spiritual and moral power, and that if it does not start with them, it will probably not start at all.

GAYA PRASAD SINGH

B.A., B.L.,

A sound nationalist and from 1924 to 1934 was an elected Member of the Indian Legislative Assembly. Other appointments during a very busy life include Member Standing Finance Committee of the Indian Legislative Assembly; one of the foundation members of the Aero Club of Indian and Burma; founder and for many years Honorary Secretary of the Town Hall Library, Muzaffarpur; at one time Sub-Deputy Magistrate and Collector; Member Municipal Board Muzaffarpur; Member Sudder Hospital Committee; and local Exise Advisory Committee, Muzaffarpur; President of the All-India (including Burma) Postal and R. M. S., Behar and Orissa Provincial Conference, Muzaffarpur, March 1933; President Burma Provincial Kshattriya Nava Yuvak Sangh, Rangoon April 1933; President Punjab Provincial Depressed Class conference, Amritsar, September 1933; President All India Arts and Crafts Exhibition, Delhi, October 1933; President U. P. Provincial Postal & R. M. S., conference, Benares, 1934; Member Governing Body of the Indian School of Mines, Dhanbad; Member Governing Body of the G. B. B. College, Muzaffarpur; Member Managing Committee Prithviraj Kshattriya High School, Lakhimpur-Kheri; Secretary Managing Committee Yuveraj Dutta High School, Oel, district Kheri (U. P.); Member Working Committee All-India Kshattriya Maha Sabha, Author of Khadder (Name Protection) Act 1934, passed by the Central Legislature; Author of "*Pictorial Kashmir*".

ABOLITION OF CAPITAL PUNISHMENT

THE subject of the abolition of capital punishment is no longer a mere theoretical one. It has now entered into the realms of practical politics. On the 17th Feb, 1931, I myself brought forward a motion in the Indian Legislative Assembly on this subject, but unfortunately it was not succesful owing to the attitude of the Government, and the weak composition of the popular element in the House at that time. It should be noted that I had expressly excluded military indiscipline from the purview of my Bill, and the same might be understood with regard to my views on the subject, which I set forth below.

So far as my information goes, the death penalty, after careful examination, has been either legally abolished, or abrogated by disuse, in the following countries :—

AUSTRIA : abolished it in 1919, except under martial law.

BELGIUM : abrogated by disuse. No execution took place since 1863, except in the case of a murder by a soldier during the War.

DENMARK : abolished in 1930, but no execution took place since 1892.

FINLAND : abrogated by disuse. No execution took place since 1826, except during the revolutionary rising in 1918.

HOLLAND : abolished in 1870, but no execution took place since 1860.

ITALY : abolished in 1889; but in 1926, following the attacks on his life, Signor Mussolini re-introduced capital punishment for cases tried before special tribunals, for crimes endangering the king, his chief minister, or the safety of the state. The restoration of the death penalty marks a stage in the present conflict in Italy, and is no doubt an application of the Fascist principle and policy. But this does not in any way alter the fact that the abolition of the death penalty in Italy during a period of nearly 37 years was accompanied by a considerable decrease in homicidal crime, as the official statistics furnished by the Italian Ministry of Justice indicate.

NORWAY : abolished in 1905, but no execution took place since 1876.

PORTUGAL : abolished in 1867.

RUMANIA : abolished in 1864.

SWEDEN : abolished in 1921, but no execution took place since 1910.

SWITZERLAND : abolished in 1874 by the Federal Government; but 5 years afterwards, the Cantons were given the liberty of re-introducing it. Fifteen Cantons out of the twentyfive have not re-imposed it, and the remaining ten Cantons have had only seven executions in the last 40 years.

AMERICA : the death penalty has been abolished in the Argentine, Brazil, Columbia, Costa Rica, Ecuador, Honduras, Peru, Uruguay, Venezuela, and in Mexico in 1929.

AUSTRALIA : Queensland abolished it in 1922 by law, but no execution took place since 1913. During the years 1916—1928 there have been but six executions in each of the three states of Western Australia, Victoria, and New South Wales; fourteen only in South Australia; and but one in Tasmania.

THE U. S. A. : the death penalty has been abolished in eight states: Michigan in 1847, Rhode Island in 1852, Wisconsin in 1853, Maine in 1887, Kansas in 1907, Minnesota in 1911, North Dakota in 1915, South Dakota in 1915. Capital punishment is retained in 40 out of the 48 States in the American Union and these 40 States have four times as many executions a year in proportion to population as there are in England. Those States which do not inflict the capital penalty stand very high among the States with the least number of murders ; and this is a fact the significance of which should not be overlooked. Major Lawes, warder of the Sing Sing Prison in the United States says :—"*Capital punishment in the United States may be regarded as practically abolished through indifferent enforcement.*"

I shall now turn for a minute to the cases of France and Germany. The fact about France is that she has never abolished capital punishment ; but during the Presidency of M. Grevy (1879—1887) and that of M. Fallieres (1906—1908) a liberal use was made of the prerogative of mercy.

A memorandum furnished by the British Ambassador in France and based upon information supplied by the French Ministry of Justice, after quoting certain figures, says that no argument could be drawn from those figures regarding the abolition of the death penalty. The increase in crimes of violence is attributed almost entirely to the increase in drunkenness proceeding at that time, and states that "*on the whole, it appears difficult to draw from French experience any very strong argument for or against the abolition of the death penalty.*"

In Germany, although the death penalty is retained on the Statue Book, in October 1928 the Judicial Committee of the Reichstag decided provisionally on complete abolition, and there have been no executions in Germany since January 1928. The official memorandum compiled by the British Foreign Office, on information supplied by the German Government, states that

> "in view of the possibility of the legal abolition of the death penalty, the Federal Minister of Justice in July 1928 informed the Governments of the German States that it would be in accordance with the views of the Federal Government if, pending a definite decision of the Legislature on this subject, death sentences were temporarily not to be carried out, but were, by means of the exercise of the prerogative of mercy, to be commuted to sentences of imprisonment."

The Report of the Select Committee of the British Parliament has recorded that capital punishment is now in abeyance in Germany. I am not referring to what the world is witnessing today.

In England, the question of capital punishment was discussed in 1819, 1833, 1847, 1856, 1864, 1874, and 1886, and a Select Committee of Parliament consisting of members of the parties was appointed in 1929 to go into the question. A large number of witnesses was examined, including official representatives from foreign countries in which capital punishment has been abolished, or is in abeyance. The Committee produced an exhaustive Report, recommending the abolition of the death penalty for an experimental period of 5 years ; and in 1931 as many as 215 private Members of Parliament from all parties addressed a memorial to the Prime Minister asking for an early debate on the subject. The Select Committee's Report was sympathatically received by representative papers in England, such as the "*Spectator*", the "*Nation*", the "*New Statesman*", "*Everyman*". "*The Church of England Newspaper*", the "*Christian*", the "*Baptist Times*", the "*Methodist Times*", the "*Daily Herald*", the "*Manchester Guardian*", the "*Justice of the Peace*", the "*Solicitors' Journal*", the "*Lancet*", the "*Law Journal*", and a large number of provincial newspapers. But official conservatism in England has not yet been conquered.

In medieval India, according to the testimony of Fabien, who visited this country about 400 A. D., and of Hieun Tsang, who visited India about 200 years later, capital punishment did not exist. During the 7 years (1804—1811) that Sir James MacKintosh presided as judge of the Supreme Court of Bombay, he entirely suspended the death penalty, and at the end of that period, in his farewell address to the Crown Jury at Bombay, after comparing the statistics of his term with those of the preceeding period, concluded ;—

> "This small experiment has been made without any diminution of the security of the lives and properties of men. Two lakhs men have been governed for seven years without capital punishment and without any increase of crime"

In Nepal, on the authority of Mr. A. Vadivelu in his book called "*The Ruling Chiefs, Nobles, and Zeminders of India*" (Vol 1 page 109e) capital punishment has been almost totally abolished with the interesting result that there is a marked decrease in crimes, which were formerly punished with death for an experimental period ; and this in spite of the fact that the country is mostly inhabited by warlike races in the interior, and wild tribes on the border.

The Legislative Council of Ceylon passed the following Resolution, on the 2nd. Feb, 1928 :—

> "That in the opinion of this council, capital punishment should be abolished in Ceylon, and the necessary amendment in the law should be introduced at any early date".

It has been calculated that the total population of countries where capital punishment is abolished, or is in abeyance, is 17,30,41,000 and the population of countries where capital punishment is still inflicted is 14,25,63,000 showing a majority against the infliction of capital punishment.

It may be argued that the power of commutation of death sentences in this country is somewhat liberally exercised ; and so there is no very strong reason for considering the wider question which is the subject matter of this article. But from the reply to a question which I asked in the Indian Legislative Assembly it appears that during the period 1926 to 1930, the Government of India received petitions against the sentences of death under Section 401 Cr. P. C., in 3083 criminal cases, and death sentences were commuted in the case of 60 persons only. No information was available as to the number of such cases disposed of by local governments which have concurrent powers under that section.

I shall now briefly turn to indicate the grounds on which capital punishment is objected to. The first point is that it is not necessary as a deterrent ; and its removal will not necessarily lead to an increase in the number of homicidal crimes.

In a memorandum communicated by the Belgian Ministry of Justice to the Select Committee of the British Parliament, it is stated that since it was definitely abandoned, the crime ratio has remained practically stationary ...... It seems inconceivable that a Minister of Justice should ever again think it possible to re-establish a penalty, the uselessness of which, to put it no higher, has been amply demonstrated.

Professor Herbert Speyer representing the Belgian Government in the course of his evidence asked what the statistics really teach us? To his mind they show conclusively that, in Belgium; the infliction of the death penalty is not necessary for the protection of society, and the reduction of crime.

Mr. Erik Kampmann, Director of Danish Prisons, representing the Danish Government said, that in Denmark, the number of murders decreased since the virtual abolition of the death penalty.

In a memorandum supplied by the Government of Finland where more than 100 years have passed since the last death sentence was executed, it is stated that the much advertised deterrent effect of the death penalty scarcely exists at all in in the case of murder.

With regard to Holland, Sir Simon Vander, Secretary General of the International Prison Commission, and formerly Director General of Dutch Prisons, in the course of his evidence said that when the death penalty was abolished in Holland, criminal statistics thereafter continued to show no tendency of increase of crime for which, in lieu of the death penalty, lifelong imprisonment may be imposed. The Government of Norway in its memorandum said that the abolition of capital punishment had not caused any increase in the number of murders. Mr. Viktor Almquist, formerly Chief of the General Administration of Prisons in Sweeden, with 40 years' experience, said the statistics lead him to suppose that the discontinuance and the abolition of capital punishment in Sweeden have not adversely affected the homicidal rate.

Mr. Lewis Lawes, Governor of the famous New York State prison of Sing Sing has, as a result of his experience become a confirmed opponent of capital punishment, and in his book, entitled "*Man's Judgment of Death*", he sets forth his grounds of objection. He shows that in practically every state in the American Union, where the death penalty has been re-established after a period of abolition, the homicidal rate has climbed appreciably.

I will refrain from quoting more opinions on this point, but will only say that no statistical evidence was produced before the Select Committee to show that abolition in any single country had caused an increase in murder. On the other hand, every murder is an example of the failure of the death penalty to deter.

If a general question were asked ; "Is capital punishment a deterrent", I might say it is. So, perhaps, was torture, the thumb-screw and the rack, in the middle ages. But the real question that should be asked is : "Is capital punishment the most effective deterrent ?" And here on an examination of the psychology of crime, and the experience of the abolitionist countries, one cannot but answer this question in the negative. In the 18th century as is well known, there were 200 crimes punished by death ; and the proposal to abolish the death penalty for these offences, raised exactly the same objection then, as is being raised to-day. But security of life and property has not diminished in modern times.

The "*Encyclopaedia Britannica*" in an impartial historical survey of the subject, states that at the end of the 18th century, the criminal law of all Europe was ferocious, and indiscriminate in its administration of capital punishment for almost all forms of grave crime ; and yet, owing to poverty, social conditions, and the inefficiency of the police, such forms of crime were far more numerous than they now are.

IRREVOCABLE

The second objection to capital punishment is that it is an irrevocable penalty, although no human justice is fallible. Is it contended that the only court that never makes a mistake is the one which passes a sentence of death?

Over eighteen years elapsed before the unjust verdict was set aside in the case of Oscar Slater ; and it took Adolf Beck seven years to establish his innocence. What would have happened if they had been executed instead of being imprisoned ? Take the case of Habron, who was sentenced to death in 1876 for murdering a policeman near Manchester ; he was a young man, and was reprieved. Afterwards Charles Peace confessed to the murder, and it was proved that he had done it. In Germany, Jakenbowaki, executed in 1926, was posthumously exonerated in 1929, and Paul Dujardin, sentenced to life imprisonment for murder in 1919, was proved innocent in 1929, released, and compensated. In Hungary, Stephen Tomka was hanged in 1913, and discovered to be innocent in 1927. In Austria, Hilsner was sentenced to death in 1899, reprieved, and proved innocent after 19 years in prison. In Holland, Tuenissen and Klundert were convicted of murder in 1923; but as Holland has no capital punishment they were imprisoned; after 6 years imprisonment they have been proved innocent. It is stated in a book called "*Penological and Preventive Principles*" by Tallock (pages 246-247) that in Lincolnshire in 1869 a woman was convicted of poisoning her husband, taken to the scaffold, and executed, protesting her innocence. Subsequently, a man on his death-bed confessed that he had entered the kitchen and poisoned the food in the woman's absence.

I need not multiply instances of such miscarriages of justice. One reason why so few cases come to light is that after a person is executed, there is no incentive on the part of any one to hunt up evidence, which might establish his posthumous innocence. But the factors which cause miscarriages of justice are present in both capital and non-capital crimes. Sir Herbert Samuel said, he did not think that we can ever say that no innocent man has been executed for murder in the past, nor can we have an absolute assurance that no innocent man will be convicted and executed in the future.

BRUTALISING

A third objection to capital punishment is that it inflicts vicarious suffering on the innocent relatives of the condemned man and also upon other prisoners, as well as on the prison officials who have to carry out the penalty. The Rev. S. R. Glanville Murray, a prison chaplain of 28 years service said he had certainly known officials to be greatly perturbed, and suffer in health and that it cannot be denied that an execution is a moral shock of such a nature that it is impossible to say what may be its ultimate effects on mind and body.

A hangman's job is both revolting and degrading to his self-respect and brutalising to his spirit.

A fourth objection to capital punishment is that it creates a great deal of morbid sensationalism, and produces a demoralising influence, and even leads to imitative crimes, by stimulating misplaced sympathy for the murderer, who is depicted as fighting for his life against all the forces of the state. Lord Brentford told the Select Committee that from the psychological point of view, it encourages morbid thoughts in the minds of other people. Young persons have been known to copy what they read in the Press about sensational murder cases.

A fifth objection to capital punishment is that it is unjust, immoral; and destroys the sanctity of human life. The best means of inculcating respect for human life is to refrain from taking life even in the name of the law. If the State declared that human life is so sacred that even in punishment it should not be taken, that example would spread. John Bright truly observed that deep reverence for human life is worth more that a thousand executions for the prevention of murder, and is in fact a greater security tc human life. The law of capital punishment, while pretending to support this reverence, does in fact tend to destroy it.

It is not death that man should be taught to dread, it is life he should be taught to respect. The true aim of criminal law should not be retribution, but reformation and the protection of society. The most effective way to accomplish the former is to achieve the latter. When the offender is reformed, society is protected in the best possible way. In a large number of cases the culprit is not an entirely free moral agent, but a victim of psychological and physical enviroments, all of which he cannot perhaps successfully resist. Vengeance is no part of the Christian creed ; its keystone is that no human soul, however fallen, is beyond the pale of reclamation.

Lord Lytton as the Governor of Bengal made a remarkable speech in the Rotary Club of Calcutta in 1926, and in its course said :—

> "The subject I want to discuss with you is the treatment of delinquency and the use and abuse of punishment in the moulding of human character. The ideal I wish you to test for me, stated in the briefest and simplest form, is just this : the substitution of reformation for retribution as the basis of our penal code. Punishment can instill fear, and enforce habits—it cannot inspire goodness. As a means of moral

regeneration therefore, it is worse than useless, and should be abandoned. A morality which is only enforced by pains and penalties, is a false morality, and those who would secure the acceptance of moral standards should employ other methods".

A sixth objection to capital punishment is that an increasing volume of public opinion is rising against it. It is a truism that the criminal law must rest for its ultimate sanction upon the consent of the community; and when a considerable section of the population regard a punishment as wrong, or unnecessarily harsh, that penalty has lost its moral sanction, and the judge who pronounces it his moral authority.

I need hardly say that in advocating the abolition of capital punishment, I need not of course, be supposed to hold any brief for the murderer, whom I recognise to be, in Dymond's phrase, a depraved and deep violator of the laws of God. But I am afraid my article may exceed the limit set before me, and so I must conclude with the remarkable words of Mr. Henry Ward Beecher :—

> "In our age and with the resources which Christian civilisation has placed within the reach of civil governments, there is no need of the death penalty; and every consideration of reason and humanity pleads for its abolition. It does not answer well the ends of justice, and often defeats them. It is the rude justice of a barbarous age".

SHRI VISHWANATH ANANT KESKAR

B. A.,

Was born in March 1880 at Mhaswad, Bombay Presidency and received his education at the Government High School Amraoti, and the Deccan College, Poona. After graduation he became a Life Member in Nutan Marathi Vidyalaya.

After working as Vice Principal for about five years he proceeded to Hyderabad, Deccan where he worked as Principal of the Government Madrasai Asafia Military College and started his own High School, the Excelsior. After six years in Hyderabad City Shri Maharaj turned to the Himalayas for yogic and spiritual training and no definite details are available about his life in the Himalayan Holy Land, as he refuses to reveal any particulars of that period. Between the years 1918 and 1926 he was seen in Benares working as Professor of Philosophy at Kashi Vidya Peeth for about a year.

After travelling throughout to study ancient holy shrines and centres of spiritual culture, Shri Maharaj sailed in 1929 for a tour of the world when he visited London, Paris, Berlin, Vienna, Rotterdam, Geneva and other cities of Europe delivering lectures on comparative religion and philosophy, and holding classes on the *Bhagvad Geeta* and bibles of the world.

He has made special researches into the unexplored regions of spiritual conditions of life after death, and gains his information about the world's great prophets, masters, saints, poets, philosophers, mystics and scientists by direct observation and experiments. He is in close touch with all the genuinely spiritual institutes that work for the enlightenment and liberation of honest seekers on the path, all over the world.

Since his return to India in 1932, Shri Maharaj has been preaching the gospel of love and service. His works include *Pillars of Life*, *The Universal Gospel* and *Vishwa-Geeta* (in Marathi).

MONOGRAPH ON PHILOSOPHY

WHAT is philosophy in general? It is a generalisation of various particulars in life and nature. It is a formulation of laws that guide operations in physical nature and in the mental world.

Philosophy is a name given to the scheme of operation of the human mind when it is developed, trained and applied to the solution of problems of relations between persons and things, and of the real ultimate nature of persons as well as of things in themselves.

The concrete mind is busy with analysing and distinguishing matters of immediate interest to man. It does not generally stop and think to ask itself why. And when it does stop, it gets easily satisfied with simple answers that offer some kind of explanation. It is too much occupied with the things visible and tangible in external nature or physical world of matter to be sufficiently aroused to look beyond. It is only when the matter-of-fact mind gets dissatisfied with the explanation offered by the senses that it looks beyond names and objects and tries to penetrate into the meaning.

The eyes look out and see objects with different forms and colours. The ears hear sounds of varying intensity. The hands touch many things and find them soft or hard. The sensory nerves carry the impressions to brain centres and then the motor nerves react. All this process of human life-activity goes on so unconsciously, and mechanically that it hardly attracts the attention of average man. Like the lungs and the heart, the two involuntary systems of the human body, the moral life of man runs simply yet unconsciously.

Man lives an animal life as far as the physical body and its needs are concerned. He tries to live a normal human life when he uses the mind as an instrument for search after truth and happiness. Here begins the path of higher evolution through intelligence, understanding and conscious effort.

The modern world has seen some remarkable results of experiments in the field of physics, chemistry, and mechanics. Research work in science and psychology, medicine and sanitation, has resulted in throwing a clear light on some of the most important and useful problems of human knowledge. Many new means of transport and comfort have come into use, but the most vital problem of real happiness has not been taken up seriously in modern times. Research works many ways in many lands, but man is still the most unfortunate and most unhappy of creatures on earth.

RELATION BETWEEN MAN AND GOD.

The question naturally arises, how is it that, in spite of the apparent vast progress in literary education and general civilization, man lives in constant fear of starvation, war, and oppression ? If progress has any meaning, it must indicate diminution of sickness and misery, and positive increase in real peace, comfort, and happiness.

Man does not live by bread alone! Man is not a body! He is not even a mind! He is something higher than both mind and body. Hence his constant search for truth about himself, about God, and about the world around him. He will not really be satisfied with anything short of ultimate truth. The struggle in daily life leaves him no time to think about this truth, but even in the case of the most worldly type of people, there is, at the back of their selfish activities, an inward urge to find and know the truth of truths, the life of lives, the power of powers, and the supreme joy of all joys. They do not know why they feel dissatisfied with the pleasures of senses after a time. They do not know what is wrong with their mode of life which they share with the majority of people around them. Something forces them into the routine of a daily round of duties, but, on occasions, they distinctly feel a lack of something they must possess, and intuitively they are impelled to find that out.

Upanishads are the most direct and most satisfactory answers yet given by God and nature to man in his search after truth and eternal happiness. They are the records of results of scientific research in the field of philosophy of human experience. They are based upon the universal principles of immortality of the soul, the law of evolution and causation, the necessity of rebirth for richer experience, and the change of forms of matter or bodies to help the changeless spirit or *Jeeva* gather that experience.

Wise sages say that God is neither being nor non-being but includes them both within Himself. He is neither light nor darkness. Light and darkness proceed from Him. He is above all qualities that mind can attribute to Him, and yet He is in every being and in every object of the universe. There is only one thing in the wide universe which bears no contradiction, and that thing is God. Being one and simple, all other things exist as compounds by His will.

He is the essence of all power that exists now and of all that may become manifest in the future. He resides in every heart. Especially in man is He more manifest than in other orders of animals. Man speaks through His power. Through His power he thinks and acts. The fundamental relation between man and God is not one of resemblance but of complete identity. Man is God unmanifest. In the case of ignorant *Jeevas*, God is in exile. In the case of those who think of the higher problems of life, God is nearer to His throne in the heart. God is firmly established on his seat for the few fortunate souls that have seen Him in the purity of their minds and hearts.

The two birds which so far wandered far from each other, sitting on the one tree of life, now meet in embrace of spiritual wisdom and become once more transformed into one. The long search has ended. Truth has been found within. The bliss of finding one's self as God, and God as self is inexpressible. Words fall back, not reaching Him. Brahma enjoys himself.

But the path of evolution and experience is a very long one. Not until all desires are eliminated and life is purified, can such a consummation become possible for man.

RELATION BETWEEN MAN AND NATURE.

Where science ends, in nature, philosophy begins. The world of objects is the stage on which man plays his part. He has many exits and entrances, but plays only one part at a time.

Natural philosophy was the name used by modern science in its early history. The term was borrowed from Greek philosophers. It represented the dignity and scope of science in true measure. In the days of domination of the church in Europe, science was made a handmaid of religion. Strangely enough, sciene is now neither philosophy nor handmaid, narrow science as such. It is as rigid and dogmatic as was the medieval church.

The reforming march of time will remove all barrieres artificially erected by the prejudice of limited intellects and man will soon emerge into his full-grown position as master of nature. He can no longer be divided into fragments. He is and will be a complete whole.

The human mind is a harmonised unity, and has many functions and faculties. But all are fused into a harmony and referred to the personality as experiences of the one. The unifying principle is the soul. Experiments in *yoga* and psychology clearly prove the marvelous power of the mind, when controlled and trained, to separate itself from the body and to study nature or the world as it is.

The mind is the link which connects the two opposite poles of man's being, spirit and matter, or body, and thus enables him to enjoy objects in nature. The world is to man what he thinks it to be, not what it is in itself. Science and psychology agree that all our direct experiences are psychological, or inner, and not physical. The mind lends its own coloring to things and objects that are perceived. These are all appearances. The reality is something differnt from, and higher than, these ; and yet, the reality itself makes these appearances possible.

RELATION BETWEEN MAN AND MAN.

All is vibrant with life. There is no such a thing as dead matter. The atoms and electrons dance in tune with the divine music of the supreme lifegiver. All grades of life are differences of degrees, not of kind.

Yet for man, man is the most interesting theme. Man is by nature a social being. He looks around and sees all kinds of creatures, and from the highest to the lowest all possess the common quality of life impulse. The domesticated animals attract his attention most and serve him usefully, but he finds real joy only in the company of man.

All creatures are God's children, but men and women are His chosen and select. They possess within them the possibility of rising to the full height of divine consciousness and thus directly sharing in His glory. Man should be a real brother to man. As members of a family group or as units in organic society human beings are intended to divide their sorrows and share their joys. They are all pilgrims on the path. The elder brother is expected to lead the youngsters gently by the hand and to teach them from his own experience the lessons of patience, understanding and constant efforts.

The creation was born in love, and out of love it is being maintained. He who understands this primary lesson of love, proceeds onward, reaches truth and finds joy in living. There are guides placed on the path. They teach and warn against dangers. Like sign-posts, they are impersonal and unselfish. They are the elders of the race. They love to serve. In them God is manifest. They reflect His wisdom and power. "*Know thyself, brother*" says the wise teacher, man's guide on the path. He who listens to the words of the worthy adviser translates them into his own personal experience, becomes a teacher unto himself in course of time and a guide to others. "*Watch each step,*" says nature or God through him. The way is long and many are the steps to climb.

MAN IS A THINKER

The modern theory of emergence comes much nearer to truth. The higher growth of man is from within, not from external knowledge. Mere possession of brain does not form a real qualification. It is true that in man this brain shows a higher quality of grey matter. This does not make man a thinker. Man is by derivation a thinker. The root man in Sanskrit means to think. The great Manu is the first thinker and therefore the first father of the human race.

Man cannot think clearly until he has removed from his mind the impurities of fear, prejudice and doubt. The average man does not think but unconsciously uses the brain. A great writer rightly remarks : Man sees in part and thinks in part. So his opinions and judgements are limited. This brings misery to individuals and nations.

A great step forward is taken, when man leaves aside the narrow conceits and prejudices of ordinary people and resolves to know the truth. He wants to reach the fountain of experience and he must be prepared to sacrifice everything he holds dear in life. Now he is a thinker, a seeker, a *Sadhaka,* in search of a reliable guide on the path.

INDIVIDUAL GROWTH OF CHARACTER

Mind being purged of sin and being concentrated on the goal of realisation or liberation, man, the seeker, finds a great change has come over him. He does not find interest in the objects of the senses, and in the normal pursuits of worldly people. The higher intellectual and spiritual delights have taken the place of sense pleasures and social amusements. This practice develops a special trait of character which marks him out from the common crowd. Now the seeker is a thinker with special character. With growth of *Vairagya* or spirit of non-attachment, and *Abhyas,* or constant practice of golden rules of conduct, he advances in understanding, discretion, and intuitive vision.

If he is fortunate enough to attract the attention of a real *Sidha* or master, he makes rapid progress under the personal guidance and care of that enlightened teacher. If he is not so fortunate, but still persistent and sincere, he receives light from great books and finds guidance from within himself. The higher law of guidance ever watches over honest struggling pilgrims and reaches them in the form of persons or as intuitive monitors. This depends on the kind and quality of his previous life or lives. Man is today what he has made himself in the past, and he will be in the future what he makes himself now. As a man thinketh, so he becomes, is a truth of deep philosophical import.

Thought is a great power. Words are facts. He who controls his mind and trains it in the right direction becomes free and happy. He who uses words with thought and care attains to perfection.

PHILOSOPHY IN PRACTICAL LIFE

Philosophy means, practically, living a life of principles. Understanding of laws, and reading of good books on philosophy are only means to an end. The end is perfection and liberation. there is a good deal of misunderstanding on this subject. People generally believe that a man who reads books on religion and philosophy, and speaks well, or writes well on problem of life, is a philosopher. Far from it! That is just the difference between philosophy and other subjects and means of knowledge. A man who knows history does know something more than others who have not studies that subject. A man of science knows more than those who have not studied science. But a man of philosophy does not necessarily know more than others who are laymen, unless he practices what he preaches. An ordinary man who lives a clean and pure life of usefulness is better than a professional philosopher who studies books for show and not for attainment. That is why in great books it is said that an ignorant man is better than a book-learned one who does not practice his philosophy.

The greatest philosopher read no books. Real wisdom that leads to liberation is living in the supreme experience of God consciousness. The test of reality is persistence in life under all conditions. He who lives undisturbed and happy under all circumstances is the philosopher, the wise sage, the *Muni*. His is the kingdom of happiness, not of him who talks on philosophy and happiness only.

HUMAN EVOLUTION AND WORLD PROGRESS

Different and varied are the theories about creation. The most rational and sound philosophically is the theory of divine will to create. A careful study of astronomy and science clearly, points to a supreme intelligence which rules and regulates this huge mass of forces and activities called the universe. A careful study of the world's scriptures and philosophical works of merit clearly proves the creation to be the result of supreme will, wisdom and power of the almighty *Ishwar*. Experiences of all great sages, saints and mystics recorded in books unanimously declare that the universe was created by the cosmic will of *Para Brahma* or God Almighty.

His will is law, and that law is evolution. The modern theory of evolution is a part statement of that truth. Evolution in its complete sense makes a circle with two arcs downward and upward. The downward arc described the descent of spirit into matter. The upward arc described the slow process of evolution from the lowest grade of matter to the highest grade of consciousness.

All life is motion and all motion is in a circle or ellipse. The starting point of evolution is supreme intelligence and the goal of all evolution and progress is reaching that intelligence consciously with a view to enjoy the bliss of existence.

All human progress is to be measured in terms of those mental and spiritual qualities which make for harmony, love, peace, wisdom, power and happiness. Physical and material achievements have no value, except in so far as they conduce to the higher advancement of man and the world as a whole.

POLITICS AND ECONOMICS

Philosophically, man is a brother to all life-bearing animals, and a microcosm in the macrocosm. He is lord of all animals below his rank and it is his sacred duty to see that lower animals are properly protected from harm. He is a brother man to all other men, and it is his sacred duty to treat them with the love and respect due to their individual merit.

Only when man treats man spontaneously, as a brother does real human evolution begin at a quicker pace. Till that time it is slow and monotonous. Political philosophy, including economics, comes into operation when towns and cities begin to grow rapidly and international trade develops.

Man is no longer an isolated individual living in a quiet corner looking only to his own personal need. He is a member of a private family group, and an integral unit in human society. He is a citizen of the world. He has many duties to perform and he must perform each of them with discretion and care. Rights of individuals and the economic well-being of all members now become the concern of each thoughtful intelligent man. Leaders are responsible for the right guidance of ordinary people. The leaders must be good, practical philosophers before they can lay down useful laws for society, and transact business with impartiality and generosity The world's greatest leaders, jurists and judges were philosophers first, and men of practical affairs next. The world to-day suffers for want of such clear thinking, and far-seeing, philosophically-minded, leaders. Politicians and economists must be wise and sober men of ripe understanding and experience. Only then can they lead safely. Duty is religion, and religion in its practical aspect is duty well performed, or *Dharma*.

PHILOSOPHY OF RELIGION

The modern divorce between religion and science is as sad as that between philosophy and politics. No one is the gainer, and the world has had to lose the best advantages of their co-operation. This conflict is due to misunderstanding on the part of leaders of thought as to the proper relation between the parts of man's being and his position in society.

Man is the world's greatest miracle. Every part of man is a marvel of skill and efficiency. The body temple is intended to shelter a living god. The marvellous mind possesses powers beyond the dreams of ordinary imagination. The soul or spirit uses these wonderful instruments for his *Leela* or sport. All these three divergent principles work in beautiful harmony and make man's life a repository of the highest experiences of peace and bliss.

There is and there can be no conflict in this universe of law and harmony. If only man used his own body temple in a religious sense of purity and cleanliness, and sanctified the holy of holies of the mind, he would be fittingly installed as god in his own world. It would then be so easy and natural to look upon all life, especially men and women, with religious love and devotion of a *Bhakta* or pious seeker. Life is a joy and a rejoicing.

REALIZATION AND LIBERATION

As a man soweth, so also shall he reap, states the law of eternal justice. Man is born in freedom and fights for freedom. For lower animals there is no freedom of thought and action. They are driven forward by the forces of mother nature, and can, therefore, commit no sin. With man, freedom becomes a birthright. He is free to go forward slowly or quickly; or he can fall back. There is no standing still. The result is that man alone among all creatures in the universe has risen to the highest peak of perfection and has fallen to the lowest depths of degradation.

Heredity and environment play a large part in moulding man's character and shaping his destiny. But the principle factor is his own will and action. Man is the architect of his own fortune and destiny. Planetary influences only indicate individual character as the result of his own past actions. A wise man rules his stars whereas a fool obeys them. When man rises step by step by obedience to laws, cultivation of virtues, and gathering of wisdom, he begins to see the reality within himself. Knowledge is power. The more he knows of truth and laws, the more power he gains for self-perfection and service to others. The purified mind reflects the light of spirit. The refined heart feels the lofty emotions of love for all and service to the lord *Ishwar*. The body, disciplined and trained in good habits, becomes a uselul instrument for service, and not a fetter of bondage as it is with ordinary people.

Life is dedicated to the will of the supreme ruler. Mind and heart are concentrated on the one goal of realization and liberation. The spirit has no bondage and therefore no liberation. It is ever free and happy. But the mind was under the impression that it was not free, but bound to things on earth or in higher regions. With the wisdom of reality and the disappearance of doubts and temptations, all becomes clear within and without. Man no longer identifies himself with body or mind, or the world of objects. He may sit in meditation in solitude without ever moving out, or take an active part in social or political affairs. He is the same stable and peaceful man, liberated, realized in truth. He has attained to consummation of human destiny. This is *Moksha*, *Nirvana*, *Kaivalya* absolute.

PHILOSOPHY OF LIBERATED SOULS

The *Sadhaka* is now confirmed *Siddha*. The pupil has qualified himself into a teacher. What stupendous heights rise before the vision of the mighty souls after they enjoy the bliss of liberation, is impossible even for the best of us to conceive. They live, move, and have their being in supreme intelligence, with full consciousness.

Some of these fortunate supermen merge into the ocean of divine bliss for ages. Others are promoted to superior offices in the management of world systems. Some others, again, by their free choice come down to earth to help their fellow men in the struggle for freedom. But realization once attained is attained forever.

These are the great brothers of superhuman orders, risen from the midst of unfavorable human conditions of life. They teach by example the greatness of man and the glory of God. 'Wake up, good pilgrim brothers,' they seem to say, 'Take courage, do not falter. Do not stop till you reach the goal.'

Aum Shantih Shantih Shantih.

GOVINDRAJ VENKATACHALAM

Born in 1895, he started his career as a journalist and was for a time special art contributor to "*New India*," a daily edited by the late Dr. Annie Besant. Was also Associate-Editor of two art journals, "*Theatre*" and "*Roopa-Lekha*." Between the years 1924 and 1928, was Secretary to an International University, the Brahmavidyaashrama, at Adyar, and also a lecturer on art and culture.

Visited Java in 1930 on a lecturing tour, at the invitation of the Dutch Arts Society, and in 1935 toured in Japan, China and Korea as a visiting lecturer from India. Was elected a member of the Nippon Bunka Renmei for cultural work done in Nippon.

Along with Dr. James H. Cousins, the Irish Poet, organised exhibitions of Indian art all over the country and lectured at several University centres and art clubs. A regular contributor to various leading journals in India, America and Japan, and is the author of the following books on Indian life and art "*The Mirror of Indian Art*," "*Modern Indian Painters*," "*Travel Diary of an Art Student*," "*Daughters of the Dawn*," "*Pen-Pictures and Sketches*," "*Unheard Melodies*," and etc.

KATHAKALI

KERALA is a fascinating bit of coastal country in the extreme south-west corner of India. It is a tropical paradise, with dreamy lagoons and dark-eyed maidens, palmfringed horizons and surf-swept beaches, and is only to be rivalled by Lanka or Java. Kerala is rich in arts too. The old temples and palaces contain fresco paintings as interesting as those of Bhag or Ajanta, and stone carvings as varied as those at Ellora or Madura. Folk arts here have met the same fate as in other parts of India, but of late some interest is being evinced in their revival, especially in the two popular folk dances *Kummi* and *Kaikottukali*, which are being taught to girls in schools. But by far the most unique dance of Kerala is *Kathakali*, the art of dancing *par excellence* in India.

Kathakali, in its present form, may be said to date back from the early 18th century, and its association with a prince of Travancore may, to a certain extent, be historically correct. But its real beginnings can be traced to a race and civilisation much anterior to the Aryan, and its antiquity must indeed be very remote considering it has certain primitive elements in its rhythm, music, make-up, dress and ornaments, and considering also that it gave birth, at a distant past, to the Javanese *Wayang-Wong* and Kandyan *Prehera* dances. It has most certainly absorbed and assimilated the whole of *Bharata Natya*, which gives it its present cultured character and form. This art is as great, in its own line, as Ajanta paintings or Sanchi sculptures in theirs.

Kathakali, as its name indicates, is Story-Play, or the narration of a story in the form of a drama. But in this case the drama is a pantomime or dumb-show, accompanied by music, song and dance. It is an unique dramatic art, as daring in its conception as it is complex in its expression, where even a whole epic like the *Ramayana* or the *Mahabharata* is presented to the public without a single spoken word but through an evolved technique of suitable gestures, poses and movements.

SRIMATI ENAKSHI RAMARAU
M.A., (HONS.) OF PHILOSOPHY

It is an open-air show, meant to be performed in a grove or *maidan* and never inside a theatre. It has, therefore, not the usual painted curtains and backgrounds that are the abominations of the Indian stage. Its settings are simple and admirably serve the purpose. Just a *shamiana* with a high roof supported by four poles, two tall bell-metal lamps burning bright all through the night, a beautifully coloured cloth helps in front, like a drop-curtain, and a stool for actors to sit upon or rest their legs as the case may be. The audience sits in front on a matted floor, and the singers and drummers stand immediately behind the actors.

The orchestra consists of two singers (narrators of the story), a *maddalam* player (drum played by hands), a *chendai* player (drum played with sticks), a cymbal and a gong man. A conch is sounded at the beginning of a show. The first impression of this music is that it is rather loud and harsh, but when the ears get used to it it is pleasing and enjoyable. Certain changes would need to be effected if it is to be played in a closed theatre as the sound would be deafening.

The play, usually a story or scene from the Indian classics, lasts a full night, from 9 P.M. to 6 A.M.; at times continuing for several nights. In its own place and among its own people this may be alright, but when it has to be presented outside Kerala and to an audience with modern tastes and ideas, there must be a time limit. This is now being introduced by the poet Vallathol, who has been chiefly instrumental in reviving this ancient art and making it known throughout the world through his *Kalamandalam* and its pupils.

The conventional form of presenting a play is as follows: First there is the announcement to the villages all around by drum-beating about sunset, known as *Kelikottu*, and this is followed by *Todayam* (when a series of interesting dances are given behind the curtain) and *Vandanaslokams* (song and prayer). The first appearance of the actor or actors is called *Purappadu*, and the interval between this and the actual commencement of the story is taken by *Melappadu*, musical contests between the *maddalam* and *chendai* players and the singers.

The stories interpreted by *Kathakali* are in poetic form, set to music. Several gifted poets of Kerala, some of them princes of the royal blood, have contributed much to this art in the form of poems or plays which the actors try faithfully to interpret. The singers here, like the *Dalongs* in Java, are not possessed of good voices, which is unfortunate, and even the drummers might try to play softer music than they now do. It would not be a bad idea if the *Edakai* (stringed drum) be introduced in certain scenes where solo dances are executed conveying *sringara* (love) or *soka* (grief) *rasas.*

There are thirty varieties of dances, some simple and some complex, and they are based on a sound knowledge of rhythmic laws of body movements. There is much footwork, in the Western sense of the word, and some of the steps are obviously primitive and powerful. The main emphasis seems to be not so much on grace or beauty as on strength, but still there is a good number of graceful movements and steps. A student of Indian sculpture can easily discover in this art the varied bends and flexions, poses and postures that he sees in stone and bronze images.

This art is not merely suggestive and interpretative but descriptive too, such as, for instance, the peacock dance. This is an amazingly truthful portrayal of the bird's moods and movements, its vanity and majesty. The composer of this dance was not only a keen observer of nature, and particularly of the life of the peacock, but also a consummate psychologist who understood something of the bird's flutterings of heart and mind. This clever imitation and representation of animal and bird life is an interesting feature of *Kathakali.* Knowledge and insight characterise most of these dances and not the whim and fancy of the artiste as in modern dances.

It is here tradition helps and keeps in check individual idiosyncracies from running riot. A sad feature of modern art is this supreme conceit and ignorance in art interpretation without the requisite genius or guidance. Tradition can both help and hinder. It all depends upon the artist and his, or her, temperament.

Abhinaya (*i.e.* interpretation and portrayal of moods, emotions and ideas through hand gestures and facial expressions) is an essential part of Indian dancing, and it is elaborated into an interesting science and art. Body movements and rhythmic steps have their own important place in Hindu dancing but not a primary place as in Western dancing. Bharata, the reputed author of the *Natya Sastra,* has evolved a system of gestures (*mudras*), now in vogue, though in a corrupt form, in the several styles of dancing existing today ; but the authors of *Kathakali,* either following a more ancient tradition or creating a new one, have considerably enriched this with a wealth of idiom, phrase and expression nearly as complete as the spoken language and capable of interpreting even abstract ideas. Some of these *mudras* are as descriptive as any picture and some as suggestive as any symbol. They are based on a profound knowledge of life and nature, and when it is considered that even epic poems like the *Mahabharata* and the *Ramayana* can be intelligently interpreted by this gesture-language, its achievement becomes almost incredible. And yet that is what has been attempted in *Kathakali.*

Being an intricate sign-language, it is naturally more elaborate than a spoken language, and it takes time to learn. The memorising of the 24 "*root-mudras*", with their endless permutations and combinations, would itself take a long time, but to be efficient in their exposition and to master, simultaneously with them, the nine movements of the head, eight glances of the eye, six movements of the eyebrows, four postures of the neck and sixty-four other movements of the whole body, as practised in *Kathakali,* is indeed a matter of several years' study and training. That is why a pupil takes at least six years to get some proficiency in the art, and no one is allowed to teach another unless he has learnt it for 12 years. The discipline and physical exercises these pupils have to undergo are very rigorous and exacting, and they have a novel method of massaging the body by the feet.

What a mockery, then, it is that after a couple of months' easy and indifferent training, young dancers come forward most brazenly to interpret the classical dances of India, expecting patronage, appreciation and applause ! Art is a jealous mistress and the aspirant must pay the price.

In the whole of Kerala, today, there are now only a few masters of this art, two of whom are well-known as the teachers of rising dancers like Gopinath, Madhavan, Sivaraman, and artistes like Shrimati Leela Desai and Ragini. They are Kunja Kurup of Thakazhi and Narayana Nayar of Kavalapara, both great dancers and good men. In any other country their genius and fame would have been proclaimed from the house-tops, but here they live and work, unknown and unhonoured, not for money but for the love of the art and its traditions. All honour to them !

Make-up and mask play a great part in *Kathakali.* This is an elaborate process needing years of practice, and there are men who specialise in it. The *Kathakali* make-up ordinarily consists of a white *Chutty* (or outline) made of rice paste and cleverly done in relief on the sides of the face from ear to ear, and the face within is painted green, red or black, (according to the character), and which serves as a sort of background for the play of passions and emotions exhibited by the actors. As a mask and a work of art this is much more intriguing than the artificial paper or pulp masks used in other lands. Women characters do not have this make-up or mask. Personally, I should prefer all actòrs, except those who represent *rakshas* or demons, to appear without these *chutties.* They are magnificent in their own way and possess an artistic merit, but they do, to a certain extent, mar the aesthetic character of the dance, and if any make-up is needed at all, a little paint of the flesh tint for the face, with attenuated eye-brows and slightly emphasised mouth will equally serve the purpose.

This change in the make-up will necessarily affect the present costumes and ornaments of the dancers, which are, truth to tell, heavy, cumbersome and barbaric. The dancers' beautiful bodies and their graceful movements get lost within the heavy folds of their present long-sleeved blouses and pleated skirts. Dances of these actors, with practically no costumes, save a piece of cloth, create a far more aesthetic impression, and reveal more fully their supple form and sinuous lines. The ornaments too, though picturesque and copied from the temple images, are not elegant and even the crowns (*mukutas*) are heavy and can easily be replaced by a more refined form of headdress, like those of the Javanese or Balinese dancers.

A bold and courageous reform needs to be introduced in all these directions, and much of the present misunderstanding about this art, in its own homeland, is due to these barbaric costumes and frightful characters presented in the plays. In representing *bhayanakara* and *bibhatsa rasas* (fear and grotesque emotions), the *Kathakali* actors cannot be excelled by any in the world, and their characterisation of demons too, is realistic and terrible. The make-up, costume, gesture, music and the tense atmosphere are all awe-inspiring.

This is only one aspect of *Kathakali*, and most unfortunately, it is this that is most often shown, and hence the impression that the dance-art is crude and inartistic. This, however, is a mistake. The *Kathakali* dancers are equally expert in presenting *vira* and *karuna rasas* (heroic and compassionate) or *sringara* and *soka rasas* (love and grief), and few actors in the world can excel them in these. But much of these finer aspects of this dance-art get lost in the conventional and antiquated method of presentation, but thanks to the efforts of cultured artistes like Uday Shankar, Ram Gopal, Shrimati Tagore, Shanta Rao, and others. *Kathakali* is now being presented to a wider world in a more attractive and acceptable form. *Kathakali* has a great future, both as a dance-art and a pantomime show, and more and more artistes from all over the world are certain to seek inspiration and enjoyment from this ancient and glorious art of India.

RAO BAHADUR C. GOPAL MENON

CERT. A. I. B. (ENG)

Elected to the 2nd and 3rd Legislative Councils by the Southern India Chamber of Commerce, Madras. He was the Chamber's Secretary for 10 years and for several years its Vice-President. Educated at Zamorin's College, Calicut, Church of Scotland Mission College and Teachers' College, Madras. Gold medalist and scholarship-holder in commerce of the Madras Government. Started life as a commercial instructor and superintendent of a commercial school in Madras and is a great exponent of modern methods of commercial education.

Mr. Menon possesses a long record of public work in the City of Madras. He was for ten years Secretary of the Madras Mahajana Sabha, the oldest political institution in India, then was its Vice-President and for four years its President. In 1914, he was one of the Secretaries and Treasurer of the Indian National Congress held in Madras.

He has also been an honorary magistrate in the City of Madras, Trustee, Madras Port Trust, Director and Treasurer of the Madras Co-operative Central Land Mortgage Bank Ltd. He is on the Board of Management, Madras Provincial Co-operative Bank Ltd and Chairman of the Board of Examiners in Commerce. For a long time he was on the Senate and Academic Council of the Madras University, and a member of the Provincial Banking Enquiry Committee and Unemployment Committee.

He is a member of the Local Board of the Reserve Bank of India, (Southern area) and has given evidence before several Commissions and Committees on Industrial Taxation, Fiscal, Economic, and Labour questions and visited Europe in 1922.

INTERNAL TRADE OF INDIA

IN the western countries the internal trade of India is supposed to be 25 times that of foreign trade. It may be noted that in those countries having regard to their climatic conditions and internal resources the need for import and export trade is much greater than in the case of India which is a tropical country of a variety of soils and climates and growing very many different kinds of vegetables, producing an equally large variety of minerals and having an extensive home market. In countries where there is a greater chance of self-sufficiency in the matter of production and consumption of goods, the scope for internal trade is much greater than in other countries. On that account one would think that the internal trade of India is much greater than 25 times the foreign trade which is the scale on which calculations are made in other countries.

But it may be pointed out that there are very many impediments in the case of India. It is a country of numerous mountains without many passes over them, numerous unbridged and unfordable rivers and it is a country of steep gradients from one end to the other. Apart from these, the railway and road mileage is comparatively smaller. In the whole of India the railway mileage is 45,000 miles and the road mileage of metalled roads is about 85,000 miles. These two sections of transport may be considered the main arteries of internal trade. There is a mileage of 225,000 miles of non-metalled roads, which may be useful for slow moving traffic.

Another great difficulty is the large number of provincial and local jurisdictions, and of Indian States through which traffic has to pass under varying degrees of restrictions. It is a great pity that as autonomy is being introduced in greater and greater measure the tendency to have a uniform policy for the whole of India is receding into the background. It was a great disappointment that the Finance Ministers' Conferences have not fructified and have not been repeated in latter years so that a common policy of taxation and reduction of inter-provincial restrictions could be obtained. Such restrictions are bad now, but it is still more deplorable that local boards and municipalities have also taken upon themselves the introduction of handicaps to internal trade within their limited areas by means of octroi and terminal taxes which are much too common in many municipal areas, particularly in North India.

LABOUR LEGISLATION

Another source of divergence between the policies of the different provinces of India and States which is culminating in a greater handicap to inter-provincial trade is the manner in which labour legislation programmes are undertaken by different governments. Although under the Government of India Act labour legislation is a central subject, with a view to give some latitude to the Provinces to adjust the central legislation to the needs and conditions of local areas a right for concurrent jurisdiction has been conceded in respect of this subject. But such discretion is being carried to inconvenient lengths by the different provinces in their enthusiasm for catering to the needs and welfare of the labour population.

Within the short time during which Provincial Autonomy has been working in the different provinces there has been a plethora of labour troubles all over the country in almost all of which the labour population was more or less sure of governments' intervention with full sympathy on its side. Courts of enquiry were set up in those cases and almost all resulted in substantial increases of wages, holidays, maternity benefits, housing facilities, medical relief and so on. But such hasty advances in labour amenities would not have been so calamitous had they been the result of a general policy of all the provinces and Indian States. Such a desideratum is yet to be achieved, but I understand that proposals are already on foot at the instance of the Chambers of Commerce for the Government of India taking the initiative in shaping the machinery to co-ordinate such legislation of the different units in India.

INCIDENCE OF TAXATION

The incidence of taxation differs from province to province and is another source of unfair competition and another direction in which internal trade is made to flow and divert from time to time. Within the last few months each provincial Finance Minister has been busy devising new taxes on the sale of goods generally, property and so on.

One undesirable feature of this tendency for new taxes is the liberty the provinces are taking to trench upon the jurisdiction so far allowed to local boards and municipalities. Such encroachments are so far visible in the matter of toll revenue, licence fees, entertainment taxes and so on, all of which are being hastily provincialised ; the local boards' claims being discharged by means of average rates of compensation which tend to cripple the resources and financial position of local bodies. It should be noted that the local bodies are the institutions primarily responsible for the upkeep of the country's road mileage and for providing the necessary facilities for internal trade. When the local boards' finances are crippled it must necessarily reflect upon their services for road maintenace and trade facilities.

INDIAN STATES TARIFF

Another disturbing feature of the present position of the internal trade of the country is the liberty the Indian States have taken with regard to the institution of tariff barriers between themselves and British Indian districts. It is true that, generally speaking, the tariff both for imports and exports in these cases does not exceed 5% *ad. valorem* but in many cases it is high enough to restrict the flow of trade and to promote localisation of industries and trade.

It is not easy to challenge the right of Indian States to the imposition of such tariffs because it provides a substantial portion of their annual revenue and because it helps the promotion of enterprise within the States.

When the Federation is established these States might agree to have compensation on some reasonable scale for the loss of revenue by the abolition of such tariffs. But it is highly desirable that such amicable settlement should be introduced as early as possible so that internal trade between Indian States and British India could run on freer lines. This is becoming a more and more urgent necessity as the most stringent conditions prevailing in

British Indian Provinces have been successfully driving out industries and enterprises from British Indian districts to Indian States for the last 10 or 15 years, and the products of these units must necessarily be marketed outside the Indian States in a large measure and it could not be done unless trade is allowed to flow in a freer manner between the States and outside.

RAILWAY POLICY

It can truly be said that the railway system of the country is the real bulwark of economic salvation. The economic progress or deterioration of the country must surely be attributed to the policy adopted by the railways. The Indian Railway Act allows a certain latitude to the railway adminstrations for fixing rates between maxima and minima rates. Nearly the whole of the capital sunk in the Indian railway system is owned by the State and a very large section of the railway is managed by the State. In the circumstances it would not be difficult for the introduction of a national policy in railway administrations. The great advance made by countries like the United States of America, Canada and Germany in the matter of industrial enterprise and export trade has almost entirely been due to the national economic policy of the railways of those countries. If this could be achieved in countries where railways are mostly run by private enterprise it should be a much easier task where the railways are practically owned by the Government.

The expenditure budget of the railways should be thoroughly rehabilitated in order to provide all available economies and the tariff of the railways should be scientifically revised by a public investigation of the necessities of the different indigenous industries and the opening of markets for their products and for the quick movement of traffic in perishables.

The investigation conducted by the Ackworth Committee in 1923 revealed many lapses in the policy of the railways. The discretion vested in the railways for the manipulation of freight rates has sometimes been used in a most disastrous manner to other competing means of transport. The present condition of the Buckingham Canal in Madras is primarily due to the policy of the railway which reduced the rates to such an exceptionally low level as to leave to the canal authorities too small a margin of profit.

Similarly the discretion is sometimes used to uphold the enterprise of certain places and put it down in other places. In this matter the railway adminstrations have paid scant attention to the standing order of the Railway Board, circulated as early as 1916, for adjusting the railway rates so as to help indigenous industries by transporting both their raw materials and their finished products, at minimum rates. Although the railways have vociferously protested against the allegation that their policy has been consistently to help the export trade of raw materials rather than of products of indigenous enterprises in internal trade there has been no authoritative refutation of the allegation. At any rate the railways are far from giving all possible help to the indigenous industries within their limits.

The Railway Rates Advisory Committee is nominally established to supervise this policy of the railways but it has no initiative and its proceedings are far from being simple and inexpensive so that the prospect reprimand of from that quarter is practically non-existent. Under the circumstances the most advisable course for local authorities would be to sustain as much as possible the competing means of transport like inland waterways and motor vehicles. Unfortunately the policy of Provincial Governments has not been entirely favourable. Recently the Motor Vehicles Act was revised so as to handicap road traffic still further by the creation of Provincial and Regional transport authorities and by giving them power to allocate classes of goods to the railways and to the road transport system and to control the rates within certain limits. The .Provincial Governments have also introduced special taxes on petrol and other fuel oils. All these things increase the cost of transportation by competing means of communication, and still further handicap internal trade and indigenous industries.

INLAND WATERWAYS

The facility for inland navigation in this country is also limited because of the want of depth of rivers and owing to their rocky beds. The result is that navigation is practically limited to the mouths of rivers and that too only for small country craft. The inland waterways transport is also exposed to the serious danger of rate-cutting by competing railways and coasting vessels.

Attempts were several times made in the Central Legislature by private members for introducing minimum rates in river traffic but all attempts proved unsuccessful and the inland waterways remain as much neglected as before.

The Madras Presidency is an example of such neglected interest. The Buckingham Canal which was built at great expense and was at one time a great artery of commerce but at present its condition is such that there is hardly two feet of water throughout its length and even country craft of small capacity find it difficult to get traffic, and in spite of the persistent appeals by merchants and boat owners the Provincial Government has not maintaned a necessary depth of water nor lowered the licence fees or penalties so as to help cheapen the communication.

COASTAL TRADE

This country having such a length of coastline has a very cheap means of alternative communication for the railways and inland waterways, but the shipping on the coast is practically controlled by foreign interests ; the coasting traffic available to Indian bottoms being about 23%. Even that percentage is handicapped by the control of the conference lines in respect of rates of freight, passenger traffic and cargo picking. It is however open to the Provincial Governments to give some help to the minor ports of the maritime provinces by way of improvements and lowering of shipping and landing charges.

Excepting seven major ports of India all the ports are under the control of Provincial Governments who have jurisdiction to improve the condition and afford cheap handling both for the import and export trade of those ports. Far from adopting such a policy the Provincial Governments have left the ports in the same neglected condition in which they found them. It is a great pity that the several demands made in the Central Legislature for some degree of reservation of coastal trade for Indian bottoms should have met with strong opposition from the Government and in the result new enterprises by Indian capital remain exposed to the danger of annihilation. This is particularly regrettable as thereby the Imperial Government would be crippling the defence operations that India can put up in any emergency on the waters of the Middle East.

In the west some degree of co-ordination between these two means of transport has been achieved but in these places the transport policy of the government is vested entirely in the governments which are national Governments. A few such attempts in India made by the Indian States, such as Hyderabad and Travancore, have also succeeded for the moment, and it is the aim of the Government of India to introduce similar measures in the British Indian provinces.

CO-ORDINATION OF ROAD AND RAIL TRANSPORT

An unfavourable development under the government's now established policy is the tendency to vest in the local boards the monopoly of running road services in their areas. Several District Boards in Madras have already been authorised to run services on their roads and others have applied for the same right. In this manner private enterprise is becoming annihilated quickly and the only result of it would be that the cost of transport to the public is bound to rise to the real detriment of the economic wellbeing of the people.

The above exposition would show that the internal trade of the country is now exposed to the jurisdiction of different authorities, central, provincial and local, and that it is paying the penalty for such diversity of jurisdiction. It should be the aim of all to develop transport facilities in the country both in volume and quickness of circulation. This can only be achieved by a co-ordinated policy of transport which aims at cheapness and prompt service to the indigenous industries and markets. The necessity for such a reorientation in the transport policy of the government is what is required most urgently as it is becoming increasingly clear that no country could wisely depend on its present connections with foreign customers for any reasonable length of time, as every day the internal barriers to trade are increasing both in number and in intensity. There must be a central machinery for handling all matters connected with railways, roads, and inland waterways and there should be a central national policy which runs through the administration of these different sections of transport.

SHRIKRISHNA VENKATESH PUNTAMBEKAR

M. A. (OXON.), BAR-AT-LAW

Professor of History and Political Science Benares Hindu University.

Professor Puntambekar was born on November 14, 1890 and received his education at Poona, Oxford and finally at Lincoln's Inn, from 1915 to 1920 he practised as a Barrister at Amraoti and took part in many educational, social and political activities, being secretary to many institutions. He was the Principal of the National College, Bombay from 1921 until 1925 taking a leading part in the public life and activities of Bombay.

In 1931 he was elected delegate to the Empire Universities Conference at Edinburgh. He is a prolific writer and has contributed numerous articles to learned magazines and professional journals. His best known published works include "An Introduction to Civics and Politics," "An Introduction to Indian Citizenship and Civilisation" (2 vols.), "Foundation of Indian Civics", "Constitutional History of England" (2 vols.).

In the article which follows Professor Puntambekar approaches history in a manner which gives one furiously to think and students of Indian and world history will do well to keep in mind the fallibility of the human factor to which the Author gives point.

AN APPROACH TO HISTORY

SOME of the great historical events which have been turning points in the history of India are the settlement of the Aryans in India; the Rama-Ravana battle; the Kaurava-Pandava war; the rise and fall of Buddhism; the Yavana, Saka and Huna invasions; the rise and fall of the Rajputs; the Arab; Turk and Mughal Conquests; the fall of the Deccan Kingdoms; the rise and fall of the Vijayanagar Kingdom; the rise and fall of the Marathas and the Sikhs; the British conquest of India, and the Revolt of 1857.

How these events were understood and approached by contemporary writers is fully recorded in their books. I will, however, take only one of them, namely, the British conquest of India, and shall try to show how this historical event is approached and understood by our Indian and English writers. It is considered an act of divine dispensation by Raja Ram Mohan Roy and Mahadeva Govind Ranade. They could not rationally explain it. British historians like Mill, Thornton, Seeley, Froude, explained it as an expansion of their racial mission or destiny, and treated the rest of Indian history, past or contemporary, as a mere prelude or subsidiary to it.

Every action which contributed to the British success was praised. Every action which delayed or opposed it was condemned. It was treated like a war between good and evil, or God and satan. The success of the British was held to be predestined, inevitable and justified. Only those who fought for Indian independence or the actors in the dramatic Revolt of 1857 thought and acted otherwise. A few of their opinions will suffice. Elphinstone says,

> "A new race of conquerors has already commenced its career which may again unite the empire under better auspices than before."

Peter Auber (1837) remarks,

> "The blessings of British rule may be long enjoyed and fully appreciated." Keene writes in his Fall of the Mogul

Empire : "what he has here written may help to remove doubts as to the benefits derived by the people of India from the Revolution under consideration."

Sir Jadunath Sarkar in his lectures on "India through the Ages" observes :

"No careful student of our history can help being struck by one supreme characteristic of the Indian people. It is their vitality as a *distinct type* with a *distinct civilisation* of their own and with a mind as active after centuries of foreign rule in the past.......It is the duty of the historian not to let the past be forgotten. He must trace these gifts (left by races, creeds, dynasties and schools of thought) back to their sources, give them their due place in the *time-scheme* and show how they influenced or prepared the succeeding ages and what portion of the present day Indian life and thought is the distinctive contribution of each race and creed that lived in this land."

I see among typical Indian writers a lack of insight into the individuality of events, into man's desire and action for freedom, toleration and real humanity. How would they view the Rajput, Maratha and Sikh wars of independence and their kingdoms, or the revolt of 1857 ? Are they merely episodes or main events in our history ? Then what are the contents and characters of this Indian culture, its *Unity*, its *common distinct type* which these historians believe in ? Why does the culture change or the Unity break down or the distinctness fade so often and continuously as it were ? Does the Hindu conception of high and low, the Muslim conception of believers and kaffirs, the British conception of civilised and barbarian contribute to this desired but unrealised result ? Which of these ideas contribute to our social, political or cultural unity ? What do the codes and laws of foreign conquerors indicate ? Do they connote unity, humanity, freedom, toleration or respect in their attitude and application to their neighbours and subjects ?

Our history writing is based on certain *a priori* conceptions and interpretations which our poets, philosophers and propogandists have propounded. Dr. Tagore and others like him believe that India has a message and a mission, a special work entrusted to her by Providence. He writes that :

"In the evolving history of India, the principal at work is not the ultimate glorification of the Hindu or any other race. In India the history of humanity is seeking to elaborate a specific ideal, to give to general perfection a specific form which shall be for the gain of all humanity. Nothing less than this is its end and aim. And in the creation of this ideal type, if Hindu, Moslem or Christian should have to submerge the aggressive parts of their individuality that may hurt the sectarian pride, but will not be counted a loss by the standard of truth and right".

Are these views and interpretations of Indian historians and philosophers justified ? Is there an inevitable law of progress or achievement in history ? Is that law an urge towards creating a oneness of human society and civilization or evolving a common but distinct Indian type of civilization or mission or maintaining permanent elements of our old and common civilization and attaining an organic unity on that basis, or is it a synthesis of diversities and a harmony of varieties of Indian life through the ages, safeguarding their liberties and inculcating tolerence and respect but not forging any solid uniformity ? Is there such an increasing purpose or meaning in our history or in all universal history ? Is an ultimate goal for India or the world predetermined ? Is history working teleologically, ethically, fatefully or causally with inevitable logic with the ideals of unity, equality and freedom of mankind moulding it ? Is there a time-spirit or a time-scheme controlling this process or evolution through ages or cycles ? If so, then are historical events or facts in this process mere incidents, instruments, causes and effects interconnected by an inevitable and desirable chain of causation, or are they something unique, free and self-existing, accidental and particular, directed by some god's plan, destiny's power or man's free-will ?

Then, is there one time-scheme in history, or a series of them, one civilization or a number of them, one pattern of unity and freedom in humanity or grades of them ? Are human experiences or historical events self-explaining or do they require a supra-historical god, idea or force to explain their manifestation or, on the contrary, does history treat only of the unique, multiple or particular ? Is it devoid of any unity and is it unconnected with the universal or general? Is there a common drama of humanity? Is there a *Sutradhara* (director) outside or is the *nata* (actor) self-directive? Such are the innumerable questions which arise in our minds demanding an answer and explanation.

Let me state that the proposition I believe in is that *history cannot forget* and the *historian cannot forgive.* History must record facts and historians must scrutinise them, understand their inter-relation, find out their causes and effects, and interpret them historically. It is the duty of the moral philosopher and not primarily that of the historian to value them ethically according to contemporary or idealistic standards. The historian's method is not that of praise or blame according to some *a priori* absolute standards or ideologies.

In order to make clear the implications of my statement I shall state what I mean by *history* and *historical facts* and examine their nature and contents. Historical study is primarily intended for three purposes; firstly, to find out and understand the past and to recover its lost values and life, secondly, to understand how the present came about from the past; and, thirdly, to interpret the mysterious flow of the interactions of man and environment in the process of human life and change. History is, therefore, a complete and accurate picture of the human past and of its process to the present giving the interrelations, causes and results of events in that process, and finding out the conditions under which they arose and the factors which determined them. A historian is to do all this. He may also interpret the sum total of human achievements and find out some law, tendency or force which underlies it or directs it. Thus history studies the social life of men in all their activities in an environment of time and place in which they are placed.

In order to understand, therefore, the problem of history writing and teaching we must first understand the problems involved in the nature and scope of historical facts. History is really not merely the past but its happening. It records continuous change and new experience. It reveals itself anew everyday. No hypothesis of ours can cover all facts. Facts are not similar. Some are common, others are unique. Some recur, others do not. Some are causal, others casual and contingent.

Some are connected, others merely contiguous or convergent. New facts happen and record change. What therefore is the nature of fact ? How does it happen ? There are two visible agencies which bring about a fact, namely, man and his environment. We must understand the interaction of man and environment in order to understand historical facts.

Man is not merely a static individual. Perhaps as an individual he does not exist. He is a changing complex. He is not merely a being but also a becoming. His responses and reactions to environment are various. They are not predetermined nor precalculated. There is a number of possibilities before him. He chooses one or the other. Man is a spirit. We may know the laws of his survival but do not know those of his arrival. Man is a being whose knowing and thinking, though dependent on his material organisation, is not restricted by it. There is in him will, reason and consciousness independent of matter. There is a play of motive and purpose also. He is the determining factor. His environment is only the conditioning factor. *Environment* is also a socio-physical complex. There is geographical environment and its variety of influence and possibilities. There is also social environment and its various inspirations and restrictions. But environment alone does not determine man's development. History shows a constant process of emancipation of man from the control of environment. Man is the hero. At first helpless, man eventually conquers nature through the processes of invention and culture.

According to *Vidal* what really in all these climatico-botanical frames is that various geographical possibilities are awakened according to the nature and initiative of man. There is an environmental challenge or possibility and a human response and choice. The result is an event or a fact. It has, however, many causes or factors behind it.

When we study *historical facts* or *events* we are confronted with a number of questions. (1) Are they mere common incidents interconnected by an inevitable chain of causation and do they follow from one another. Are they a consequence ? Or (2) are they something unique, free and self-existing, accidental and particular, mere matters of chance or caprice residing within them, and do they merely follow one another ? Are they merely a sequence ? For my purpose I take historical facts as not merely connected and causal incidents but also as causal and contingent accidents. They are of both types. An event is not the product of a single cause but the interaction of several causes, coincidences and contiguities. It does not produce a single effect but combines with other events to produce many effects. Therefore, historical events are not simple entities but complex unions of different factors springing from a multiplicity of facts. Hence they cannot be isolated. They are pluralities not predetermined but possibilities. They may occur and recur or they may not recur at all. Therefore, events in history are either actually willed or accidental or caused by some inner logic.

The conception that the historical facts are absolute, precise and unchangeable entities which can be discovered and which in any situation are invariably the same and uniform is an illusion. History in a larger sense does not repeat itself. Henri Berr, a famous French historian says :—

> "that the facts of which human evolution is woven can be grouped in three distinct orders. The first are the *contingent*, the second the *necessary* and the third those that relate to some *inner logic.* The whole content of human evolution falls into these general divisions of *contingency, necessity* and *logic*.......History disentangles three kinds of causal relations : *mere succession* where the facts are merely determined by others : *relations* that are constant, where the facts are linked to others by *necessity*, and *internal linkage* where facts are *rationally connected* with others." Prof. Becker in his paper on "What are Historical Facts" says—"the simple historical fact turns out not to be a hard, cold something with clear outline and measurable pressure like a brick. It is, so far as we can know it, only a symbol, a simple statement which is a generalisation of a thousand and one simpler facts which we do not for the moment care to use and this generalisation itself we cannot use apart from the wider facts and generalisations it symbolises."

Therefore the data of history are not absolute, precise unchangeable historical facts, which in any given situation are invariably the same and may be viewed uniformly by all honest investigators. It is impossible for us, therefore, to praise or blame a fact or event because it is in its nature a complex having sociocultural content and relations with a number of causes and results. Any distortion of it may falsify the nature and understanding of historical development. A study of facts merely determines the nature of facts, their causes, connection and effects. It does not afford a standard for a critical estimate of actual conditions nor a correct basis for reforms.

The human mind is complex and diverse. There are mixed motives and forces behind it. We cannot, therefore, know the real facts and the complete chain of causation. They always present a part of the human picture for us. History, however, as a science consists in the synthesis of facts with ideas so that facts become the expression of ideas. Therefore we shall have to find out facts and ideas and forces behind them.

One writer says that "every great historical occurrence involves the complicated interaction of millions of different events, of millions of conflicting psychological results based on unknown and unknowable internal factors, of millions of currents and under-currents social, political, economic, physical, psychical, of which very little can come to the attention of a historian, much less be subjected to his analysis." He can see sequence but not the causes and contingencies in full. Therefore in order to do this work a fully equipped historian is necessary. He must be well conversant with the results of social sciences as they will help him in understanding the nature of facts and ideas behind them. Facts may be of political, social, economic, cultural, religious importance or of a mixed type. With the help of social sciences he can elucidate them. Social sciences have a great place in historical studies. Social sciences of politics, economics, sociology, psychology, anthropology and ethnology and jurisprudence, natural sciences of geography, biology, geology and palacontology have all helped to elucidate the origin, growth, nature, structure and function of social facts. One group deals with man, the other deals with environment. They have also given provisional conclusions about them. These help the historian immensely in determining the nature of historical facts.

The difficulties before a historian are generally threefold : how to select facts, how to elucidate and determine their nature, and how to interrelate and to interpret their values. He has to give a picture of man's multifarious activities as a member of changing and developing social groups and cultural complexes. Therefore he should be adequately grounded in the various social sciences and allied natural sciences which will elucidate for him the nature of various and complicated social and cultural events and situations in which men have been placed or have acted in the past. He will have to acquire a comprehensive grasp of the various aspects of human development in the past. The general cultural and social setting of the past is very different from that of the present. The historical writing of every age represents the dominant interests of that period. But the study of social sciences, as such, and the subordination of history to them cannot compensate for the study of history independently and as a major subject. History is not merely illustrative or episodical or informative in character. It has a flow, a continuity and an inspiration of its own. Theories of social scientists cannot cover and connect all the facts of history, rational and irrational, common and unique. The attempt to impose rationality upon historical facts, more than those facts will bear, will result in discovering in the diversity and flow of human phenomena more identity than really exists in them.

No doubt there is some kind of continuity discernible in history between all aspects of human life but it is an abstract conception of life. It does not indicate its spontaneity, its actual variety, its growing complexity, its breaks and its free happening. There is a *naturalistic school* which assimilates history to sciences. According to it historical reality consists of certain events of certain kinds. A cause of one kind produces an effect of a corresponding kind. It is the business of the historian therefore to discover the universal laws connecting cause and effect.

The *individualist school* believes in the individuality of historical events and agents. It does not allot an event or agent to any class. To it there are no uniformities or laws. It recognises the decisive actions of individuals, roles of prominent men which sociology falsely eliminates for the sake of generalities. General principles do not account for a particular sequence. They embody necessary *conditions* but there is a chapter of accidents also in historical occurrence. Historical occurrences are what men have done, thought and felt. They have a validity of their own. They did not happen merely in order to be antecedents or preludes to lead up to us. "We are not *final* in time any more than we are *central* in space". History has a past not a cause. It is a sequence and not a consequence.

The next difficulty of the historian is the selection of facts. I mean guiding facts. Facts as they are, we do not know well. Facts as we want them to be do not count. Facts as we think they are alone count with us. This vitiates our understanding and conclusions. Our knowledge of facts depends on the state of our knowledge. When it advances, the range and meaning of facts also advances. New physical and social sciences have increased our knowledge and range of facts, and the methods of understanding them. But the stage of our culture has influenced the general position, the direction and mode of our understanding. Our intellectual attitudes and approaches also influence our knowledge and understanding. Facts are not only selected for their truth but also for their utility and importance. There is a wide difference of opinion as to the importance of facts according to the understanding and outlook of the chroniclers and historians. Facts are relevant only as elements in a larger historical totality which a historian conceives of. Prof. Goldenweiser says

> "The historian is of necessity a selector of events. His interpretation, moreover, is not separable from the selection, rather does the former determine the latter, at least in part. The facts do not speak. The historian speaks for them or makes them speak, and what they say depends upon the magic of his wand." Mr. Joad says, "The writing of history, I am well aware, must from its very nature be informed by a subjective element. For written history is a record of events seen through the spectacles of Mr. X. Y., a limited and partial personage living in a particular age, a member of a particular civilisation, the child of a particular environment, and the inheritor of a particular culture.........Accredited historians make every effort to minimise or at least to disguise this element of the personal and to present as objective a record as in the nature of things is possible."

Selection involves preconception and distortion. The historians selection determines the nature of facts and his interpretation determines the selection of facts. Therefore, every fact of history has its relative significance with respect to (1) its importance in the age of which it was a part ; (2) its bearing upon the origin and growth of contemporary culture and (3) its utility in the eye of the chronicler. There is no absolute test for fact for as one writer has put it historical fact is at its best what the historian thinks of what someone else thinks, he saw or said or did or heard. At its worst it is a paltry third or fourth hand judgment.

The historian's mind plays a large part in showing the connections between facts, finding out motives, causes, effects changes or connections. They must select, order, and interpret the facts according to some theory or way of looking at history, explicit or implicit, old or new.

The next problem before the historian is how to interpret the facts. There is no simple solution for this, because causation in human affairs in multiple. Every event has many causes and leads to many results. There are many motives, factors and beliefs behind it. There are conditioning factors and determining factors. In history we cannot refer phenomena back to a first cause and ignore secondary causes. Historical interpretation has suffered from monistic approach and dogmatic theories. Geographical and racial, theological, ethical and metaphysical, materialistic and technological, psychological and sociological determinisms have been found to be inadequate and misleading. No single category of causes is sufficient to explain all the phases and periods of historical development. Unless we study the collective psychology of a period, it is not possible to determine the historical development of that age. It is therefore, necessary for the historian to find out, to value and to state the chief factors which underlie and mould the collective view of life and to determine the nature of social struggle in that period.

We must not make geography or race, an idea or mere matter, a tool or a social relation, the absolute or determining factor. They are merely conditioning factors. We cannot establish any simple unilateral evolutionary schemes of universal applicability, by overlooking discrepancies. This results in a serious misrepresentation of facts and their interrelation. We cannot brush them aside as disturbing agencies because some religious, racial, cultural, national or socialist prejudices are threatened. Therefore, we cannot tamper with facts and their interconnection by selection, suppression or distortion. We cannot fit facts of history to suit our pet scheme or attitude or outlook in life. We cannot understand human history unless we recognise in persons and events a certain amount of irrationality and diversity, particularity and fresh possibility. We must avoid any attempt to find out a single cause for all events. We must allow the existence of many causes acting simultaneously and possessing intricate corelations. History must convey all the complexity, the indeterminateness, the flow and cross currents of the past.

History does not seem to work in a cycle as Spengler in his *Decline of the West* propounds, or according to a law of inevitable and desirable progress as nineteenth century historians conceived.

According to Prof. Bury general causes did not usually explain the great events of history. Causes of great events are not simple, and ascertainable. These are coincidences of events which may result in great consequences, but there is no inevitability in the coincidence, the general laws are insufficient to account for any particular historical development or personality. There is the part played by coincidence and the part played by individuals, general principles cannot account for a particular set or sequence of events. There is a chapter of accidents with certain conditions. Historical development does not lie in a particular or right line. There are possibilities of diverging from the course. Several roads are open. One is chosen. Why ? We cannot say. The professor states that no given transformation can be proved to be necessary or determined. Types of development do not represent laws, but only possibilities chosen.

The course of history seems to be marked at every stage by contingencies, some greater, some smaller, according to Prof. Shotwell of America. In some cases they produce a situation to which antecedent situation does not lead. Origin of man (*homo sapiens*) is itself a primordial contingency according to him. Professor Fisher in his *History of Europe* remarks :—

> "One intellectual excitement has, however, been denied to me. Men wiser and more learned than I, have discerned in history a plot, a rhythm, a predetermined pattern. These harmonies are concealed from me. I can see only one *emergency* following upon another as wave follows upon wave, only one great fact with respect to which, since it is unique, there can be *no generalisations*, only one safe rule for the historian, that he should recognise in the development of human destinies the play of the *Contingent* and the *Unforseen*. ......The fact of progress is written plain and large on the page of history, but progress is not a law of nature. The ground gained by a generation may be lost by the next. The thoughts of men may flow into channels, which lead to disaster and barbarism."

History is concernd with concrete deeds, individual agents, and with particular situations. It does not deal with the universal or general as such. The individual fact is the end ; and the general law is of use only in so far as it helps to understand the individual fact. The historian cannot ignore the study of the individual characteristics and differences, which determine the course of events in accordance with the personalities of the actors. The historical method of scientists is not able to explain correctly the arrivals of events or facts. It merely takes into account their survivals and then tries to trace causes and connections. And in explaining those survivals it enters into geographical, racial, psychological and sociological explanations which do not elucidate the whole event, and ignores its individuality and uniqueness, its inner urge or creative power.

Therefore, a view of history which is purely unitary is not correct. A pluralistic or collective approach is necessary. The idea of inevitable progress, of the unity of humanity and civilisation, of the realisation of reason and freedom or the absolute in history are misdirecting the study of history. These interpretations may be desireable, useful, and possible under some pre-possessions, but not inevitable or necessary or correct. History does not repeat itself even in events, much less has it established laws for their occurence or for the process of their happening. History is concerned with the investigation of something unique which cannot be repeated. It tries to find out to relation of the unique, the singular, the individual to general uniformities. Historical facts are not merely incidents (causal) but incidents (casual) which may divert the course of history.

Was Shivaji or Clive, Alexander or Napolean, mere results of causes in chains of progress, rational and determined? Can their lives give us a calculus for the future? Great men are not only accidents but unforeseen and extremely disturbing accidents. Similar are the great ideas of a Buddha or a Christ, a Muhammad or a Marx. They are largely self-sufficient and prevent social and economic conditions and forces from working according to the traditional, general or assumed laws. Take men like Lenin, Mussolini, Hitler or Gandhi. We see that the action of their individual wills has been a determining and disturbing factor, too significant and effective to allow history to be grasped by sociological or ethical formulae.

Thus we arrive at the following conclusions. According to the old school of dogmatic approach to history all the component facts of history can be accounted for historically, just as those of the physical world can be accounted for physically. To it historical connection is strictly causal as chemical or biological connection. The result of this view is that man as an individual does not exist, he is merged in some law, or force or idea, The other pragmatic approach recognises the individuality of man and its uniqueness and believes in the contingency of events also. It does not believe that history repeats itself. It does not trace any laws or mission in history or any fixed message or course in their happening. To it historical facts are not merely causal incidents but also casual accidents which divert the course of history.

Many historical generalisations of yesterday have become the fallacies of today. Therefore the chief function of the historian is the discovery and collection of historical facts and the constant testing of their interpretations, so as to eliminate false generalisations or estimates,

History should not enslave us to the laws or lessons of the past. How little is the human past! How vast is the human future ! History should not aim at producing infallible laws, but should aim at a comprehensive knowledge and a better understanding of all facts and aspects of human life and its individualities. Mr. H. G. Wells says that man is still only adolescent. As yet we are hardly in the dawn of human greatness and that what man has done forms but the prelude to the things that man has yet to do. To explain the past in terms of an ideal future would be as much a form of propaganda as to explain it in terms of the present.

Great modern historians of the west have come to the following conclusions with regard to lessons from history. They say that truth is what is true now because man has no fixed nature but history, and environment is a number of possibilities. Man is life, a happening. He is not a mere being but a becoming. *Not that man is, but that he lives. Man is not. He goes on being this and that.* Human life is not an entity that changes accidentally. It is itself a change, a drama that happens. History is the past summoned to the present. It has to be approached pragmatically, relatively and in a pluralistic way. There is no fixed causation or determinism in history. No one law or category of historical events and facts can serve as the basis for the organisation of historical causation. At times one or another factor may rise to the position of transcendent importance, but no single cause or influence or purpose has been dominant throughout human history.

Thus we see in history a law of relativity with regard to the importance and nature of events, a law of indeterminism with regard to the play of contingency in events, and a law of discontinuity with regard to progress or evolution of events. There is no unity in history and there is no finality in history. History will contain a record of a country's failures, blunders, disasters and humiliations as well as of its glories and achievements in all aspects of life. It will contain a warning as well as an inspiration. Only in this sense is history a school for the statesman or the citizen. It should create a vivid consciousness of the past, its success and failures. But there can be no such thing as a final verdict in history.

Unbiased accounts of historical events are not obtainable since they are recorded and handed down by men who have their own predilections and prejudices. Documents, however complete and circumstantial, may be imperfectly drawn up. They may be set down in the interests of some cause personal, communal or national. Thus there is a large possibility of bias in the recorder, of bias in the interpreter of events and facts, besides the bias or spirit of the times, the teacher and the reader himself. *Truth* to a historian is essentially that which *makes sense* of all data to hand. But the accumulation of fresh data often calls for a fresh examination of all facts and a new conception of truth. Sometimes the new data are widely divergent from anything which the past has produced and actually prove that the *old truth* was wrong. Therefore the *historian's truth* or synthesis rests on a balance of probabilities understood at the time of writing history.

The danger in historical writing and teaching may arise out of the idolisation of nationlism, imperialism, religion and socialism This leads to a deliberate telling of lies about past events. It leads to a choosing of suitable facts or to their distortion, suppression and falsification. We must therefore be able to distinguish between facts and their partisan interpretations.

Devotion to reform also leads to search for a golden age, a philosophical age, a natural age in the past which the reformer wants to revive and restore. Lastly, the outlook of *present-mindedness* causes us to see the past through the distorting medium created by our own standards, presuppositions, and utilities.

Really speaking historical occurrences have a validity of their own. They did not happen merely for our sake. We are merely a stage or state in that happening. We are not the final end of the journey or destiny. We must study the past for its own sake. What then should be our outlook in writing or teaching history. We cannot deal with our past with the outlook of any contemporary "ism"—radical, reformatory, revivalist or revolutionary. We can however, have some provisional standards of judgements in estimating and elucidating our past, without adopting contemporary philosophies for our judgement. We can adopt certain human considerations and virtues with which we can estimate past situations, institutions and personalities.

SRIMATI ENAKSHI RAMARAU

M.A. (HONS) OF PHILOSOPHY

Has the distinction of being the first high class Brahmin girl to take up films as a career. She is the daughter of the late Rao Bahadur B. RamaRau (District and Sessions Judge) and the grand-daughter of the late Justice S. Doraswamy Iyer, Chief Judge of the Cochin High Court. In private life Enakshi RamaRau is the wife of Mr. Mohan Bhavnani one of India's leading film directors and producers and the proprietor of the well known and widely shown Bhavnani Productions. Of the many successful roles she has portrayed perhaps the most widely known was her starring in the British Instructional of films "Shiraz."

Enakshi RamaRau has also made an intensive study of Indian classical and folk dancing the schools she has studied including the Tanjore School (based on the famous *Natya Sashtra* by Bharata), the school of the Kathakalis of Malabar, Kathak (performed in North India) the dance of Manipur ; and the folk dancing of Rajputana and the Kathiawar. She has been invited by the world famous dancer Uday Shankar to join as a solo dancer in his world tour, and when she was last year the guest of Dr. Rabindranath Tagore at Shantiniketan, he saw her dance and said, "Srimati Enakshi RamaRau delighted me with her exhibition of Manipuri dancing. She has mastered the technique of the dance. Subtlety of movement and rare grace characterise her dancing." After that Enakshi was invited to give an exposition of her dances before the Oriental Society of Indian Arts, by the President and Committee and also at the Bengal Music Conference, the most important all-India gathering of song, music and dance exponents.

She made important public speeches when she opened the South Indian Film Conference and when she addressed a large gathering at the Indo-American Club on the occasion of the American Independence Anniversary Day Dinner. Her theme was that eventually it was the artistic and cultural side of people that would bring the nations to a better understanding ! Notable among her radio broadcasts are her talks on the special significance of gesture language in Indian Dancing, the revival of India's dance and her trek to the Himalayas.

Enakshi RamaRau, who is considered one of India's greatest exponents of the Hindu dance, has given more than twenty-five dance recitals in the leading cities. Her contributions to the papers, include articles to the '*Hindu*,' '*The Madras Mail*,' the leading film journals and to the '*Illustrated Weekly of India*.' Her articles include 'Films a career for cultured girls,' 'My experiences in Vasantasena,' 'India's Classical Dance,' 'The Sacred Cave of Amarnath,' 'Manipur's Terpsichorean Art' and 'The Masked Dancers of Sikkim.'

Requested to submit an article on classical and folk dancing of India Enakshi RamaRau has written the following specially for "*What India Thinks*."

INDIAN DANCES

RHYTHMIC showing or Natya has always played a prominent and inspiring part in the arts of India. The Indian classical dances as explained by Bharata in his *Natya Sashtra* were composed of a series of enchanting combinations of the three main elements of bodily gesture ; namely the limbs, the whole body and the entire face. These great divisions had to express between them, one uniform whole, in which swiftness, symmetry, versitality, and glances followed in a natural stream of such perfect unison as to produce a unique and marvellous effect of the essence of emotional exhibition.

This outward symbolic structure as a whole outlined the manner by which the meaning of the dance was to be expressed ; the expression was detailed in the Mudras or hand poses ; the Bhava or mood of the dance tenderly described by the glances and head movements, and the rhythmic timing or tala by the feet. And each single token of expression passed and repassed in one circle, the significance of which was that where the hands moved, the glances wandered accompanied by the quivering sensitive brows ; where the glances and brows strayed, the mood swept along, and thus the Rasa or flavour of the dance unfolded its mysterious and complicated self. When this stage of Natya was reached by the dancer, she had attained the acme of perfection and was considered to express with ease the soul of her inner life in its manifold suggestions, while technical perfection was always a necessity as the background from which the dancer could give her fullest to the style of expression.

At the outset, these classic dances had always a devotional trend about them, though the themes varied. South India, which has preserved intact the dance as described by Bharata in his *Natya Sashtra*, is famous for its temple or Devdasi dances. Just as in early Greece, these fair tenders of the temple in India had the same duties as the vestal virgins. They were the brides of the god, worshipped him, sang to him and danced for his delight. It is these pure, natural and religious dances that deserve the true apellation "classic."

In Tanjore, in Southern India, with its age-old carved temples and its spirit of real Hindu culture, the classic dance has best been preserved. It is here in particular that the statuesque, exquisite interpretation of how the body can be used in every feeling of a human being, is truly revealed. Historically it is believed that the great Chola kings of the Tamil country who ruled some time in the 10th and 11th centuries, first gave impetus to the renaissance of the dance. They tried to maintain the original position of honour for the dance and its exponents by recognising the art in the Vishnu temples and giving a place of dignity to the institution of Devdasis in the Shiva temples. Becoming absorbed in the beautiful ideals and conceptions laid down in the *Natya Sashtra* which formed a part of the Vedas, the great teachers of the dance transferred to their dancing all genuine sublimity of a religious significance, where gods and goddesses, the heavenly counterparts of human beings, began to play an important part. The perfect angles that arms and waist-line take ; the swing of the head ; the mere walking at times in Tala and the precision of the combination of foot work and hand gestures made the dance appear as if the immortal temple carvings had come to life and melted from one pose into another to the accompaniment of the Padams or lyrical verses. Perfect grace and suppleness stood supreme in the gradual changes that took place from posture to posture and each little piece of the dance made a series of petals in the complete flower of the dance ensemble.

Their dancing, like all Indian dancing, is divided into the Tandava, which is vigorous and forceful and the Lasya which is sweet and gentle. The most unique feature of the dance is its perfect timing. It is kept so by playing on the mirdang and accompained by song, the padams (in lyrical form) and the sweet tones of flute, cymbals and clarionet. Each step of the dancer has to find its absolute counterpart in the echoing drum beats. The dances of Tanjore have a complete and comprehensive tabulated form of hand-poses. These, with various combinations of fingers in various sequences and numbers used with both hands and singly have been tabulated to convey meanings of greeting, prayer, offerings, flowers, garlands and nearly every possible word. They use the full arm, the forearm and wrist in varying angles to stress the moods. The dancer has to feel the inner urge to dance ; a divine mood should possess them. They are imitating the movements as the deities of heaven would have acted. These exquisite dances, full of technical excellence, their ever-varying poses, and feet movements maintaining a great frequency of intricate stepping which pass from the flat of the foot to the toes ; toes to heels ; the heels to the ball of the foot ; and again to the edges of the foot are India's purest gift to posterity. Their dance themes can be counted by the hundred, and are danced in solo, sometimes in duet and occasionally in groups numbering even twelve. One of the famous dance themes depicts that of the goddess Parvathi, daughter of the Himalayas as she danced on mount Golden before an assembly of gods and goddesses, heavenly musicians and nymphs.

"He with the matted locks and head from which flows the Ganges in a sparkling cascade ; on his wide brow, the serpent and the crescent moon."

"Spread his glory. With a garland of skulls, he dances on the earth upheld by the snake of Vishnu : victory to Shiva ; victory to Parvathi's lord, victory, victory."

In sparkling raiment she is clothed :
Her gentle breast rises and falls with tender thrill.
Her little feet with magic stress rhythmic ecstacy
A smile divine lights her face faintly and all
The colour of nature has painted her with heavenly hue
To please the assembly of gods and goddesses
Victory to the divine Parvathi ; victory, victory.

Her twinkling feet speak almost words
A lilting song they form,
Parvathi, the pale Uma dances as in a dream,
Her mood sweeps all those present
And fills the winds of heaven.
So gentle is the flow of her body,
Like a serenade it joins the music,
And every cadence strikes sweet harmony.
Glory, glory to Parvathi......glory.

The madole drum rings forth it's low base notes
The cymbals clink in lightly.
And in the music join her little ankle bells.
Loud booms the mirdang drum.
While gods and goddesses and all the
Company of heaven sit transfixed by
The chorus of instruments and spiritual dance.
Hail Parvathi......hail Parvathi.

These words are chanted in lyrical verse and the dancer with her languid movements of the body, the fan-like swift pushing from side to side of the head, forming a unison with her hand gestures, the glances of the eyes and her postures illustrates each word.

Again there is quite a different theme, when Radha, the beautiful impersonation of womanhood awaits Sri Krishna in the scented bowers of the malika blossomed groves. The Gopis passing with their milk jars see her and take this message to the divine lover :—

The lovely fair-eyed one awaits thy presence
The malika blossoms are scenting the air.
Faint stars smile at the starry flowers,
And reflect themselves in the lotus-eyes
Of the maid who waits in patience.........

Raja Gopala ! Sky clad art thou
She too is dressed in indigo, with vermillion
On her brow and golden ornaments
Awaiting thy presence.

The Varnam is one of the most beautiful and highly elaborate dance conceptions in the southern classical Natya. It is composed of gestures with rhythmic cadences and can be compared to a musical prelude, wherein the pure dance is described and depicted in a series of interludes. In this exposition, with it's dramatic finales, is embodied Natya (the dance) Nritta (dramatic expression) and Abhinaya (gesture description with mood and song). And with it is the other important Lasya (gentle) dance style called Tillana. This is the essence of grace and feminine charm accompanied by all the elements of bodily gesture.

In north India, the classic dance is known as the Khatak. In this dance also, as all over India, the themes are all interpretative and suggest various emotions and feelings. The stepping again is rhythmic and patterned as in the South, though here more of the swift movements are done on the flat of the foot, the toes and in pirouetting, so that the wide dancing skirt spreads out like a scalloped blue-bell turned upside down, and each step has to be timed and regulated so that every little "Thora" or piece fits into the timing and coincides with the tablah as it sounds out the corresponding Bol or tablah words.

Kathakali, the portrayal of the exquisite dance dramas of Malabar is performed by the people of the village in the open air under spreading trees. The performances start at six in the evening and continue the whole night, with the gentle breeze sighing through the foliage, and dozens of little oil lights flickering in shining brass candlebra. Whole episodes are danced from the *Mahabharata* and *Ramayana* with a detailed hand gesture or mudra language that embodies about eight hundred in number.

Though the dance is full of a tabulated form of Mudras, a strict style, and is purely traditional, it must be classed as one of the most unique forms of folk dance prevalent in India. Unlike Tanjore which in it's classic tradition, combines abhinaya and dance in one movement; the school of the Kathakalis talk for hours with their hands walking about the stage and divide up the dance conversations with pure dance interludes; thus giving the whole a system of drama and dance combination. With their elaborate facial masks made of rice flour and their gorgeous costumes, the powerful play of eyes and eyebrows, the gesture language becomes almost a vivid speech. Often song accompanies them and drums keep the rhythmic balance. Every dance drama is introduced by a prologue known as the Purappad done by a man and a woman in character as an introduction to the dance play which is to follow. It contains briefly the basic principles of the pure Natya or dance. Full of force the men express pure vigor and the women in their mohini atam, kummi, and shari dance show perfect feminine grace. Famous among their themes are the stories of Rugmangada, of Lalita and the baby Krishna, of Rama and Sita, of the killing of Dussasana, of Arjuna and all the famous episodes of Hindu religion and mythology.

Folk dancing throughout India is seasonal, and where the classic dance tends to be in a definite order, has a strictly recognised form and a complicated system of footwork. The folk dancing is far more spontaneous. One of the most beautiful and vivid types of folk dancing is that of Manipur. Strict Vaishnavites by religion, they have transferred to their dancing all the episodes centring round the lives of Sri Krishna, Radha, the Gopis and Gopas as they lived and danced on the banks of the silvery Jamuna river and under the Kadamba tree at Brindaban. Their dancing, too, like all Indian dancing is divided into the Tandava or vigorous type and the Lasya or soft type. But in both styles, the movements are full of a rare grace, with a lilting movement of the body and a gentle waving of the head in a circular motion forming a rhythmic unison of hands and figure. Being folk dances, they have not such a complete and comprehensive gesture language in a tabulated form of particular mudras. But they have certain very expressive gestures which convey meanings and they use the elastic circling of wrists with supple undulations of the whole arm. They take into consideration the fact that, according to their teachings Sri Krishna and the Gopis only danced when they felt the inner urge to do so. The people of Manipur have shown in every turn this inner feeling or Bhav ; this bliss or Anand.

Usually the dances are danced at night on a maidan, where a kunja or dance house, constructed with dry corn stalks and decorated with bunches of hanging leaves and flowers has been erected or else in a big paved courtyard called the Natya Mandir, built so that it faces the actual temple. Among the famous motifs of the various Ras Leelas described in the *Srimad Bhagvatha*, their religious book, is the dance of Maha Ras, a marvellous feat of technical brilliance, full of swift turns, leaps and eloquent poses coupled with melting arm movements. It is taken from the theme that one night when Sri Krishna was walking in Brindaban, the full moon spread it's soft radiance all around the shining white sands of the river, a gentle breeze fluttered over, wafting the scent of the thousands of creamy malika blossoms that peeped like many stars everywhere. A whispering stillness pervaded the atmosphere, and he was filled with an inner joy to dance. So he began to play sweet music on his magical flute which could only be heard by Radha and the Gopis and none else in the world. They heard it and came forth to bow in worship to his will and danced with him in pure rapture. He danced too, and so quickly did he move, that every maiden seemed to feel that he was at her side.

In Rajputna and Marwar, there is the dance of the Vanjaras, a tribe of gypsies. Their springtime dance, celebrating the festival of blossoms, is fascinating. Forming into a square and hitting their sticks criss-cross, their anklets clinking and the sunshine making jewel-like lights from the moving shades of colour, they look like wind blown poppies sweeping along with unconscious grace. Again, the famous Kijri dance which is performed during the rainy season; a dance of propitiation to the rain god so that he may bless them with a very successful harvest. It is during this season that dances are done for little Ganesh the fortune-giving elephant-headed god.

The spring festival, however, is a time of merrymaking. It is the time when nature is bright with colour and the Vasant-utsava is celebrated. Gay songs and dancing thrill the air. Closely allied with it is the Holi or Carnival of Colours; when the sprinkling of coloured liquid and tinted flowers is done to celebrate the coming of the budding blossoms and the mysteries of awakening nature. Coloured powder is moistened and thrown by people at each other, and groups of them start dancing and singing, calling forth nature, which is alive with the pale mango buds. Their fast movements and clapping hands extol the feeling of love and adoration for Mother Earth, which is bursting within themselves; impregnated as they are with the consciousness to the changing phases of their native environment. Similar is the song and dance connected with the Jhulan Leela or play of the swing. This is the time when the baby image of Lord Krishna (the impersonation of eternal youth) is placed in a cradle and rocked. It is an autumnal festival, when all the leaves are turning red; the fields are like waving green carpets, and the rains are nearly over. On a decorated swing scientillating with coloured flowers and tassels, they place the small image and sing and dance around, in majestic stepping, so that they seem to look like a flaming garland. Their gestures depict this pretty song

Little baby Krishna, I rock you in a cradle,
Under the shady banyan tree,
Whose green crisp leaves are playing cymbals with
each other ;
So go to sleep my little one.

Little baby Krishna, I have fastened your cradle with
silken strings,
And made for it a silver stand
Decorated with tassels and flowers ;
So go to sleep my little one.

The breeze is kissing the scented buds,
And with the perfume weaves a garland for you.
The milkmaids with tinkling anklets,
Are bringing your'curds and bread,
So go to sleep my little one.'

Then comes the festival of the Divali or Thousand Lights, when whole villages are lighted with hundreds of little oil lamps. The peasants sing and dance as they go to worship. Crackers are fired and fireworks fill the air with noise, so as to drive away all evil spirits and to celebrate the conquest of Lord Vishnu (the preserver) over Narkasur the demon of hell. The songs accompanying the pageant of dance are in praise of peace and good will on earth and the fact that because the days are getting longer and fuller, the people will spend happy days of harvesting.

Folk dancing has its root in nature. Being people of the soil, the peasants live and move and have their being in natural surroundings. To them, the seasons of nature are like the human phases of life. Their dance is the outward evidence of their inner feelings, emotions and simple religious beliefs, Their movements are a pantomime of what nature would say if we could understand her language. It is the same with the dancing of even the people of the hills ; the Gonds, the Bhils, the Todas, the Santhals and other who dance essentially to express a particular emotion. Herein lies the essence of Indian folk dancing ; its material yet symbolic depiction of beliefs founded on religion like the classical dance, but still its unbounded contact with nature which keeps something personal for the free development of the imagination.

Indian classical dancing has, within the last few years, begun to play a very important part in the country. The renaissance, as it were, has become so universal that amateurs and professionals alike apart from each other have taken it up seriously. And in a short time, it has come to play an equally important part in films as well. Light beautiful songs are illustrated with dances and have lent enchantment to the scene. And it is possible to do a great deal in spreading this dance art through the films. By their exhibition, much of provincial tastes in dancing has been overcome. The exquisite statuesque dancing of Tanjore, has been shown through pictures and greatly appreciated by thousands throughout the other provinces. The dance of Manipur, is now known and praised everywhere. It has been the same with the folk dancing of the Kathakalis, of Rajputana, Marwar and other places. Presented artistically, danced with feeling, bodily grace and rhythm the films have been able to make the dances of India, all-India's. In stories of village life, folk dances have played more than a mere artistic part. They have created a reality of atmosphere and lent a meaning to the theme, which every person in the audience has been able to understand. And with the growing urge for dance recitals in the main cities of India, with the realistic beauty of settings, colour, lighting and the pageantry of costumes, the Indian dance will become once more a matter of national pride. It embodies Indian culture which has come through centuries ; the essence of philosophical thought in its conceptions effects the background of sculpture and paintings, and portrays the outward expression of human emotions.

PROFESSOR BENI PRASAD

M. A., PH. D., D. SC.,

Was born near Agra on the 19th February 1895. He began his education at the village school and continued it at Agra, Allahabad and Cawnpore standing first in most examinations and winning numerous prizes and scholarships. Passed the Sanskrit Prathama and Madhyama examinations in 1911 and 1915. Research scholar in history from 1916 to 1918 and Assistant Professor in History from 1918 to 1923. Studied and travelled in Europe from 1923 to 1926 taking his Ph. D., and D. Sc., (Econ.) from London University in 1926 and 1927. Head of the Politics Department in the University of Allahabad since 1927.

Dr. Prasad has published numerous articles in Hindi journals and periodicals and his books include "*History of Jahangir*", "*Theory of Government in Ancient India*", "*The State in Ancient India*", "*The A B C of Civics*", "*The Democratic Success*", all of which are in English. In Hindi he has published "*Surasagar*", "*Gulistan*", "*The Ancient Civilisation of India.*"

His public activities include the editing of "*Pratap*" at intervals from 1913 to 1918, and association with the All-Indian Seva Samiti, Allahabad since 1921 and with educational and literary institutions.

THE EDUCATIONAL STATE

ALL social life and organization is implicit with bye-education and has an intimate bearing on formal education. The home, the neighbourhood, the vocation, the state, the religious congregation, the currents of opinions and feelings, the traditions and prejudices, relationships, friendships, animosities all affect the development of personality, the formation of character, the acquisition of knowledge and habits of thought and action. They determine the spirit, the ethos, of society and may neutralise or seriously modify the influence of school and university. But, in spite of being interconnected, they rarely constitute a harmonious whole. Partly, they represent a clash and compromise of interests and tendencies. Some of the latter are likely to accord with the influences radiating from the school and would, therefore, be strengthened by them. In this context formal education represents in itself a social influence, operating in close conjunction with all the other social influences.

ASSOCIATIONS

The character and results of education are affected by all the associations through which social life expresses itself and which themselves reflect the salient features of social stratification, distribution of wealth and diffusion of knowledge. Education has been dominated through the ages mainly by the ideals of the church, the state or powerful political parties.

In ancient India education was religious in its foundations and placed the chief stress on a study of sacred lore. *Inter alia* it inculcated the sanctity of the social order as instituted by the gods or by the sages under divine inspiration. Chinese schools taught the worship of ancestors and the ethical life as defined by the ancient saints. Until the nineteenth century every boy in an Islamic country began with the *Holy Quran* and if he pursued his studies far enough, was expected to master the *Hadis,* in preference to anything else. During the Middle Ages European education was controlled mainly by the church and laid the highest store by theology. Medieval scholasticism comprised the study of logic and metaphysics but it could never free itself from dogmatism and the time was spent in justifying faith through dialectical reasoning.

There is one other influence which theology has exercised on education. It has often painted human nature as essentially evil and sanctioned harshness in methods of instruction. Asceticism has placed a premium on monotony and drudgery in instruction.

The progress of science has gone a long way to secularise the outlook but the religious congregations have not yet relinquished their hold on education. In India they have established separate schools, colleges and even universities partly to confirm the young in the faith. The various Christian missions have established schools with a religious bias in many countries in the world. The control of education by the churches has occasionally been one of the major issues in politics in several countries such as France and Spain. And in spite of reverses, the Church still asserts its claims. As late as 1930 the Encyclical letter of Pope Pius XI on the Christian Education of Youth, while recognising the concern of the family and civil society in education, stated that the right of the church is "*absolutely superior......to any other title in the national order*".

MILITARISM

Next to religion, militarism has been the most potent influence in the history of the school. It has stressed training in arms and also a number of pastimes to fill the long gaps of leisure in the life of captains and soldiers. Archery, swordsmanship, tactics and strategy formed the chief items in the education of Kshatriya youths in ancient India and, *mutatis mutandis*, in the training of the sons of warriors and other would-be soldiers all over the world. Not to speak of Sparta, where all education was dominated by the barrack, the only direct provision made for education by the government in Athens concerned the military training of youths between sixteen and twenty. Roman education was always militaristic in ideals.

* cf. Edmund Holmes, *What is and what might be*.

Scions of the European nobility during the middle ages often served as pages from seven to fourteen, and then attached themselves as squires to knights until twenty-one. The education of a knight consisted of seven arts—reading, versification, chess-playing, swimming, hunting, tilting and archery. The squire attended on the knight in tournaments as well as in battle.

The influence of militarism is perceptible also in the assimilation of the discipline of the school to that of the barrack. Harshness has been upheld as conducive to hardihood. The public school system in England was deemed to have received the highest compliment when the Duke of Wellington observed that the battle of Waterloo had been won on the playing fields of Eton. Literature itself has been one of the most persuasive means of militarist propaganda. The epics and ballads cultivated in the seats of learning have sung the glories of war. History, as it has been studied so far, is largely a record of wars and battles.

THE STATE AND BYE-EDUCATION

The state has usually been the most powerful of associations, with comprehensive and compulsive membership, wielding physical force, maintaining a social order and co-ordinating the spheres and working of other associations. But it has occasionally been overshadowed by church or functional associations; oftener it has stood in close alliance with one or more of them and in any case it has reflected their influence. Its organisation has radiated an educative influence in accordance with its principles. It has, to borrow the language of Aristotle, fostered a type of virtue in citizens in harmony with the spirit of its constitution. The Greek philosopher felt that citizenship differed necessarily under each form of government. Two thousand years later Montesquieu echoed the same opinion.

THE STATE AND EDUCATION

It is, however, not merely the bye-education which is profoundly affected by the state. Government, as its executive organ is called, has a share in determining the facilities, the scope, the methods and the tone of the education imparted in schools, colleges and universities. It pays at least some of the pipers and calls the tunes; it favours or discourages, rewards or penalises, the inculcation of certain views; it permits or prohibits the adoption of certain techniques of teaching and discipline. If the state were based on the principle of creativeness of personality to the exclusion of all contrary influences, it would universalise education, psychologise it completely and refrain from imposing any dogmas whatever. But the control of education by a centralised bureaucracy facilitates indoctrination, hampers reform and encroaches on the legitimate freedom of teachers. Education inevitably suffers when teachers have no voice in the control of their profession and have merely to carry out orders. To the extent that the state departs from the principle of creativeness and violates the dignity of man as man, it restricts the facilities of education to the few, dominates the school in an autocratic manner and perverts the methods to suit its real or supposed interests. But no state however powerful and well-organised, can succeed completely or permanently, in controlling the forces which even imperfect education is calculated to set in motion. There results a dualism between the principle of education and that of the state which works injury to both, generates discord and provokes revolutionary explosions.

DIFFUSION OF EDUCATION

No government can, specially in modern times, dispense altogether with education, lest the supply of ministers, officers and clerks be dried up and social and economic life be reduced to a fatally low standard. But a despotic government, haunted by a sense of insecurity, fighting shy of all change and, therefore, wedded to the *status quo* often aims at the restriction of education to a few classes.

The Holy Alliance which sought to render revolution impossible after the Congress of Vienna deliberately narrowed the facilities of education. Pobyedonoscev (1827—1907) who weilded considerable influence under two Czars in Russia argued that if the peasant learned to read he would only gain the consciousness of his poverty. Accordingly, the mighty minister strove earnestly for the preservation of ignorance among the Russian masses. Gentile, the philosopher of Italian Fascism, declares that secondary education is by its nature aristocratic, made for the few and imparted by the few.

Democracy, on the other hand, tends to bring home the necessity of mass education. We must educate our masters said Robert Lowe on the morrow of the Reform Act of 1867 which admitted nearly a million new votes to the franchise in England. Within four years the Gladstone ministry placed a measure for compulsory primary education on the statute book. The advances towards responsible government in Europe, the United States and the British Dominions were accompanied by expansion of educational facilities. When Japan modernised her government in the seventies and eighties of the last century. The reformers urged that there should be no village with an ignorant family and no family with an ignorant member.

GOVERNMENT AND SCHOOL DISCIPLINE

Government has often sought to imprint its own spirit on the educational institutes organised or permitted by it. For instance, Spartan militarism was writ large on the training of youths between seven and thirty. They were to be brought up in courage, endurance, obedience and loyalty but not into culture and refinement.

The government of Prussia forbade the kindergarten of Froebel in 1851 because its freedom was antithetical to its own autocracy. The Czarist government forced the resignation of N. I. Pirogov, curator of the Kiev Educational Region who dared to introduce pupils' courts as a measure of student government in schools in his jurisdiction in the sixties of the nineteenth century. Apart from specific prohibitions and prescriptions, the school discipline tends to assimilation with the spirit of social control. If the latter is harsh, the school is marked by repression and severity of punishment. If, on the other hand, social control is true to the constructive role and relies on persuasion rather than force, the school fosters the expansion of personality and punishment recedes into the background.

It is doubtful if the advance of educational psychology would have sufficed, without a move towards democracy, to transform the methods of school discipline in the nineteenth century. Quintilian in ancient Rome, Comenius and Lock in modern Europe as well as many others perceived the evil of corporal chastisement, but their ideas had to be revived by Russeau, Pestalozzi, Froebel and Herbart in a more congenial environment before they were translated into practice on a wide scale. As Herbert Spencer put it, the style of school discipline approximates to that of the contemporary rational government. If adults are fit only for political tutelage, children may be deemed fit only to be beaten. If government is based on distrust of the people, education is liable to be based on distrust of the child, resulting in needless restraint, repression and demoralisation.

NATIONALISM

Since the French Revolution and Napoleon, the school and the university have been harnessed openly into the service of nationalsim or imperialism, sometimes in conjunction with other ideals. During the reign of Czar Nicholas I, Count Uvarov, minister of education from 1833 to 1840, summed up his policy by proclaiming to all educators in Russia that the general task consisted in establishing such education for the nation as will unify in itself the spirit of Orthodoxy, of Autocracy and of Nationalism.

The Russian, Prussian and Austrain governments utilised the school ruthlessly to assimilate their Polish subjects to their own culture, outlook and interests. Everywhere in Europe and America the school has been pervaded by the spirit of nationalism. Textbooks of literature, history, civics, and even geography have inculcated national pride. For instance, the report of a committee on studies and textbooks of the public schools of New York City laid down in 1922 that the textbook must contain no statement in derogation or in disparagement of the achievements of American heroes. It must not question the sincerity of the aims and purposes of the founders of the Republic or of those who have guided its destinies......*

In countries with overseas possessions, imperialism tends to become the creed of the school. The Scout Movement, in-

* See C. Hoyes *Essays on Nationalism*, p. 114.

augurated in Great Britain by Lord Baden-Powell has been tinged with imperialism. Bertrand Russell cites the case of a teacher who was dismissed from her post in a school at Coventry because she declined to salute the flag on Empire Day. *

In overseas possessions the dominating powers have sought to inculcate loyalty in the schools, distorting the history of the subject peoples in the process. Incidentally, it has involved the discouragement of indigenous scholarship. In 1935 for instance, the British Government in Burma appointed a committee to inquire how the imperial idea might be inculcated and fostered in educational institutions. The committee recommended, *inter alia*, that the chairs in the Burma University connected with imperial studies, e. g., civics, history, geography and economics, should for the most part be held by men of British descent trained in a British University.

On the other hand, a subject people, following the law of psychological compensation, locates its utopia in the somewhat distant past and gives a strong revivalist tinge to its own independent schemes of education. Here the danger is that education may lose touch with the trends of modern life. Imperialism, and the resistance it provokes, are calculated often to introduce racialism at the expense of humanitarianism into education.

LOYALTY TO GOVERNMENT

Many a government, specially of the non-representative type has insisted on loyalty to itself as an article of faith in education. An extreme illustration is furnished by the case of a Japanese professor who suffered dismissal, boycott and ruination in 1912 for daring to question the necessity of the suicide of a station master who had been responsible for delaying the Mikado's train for an hour or two. The *hari kari* was so noble a manifestation of devotion to the throne that it was a sin to regard it as erring on the side of excess.†

Certain official regulations in pre-war Germany laid down that teachers must be qualified to rouse and nourish in pupils

---

* *Education and the Social Order* p. 144.

† E. C. M. Joad, *Liberty Today*.

love for the Fatherland and for the ruling dynasty. According to an order of Kaiser William II the schools were to create in the youth the conviction that the doctrines of socialism are contrary, not only to God's decrees and Christian móral teaching, but are in reality incapable of application and are destructive both to the individual and the State.

From 1906 onwards, a number of students have been expelled, teachers dismissed and school managers forced to resign in India because they were wanting in loyalty to the government of the day. A strong tradition of liberty of thought has been established in Western and Northern Europe and in the United States but teachers or students there can profoss communism only at their peril. Every one is expected to bear general loyalty to the foundations of the social order of which government is a part.* Government now touches life at so many points and engages in so many activities that it tends to represent a working philosophy of society. A rigid demand of loyalty to government may resolve itself into a demand for allegiance to a very extensive body of social, economic and political doctrine.

EDUCATION AND POLITICAL PARTIES

Napolean Bonaparte stated frankly that his principal object in founding a teaching body was to have a means of directing political and moral opinion. This tendency itself reaches its climax when political parties with totalitarian philosophies attain to power and begin to control the entire educational organisation for the propagation of their doctrines and the perpetuation of their hold on the coming generation. As the Russian diplomat Rakovsky said, "*We are a congregation*".† The Communist dogma reigns supreme, unquestioned and unquestionable, in every school and university in Russia. It is reported that a young Communist, Sten, ventured to observe that every

*Compare the broad generalisation of Kant who declared that "rulers are simply interested in such training as will make their subjects better tools for their own intentions."

† See also Sidney Webb, *Current History*, February, 1933 p.536, for the pose of the Communist Party as the spiritual power in Russia. Also W.H.Chamberlain, *Foreign Affairs*, January, 1932, p.291, Arthur Feiler, *The Experiment of Bolshevism*, tr. S. S. Sterning. pp. 188 ff.

S. SARDUL SINGH CAVEESHAR

young communist must seriously work out all questions by his own experience and thus become convinced of the correctness of the general line of the party. The proposition was promptly denounced by the official organ of the Union of Communist Youth as at best the formula of a petty bourgeois revolutionary individualist, not the formula of a Bolshevic. Sten's young communist is some sort of critically thinking personality, who has no concern with the collective experience of the party.* Close observers of Russian education hold that concentration on propaganda lowers the quality not only of general but also of vocational education.

ITALY

The Fascisti Government in Italy signalised its accession to supremacy by re-organising education. The schools are to turn out good Italians, with patriotic minds and hearts and with Fascist convictions. A few years ago a decree made it compulsory for university teachers to swear allegiance to the king, his royal successors and to the Fascist regime. *I promise loyally to obey the constitution and other laws of the State, to teach and to fulfil all other academic duties with the purpose of educating honest citizens, faithfully to the country and to the Fascist regime............"*

During the last fourteen years a number of school masters and professors have been dismissed for their hardihood in criticising the policy of the Fascist Government. †

GERMANY

An identical policy has been followed, only with greater rigour, by the Nazi dictatorship in Germany since January, 1933. Several years earlier the original Nazi programme of twenty-

*W. H. Chamberlain, *op. cit.*, p.233 ; on want of freedom, also Arthur Feiler, *op. cit.*, pp.194 ff. Compare also Julian Huxley *A Scientist among the Soviets*, p.38.

†As an instance of the general policy of dominating the mind it may be mentioned that in March 1926 the Mayor of Milan suspended the Italian National Convention of Philosophers because their discussion had centred on the problem of freedom of thought. The Italian minister of Education congratulated the Mayor on "having taught an elementary lesson to the philosophers." (See *Current History*, 1931, p.535.)

five points had advocated the suppression of liberty not only of the press but also of education. Herr Hitler was reported to have declared that the most important issue for the National Socialist Party is not the taking over of power, but education Education in the Fascist corporate state is not education in the school alone, but in every milieu (path) or society.

The chief aim of education is defined in "*My struggle*" as physical fitness and preparation for National defence in the spirit of 1914 by means of obedience and absolute subjection to the will of the leader which must be expressed by the teacher..........Only after that is the acquisition of knowledge.

To this supreme necessity intellectual honesty is frankly sacrificed. According to Dr. Frick, German Minister of the Interior, the effort of educationists must be to produce the man political, who in all thoughts and actions is rooted in his nation and inseparably attached to its history and faith. Objective truth is secondary, and not always to be desired.* On the 19th of July, 1934, the newpapers reported a speech by Herr Friendrich, Storm Troop leader, in the course of which he told the Hanover High School that the criticism of the Nazi ideals must cease and to rather be wrong with your leaders than right against them.

In this background it is not surprising that the Bavarian Teachers' Union adopted a decree to the effect that the task of the Teachers' Union is to develop the school in the patriotic and National Socialist idea ....There must be training to blind obedience to the teacher.†

---

*C. E. M. Joad, *Liberty Today*. p.114 Cf. also the following from Herr Rust, Prussian Minister of Education : "I except from the teachers that they give to their pupils the fundamental principles of the philosophy and the idea of National Socialism.........Not to remain neutral and objective in the school, not to make the child into a cold observer, but to awaken in him enthusiasm and passion. It is a question of eternal and divine values and not one of cold reality."

†C. E. M. Joad, *Liberty Today*, p.189 also quotes a letter from Elizabeth Bibesco to the *Times*, May 11, 1934, reporting that a professor of ethnography in a German University went into exile in Switzerland because he was threatened with imprisonment for refusing to obey the command to teach that the Japanese were Aryans. Even before the inauguration of the Nazi regime, Dr. Becker, once Minister of education, propounded the theory that the teacher was essentially a state servant and was in duty bound to influence children towards the official point of view.

During the dictatorship of Marshal Pilsudski it was dangerous for a teacher to question the propriety of strong government in Poland. The modern dictatorship endeavours to control thought and emotion through text-books prepared to order, lectures specially doctored for the occasion, a press in leading strings and the radio sounding to the prescibed tune.

THE STATUS QUO

Not only government but society at large has often insisted on the school assisting the maintenance of the *status quo*. It has been openly avowed that education is the means of transmitting national or group culture and ideals as they are and that it must promote national or group solidarity.

It has, therefore, been characterized by artificial conformity to the received traditions and dogmas.* It has tended to become a matter of external forms. Success in examinations passes for culture ; correct behaviour is mistaken for strength of behaviour ; information masquerades as knowledge and mental discipline is upheld as an end in itself. Sanskrit and Arabic or Persian in India, Greek and Latin in Europe were regarded for long as the supreme subjects of study because they were supposed to involve discipline. Mathematics was justified on the same ground for those who seemed to possess no aptitude for it. Science was excluded from the curriculum of a liberal education because it was not disciplinary enough. It has often been forgotten that it is the transmission of *life* which is really

After the Nazi revolution, instruction is given in racial questions ; great emphasis is laid on the glorious history of Germany and the shame of 1919-32. 'Non-Aryan' professors have been turned out. On April 25, 1933 a law was promulgated against the overcrowding of the German universities. Students are admitted only in numbers consistent with the opportunities in the professions for which they wish to prepare themselves.

Candidates for admission to German universities may be debarred on the score of political heresy. All Markist and anti-national students were ousted from Prussian universities. Non-Aryans are not admitted to the inner student life of the university.

* Sociologists complain that ideas which shock prevalent habits of thought incur social and even academic opposition and endanger one's position in the University (C. H. Cooley, *The Social Process*, p. 367).

important* and that culture itself is imperfect unless it assists the adaptation of old traditions and philosophies to the new environment and its possibilities.

SUBORDINATION OF EDUCATION

The subordination of education to theology, social order and, specially, to the exigencies of politics has been reflected in social philosophy from the earliest times. Political theory often assumed that education is a means of realising political ends and should conform to the spirit of the constitution for the time being. Plato, dominated by the ideas of class and heredity, elaborated a great system of education for the guardians and made it the principle business of their life, but he was content to prescribe humble and spasmodic training for the farmers, not to speak of the slaves.

Aristotle believed that the art of education was subordinate to that of politics and that the educator must take his orders from the statesman as to the sort of character to be produced in the souls of the citizens. Both to Plato and to Aristotle, education is a branch of administration, like sanitation. The Greeks believed that good life and good citizenship involved each other but their conception of good life was somewhat narrow. Montesquieu observed that the laws of education would differ under different forms of government holding that "In monarchies they will have as their object honour ; in republics virtue ; in a despotism, fear. Montesquieu felt that the education of a people ought to be relative to the principles of good government.

Since the eighteenth century many philosophers have argued and politicians have quietly assumed, that as Hegel declared education is to form the citizen, not the man, thus shifting the emphasis from freedom to artificial discipline.

INTERDEPENDENCE OF EDUCATION

The subordination of education to political exigencies reflects the domination of forces which hamper the development of personality of all or some of the people. Apart from

* Cf. Thring who defined teaching as "The transmission of life through the living to the living."

ignorance of the true nature of education it represents an aspect of the pervasive and partly unconscious attempt to buttress a given set of social relationships. If the social order were based on the principle of full self-relation on the part of all the principle of equal and maximum opportunity it would foster education as if it were an end itself.

Education as guided growth would harmonize with the principle of social organisation and there would be no question of subordinating the one to the other. But if the social order is based on the denial of personality to some, it threatens to disintegrate at the touch of true education. Plato perceived that when modes of music, that is education, change, the fundamental laws of the state change with them. A defective social order seeks to pervert education, to dilute it with elements contrary to its true nature with dogma, unreasoning loyalty, mechanical conformity, false perspective, passion and prejudice. Social stratification affects the distribution and character even of vocational education.* Perverted education in its turn assists the maintenance of social perversions, though, it may be, only for a while. The two are interdependent.

There can be no doubt that the acquiescence of many peoples in the curtailment of liberty of expression and action during recent years has been partly to the persistence of obsolete method of education. Popular government was so imperfect that it failed to bring public instruction into accord with those principles of universal self-realization for which true democracy stands.

SOCIAL MOVEMENT

The search for the solution of the deeper problems of society always returns to education. At first sight things seem to move in a vicious circle. Social reform depends on the diffusion and reform of education while the latter depends on social reform. But the circle only illustrates the interdependence of all the aspects of life. Every phase of social organisation, traditions and institutions represents something like an integrated whole, because men adjust themselves to one another. But history has shown that the circle is liable to be broken at many points. The flow of thought cannot be damned completely ; reflection

* John Dewey, *Democracy and Education* pp. 372—73.

suggests changes ; discovery and invention lead to new occupations and new classes; ideas gather momentum ; contact with different ways of life and thought prompts reorganisation. Energetic agitation by a majority, or a determined minority may lead to a revolution. Gradual or sudden transformation in one sphere of social life affects all the others and results in a new alignment of social force. Every step in the revision of traditions, every change in the working of institutions, exercises a repercussion on the facilities and on the character of education. Similarly, the expansion of education, affects the tone of society and the character of its institutions. The social whole moves continuously to new wholes, though often with jerks, temporary dislocations and explosions.

RAPIDITY OF CHANGE

Change is affected in the modern age with a rapidity beyond all precedent. The facilities of transport and communication have created numberless contacts between groups and cross-fertilized all cultures. The advances in knowledge and invention have altered the basic condition of social life, multiplied wealth, created new vocations and classes, and affected the outlook on life. New possibilities of comfort, enlightenment and happiness for the whole of humanity have been revealed. Progress and retrogression in one country or sphere of life react on others with marvellous dexterity. Education cannot, therefore, stand still. At the same time education is now equipped with inner springs and engines of movement. It has become a science and progresses through investigation, observation and experiment. Educational psychology and child psychology have become disciplines in themselves. A vast number of educational experiments is being tried all over the world, and their results are being gradually incorporated in national schemes of education. As the new generation grows up, it is likely to live a life different from that of its predecessors.

SOCIAL ORGANIZATION

Education touches social life at all points so intimately that no reform in society can be permanent without a corresponding expansion or reform of education. For instance, the reforms projected by the court in Spain and by Joseph II in Austria in the eighteenth century miscarried because the people were not educated enough to appreciate them much less to sustain them. The political or economic gains of many revolutions have been largely lost because those who seized power for the time being failed to realize the imperative necessity of a wide diffusion of education. Democratic government has not fulfilled the expectations formed of it in the middle of the nineteenth century, *inter alia*, because the standards of education have not been high enough.*

The very moderate projects of rural uplift, co-operative credit and agricultural improvement launched by official or non-official agencies more than once in recent years in India have yielded little tangible result because they have not been accompanied by an attack on illiteracy. It has been forgotten that education alone can enable the agriculturist to retain the gains of improved methods ; otherwise they would be appropriated by those who seek to exploit him. Education furnishes the most effective of all incentives to improvement. Nor has it been adequately realized in India that education alone can habituate the pupil to a higher standard of living which is of the essence of the matter.

THE UNIFYING PRINCIPLE

Mass illiteracy, with its inevitable accompaniment, mass poverty, necessarily lowers the standards of honesty and efficiency in government and public life. Conversely, educational reform lacks stability until social organisation has been brought into line with the principles of equality of opportunity. T. N. Carver, (*The Economy of Human Energy*, 1924) describes the social process as "*a transformation of energy and its redistribution* ; *civilization is nothing but an accumulation of this transformed*

---

* "A free constitution which should not be correspondent to the universal instruction of citizens, would come to destruction after a few conflicts and would degenerate into one of those forms of government which cannot preserve the peace among an ignorant and corrupt people." Condorcet.

energy ; and progress, its better and better utilization". Education is by far the most potent agency in this transformation, redistribution, accumulation and utilization of energy.

The practical conclusion to which the interdependence of education and social organisation leads is that they are true to themselves in the fullest measure and escape the risks of perversion only when both of them conform to the principle of equal and maximum opportunity of self-realization to every member of the human race. If education were restricted or faulty, it would hamper the efforts of statesmen to improve the quality of social life. If social organisation were based on privilege and error, it would prevent education from being universalised or improved. If business were dominated by selfish motives of profits, if government were corrupt and tyrannical, it is not educative.

Progress is best achieved through simultaneous reform on all sides. Education is the art of fostering the internal order, harmony and balance. Politics is the art of maintaining conditions favourable to this development of personality. But the fundamental sociability of man renders internal development and external conditions interdependent. Men can neither understand nor uphold the requisite conditions unless their own personality has attained to a certain stage of development. Politics should furnish incentives to education ; education in its turn should strengthen the political impulse, the impulse to cooperate in promoting social welfare. Together they would make man master of his destiny.

EDUCATIVE ORGANISATION

The type of education outlined in the foregoing would foster the growth of personality in energy, aspiration, creativeness and variety of interests. But these traits can be sustained only if the social organisation offers scope for their expression. The bye-education emanating from society must harmonise with the education received in school and university. We return to the proposition that political and economic institutions should be so organised as to offer continuous opportunity for education. They must maximise the fruitfulness of experience and generate the maximum of power for social advance.

Civilisation is the ordering of society ; education is the ordering of civilisation. It is social life as a whole which must be educative in more than the intellectual sense of the term. Institutions rooted in the silent exertion of force by one group against another inspire fear or vanity and depress or pervert personality. Privileges and disabilities attached to birth generate a sense of injustice and diminish the chances of self-realization of large numbers. Social stratification which reduces the points of social contacts mars the educative value of living together. In multiplying interrelations, democracy furnishes the most effective antidote against retrogression.*

There is something wrong somewhere in social organisation unless it makes every person feel that he counts for something and that he is welcome to contribute his quota to social welfare. The political impulse, if it does not find the proper scope, degenerates into intrigue or gives way to spasmodic charity, reverie and contemplation of art for its own sake. In such a social content education becomes a means of personal aggrandisement in terms of the *status quo*.

THE EDUCATIONAL STATE

In this background a momentous duty falls to the state as by far the most powerful of associations in the modern age the duty of undertaking functions which require nation-wide organisation or international co-operation. These functions have to be so performed, and those of the other associations so co-ordinated, as to develop the personality of all. So emerges the concept of the educational state, the state resting on the principle of education in the fullest sense of the term, and, therefore, on the principle of self-control from within as contrasted with that of coercion from above. Education is the culminating point of politics because it is calculated to rationalise social direction. There follow three practical corollaries.

Firstly, the state should be so organised as to stimulate aspiration ; to furnish an incentive to knowledge and judgment ; to provide forums of discussion and means of participation in social life. In order to conform fully to the educative role,

* J. A. Thomson, *Gospel of Revolution*, p. 198.

government should not only be democratic but should also be conducted on rational principles. Aspirants to authority sometimes put a premium on non-rational elements. Thus Adolph Hitler announces that "*Propaganda is not science. The appeal must be directed to the emotions and only in a very qualified manner to so-called intelligence*".* If social, intellectual and international conditions are not ripe for democratic government, it means that conditions are not favourable to perfect education. But it does not controvert the proposition that fullness of education is impossible without democratic government.

Secondly, the functional, religious, cultural and other associations (including the family) must similarly be organised on the principle of education. It is the maintenance of this principle which is the chief aspect or function of co-ordination which falls to the state.

Thirdly, the state must universalise primary, secondary and university education and also place ample facilities for education within the reach of all adults. This, indeed, is the duty which the state owes not only to the cause of human progress but also to itself. Unless it universalises education, it is doomed to very low standards of efficiency and integrity.

Civilisation involves a strain on the mind ; the greater its advance, the severer the strain. Education is necessary to enable the people to bear that strain. Otherwise, civilisation would be accompanied by nervous breakdown. Education is adjustment to civilisation and must rise higher.

In the course of a telling criticism, George Bernard Shaw has said that "*there is no way out through the schoolmaster.*" But it will be more correct to say that there is no way out without him.

THE EDUCATIONAL SYNTHESIS

The educational synthesis implies the widest diffusion of education up to the highest grade ; the foundation of education on psychological principles and the conformity of social institutions to the educative role. To all this there is an international aspect. Social organisation and education are perverted

* Adolph Hitler, *My Struggle*.

from their true purpose and principles by militarism and imperialism which flourish on the weakness of other peoples, due *inter alia* to imperfect education and organisation and on the jealousies occasioned by the temptation to aggrandisement.

The recent inroads on education, for instance, in Italy and Germany are clearly traceable to the nationalistic fervour which foreign affairs, the prospects of revenge, redemption or aggrandisement have raised to white heat and which is embodied in absolutist regimes. Education has come in for its share in the general regimentation of life in the national interest in Austria, Poland, Japan and elsewhere.

The development of personality suffers yet more grievously in subject countries ; illiteracy, depression, frustration of life are the lot of multitudes. As in the realm of economics, so in that of education, the fortune of countries and nations are bound together. Enlightenment in the backward regions is a necessity not only to the good life of their inhabitants but also to the true and lasting welfare of the rest of the world.

The present disparity between the actualities of social organisation and the principles of education must disappear from every country and every group. The educational state cannot be safe in one region unless it is safe everywhere else. The educational synthesis, whether in the wider or in the narrower sense of the term, is an all-comprehensive and world wide synthesis. It would inaugurate the reign of reason and eliminate force from processes of social change. If education follows right principles, it enables the individual not only to adapt himself to the world as it is but also to change the world, to discern the possibilities of fuller life and to contribute to their realization.

Aristotle observed that the state was a plurality and that it was to be converted into a community by means of education. It is the educational synthesis which would make a community out of the nations which are at present in a state of nature, as Hobbes would say. Mankind today is living anywhere between the twentieth century B.C. and the twentieth century A.D. Universal and intensive education would make them a community. Parents educate their children neither for the world as it is at the moment nor for the world as it may be a century hence but for the world as they think it likely to be by the time that they reach manhood. If there is a tempo of reform they would prefer education for a reformed world to education for the world as it is. In the education for life at its highest, the antithesis between the education of the citizen or the national and that of the individual vanishes.

ORGANISED DEVELOPMENT

General Smuts observed that humanity "*has struck its tents and is once more on the march*". A transformation is inevitable but the possibilities of wrong moves and consequent wrangle and misery are also immense. The course of events since 1914 has demonstrated that the facilities of communication on which rest the hopes of educators have rendered possible new ways of dominating minds. Universal education would strengthen the sense of discrimination, steady and accelerate the march to higher and higher destinies. It would facilitate the realization of potentialities which have so far lain dormant with the vast majority.

As Stanley Hall said, man is "*the tadpole of what he is to be*". But none can attain to the highest point he is capable of, unless the whole of mankind raises to a high level of life. Civilisation is essentially a co-operative venture. Ignorance, error or perverted education in some regions lower the tone of life not only in those regions but also in a greater or lesser measure all over the world. The traditions that grow up in this enviroment tend to narrow down pleasures to animal appetites and to uphold force as an instrument of social relationships. It becomes difficult for ordinary people to follow the great personages, because they are not equipped for the enterprise. "*Progress itself*", said Novicow, "*is nothing but an acceleration of adaptation*". Education is the one sure means of adaptation to actualities and potentialities. Man is never satisfied with mere life ; he aspires, by the very nature of his being, towards good life. The distinctive character of human evolution is that adaptations to the environment contains possibilities of further development and a decisive point is reached when society becomes conscious of the various posibilities, exercises an intelligent selection among them, and organises them into a process directed towards well-thought out ends. It is the role of education to enrich the possibilities and to infuse breadth and foresight into the selection, the organisation and the ends.

CHUNILAL B. MEHTA

J. P.

Mr. Chunilal B. Mehta who was the Sheriff of Bombay for 1935-36 was born in 1888 and educated in the city which he has served so well. During his career Mr, Mehta has held the following appointments :—President of Bombay Shroffs' (Indigenous Bankers') Association ; Honorary Treasurer of the King George V Memorial Fund ; Editor of "*The Financial News*" ; member of the Governing Body of the Imperial Council of Agricultural Research and of the Executive Committee of the Federation of Indian Chambers of Commerce and Industry ; member of both the Managing Committees of Indian Merchants' Chamber, Bombay and Ramwadi Free Eye Hospital ; member of the Indian Central Cotton Committee ; on the General Committee of the Bombay Presidency Branch of the Indian Red Cross Society ; member of the Anti-Tuberculosis Committee ; Director of Alcock Ashdown & Co., Ltd, Bombay Bullion Exchange Ltd, Bombay Talkies Ltd, East India Cotton Association Ltd, Scindia Navigation Co., Ltd, Narottam Ltd, Narottam & Pereira Ltd and the Managing Director of Chunilal Mehta & Co., Ltd. He travelled round the world in 1917 and in 1930 he visited Europe and America.

In the following article Mr. Mehta deals with the problem of agricultural finance and in so doing expresses the hope that due consideration will be given by those concerned to the points he brings forward.

AGRICULTURAL FINANCE

THE problem of agricultural finance, put baldly, is that of meeting the credit needs of the agriculturists. These needs have been divided into three categories—short-term, intermediate, and long-term credit needs. The meeting of these needs, with minimum cost to the agriculturist and maximum safety to the lender, forms the crux of the problem of agricultural finance.

How best can they be met ? Commercial banks, here as elsewhere, do not as a rule take part directly in the finance of agriculture. In India, especially, loans to agriculturists fail to satisfy one essential condition requisite for bank advance *viz.*, credit worthiness according to the commercial banks' standard.

Co-operative credit societies fill the gap to a large extent in many countries. Our own experience of co-operation has, however, been none too happy. In fact, in spite of the illusive expansion in its nascent stage, it is doubtful whether co-operation has taken firm root in the country. The latest available figures, which are for 1934-35, show that agricultural credit societies in India numbered then about 80,000 with a membership of about 21/2 millions. The movement has, therefore, barely reached 5 per cent. of the rural population of the country. Nor were the existing societies in any way thriving. About one-third of them were not working properly, or were on the verge of liquidation at the time. Quite apart from all this in Australia, where co-operation is supposed to have been a great success, it has failed to meet all the credit requirements of the country, and the Australians have tended more and more to ask for and receive assistance from the State. In India, therefore, where the movement is admittedly tardy, we have to look beyond co-operation to satisfy the credit requirements of agriculturists

The Land Mortgage Bank is the natural complement of the agricultural co-operative credit society, in that, whereas the latter provides for the short and intermediate credit requirements of the agriculturist, the former is professedly a long-term credit institution. Here, at least in one Province, Madras, it has made considerable headway and has played a not inconspicuous part in helping to liquidate a portion of the rural indebtedness of the Province. But as, professedly, such banks are intended to cover only a part of the credit needs of the agriculturist, they cannot meet the situation in its entirety.

So then we come to the indigenous bankers, that much maligned community, with whose help, nevertheless, the major portion of the agricultural financing of the country is done. The indigenous banker was here before the joint-stock banking system and even now forms the most important financial institution in India. Very many towns in India have no banks, or branch of a bank, and in such places the indigenous banker is the primary sourch of credit. A strike of the indigenous bankers would leave an unbridgeable gap in the credit oaganisation of the country. The most important problem of the day is to make the indigenous bankers an essential part of the banking structure. It has definitely been said by the Indian Central Banking Enquiry Committee, and by Sir George Schuster, that without bringing the vast number of indigenous bankers within the structure of the Reserve Bank, it will not be possible for the Central Banking institution to control the money market of India, especially in the interior.

The subject of linking up the indigenous bankers with the Reserve Bank is taken as closed by the Reserve Bank, which derives the technical satisfaction of having fulfilled the statutory obligation of reporting within three years to the Government of India. Some of the conditions laid down by the Reserve Bank as being necessary for their incorporation into the banking system are :—

(1) they must confine their business to banking proper as defined by the Indian Companies Act ;

(2) they must maintain proper books of accounts and have them audited by registered accountants ;

(3) they must file with the Reserve Bank the periodical statements prescribed for scheduled banks ;

(4) the Reserve Bank will have the right of regulating the business of the bankers on banking lines, when necessary ;

(5) if an indigenous banker does not incorporate himself under the Companies Act, his liabilities in respect of his banking commitments will be unlimited.

The indigenous bankers have taken very pertinent exception to some of these stipulations. The Reserve Bank makes a great point of insisting that the indigenous bankers confine themselves strictly to banking business. In reply to that it is pointed out that the indigenous banker does in the main conform to activities covered by section 277 (F) of the Indian Companies Act. Where, in cases, they do conduct other business, it is pointed out that it would be greatly unfair to the indigenous banker to ask him to shed such business all of a sudden. For example, if an indigenous firm of bankers, besides banking business, is dealing in gold and silver ornaments and silver utensils as merchants, is it seriously suggested that, after linking, such business should be dropped? On the other hand, in some cases the dropping of such ancestral business would involve not only the closing up of a lucrative source of income, but might well prove a blow to the prestige of the indigenous banker in the locality.

The Reserve Bank must wait till it has started dealings with these persons, and till it is demonstrated to the Bank, in each individual case, that the continuance of a particular business would entail for the banking business such serious risk as to demand its discontinuance. The result which the Reserve Bank authorities desires to see at once, *viz.*, the elimination of all other business would be achieved in due course as the volume of banking business increases. When, after some years, some of the bankers on the register find that their banking business is of sufficient volume to make it attractive for them to shed all other business they will not need very serious persuasion to do so.

As regards the requirement of publishing the returns prescribed for banking companies by the Companies Act, it is pointed out that the publication of such returns, so that all and sundry may know them, would do more harm than good. However, it is explained by the indigenous bankers that all particulars wanted by the Reserve Bank authorities themselves will be readily supplied. They only say that the Reserve Bank should not rigorously insist on the publication of periodical returns.

In respect of other conditions stipulated by the Reserve Bank the indigenous bankers are in perfect agreement. They are willing, and prepared, to have their account books audited by registered accountants; they have conceded the right to the Reserve Bank of regulating their banking business, when necessary. As regards the question of unlimited liability to be borne by those who do not incorporate themselves under the Companies Act, indigenous bankers know it and undertake it with full responsibility.

Under the circumstances, when the indigenous bankers have gone more than half-way to meet the Reserve Bank, the Reserve Bank owes it to itself and the country to accept their point of view and work the scheme as slightly amended by them. The indigenous bankers are a force and a necessity in the Indian economic structure and it is the duty and responsibility of the Reserve Bank to do all it can to bring them within its fold.

Not only the Reserve Bank but other quarters also seem to view the activities of the indigenous banking community with disfavour, if not with actual hostility which is largely inexplicable considering the important role they play in the finance of agriculture. This seems to be because they are branded in the public mind, as an usurious, tight-fisted, money-grabbing lot who would do anything for a mess of potage. This stigma still remains inseparable from mention of their name. It is not generally understood that in spite of the so-called usurious rates of interest, charged by indigenous bankers on their loans to agriculturists they are losers on the whole.

The indigenous bankers, therefore, have viewed with great disquiet the recent debt conciliation Acts and Bills passed, or waiting to be passed, in the different provinces of the country. Most of the provisions of these bills are against the creditors and in favour of the debtors They seem to be conceived with the idea of penalising the indigenous bankers, who are, apparently, thought of as persons fattening on the sons of the soil. This is by no means the whole truth of the matter. On the other hand the village *sowcars* are in an even worse plight themselves than the agriculturists. They are heavily in debt, having had to borrow from town *shroffs*, and others for the conduct of their business. This debt can be liquidated only by the realisation of the amounts *owing* to them by the agriculturists. If obstacles are placed in the way of realising such amounts they will be reduced to a very sorry plight indeed. This phase of the matter seems to have been ignored completely by the sponsors of the various bills in the provinces. The result of putting such measures into operation is likely to cause the indigenous banker to withdraw from his age-old business, to the serious detriment of the national economy, for co-operative banks cannot fill their place completely, at least not in the near future.

It is fervently to be hoped that due consideration to this aspect of the matter will be given by those who are responsible for guiding the destinies of the nation.

J. C. KUMARAPPA

M.A., (COLUMBIA) B.SC. (SYRACUSE) F.S.A.A. (LONDON)

Mr. Kumarappa who was born on the 4th January 1892 received his early education at Doveton and Wesley College, Madras completing it at Columbia University and New York and Syracuse University. After graduating he served articles in London and qualified as an Incorporated Accountant in 1918 going into practice as such in London and afterwards in Bombay.

During his career Mr, Kumarappa has carried out an economic survey of Matar Taluks in connection with the Gujarat Vidyapith in 1922. He was in editorial charge of "*Young India*" from May 1930 to February 1931 and was appointed, after the Karachi Congress, as a Convener of the Select Committee on the Financial Obligation between Great Britain and India, publishing the report in July 1931. He was again in editorial charge of "*Young India*"from October to December in 1931 and was sentenced to one year's imprisonment in the same year and to two years in 1932. He has been a member and an internal auditor of the Managing Committee of Bihar Central Relief Committee. He was authorised by the Bombay Congress to form, under the guidance of Mahatma Gandhi, the All India Village Industries Association of which he is now the organiser and Secretary.

His publications include "*Public Finance and our Poverty*", "*A Survey of Matar Taluk*", "*Organisation and Accounts of Relif work*", "*A Brochure on Publice Debts of India*", "*Philosophy of the Village Movement,*" "*The Nation's Voice*" (as Joint Editor) and the Congress Select Committee's Report on the Financial Obligations between Great Britain and India.

In the following article Mr. Kumarappa analyses certain conditions which he considers are conducive to world peace and goodwill between nations.

CONDITIONS FOR WORLD PEACE

AT a time like this when life on our planet is under the gloom of ever-deepening war clouds it is well for us to pause for a moment to consider the source and significance of conflicts between nations.

We are often told that wars have always been and will always be as long as human life lasts and that it is no good attempting to fight against nature. Is this defeatist mentality justifiable? Has war been caused by the same conditions throughout the ages?

IN FORMER TIMES

History teaches us that the wars of ancient times were mostly waged to satisfy the personal avarice of individuals. Nadir Shah cast his greedy eyes on the hoards of India. Alexander hoped to become the conqueror of the world. Napoleon had his heart set on Moscow. Others there were who had family feuds to settle or entered on them through mistaken religious zeal. Such wars were limited in time and space. Rarely do we come across a conflict between a nation and a nation. Nor do we find in the past the every day life of the people organised and lived on the basis of war as a permanent factor. Wars swept over humanity once in a while like thunderstorms, carrying death and destruction in their wake. But such disturbances did not become the basis of normal life. Hatred and suspicion were not abiding factors in national life.

AT PRESENT

As we look around we find no such personal reasons for modern struggles. An analysis will show the root cause may be traced at present, to economic reasons—to control raw material supply, to secure markets and to undermine competition.

If it is possible to trace the root cause of war it will be simple enough to prescribe the conditions for peace. So far we have diagnosed that wars at present are the outcome of economic conditions. If the prevalent system of economic organisation calls for periodic wars then the remedy lies in changing such a system and not in patchwork peace negotiations which cannot be lasting. We cannot be content with merely treating the symptoms. A further study will show wherein lie the interests which stand to gain and how it is only these interested parties that organise wars. With clever propaganda a whole nation is led into believing that it goes to war with another nation while, in reality, it is only vested interests that are in conflict with one another and array the common people against each other in battle formation to fight the cause of the vested interests.

AVARICE

The object of such vested interests is to make profits by their economic activity. Therefore, they choose such fields as are likely to pay best. Production of raw material does not pay as highly as the production of finished goods. So those interests do not concern themselves with the business of raw material production but confine themselves to the production of finished goods. Even here goods for satisfying primary needs do not pay as highly as luxury goods. Hence it is that we see the paradoxical position of dire poverty and over production at the same time. Thus these interests have organised themselves so as to skim the cream off for themselves. Successfully to do so it is necessary to compel others to take up the less paying lines. There must be raw material producers to supply the needs of these interests. Such compulsion is best applied conveniently by political control of such people. Political control can be secured only by organised violence. Having once obtained political control it is simple enough to regulate railway rates, currency and exchange and customs so as to make raw materials flow to places where they are needed and to set in a current to take back the finished goods manufactured by these vested interests.

POLITICAL

This political control entails maintenance of armies, navies, air forces, safe-guarding of ocean routes by sprinkling forts and strongholds at strategic places, building railways and roads for the rapid movements of troops etc. All these are fundamental needs of such an organisation and they cost money. It will not pay to debit all these to cost of production and so with the political power at the disposal of the vested interests these are charged up against the taxes. These are wrong charges as they are part of the expenditure of the economic organisation itself. As long as these legitimate and proper charges of production are not debited against the costs of production, the profits shown are false and the taxpayer bears the burden of such an economic organisation while the vested interests enjoy the fruits of it.

HIGH STANDARDS OF LIVING

Without such subterfuges it is not possible to make centralised mass production pay. It is often claimed that mass production makes for higher standards of living. This is illusory. It helps a higher standard of living to be maintained in one country at the cost of lowering the standards in another. Hence, looking at the situation as a whole, it cannot be said to be advantageous. If Italy wants a high standard it has to make Abyssinia a raw material producer for her factories and a ready market for her goods. This is the secret of economic imperialism and modern warfare. Even if Italy conquered Abyssinia to get the raw materials from Africa to Milan it has to control the Suez. This brings Italy into conflict with other peoples who also depend on Suez.

COSTS

This cheapness of mass production is not a reality when the cost to the nation is taken into account. Apart from paying for it through the taxes, the nation loses on many counts. A good many able bodied persons who would be otherwise engaged in production have to be detailed to learn the science of destruction in the army etc. It is not possible to compute in terms of money the cost of these lives which will have to be thrown away in case of a war. These items also should enter into the computation of cost of production but they are invariably left out. During the European war of 1914-1918 England emptied its universities to send her youth to the war front. Many of these young men were killed. Had they survived they would have been the generation that would have been at the helm of affairs today. Who shall say that the bankruptcy of statesmanship we witness in England at present is not the cost that England pays as her contribution to the loss of culture caused by that war ?

So far we have seen the direct costs of mass scale production which through political power are charged against the taxpayer and the nation to make the product sell cheap. Now we should turn towards partial burdens which are taken off indirectly.

Plant and machinery for the production of standardised goods on a mass scale have to be worked at a definite speed. Both at a lower speed than this or at a higher speed it will not be economic to run them. This means, that in practice, production of goods takes place at a rate determined largely by the capacity of the plant. Unhindered competition goads producers to capture as much of the market for themselves as possible and hence the capacity of the producing plant is generally greater than what the market calls for. This situation leads to over-production and forced selling.

This excess production is taken up in two ways, (1) by forcing the goods on to other people with the help of political power and (2) by turning to the supplies of the Army which is not only a non-producing unit of society but is definitely a destructive factor. Hence the latter provides a convenient outlet for the excessive productive power. An ordinary consumer will resist forcing more than his needs on him but he can be made to pay taxes which can be utilised for purchasing goods or maintaining services for military purposes.

SPREADING COSTS

In our own country the railways and trunk roads which play an important part in military equipment, are largely paid for as current expenditure by the taxpayer. The military aspect of it is forgotten. We need only lift the seat in a third class railway compartment to know the real purpose of it. Under the seat will be found brackets for keeping rifles. If the railways were charged up as military equipment the taxpayer will kick at it, so the cost of such equipment is spread out and is partly paid for by the passengers.

Heavy production plant can make bicycles in peace time and armaments during war. If such plant were meant only for bicycles, it would not pay. On the other hand we cannot be making armaments during peace time as such products will become waste if they become out of date after a while. It is, therefore, necessary to produce armaments only when required. It is impossible to put up the plant at short notice and hence the plant has to be kept always ready.

These considerations show the mutual dependence of mass production and war on each other. The one cannot exist without the other.

Thus, present day wars are the outcome of economic causes inherent in the prevailing system of economic organisation which locates its plant in one place, gathers its raw materials from the four corners of the earth and distributes its products back again to the rest of the world. This necessitates :

1. Control of raw material production to ensure that the plant works steadily at its economic speed,
2. Control of the routes and methods of transport of raw materials,
3. Control of labour force,
4. Control of markets for finished goods,
5. Control of accessibility to such markrts
6. Spreading of the cost over a larger number of persons thån the consumers only.
7. Safeguarding investments abroad.

This situation calls for political control over the lives of other people.

All these requisites cannot be obtained without compulsion and force.

These then are the causes of war.

REMEDIES

If we are clear as to the causes the remedy will follow easily. Any remedy to be effective will have to be based on the malady.

It has often been suggested that all countries should enter into a pact to disarm. As long as centralised methods of production are allowed to be used freely, the need for war is there and disarmament will, at the most, be only a lull. The evil will come to a head some day. Agreements to create a balance of power or a League of Nations will only open up more doors of intrigue.

A permanent cure lies in banishing the cause of war. Our analysis shows that mass production by centralised methods needs as a prerequisite control over the lives of others and other nations and this ultimately leads to war. The motive force for mass production is profit and this is needed to obtain a high standard of living. A high standard cannot be maintained without exploiting others. Therefore, the remedy indicated is to reserve the centralised methods of production in the hands of the state which alone can afford to take a detached view and to confine the production of everyday needs to decentralised small units. The attempt made by some schools of thought to change human nature to an extent where everyone will think of the common good and submerge self interest in such national interest is no doubt idealistic but human nature being what it is, a certain amount of profit motive has to be allowed for. As it has been proved repeatedly that profit motive in centralised production has been disastrous to the nation, it is necessary to use this method of production devoid of profit motive and so it has to be left entirely to the state.

As against the disarmament school of thought there are those who say "*If you desire peace prepare for war*". Our recent history has demonstrated clearly that armament has never saved a nation. Germany in 1914 and Czechoslavakia in 1938 were highly armed but armaments did not save them. Armaments not only direct production from creation to destruction but also take away the productive manhood, develops a mentality of hatred and suspicion and lowers the value of human life.

Therefore, we are driven to the conclusion that there can be no peace until nations realise that they can raise the standard of living of their own nationals above a certain limit only at the cost of other nations, that profit motive should be taken out of centralised production but allowed only in small decentralised units, that the progress of humanity does not depend on and is not commensurate with the multitude of things possessed, that work has a definite contribution to make to the cultural development of humanity and that war dehumanises man. We should educate the people in standards of values that really help to bring about a civilization where our duty to others will be emphasised more than our own rights and a simple life rather than a complex one. When we are able to achieve this we shall have attained conditions conducive to world peace and good will between nations.

BALKRISHNA MADAN,

M. A., PH. D.

Was born 13 July, 1911, in Sialkot and educated at Arya High School, Bhopalwala (Sialkot) and the Dayanand Anglo-Vedic College, Lahore. Stood first in the Province at university examinations; Intermediate (1929), B. A. (Honours) in Economics (1931) and M. A. Economics (1933), with a high first class and record marks in the last examination.

He was the Founder-Secretary and President of the Punjab University Economics and Political Science Society (now two Societies); Research Scholar in Economics, 1 January 1934, Research Assistant in the Economics Department, 1 April 1935; University Lecturer in Economics, April 1936; Officer on Special Duty for enquiry into Resources, Punjab Government, July 1937; first to obtain the Doctorate degree (in Economics) of the Punjab University, February 1938; elected Member of the Executive Committee of the Indian Economic Association, December 1938, Officiating Honorary Secretary of the Indian Economic Association, May to September 1935; Author of '*Some Aspects of Rural Economy in the Punjab*' (1934); '*Sales of Gold in 120 Punjab Villages*' published as Pamphlet No, 1 of the Punjab Board of Economic Enquiry; "*India and Imperial Preference : "A Study in Commercial Policy*" published by the Oxford University Press, London, 1939; and numerous articles in economic and financial journals.

THE POSITION AND PROSPECTS OF INDIA'S FOREIGN TRADE

AMONG the many changes in the economic sphere during the last decade not the least important have taken place in the field of international trade and trade policy. Indeed, far reaching shifts have occurred in the volume, character and direction of international trade at once consequence and cause of developments in policy which have necessarily had their repurcussions in this country.

TRENDS IN VALUE, VOLUME AND PRICE LEVEL, COMPOSITION AND DISTRIBUTION

The table on p.444 gives a general conspectus of the position of India's trade during the last ten years.

Table Showing the General Position of India's Sea-borne Foreign Trade during Twelve Years, 1927-8 to 1938-9.

	Quantum of		Price-Level of		Terms of Trade (Indices of imports received for a given quantity of exports)	Value (Rs. crores of)		Balance of Trade in Merchandise	Balance of Transactions in Treasure (Gold and Silver)	Total Visible Balance of Trade	Percentage of Trade with the U. K.	
	Exports	Imports	Exports	Imports		Exports (including re-exports)	Imports				Exports	Imports
1927-8	100.0	100.0	100.0	100.0	100.0	319	250	+69	...	...	...	...
						(292)	(255)	(+37)				
1928-9	106.1	105.2	97.5	96.4	101.1	338	251	+86	−34	+52	21.4	44.7
1929-30	108.0	103.4	90.2	93.2	96.8	318	239	+79	−26	+53	...	...
1930-1	96.6	82.5	71.5	80.0	89.4	226	164	+62	−24	+38	...	...
1931-2	82.5	70.6	59.2	71.7	82.6	161	126	+35	+55	+90	27.9	35.5
1932-3	74.9	81.4	55.3	65.2	84.8	135	132	+ 3	+65	+68	28.0	36.8
1933-4	86.2	72.9	53.5	63.5	84.3	151	115	+36	+57	+93	32.2	41.3
1934-5	87.8	84.1	54.1	63.0	85.9	155	132	+23	+52	+76	31.6	40.6
1935-6	88.4	86.6	56.9	62.1	91.6	164	134	+31	+36	+67	31.5	38.8
	(89.4)	(91.3)				(154)	(149)	(+5)			(29.9)	(31.7)
1936-7	107.4	79.8	57.2	62.8	91.1	202	125	+78	+14	+92	32.2	38.4
	(109.9)	(86.1)				(192)	(142)	(+50)			(31.0)	(31.0)
1937-8	103.1	95.7	62.9	71.1	88.5	189	173	+16	+14	+30	33.3	29.9
1938-9	...	...	...	...	...	169	152	+17	+14	+31	33.7	30.7

Figures within brackets refer to the trade of India proper (excluding Burma), i.e. in respect of exports, they include Indian exports to Burma, but exclude Burman exports : in respect of imports, they include Indian imports from Burma, but exclude imports into Burma. For 1937-8 of course all figures relate to India exclusive of Burma. The separation of Burma has effected the Indian balance of trade adversely to the tune of about Rs. 15 crores : in 1937-8, exports to Burma were worth Rs. 11 crores, while imports from Burma were valued at Rs. 26 crores. India's exchange position is not however, immediately effected thereby, since India and Burma form one currency and exchange unit.

A familiar fact brought out in the above table is the great reduction with the onset of the depression in the value of India's export and import trade as a result of a fall both in quantum and price level. Indian exports declined by nearly 60 per cent. from an everage of Rs. 325 crores during the triennium 1927-30 to Rs. 135 crores in 1932-33, the lowest level touched during more than a quarter of a century. In 1936-37, they had revived by nearly 50 per cent. to Rs. 202 crores still only 60 per cent. of their pre-depression level. Much of the earlier decline in value up to 1932-33 was due to a fall in the price level (45 per cent. since 1927-28 against an equivalent fall in quantum of 25 per cent); most of the later increase in value has come from a recovery in quantum (43 per cent. in 1936-37 since 1932—33).

Imports declined no less severely from Rs. 247 crores on an average during the three years 1927-30 to Rs I15 crores in 1933-34 and have experienced small recovery since, being only Rs. 134 crores in 1935-36 and Rs. 125 crores in 1936-37. As compared to exports, the fall in the value of imports was due relatively more to a fall in quantum (over 29 per cent. in 1931-32 and 27 per cent. in 1933-34) and less to a fall in the price level (35 per cent. in 1933-34). A slow fall in the price level of imports continued after 1933-34, when a slow rise was taking place in the price-level of exports. The index of quantum of imports improved from over 70 in 1931-32 to 81 in the next year, fell again to 73 in I933-34 and revived to 87 in 1935-36 dropping to 80 in 1936-37.

BALANCE OF TRADE

The terms of trade, or the index of the price-level of exports in terms of imports moved against India up to 1933-4 to the extent of nearly 16 per cent. This meant that India had to part with a relatively larger quantity of her exports in order to obtain a given quantity of imports, or in return for a fixed quantity of exports India received year after year a smaller quantity of imports. From 1933-4 to 1935-6 there was a distinct improvement in this respect, but in 1937-8 again there has been a small unfavourable reaction.

A direct consequence of the enormous shrinkage in the value of export and import trade was the practical disappearance of India's favourable balance of trade in 1932-33—when it was only Rs. 3 crores—and its slow reappearance since.[1] India's large export surplus in commodity trade has been used to finance her vast invisible imports of civil, military and political, shipping and commercial, banking and financial, services.[2] The gap created in the balance of payments by the reduction of the surplus of merchandise exports over imports has been filled by large exports of gold since the first devaluation of the sterling and rupee in September 1931. Altogether, exports of gold from that date to the end of March, 1939 have totalled Rs. 335 crores. This enormous outflow of gold also marked the reversal of a long continued inflow which had won for India the unenviable reputation of a sink for the precious metals.

The accumulation of large foreign currency reserves out of the combined excess of commodity and gold exports over imports upto 1936—7, the sustained firmness of the exchange value of the rupee in consequence, the slackening of the stream of gold exports thereafter and the failure of the balance of trade (for India and Burma together) to improve, with the resulting strain on the rupee's external value—are incidents of a parallel story in a complicated context. The almost permanent deterioration in the balance of commodity trade (even including Burma) together with the uncertain prospect of gold exports being maintained at their present level may make a downward adjustment in the exchange value of the rupee imperative. Such a change will however immediately magnify the huge sterling liability in terms of rupees and is likely to be put off until it becomes inevitable.

INDIAN EXPORT TRADE AND WORLD TRADE

It may be of interest to relate the changes in India's export trade to world trade as a whole. The proportion of the gold value of world trade represented by India fell abruptly from 3.56

1. The year 1936—7 would appear to have been exceptionally favourable to Indian exports, and the heavy balance of trade in India's favour in that year was rather abnormal.

2. The annual foreign obligations of India in these various respects have been estimated at anything from 50 to 75 crores of rupees.

per cent in 1929 to 2.76 per cent in 1932, this was accounted for largely by the special severity of the slump in the prices of India's staple exports, though the fall in quantum was also greater than in the case of world trade (nearly 32 per cent against 25 per cent.). India's share of the value of world trade improved to 3.19 per cent in 1936, but receded again to 3·07 per cent (including Burma) in 1937 : this improvement was due mostly to a relative increase in quantum (43 per cent. in India's export trade as against only 15 per cent. in world trade up to 1936) ; the price-level recovered little.

CHARACTER AND COMPOSITION OF TRADE

The character of commodity composition of India's export trade has also undergone important changes in conformity with changes in world trade. The most outstanding change in the latter in this respect has been the increase in the share of raw materials of the total value of world trade from 33 per cent. in 1932 to 39 per cent. in 1937, a corresponding decline in the proportion of foodstuffs from 29 to 23 per cent. between the two years and no change in the percentage of manufactured goods, 38 per cent in both years.

Correspondingly, the share of raw materials of India's export trade increased largely from 42 per cent in 1932-3 to 50 per cent. in 1935-6, that of foodstuffs declined appreciably from 28.5 per cent to 23 per cent. between the two years, and of manufactured goods fell slightly from 29.5 to 28 per cent. The decline in the relative importance of foodstuffs in Indian exports as in world trade is evidence of the trend to self-sufficiency in respect of food in the former food importing industrial areas of Europe. The increase in the porportion of raw materials made up of a relative increase in both quantum and price level is characteristic of the phase of economic recovery since 1932-3 and is in part the reflex of the earlier decline in the same from 1929 to 1932.

COMMERCIAL POLICY

The reduction of international trade has been accompanied by an important redirection : tariffs, quotas, exchange controls, clearing and compensation agreements, contingents and licensing systems, prohibitions and monopolies besides the manifold devices of administrative restriction and descrimination have canalised the relatively shrunken volume of trade.[1] International economic specialization is at a discount. The courses of trade are governed less by the principle of comparative advantage and more by strategic, political and sentimental considerations, than before. Deliberate policy and non-economic objectives dominate the field of international economic relations. More perhaps than at any previous time economics is made a real hand-maid of politics.

BILATERALISM

An important new development arising out of the above factors is the bilateralisation of trade, the equalization of the value of commodity exchanges or of total trade and financial claims between individual countries. Bilateralisation cuts at the roots of the natural division of economic functions between different regions variously equipped in respect of productive resources to contribute to the sum total of the world's wealth. Of peculiar severity has been the incidence of bilateralism on Indian trade : there has been almost a complete disappearance of the familiar triangular trade between India, Europe and Great Britain. The result can be described as nothing short of a revolution —so swiftly did it come about : India's large import in commodity trade with the U. K., Rs 34 crores in 1929—30, surplus has been replaced by an appreciable export balance—Rs. 16 crores in 1936—37 and Rs. 12 crores in 1937—8. In direct contrast the huge favourable balance of trade with Europe, Rs. 35 crores in the former year has contracted to a relatively modest figure—Rs. 16 crores in 1936—37, and a bare 7 crores and 4 crores respectively in 1935—6 and 1937—8. Accordingly, the proportion of Indian exports taken by the U. K. steadily advanced from 21.8 per cent. in 1929—30 to 28.9 per cent. in 1931—32 and 1932—3 and 32.2 per cent. in 1933—4. It fell slightly in the two years following but revived to the same level in 1936—7. The share of five most important European customers—Germany, France, Belgium, Italy and Netherlands—declined from 24 per cent in

1. Though world trade has increased recently, the revival in trade has lagged behind recovery in production and there has been on the whole an important diminution in the relative importance of international trade and transactions as compared to home trade and transactions.

1929—30 to 22 per cent in 1932—3 and 16 per cent. in 1934—5, and stood at 17 per cent. in 1936—37. The continued tendency to increased dependence on the U. K. market appears particularly noticeable in respect of figures of trade for India proper (excluding Burma) : the share of the U. K. increased from 29.9 per cent in 1935—6 to 33·3 per cent in 1937—8 and further to 33·7 per cent in 1938—9. It is interesting to note that the greater part of the increase in the relative share of the U. K. of India's export trade had occured by 1931—2, i.e., *before* the coming into force of the Ottawa preferences in the U. K., while the greater part of the decline in the relative share of European countries took place *after* the Ottawa preferences began to operate in 1932—3. The important indirect repurcussions of the U. K.'s Imperial preferential policy on India's export trade to other countries, are here brought into significant light. It also appears how preference was less important than other factors taken together in enlarging the U. K.'s share of India's export trade.

RECIPROCAL PREFERENCES

The exchange of reciprocal preferences over a wide range of trade between the U. K. and India has, however, been an important factor responsible for the distinct division of India's trade towards the U. K. more in respect of exports than of imports : the proportion of preferred Indian exports consigned to the U. K. increased from 33 per cent. in 1931-2 to 42 per cent. in 1934-5 and 40 per cent. in the next two years, that of preferred Indian imports went up from 40 per cent. in 1932-33 to 46 per cent in 1933-4 and receded to 44 per cent in the two years following. The relative share of the U. K., however, increased in the case of non-preferred exports as well : it went up from 17 per cent in 1932-3 to 23 per cent. in 1936-37.[1]

PROTECTION

Not less important than preference in the redirection of Indian trade has been the influence of protection. Its effect has naturally been manifest on the side of Indian imports. For one

1 See Madan, B. K., *India and Imperial Preference*, Oxford University Press, London, 1939, Chapter VI.

thing, the protection of sugar has wiped out a large item on the import side, almost entirely imported from non-British countries and consequently increased the relative share of the U. K. even in respect of non-preferred imports from 36 per cent. in 1932-3 to 39 per cent in 1933-4 and 1934-5.

Though reliable statistics are not available, it is apparent that the volume of industrial production in India has rather rapidly risen during the depression, the severest effects of which have been confined to Indian agriculture.

FOREIGN TRADE AND INDUSTRIAL DEVELOPMENT

The reference to industrial expansion in India behind a protective traffic with some consequent reduction and redirection of foreign trade naturally brings us to a consideration of certain vital questions. What is the proper place of foreign trade in the national economy of India? Where is a compromise to be effected between a policy of finding wider markets for Indian exports abroad, and industrial expansion at home? How is the industrial development likely to affect the volume of foreign trade and the degree of economic touch with the outside world? To what extent is the volume of international trade a measure of the aggregate economic prosperity of this country? Wherein consists the special urgency of fostering the industrial development of a country like India? No review of foreign trade, however brief, can be fruitful without a reference to these fundamental aspects.

INDUSTRIALIZATION

To take the last point first, the case for industrialization of India has been often and ably put. It hardly needs restatement. Only a few considerations which have not been generally emphasized need to be pointed out here. 'Industrial expansion presents a general solution of all the most difficult problems of the agricultural countries.'[1] As the process spreads it enlarges the internal market for agricultural products and reduces the external dependence of the farmer. It compensates—and the more so the more it spreads—for the contraction of foreign markets. It insures higher prices to the agricultural producer

1. *The World Agricultural Situation*, Rome, 1934-5, p. 11.

than he would obtain otherwise. It tends to make the economic system more balanced, more capable of absorbing shocks of violent economic disturbance abroad.

India is among the very few agricultural countries which possess all the essential requisites for the development of a fairly balanced economic organisation within their limits, other countries suited for all round development, and more or less ahead of India in many respects being the United States, Russia and China.

But at present Indian exports consist for the most part of low priced primary products which are little touched by human hand or skill, and contain a much higher proportion of value contribution by nature than the products she imports. Thus in effect India allows easy access to her natural resources to the enterprise, technique and organisation of other nations, while her own human resources remain definitely and appreciably underemployed.

It may, indeed, be argued that any attempt to hasten industrial expansion would only result in uneconomical transfer of labour and capital and throw more resources out of employment than it would bring into employment.[1] But this argument overlooks the fact that much of the skill, enterprise and organisation that could be employed in potential industrial enterprise are hardly ever employed otherwise. They do not in fact exist in the measure in which they are bound to develop with industrial expansion, with 'the stimulus and culture of a nervous town life' in 'the busy hives of industry and thought.' Industrial expansion will not, therefore, simply transfer resources but create new factors and awaken fresh faculties.

Moreover, broadly in the world as a whole there has been going on a continuing shift of demand away from the products of agriculture. With a rising standard of life, the proportion of income spent on the necessaries of life, and among necessaries of food, tends to decline. An increasing part of income tends

1. For some recent views on this point see H. L. Dey, *The Indian Tariff Problem*, 1933, pp. 29-31 ; B. N. Adarkar, *The Indian Tariff Policy*, 1936, Chap. 1 ; *Indian Journal of Economics*, April, 1937, articles on "Tariff Policy in India" by C. N. Vakil, "Some Second Thoughts on our Fiscal Policy" by B. P. Adarkar, "Tariff and Employment and its Nature," by Ch. Sitaram Shastry.

to be directed towards articles of comfort and recreation for the employment of leisure. Accordingly there has been a tendency for agricultural wages, at least in the old countries, to be maintained permanently below those in manufacturing industries. And the special stimulus low wages afford to production tends to perpetuate them. "There is thus a *prima facie* case for giving some compensating artificial stimulus to manufacturing industry in general, especially in countries which are not already encumbered with an intense manufacturing development."[1]

Besides, the production of agricultural products by primitive methods is subject to diminishing returns or increasing costs. The elasticity of the supply of India's exportable products is therefore small. The terms of trade are, in consequence, less favourable to this country than they would be if her production were carried on under returns which diminished less sharply, or if the supply of her products were more elastic. For "if a change in the scale of production of the home country very materially alters her cost of production, so as quickly to bring it into line with foreign prices, the gain from trade is on a small scale, and is more or less fortuitous. But if when big changes are made in the scale of operations the comparative costs at home are altered little, that means that the fundamental economic structure of the country is such as to provide a permanent and solid basis for gainful trade."[2]

The application of modern methods to agriculture in foreign countries has effected a marvellous improvement in its efficiency and greatly lowered its costs of production. Indian agriculture is still carried on predominantly by primitive methods with rude implements. Moreover, any large scale application of machinery to Indian agriculture is not practicable : man power is very abundant and cheap and has no alternative employment if replaced by machinery. Indian agriculture thus works under a more or less permanent handicap. And the weight of this handicap is likely to grow, if the pressure on the land is unrelieved. Industrialisation by alleviating the burden on the soil may check the relative retrogression of Indian agriculture.

---

1. R. F. Harrod, *International Economics*, p. 53.
2. R. F. Harrod, op.cit., p. 34.

But how is the industrial expansion of India likely to affect the volume of her foreign trade, and how will changes in the volume of trade affect national economic well-being?

INDUSTRIAL EXPANSION AND VOLUME OF TRADE

The effects of the industrialization of India on the rest of the world are likely on balance to be beneficial in the long run.

In the short period some contraction of the volume of trade may take place on account of the substitution of home output for imports. But this effect would tend to be counteracted by the special stimulus afforded to imports of producers' goods like machinery and plant, raw materials and semi-manufactured goods which might be imported in increasing quantities. This tendency is indeed already in evidence. In course of time such imports may also be progressively replaced by home production, but the resulting increase in the purchasing power of the population and in their standards of life will create an effective demand for new imports of high grade goods for final consumption. The older and more industrialised countries will also be continually moving forward to higher and higher forms of production, and the products of their specialised skill may continue to command a ready market. International trade may increasingly tend to become a specialised interchange of a varity of manufactures instead of a simple exchange of raw materials for manufactured articles; as the industrial substructure becomes more and more elaborate the superstructure of trade may also tend to assume a more and more complex aspect. But the ultimate effect of industrial expansion on the *volume* of foreign trade need not be adverse, and may indeed be directly favourable.

TRADE AND NATIONAL PROSPERITY

Even if industrial development should result in a contraction of foreign trade, however, the effects on the position of the agricultural producer need not be adverse. For it must be pointed out that the extension and development of the export trade is only part of the general problem of finding wider markets and better prices for the products of Indian agriculture. The markets may be external or internal. The immediate problem under examination on which commercial policy mainly fixes its attention is that of widening the foreign sources of demand for Indian products, but industrial expansion may afford the better solution of the general problem : it might do within the country what commercial policy seeks to do abroad.

This is only to repeat in other words the well-known dictum that the volume of foreign trade is not a true index of the economic prosperity of the country. This has become a commonplace of foreign trade theory, but needs to be kept constantly in mind in the study of Indian commercial policy. A large foreign trade is not an end by and in itself :[1] it must subserve the general economic welfare. Foreign trade is the measure of the degree of external dependence of a country. But a high degree of external dependence may indicate deficiencies in the national economic system, or testify to the efficiency and energy of its industry : it may be the sign of economic weakness as of economic strength. The extaordinary decline during the depression in the value of India's external trade has of course coincided with, and caused, extreme economic distress. But a decline in foreign trade may also accompany or directly follow from an increase of economic prosperity.

As Dr. Marshall has observed : "a country's foreign trade is likely to be increased by rapid advance in those industries which are already ahead of similar industries in other countries ; because such an advance increases her power of producing at a profit. But her foreign trade is likely to be lessened, or at all events its growth is likely to be checked by an advance in those industries in which she is relatively weak, because such an advance will tend to diminish her need of imports."[1]

I. Dr. Bowley and Mr. Robertson in *A Scheme for an Economic Census of India*, 1934, (p. 2) incidentally take into account the possibility that the policy of the country may well be the orderly contraction of India's foreign trade rather than its expansion.

I. Marshall, *Industry and Trade*, p. 15. Joseph Grunzel in his *Economic Protectionism* observes in an illuminating passage that "when an amount equal to or exceeding that which is gained in foreign trade is lost through the restriction of home production, then there is no gain, but eventually a loss is suffered. Importation and exportation do not stand in relation of direct communication, but are separated from each other by production and consumption, and hence a continually favourable inner balance may be able to offset an unfavourable outward economic balance." (p. 131).

It is common knowledge in India's economic history that the rapid growth of her foreign trade, beneficial as it was in many ways for the improvement and diversification of agriculture, also brought many evils in its train—the decay of indigenous industries, progressive ruralisation of the country, and an increase in the pressure of population on the soil. As an impartial observer of India's foreign trade remarked long ago : "the annual returns of the commerce of the U. K., the United States, Germany, and a host of other countries, are regarded as a barometer of the progress and prosperity of the nation. As far as India is concerned these afford us true indication of the industrial weather."[1] Again, "unlike most British possessions and specially the self-governing ones, the welfare of India depends far less on external trade than on internal development."[2]

CHARACTER OF TRADE

In judging of the effects on national welfare, the character of foreign trade has to be considered as well as its volume, and that is determined to a large extent by the character of a country's economic activity. Industrialisation may effect a favourable reaction in this respect and mitigate the predominantly agricultural nature of the export trade.

GENERAL AND FUNDAMENTAL CONSIDERATIONS

At this point, attention may be directed to the really potent means for the promotion of foreign trade as apart from artificial and subsidiary aids to development like tariff preferences and trade privileges. The only durable basis of a large and flourishing export trade are (i) an efficient and economical productive system ensuring quality and cheapness in the products ; (ii) an up-to-date system of trade intelligence and organisation to meet the varied demands of a ramified economic community ; and (iii) access on fair and 'equal' terms to the markets of the world.

LIMITATIONS OF PREFERENCE

It is necessary to remember, in the first place, the close resemblance between preference and production. Preference is

1. J. W. Root, *Trade Relations of the British Empire*, p. 161.
2. Ibid, p. 153.

production against foreign competition in the market of a third country. It is an artificial shelter based on discrimination. It places the preferred exporter in a position of unequal advantage against his competitor. It is not altogether an unobjectionable mode of fostering foreign trade, and not fully efficacious in all circumstances : preference of imports from one source implies penalization of other imports : preference of exports in one market breeds penalization of exports in other markets. Preference confers special benefits on a part to the trade and involves special burdens on the remaining part.

Whether the benefits outweigh the burdens of preference depends upon the relative importance of the preferred part of trade, the general tone of the economic situation, the importance of a country's foreign trade relatively to world trade, and the influence that changes in its commercial policy may exercise on international commercial policies in general. In this aspect the intermediate value of preference may be considerable. But altogether preference holds no promise of durable advantage comparable in the long run to that which attention to more fundamental factors may bring.

PRODUCTION AND MARKETING

Turning to a brief consideration of these fundamental factors, there is an urgent need, in the first place, for improving the quality of India's staple products as a means to the expansion of their exports. Particularly in the U. K. the fiscal advantage should be followed up by a determined effort to organise the marketing of products on a scientific basis in its commercial side. As the Indian Trade Commissioner remarked in his Report for 1928-29 and 1929-30 : 'a wide disparity exists in many markets between the prices offered for superior and inferior grades of the same commodity and this disparity may also apply to different articles competing with each other as alternative raw materials for the same industry'. (Section I). In some cases India produces and supplies the superior grade, e.g., linseed, in others the inferior quality, e.g., Broach cotton, and in still other cases, India provides both the fine and inferior varities. Now the differences in quality which are reflected in the price differentials may be due to climátic or other factors beyond human control. Sometimes, however, an unfavourable price is due to bad preparation for the market. Thus, for instance, Indian hemp for a long time arrived in the London market in a dusty condition; cotton has been sold mixed and therefore of irregular staple and sometimes also carelessly ginned; wheat and oilseeds occasionally contain foreign grains or dust; hides and skins are carelessly flayed; shellac contains dust and sand; tea often includes a high proportion of broken and powder. These instances are only meant to be illustrative and do not purport to be comprehensive. The point to note is that high quality almost invariably commands a premium, and the additional cost of better preparation for market is more than repaid by higher price secured as a result.

The Indian Trade Commissioner in his Report for 1932-3 observes that "where India loses ground is not through any deterioration of her existing standards but through failure to improve them as rapidly and as consistently as her rivals are improving theirs". (Section 1).

COMMERCIAL INTELLIGENCE AND PUBLICITY

Another important point which requires consideration is the appointment of Indian Trade commissioners in countries with which we have important trade relations. As competition becomes keener and the need for pushing trade by special efforts more imperative the development of a Trade Commissioner's service becomes a matter of urgency.

Indian Trade Commissioners have for many years been established at London and Hamburg; one Trade Commissioner was set up in Milan during 1934-5, and others have been stationed more recently at Tokyo, Zanzibar and New York. Trade Commissioners can play a useful part in the extension of export trade by steady and efficient organisation of commercial intelligence and publicity and forming of trade links. More and more, a foreign Commercial Councillors' service is becoming an indispensable adjunct of the machinery of trade development.

Lastly, and above all, it is necessary to secure equality, or as a large a measure of equality of treatment as possible, for Indian exports. Equality of treatment alone forms a satisfactory basis for a flourishing international trade. It represents the reign of law, the framework of order in international trade relations. Without it inequality, discrimination, and exclusion with consequent ill-will, suspicion and retaliation govern international economic relations. Of course inequality in commercial treatment is as much a cause as consequence of mistrust and mutual misunderstanding between nations. And a simultaneous attack on the sources of political and economic friction can alone establish political peace and commercial equality on a firm foundation. But in the absence of a bold and concerted advance along the whole front, even a limited approach to a large measure of equality of treatment, so far as conditions in the country and abroad permit, is certainly desirable.

EQUALITY OF COMMERCIAL OPPORTUNITY

The unconditional most-favoured nation clause is the sign and symbol of equality of treatment. It is the instrument for enforcement of the latter. Recently, however, serious rents have appeared in the fabric of equality, and the efficacy of the instrument has been considerably impared. Multiple devices of restriction and discrimination, apart from tariffs, have been employed to regulate trade and to evade the obligations of the most-favoured-nation clause : to an extent, indeed, they are fundamentally inconsistent with the maintenance of trading equality as traditionally understood. The task of repairing the damage done to the principle of equality can only be accomplished by the joint exertions of the most important commercial nations. Nevertheless, it would be an advantage if in the course of negotiations with other countries for securing wider opportunities for trade through trade treaties, the constant aim of Indian commercial policy were to be the promotion of a larger measure of equality than exist at present rather than the prepetuation of existing inequality.

When all is said, however, the factor of first importance in the immediate framing of tariff and trade policy remains, as has been already observed, the tone of the general international situation and the economic temper of the world. International trade may flourish and normal economic development proceed, if peace is assured and an underlying basis of confidence in the political field is established. So long as the constant shadow of war stalks the world, the essential base for successfully operating a liberalist commercial policy is lacking. And commercial policy must continue in an unusual degree to be a compromise of the ideally desirable with the practically attainable.

DR. MISS C. MINAKSHI
M. A., PH. D.

Has the distinction of being the first lady to obtain the Doctorate in Indian History from the Madras University which was awarded her for her thesis "*Social life under the Pallavas*". In response to our request for an article for "What India Thinks" Dr. Minakshi has sent us a portion of the thesis which procured for her the degree of Dr. of Philosophy in 1936 the full text of which has not so far been published.

The Kailasanatha Temple at Kanchi is a picturesque study of fact and it is a matter for some regret that we are unable to publish in this volume the beautiful photographs which Dr. Minakshi sent with her article.

THE KAILASANATHA TEMPLE, KANCI

"Nayorjjitaparakramarjjitamanena Sarvajjagannrpena
Ha takantakam pranatarajakam bhunjata :
Yasah sadrsamatmano bhavaname taduthapitam
Harasya harahasarupama timanamatyat bhutam."

"While this Prince (Rajasimha) enjoyed the whole world, which he had conquered by valour combined with polity, and in which he had killed rebels and humbled kings, he erected this extensive and wonderful house of Hara (Siva) which resembles (in its whiteness) his fame and the laughter of Hara."

—V. 10, Rajasimhesvaragrham Insc.

TO the west of the city, away from its noise and bustle, in the midst of paddy fields and tall grown prickly pears, stands Rajasimhesvaragrham of the Pallavas ; the Tirukkarrli of the Cola inscriptions and Tamil literature ; and the well-known Kailasanatha temple of the present day.

The great grandson of the great Pallava king Mahendravarman I, Rajasimha, the only hero on earth (Ekavirah) who bore on his head Siva as his crest jewel (Sivacudamanih) built in his capital city, Kanci, a magnificent abode for Sthanu more splendid than the Kailasa (Kailasalilamapaharati) and round its plinths inscribed in bold and beautiful characters of the period, a dozen verses which glorify his valour as a Ksatriya and praise his piety as a Parama Mahesvara.

RAJASIMHESVARAGRHAM

The Linga or the God of the temple was known as Rajasimhesvara and the shrine itself Rajasimhesvaragrham after its builder. Instances are not lacking to prove that it was the fashion of the Pallava monarchs to bestow their own names or surnames on the shrines constructed by them.

The Mandagappattu cave is known in epigraphy as Mahendra Visnugrham after the royal excavator Mahendravarman I ; the shore temple as Atiranaccandesvaragrham after Atiranacanda alias Rajasimha, and the Vaikunthaperumal temple as Paramesvaravinnagaren after Paramesvara alias Nandivarman Pallava Malla. Contemporary records maintained the name Rajasimhesvaragrham and this name continued to exist in epigraphy as late as the 13th century A D.

TIRUKKARRALI, ITS WRONG IDENTITY

The more popular name by which the temple of Rajasimha was known is Tirukkarrali ; and the part af Kancipuram in which the temple stands was called Tirukkarralipuram in a few Cola inscriptions from the temple. A great confusion has been caused by the mistaken indentification of the Tirumerrali, the sacred western temple, with the Tirukkarrali the sacred stone temple by the late Professor P. Sundaram Pillai.* He says "Since the above was written, epigraphy has offered a direct solution of the long standing question as to the age of Tirugnanasambandha. Visiting Conjeevaram in December 1895, I found that the archaic Pallava temple, now called Kailasanatha is the same as the one called Kachchi Mettali in the Devara hymns. If Mettali means the "western shrine", the name is certainly well suited to the direction in which the shrine

* In his '*Some Mile stones in the History of Tamil literature*' forming No. 3 of the Tamilian Archaeological Society Series.

now stands. But I am afraid it is a mere mistake for Kattali or 'Tirukkarrali' a name which occurs in several of the inscriptions of tbe temple. The substitution of 'Tirukkarrali' for 'Tirumerrali' wherever found in the hymns only improves their rhythm. The local Oduvars or habitual reciters of the hymns know of no place in Conjeevaram answering to the name 'Tirumerrali' and patient enquiry on the spot leads to the same nescience. We have, therefore, either to suppose that the temple of Tirumerrali celebrated in the Devar hymns is now gone to such ruins as to leave no trace whatever of it behind or to take that name to be an error for Tirukkarrali. I decidedly prefer the latter course, as the result of all the enquiries I was able to make at the spot. Other temples commemorated in the hymns are yet in existence and if Tirukkarrali were not Tirumerrali, there would be no mention in the Devara hymns of the one temple in Conjeevaram which, of all the shrines, is the most ancient-looking."

Having wrongly identified Tirumerrali with Tirukkarrali, Professor Sundaram Pillai goes to the extent of correcting the Tevaram hymns. Though he has added a note from Hultzsch's reports that there exists a temple named Merrali in the weavers' quarters, in Conjeevaram, yet he has failed to utilise the information given by that epigraphist and permitted himself to make inferences from the ignorance of the local Oduvars.

We shall see in a moment that these two temples are distinct from each other and that both of them have existed in Kanci since the Pallava days. I had the opportunity to visit the Tirumerrali and examine the inscriptions and its architecture. It is now one of the humblest of the temples in the town and is situated in the Pillaipalayam village. The inscriptions of the temple were copied by the Epigraphy Department in 1921, and the earliest of them belongs to the reign of the Pallava King Dantivarman. It is found on a slab built into the floor at the entrance into the temple and is much damaged. The regnal year of the king is lost, but mention is made of a certain Muttaraiyan chief who had petitioned for some charities for the Merrali as well as a Matha attached to it. The interesting points in the inscription are the mention of the name Tirumerrali and the reference to the Matha. Another Tamil inscription on the wall of the temple belonging to a Sambuvarayan confirms the name Tirumerrali. Therefore, there is no doubt that this temple existed sometime prior to the reign of Dantivarman.

The very fact that Appar sings of the Tirumerrali at Kanci proves that the temple was in existence as early as the day of Mahendravarman I whose contemporary the saint was.

Sundarar's detailed description of the same temple as situated in the midst of fields just outside the city of Kanci agrees well with the location of the present temple to the west of the town. It is perhaps the antiquity of the temple that reminded Sundarar of the glory of the early Pallavas and inspired him to speak of Kanci as the one city on the earth, the city of the Pallavas surrounded by a fortified wall.[1]

That the Tirukkarrali must be different from Tirumerrali is evident, and that the Tirukkarrali is none other than the Kailasanatha temple at Kanci is also certain from several Tamil inscriptions belonging to the same temple. Now a question arises as to why it was so called. The possible explanation that can be offered is that the construction of temples of sandstone and of granite was indeed a novelty at that time. The earlier temples had been built of brick and mortar and other perishable materials.[2] And the predecessors of the Pallava king Rajasimha. Narasimhavarman and Mahendravarman, chiefly confined themselves to the excavations of monoliths and caves out of rocks. A structural temple of sandstone and granite such as the Kailasanatha temple with its lofty Vimana enclosed all round by a number of beautiful shrines adorned with imposing sculptures and rich fresco-paintings ; this great and wondrous house of Hara was indeed a unique architectural achievement. And hence the name, the beautiful stone temple, found in the contemporary Sanskrit charters of both the Pallavas and the Calukyas and in the later Tamil inscriptions of the Colas.[3] It

---

1. Parur Pallavanur Madir Kancimanagarvay.
2. Cf. The Mandagapattu inscription of Vicittracitta.
3. "Silamayam Vesma Sasankamauleh
Kailasakalpanca Mahendrakalpah."—Velurpalayam Plates ; V. 18.
"Silamaya Rajasimhesvaradi Devakula" etc.—Kendur Plates of Kirtivarman II.

See also the Vakkalari grant of the same King.
The Cola Inscriptions of the Kailasanatha temple :
Nos. 82-84. S. I. I. Vol. I.

GAYA PRASAD SINGH
B.A., B.L.

evoked the admiration of even an enemy king. Vikramaditya II, whose artistic sense and piety are attested by ths endowment he made to the temple during his invasion of Kanci.

THE TESTIMONY OF THE PERIYAPURANAM

The Periyapuranam, a work of the 12th century A. D., makes a reference to a temple 'Kaccikkarrali'. An examination of the circumstances under which it is mentioned and a presentation of a short biographical sketch of Pusalar Nayanar as given in the Periyapuranam will enable us not only to realise that it is the Kailasanatha temple that the work speaks of but also the fact that the Saiva Saint Pusalar Nayanar was a contemporary of the Pallava King Rajasimha.

Pusalar Nayanar, a Brahmin resident of Ninravur (Tiruninravur) in Tondamandalam wished to erect a temple for Siva and attempted to realise money for the same. But not succeeding in his attempts to raise the necessary funds, he began to build a temple for the deity in his own mind in all its details such as the foundation, the compound walls, towers etc., and in the end fixed a day for the installation of the deity in the temple. At the same time, a Pallava king in Kanci was also building a Karrali (a stone temple) for Siva at a great cost. He also fixed a day for the installation of the deity therein and these two days happened to coincide.

On the previous night, Siva appeared to the Pallava king in his dream and asked him to change the date of the installation at Kanci as he was on that day to be installed at the temple built by Pusalar.* The bewildered Pallava king next morning went in search of Pusalar and eventually learnt from him the truth of the dream. The Pallava monarch returned to Kanci after

---

*"Kadavar koman Kaccikkarrali yeduttumurra
Madalan Sivanukkaka perunselvan vakuttal Seivan
Nadamalariyadarai tapikku mannal munnal
Yedalar konraivendariravidaik kanavilaidi."
"Ninravur pusalanban neditunal ninaindu seyda
Nanruni dalayattu nalainam puguvoin niyin
Konriya seyalainalai yolindupin kolvayenru
Konraivar Sadayartondar koilkondarulappondar."
—'Pusalar Nayanar Puranam, 'Periyapuranam' verse 9 & 10

paying his respects to the Saiva Saint. This is in short the story of Pusalar Nayanar. The dream of Rajasimha seems to be recorded even in the contemporary inscription in the Kailasanatha temple. The verse runs thus :

> "If in the Krita (age) kings like Dusyanta who saw the gods and were engaged by (saints) like Kanva would hear a heavenly voice without body that is not a matter of wonder ; but ah ! this is extremely astonishing, that Sribhara has heard that voice in the Kali age, from which good qualities keep aloof."*

The Periyapuranam account together with the reference in the inscription not only enables us definitely to fix the date of Pusalar Nayanar as the later half of the 7th century A. D., but also to identify with certainty the Kaccikkarrali and Tirukkarrali with the Kailasanatha temple at Kanci.

EDUTTAYIRAMUDAIYA NAYANAR

Yet another name by which the Kailasanatha temple was designated is found in three Tamil inscriptions† of the Vijayanagar period from the said shrine and whose texts are published by Dr. Hultzsch. These three contain orders issued by one Koppanangal or Koppanam to the authorities of the temple. Dr. Hultzsch identifies Koppanangal with the executive officer of Kambana Udaiyar at Kancipuram.

What we are concerned with is the new name of the shrine of Rajasimhesvarmudaiyar, also called Edudattayiramudaiya Nayanar. The latter name as it stands conveys no sense and what strikes one is that it is a misreading of the name Eduttayiramudaiyar Nayanar. Sine the 'Ta' in two of the three inscriptions is written within brackets in the texts published by Hultzsch, we may almost be certain that it is Eduttayiramudaiya Nayanar and not Edudattayiramudaiya Nayanar ; the former

---

* "Dusyanta pramukhaih srutambaragata vani sariram vina
Ksmanathaih suradrsvabhiryadi krite Kanvadibhih svikrtaih
Tannascaryamidam punah kaliyuge duribhavat sadgune
Sosransiditi tam giram mahadaho vismapanam sribharah."

S. I. I. vol I p 12.

† S. I. I., vol. I. pp. 118., 120, 123 & 125.

may be understood to mean the God who is praised with a thousand namams. The Hindus never conferred a meaningless name on sacred shrines and even the most popular one Kailasanatha for our temple may find an explanation in Pallava Epigraphy.

KAILASANATHA

Of the Kailasanatha temple we read in the Velurpalayam Plates : "Silmayam Vesma Sasanka Mauleh Kailasakalpanca Mahendra kalpah"—"(This king) equal to Mahendra built of stone a house for the mooncrested (Siva) which was comparable with the "mountain Kailash"; we have also in the inscription of Rajasimha a comparison of the shrine to the Kailasa mountain both in its height and in its beauty. "He (the king) erected this extensive and wonderful house for Hara which resembles (the king's) fame and laughter of Hara." This description is not a baseless panegyric but a picturesque study of a fact, namely, that the superstucture of the temple being constructed of soft sandstone did acquire a brownish-white colour.

Thus, it is clear that the comparison of Rajasimhesvaraghram both in its form and beauty to the mountain abode of Siva—the Kailasa mountain—sufficiently explains the present and the popular name Kailasanatha for the temple built by Rajasimha.

MOHMED ALI JINNAH

M. L. A., BAR-AT-LAW

Born on 25 December 1876 at Karachi and was educated in that city and in England. He married the daughter of Sir Dinshaw Petit. In 1906 he was enrolled as an Advocate of the Bombay High Court and was Private Secretary to Dadabhoy Naoroji in the same year. Member of the Imperial Legislative Council in 1910 resigning in 1919 as a protest against the passing of the Rowlatt Act.

During his career he has been President, Muslim League (Special Session), 1920 ; Member, Reform Enquiry Committee from 1923 to 1925 and Member Sandhurst Committee from 1926 to 1927. He was Leader of the Independent Party in the Assembly and a Member of the Round Table Conference ; President Muslim League in 1934 organising Muslims all over India on national platform to contest the elections to Reformed Legislatures in 1936.

As a contribution to "*What India Thinks*" Mr. Jinnah has selected the text of his Presidential Address to the Sindh Muslim League which he delivered in 1938.

AN APPEAL FOR UNITY

I thank you for the honour you have done me by asking me to preside over this All Sind Muslim League Conference. Sind has a wonderful history behind it and it gives me a peculiar pleasure that I should have the privilege of presiding over a great conference of Muslims.

I most heartily congratulate you for having established the District Muslim Leagues in almost all of your Districts and having organized the Musalmans of Sind in the manner in which you have done within such a short time. This great political consciousness and awakening that has taken place among the Musalmans of Sind is a great pointer and I feel confident that with the help of your selfless leaders and workers Sind will come into its own and set an example to the rest of India.

You know the efforts of the All India Muslim League to separate Sind were seriously started in 1927 and the demand to separate Sind was incorporated in the Delhi Muslim League proposals in March 1927. It was a hard and arduous struggle but, notwithstanding the strenuous opposition from various quarters, it was ultimately decided to separate Sind from the Bombay Presidency as an independent Province with a constitution on an equal footing with the rest of the Provinces of British India. Now that your Province is an independent entity the greatest responsibility rests on the shoulders of the Musalmans of Sind for its welfare and progress.

Not long ago the Musalmans in Sind were divided and torn into groups but I am happy to find today a wonderful public spirit, solidarity and unity demonstrated and with proper organization. If you mobilize and harness your powers there is nothing to prevent the Muslim League of your Province. It is now in your hands. You must remember that it is your duty and responsibility which calls upon you to conduct the affairs of the Government of Sind. The constitution enacted by the Government of India Act of 1935, although it incorporates many objectionable features, should be utilized with your majority strength successfully for the economic, social, educational and political uplift of the people of Sind and in particular of the Musalmans. I feel confident that the Musalmans of Sind and right thinking Hindus will realize that the progress and the welfare of the Province lies in maintaining high principles of justice, fair play and friendly co-operation amongst the people of Sind.

While speaking in this great city and the capital of Sind, Karachi, with the magnificent position it occupies, the wonderful sea port, and, constituting as it does the first homeland of Musalmans, it gives me no small pleasure that I should preside over a conference of this kind the like of which has never before taken place in Sind and you can well imagine my emotions when I tell you that Karachi is my birthplace and I cannot adequately express how deeply anxious I am for its welfare and how cordially I wish your Province to rise to its full stature and play a great and rightful part in the counsels of Muslim India.

Musalmans of Sind have another sacred duty to perfrom and a far graver task in front of them and it is that aspect which I want to impress upon you. In the all India Muslim struggle against the various forces which are out to destroy and divide the Musalmans by means of corruption and dishonest propaganda you have to guard yourself and stand solid behind the All India Muslim League which is the only authoritative and representative organization of the Musalmans of India. It is an irony of fate that the two Provinces for which the All India Muslim Leage fought successfully, that is Sind and the North West Frontier Provinces, should remain outside the ken of the All India Muslim League. But I am glad that Sind Musalmans have now realized, and the wonderful rally on their part is a bright sign and new chapter in the history of the All India Muslim League. The North West Frontier Province for which the Muslim League fought, including the opposition of the Congress itself against our demand that it should have the constitution and reforms on an equal footing with all the other provinces of the British India, should remain, when libereted from the heel of Wardha.

I feel confident, however that it will not be very long before the Musalmans of the North West Frontier Province come on the platform of the All India Muslim League and work as loyally and faithfully as any Musalman under the banner and the flag of the All India Muslim League and those who have, and are still, misleading the Pathans will meet with their *Nemesis*.

The struggle that we are carrying on is not merely for loaves and fishes, ministerships and jobs, nor are we opposed to the economic, social and educational uplift of our countrymen as it is falsely alleged. We want to make every contribution to the uplift of our people particularly the Musalmans. Do not believe when you are told that the policy and programme of the League is reactionary. No honest man who has studied the policy and programme of the League can conscientiously and truthfully say that it is anything but fully national and most progressive. Yet the Muslim League and its leaders are daily misrepresented and vilified. Truth is supressed and falsehood is broadcast in the Congress press and news agencies ; we of course having no press. The greatest misfortune of India is that High

Command of the Congress has adopted a most brutal, oppressive and inimical attitude towards the All India Muslim League since it secured a majority in the six Provinces. After they decided to accept office and work the constitution when we were ready and offered our co-operation as we had already made it clear before and after the elections the first demand was that the League must liquidate itself and we were told that it represented nobody except a few estimable middle class gentlemen; secondly, the decision was taken that we must be treated as an anathema and the League groups in the various legislatures were boycotted by the Congress; the members of the League party in the legislatures were to be treated as untouchables and no one was to be included in the ministry of those provinces from amongst the representatives of the League party unless they unconditionally signed the pledge, the policy, and the programme of the Congess which, honestly speaking, is much worse than that of the All India Muslim League and more communal. In fact except that, we stand for adequate and effective safeguards for the rights and interests of the Musalmans and that we do not agree with false creeds of "truth and nonviolence" which is observed and honoured more in breach.

They were asked to abjure their party and forego their creed, policy and programme which is far more honest and straightforward and practical. They started in the legislatures with a song of "*Bande Matram*" which is not only idolatrous but in its origin and substance is a hymn to spread hatred for the Musalmans. And they, in their wisdom, tried and are persisting now and compelling the school authorities to sing "*Bande Matram*", at congregations and school gatherings although it is admitted that it is not a national song. They have persistently hoisted tri-colour flags in a most aggressive and offensive manner on all Government and public buildings irrespective of the feelings of others although it is admitted that it is not a national flag. They started the "Muslim Mass Contact" which is not only silly but dangerous and some wiseacres among them think that this will bring aid in the destruction of the Communal Award or, at any rate, nullify its object and destroy the true strength of Muslim representation in the various legislatures, and thereby further force every Muslim to submit to membership of the Congress.

They have been forcing radical changes in the educational system of the Provinces and have to run the department on the Wardha scheme which has assumed the name of "*Vidya Mandir*" and make Hindi compulsory in the guise of Hindustani but highly Sanskritised as the "Lingua Franca" of India and leave no stone unturned to suppress Urdu which is the language of the largest number of Musalmans in India and thus give a death blow to their culture and their solidarity. Every available post or job is reserved for the Congressmen or those Musalmans who are prepared to desert or vilify the League. The "Civil Liberties" has assumed a new definition. That in the absence of "Swadeshi Laws" "lawless and reactionary laws" such as the "Criminal Law Amendment Act" and "Section 144" are to be freely utilized against those persons who disobey or differ from the Congress ministries and particularly in the case of the members of the Muslim League. Measures are brought in, bills have been passed and laws have been enacted which are obviously detrimental to the interests of the Musalmans.

For instance, amendments of the franchise system of voting, and representation of minorities in Municipal, Local and District Boards. The Muslim Press is terrorised under threats of forfeiture of securities and in some cases the obnoxious executive orders have been passed and securities of some Muslim Urdu papers have been forfeited. Is this the national programme that is being pursued for the advancement of the people of this country which will achieve freedom and independence of India? If this is a foretaste of the limited and restricted authority and power enjoyed by the Congress, I shudder to think what would be the fate of the ninety millions of Musalmans in this country if the congress were in charge of full and plenary powers of the Government of India; and yet, the other day, the President of the Congress had the temerity, in speaking at the Haripura Congress Session in February 1938, solemnly to ask "*I would put it to the members of the minority communities in India to consider dispassionately if they have anything to fear when the Congress programme is put into operation*".

So far I have not dealt with the cases of maltreatment, tyranny and persecution regarding which columns and columns have been filled by newspapers—specially in Bihar, the U. P.

and the C. P. and we are awaiting the report of the committee that has been appointed. I hope that the report will be out before the next Session of the Muslim League in December 1938.

It is common knowledge that the average Congressman, whether he is a member by conviction or convenience, abrogates to himself the role of a ruler of this country and although he does not possess the educational qualifications, training, culture and traditions of the British bureaucrat he behaves and acts towards the Musalmans in a much worse manner than the British did towards Indians. The supreme command may well deplore corruption, untruthfullness and violence and may further deplore the faked register of membership of the Congress by "convenience".

These are a few characteristic features of the Congress programme regarding the Musalmans. But we were recently told in your city by a high authority that surely the fact that the Governors have not yet thought fit to interfere or exercise their special powers is proof positive and shows that the Musalmans are not only justly and fairly treated but they are dealt with handsomely and generously. I know that Governors and the Governor-General have failed the minorities and specially the Musalmans. But on the other hand we are told that there is a gentlemen's agreement and a secret understanding between the British Government and the Congress in consequence of which assurances were given that such powers will not be exercised, and so it is obvious that the Congress Ministries are getting the longest rope with the result that the foolish policy of the Congress is responsible not only for intense bitterness between the two sister communities but among the various classes and interests. It has resulted in serious clashes, conflicts and ill-will, and is bound to recoil in the long run on the progress and welfare of India. It seems that Congress is merely tumbling into the hands of those who are looking forward to the creation of a serious situation which will break india vertically and horizontally.

But this is not all. Let us turn to Bengal, the Punjab and Assam. In these Provinces there happens to be a predominant Muslim voice in the Ministries and they are thus made the target and object of final destruction by the Congress high command. In Bengal the move to defeat the Fazl-ul Huq Ministry has ignominiously failed. In the Punjab various efforts are made to weaken the Ministry of Sikandar Hayat. But in Punjab they have not yet dared to table a no confidencc motion because the Punjab Ministry cannot yet be bent. In Assam Mr. Saadulla's Ministry resigned. Immediately the Congress President went post haste with his henchmen and agents to help at the birth of a so-called Congress Ministry in utter disregard of all their previous professions and declarations and contrary to their avowed determination to have nothing to do with coalition. In forming the Ministry Mr. Bordoloi was not able to announce the name of even one of the three Muslim Ministers who were to be included. The methods adopted to move the President for the adjournment of the Assembly '*sine die*' was hardly creditable and, for a great party not to face the legislature knowing full well that they had not the majority at their back, was sheer cowardice. It was under threat of suspension of the oath taking ceremony that the President and Congress party agreed to the sessions of the Assembly being called at an early date, and up to the present moment Mr. Bordoloi has not been able to get more than one of the three Muslim Ministers. He is still hunting for the remaining two. When 56 members of the Assembly out of 107 are not only against the so called Congress Ministry but have tabled a vote of no-confidence. I congratulate the President, Mr. Bose, for his statesmanlike achievement for this still-born child which he is now anxious to feed by means of oxygen and bring it to life by appealing to the European planters to come to his rescue.

The Congress high command is obsessed with one idea and is determined to divide the Musalmans and particularly to break the solidarity of the Muslim League, no matter how low they may have to stoop. They have no scruples or any standard or principle in their methods. Their policy is based on arrogance and opportunism and unfortunately they are at the present moment getting the support of a large body of Hindus who have respect for the Congress and are being fully exploited.

Not only that but even Mr. Gandhi, who has acquired a spiritual influence over a large body of the Hindu public and with his halo of Mahatma, is used by those who surround him.

He often tries to get out of awkward corners by falling back upon his inner voice or the voice of silence and relies upon the fact that he is not even a four anna member of the Congress; he deplores corruption, untruthfulness and violence and pleads his utter helplessness in the decisions of Congress high command. This grand fascist council, the Working Commitee (which is named "the shadow cabinet" of a parallel Government of India) is supposed to speak on behalf of the Indian Nation. Some of its antics remind one of a clown imitating the artist in a circus. During the critical situation about the end of September last this so called shadow cabinet continaully sat in sessions and kept vigil as the All India Congress Committee had entrusted them with powers to take such decisions as they thought proper with regard to the question of India's part in the event of the war breaking out. So to begin with a sympathetic message was sent by the high command to the Government of Czechoslovakia and the Mahatma and the Working Committee were continuing the vigil waiting for Whitehall to aproach Mahatma Gandhi. But war was averted and soon now the vigil will terminate and India will breathe a sigh of relief as she is saved from the Congress decision with regard to the war for the moment.

This is the situation and position that we have to face. It is no use relying upon anyone else. We must stand on our own inherent strength and build up our own power and forge sanctions behind our decisions. Today we are told that for the purpose of a settlement of the Hindu-Muslim question we do not represent the Musalmans of India and we are required to prove our position and status by "service and merits" before the mighty high command.

Gentlemen! the meaning is clear. It is no use our blaming others. It is no use our accusing our opponents only; it is no use our expecting our enemies to behave differently. If the Musalmans are going to be defeated in their aspirations it will only be by the betrayal of the Musalmans among us as has happened in the past. For the renegades and traitors I have nothing to say. They can do their worst. But I appeal most fervently to those Musalmans who honestly feel for their community and its welfare and those who are misled or misguided and indifferent to come on to the platform of the Muslim

League and work under its flag ; and please close your ranks and stand solid and united at any and all costs and speak and act with one voice.

Here I wish to make it clear that I am not fighting the Hindu community as such nor have I any quarrel with the Hindus generally for I have many personal friends among them ; but the Congress high command is, in my opinion, the greatest enemy of India's progress and for the matter of that even in the interests of Hindus. Although there are many Hindus who entirely condemn them and are completely fed up with them yet a large body of the Hindu public is still hypnotised and mesmerized by their seductive and abusive propaganda, disingenuous catchwords and slogans. Will they get their freedom of judgment and action ?

With regard to the tragedy of Palestine that is going on at present and the ruthless repression that is practised against the Arabs because of their struggle for the freedom of their country, I need hardly tell you that we had most convincing proofs demonstrated all over India that the heart of every Musalman is with them in the brave and wonderful struggle that they are carrying on against all odds and in spite of their being defenceless, According to the resolution of the All India Muslim League Council, the 26th of August was observed all over India as Palestine Day and from all accounts I can say, without exaggeration that thousands and thousands of meetings were held all over India fully and fervently sympathising with those who are fighting for their country's freedom. Musalmans' hearts are wounded and lacerated when they hear the news of ruthless and tyrannical oppression and repression of those brave Arabs and I know that the entire Muslim world is watching the doings of Great Britain there.

I may inform you that the Muslim League Council appointed a special committee at their meeting of the 30th July 1938 to consider the question of sending an official deputation to Palestine and England and directed the committee to consider ways and means by which effective pressure can be brought to bear upon the British Government. That committee recently met at Badaun and have, in response to the invitation from the Egyptian Parliamentary Committee for the Defence of Palestine, chosen five representatives on behalf of the All India Muslim League to attend the Parliamentary Congress of Arabs and Muslim countries which will be held in Cairo starting from the 7th October 1938 with a view to consider the present situation in Palestine. Three of our representatives, Mr. Khaliquzzaman, Mr. Abdur Rahman Siddiqui and Maulana Mazhar Uddin out of the five appointed have already left India and are on their way to Cairo. We shall await the result of the deliberations and the decisions of that Congress and then I may assure you that the All India Muslim League will do all that lies in its power to help the cause of the Arabs in Palestine. I am here glad to note that the Congress Working Committee also at Delhi have passed a resolution : that having regard to its importance it was moved by the chair without any comments. This is an indication of the superfical interest the Congress takes in matters which the Musalmans consider nearest and dearest to their hearts.

I am sure, His Majesty's Government and British statesmen are not under any delusion that Congress represents the people of India or the Indian nation for there are 90 millions of Musalmans. And I would draw their attention and that also of the Congress high command and ask them to mark, learn and inwardly digest the recent upheaval and its consequent developments which threatened the world war. It was because the Sudeten Germans who were forced under the heel of the majority Czechoslovakia who oppressod them, suppressed them, maltreated them and showed a brutal and callous disregard for their rights and interests for two decades hence the inevitable result that the Republic Czechoslovakia is now broken up and a new map will have to be drawn. Just as the Sudeton Germans were not defenceless and survived oppression and persecution for two decades so also the Musalmans are not defenceless and cannot give up their national entity and aspirations in this great continent. Here also I may mention the Frontier policy of the Government of India which the sooner it is given up the better and methods of reconciliation are resorted to instead. I will therefore appeal to the British Government to review and revise their policy with regard to Palestine, Waziristan and Musalmans of India and the Islamic powers generally. It is in the interest of Great Britain seriously to consider the reorientation in the light of the developments that have taken place during the last two decades.

To the Musalmans therefore I say go forward and organize your people all over India and if the reasons and arguments fail our ultimate resort must depend upon our own inherent strength and power. I do not despair nor need we fear the consequences in this great struggle of life and death which involves the destiny of 90 millions of our people.

GOVINDALAL D. SHAH

B.A., LL. B.

Is the Editor of "*The New Outlook*" and "*The Childrend's News*", Ahmedabad and was born on December 15, 1911. He married Satyavati Mashruwala, in November 1933. He contributed articles to various journals in India and Overseas, such as "*Unity*" of America. "*Forward*" of Glasgow, "*Passing Show*" of England, "*English Poet*" of Czechoslovakia, etc., He was Honorary Associate Editor of "*The Leisure Hour*", "*The Student*", "*The Brotherhood*", "*The Mercantile Miscellany*". He has been a member of correspondence and literary clubs all over the world and is now a member of P. E. N. (India Centre). He was the founder of "The Writers' Guild".

WORLD AND INDIAN ASPECTS OF THE UNEMPLOYMENT PROBLEM

UNEMPLOYMENT is the barometer with which we measure the depth of a trade depression. More or less it is co-existent with a trade depression and forms an arch in the vicious circle that defies all analysis. For good or for bad they mutually act and react on one another and to seek to decide whether unemployment results from depression or depression from unemployment is akin to setting ourselves the proverbial problem chicken or the egg—which came first ?

However, we can safely assert that unemployment bears a direct relation to trade depression and that unemployment figures rise or fall as trade improves or slackens. There are more causes than one for unemployment and the problem is many faced. Differences in the problem exist not only because of different causes but differences of time and place often create wide divergencies. It would be futile, therefore, to be dogmatic in a problem that is as old as industry itself.

However, as I view it, I have not the least hesitation in saying that there is a marked divergence between the world and Indian aspects of the present unemployment problem. It would be presumptuous on my part to assert that there are no common grounds, but it would be equally ill-considered and unwarranted to say that they are identical Notwithstanding all their resemblances, I am certain that the difference between the two is not of degree but of kind; in the case of the world the present is but a 'circumstantial' aspect, but in the case of India it is a 'fundamental' one. While the problem of unemployment for the world is only a co-runner of the present trade depression, in the case of India the problem goes to the very roots of her present structure; it is almost a daily phenomenon. Thus, while the world problem can be set right by a little tinkering and adjustment here and there, the Indian problem needs a complete overhauling of the entire structure.

Taking the world aspect first, I would say that the problem of unemployment is largely the problem of the revival of world trade. The discussion of the present trade depression is a subject by itself and, for obvious reasons, I cannot enter into a detailed discussion here. It may, however, be noted that everything that reduces the sting of the present depression also reduces the intensity of the unemployment problem. It may be noted that under-consumption and bad distribution necesssitate the restriction of supply which in turn brings about greater unemployment which is rightly the parent of so-called over-production. Over-production and unemployment form a vicious circle which must, somehow, be broken if we are to save our selves from what Arthur Henderson terms 'the starving thirties'. It may also be noted that failing prices always bear as pointed out by Prof. Irving Fisher, a close relation to unemployment figures and if the abnormally low prices of commodities are accompanied by high unemployment figures there is, rightly speaking, nothing to wonder at.

Following upon the world-trade depression there is a contraction of credit which fetters the normal working of industrial dealings and which necsssitates restriction of industrial pursuits which is accompanied by increasing unemployment. The gathering of the war-clouds on the eastern as well as western horizon, the general distrust among nations and a race for armaments have all resulted in credit contraction. The problem of unemployment and the problem of trade revival are only two phases of one and the same problem and both of them will be knocking at the door for solution as soon as those who have the strings of the nations' purses, collectively put their shoulder to the jammed wheel. The recent frenzied race for armaments may possibly show a trade revival and business activity, but it is the momentary brilliance of a dying order and cannot be welcomed as a healthy recovery. The mad race for armaments will either be put an end to by some international agreement or will result in a world conflagration which will make our economic confusion worst confounded. Conscription and other measures may possibly show a reduction in unemployment figures, but they are not a sign of relief and, so far as the problem of economic and political stability is concerned, it turns its back to the real problem which still remains unsolved. Leaders of nations as well as leaders of men cannot hide their heads in the sand like an ostrich and the problem of unemployment will ever give them troubled heads until it is solved on the basis of economic and political peace and stability.

The currency manipulations of certain nations, which upset the equilibrum of their external and internal prices, also resulted in bad trade and increased unemployment. The hoarding of gold by two nations made the working of the gold standard an impossibility and as long as the countries dragged at its chariot wheels this also, like currency manipulation, stimulated unemployment. In the abandonment of the gold standard, if it was not accompanied by artificial inflation, there was a hope of relief, but that hope has not been fulfilled.

In the restoration of the purchasing power of the people by a better distribution of wealth ; in removing the mists of distrust by setting in motion the ice-breakers that will revive frozen credit, and in turning the 'armed-camp' into a co-operative factory lie the panacea of trade depression and of unemployment and not till these things are done can there be any solution of the problem. In the fact, these are the very minima that can keep the present system working, for according to some, unemployment is not a passing but an ever recurring phenomenon and they hold, and not without reason, that so long as capitalism is there, there is no remedy which can, or will, eliminate the distressing problem. They suggest substitutes ranging from socialism and nationalisation to co-operation and profit-sharing and not until some such plan is adopted can we look forward to a well regulated working of national and international business machines and industrial plants. Some such co-operative scheme is now the necessary lubricant which alone can ensure the smooth running of the world trade mechanism.

Coming to India, we find that the trade depression, with all its attendant ills is over-shadowing the entire country. Add to this the uncertainty of the political situation ; the fall in the price of silver and the consequent loss of purchasing power, the manipulation of currency, the transitional stage of the country in its march from agriculture to industry and rationalisation and we have a picture which is dark indeed. But darker than this surface darkness is the that which lies at the very root of the present structure of the country. It is my well-considered opinion that no analysis which does not lay stress on this inner disease can ever be worth considering or can ever bring relief. The assumption of the reins of power by the Congress in the provinces is a happy thing but their task is the task of an Hercules. The Augean stables, which have collected dirt and disease, not only in their pigeon holes but also in the hearts and heads of their keepers, have to be cleaned and it is a task to which the Congress ministries in all provinces have set their faces. With their national outlook, with their programme of prohibition, with their drive for literacy, with their efforts for village reconstruction and indigenous home industries and the like they have embarked on their task wisely and well. But, they have only been in office for two years and the fruits of the seeds they have sown will yet be long in maturing. They are only a silver lining of hope to the dark and dreary picture that is India.

So far as grim realities go unemployment 'this modern form of famine' as Prof. Rist terms it is an ever existing fact in this country. To those who reside in India no array of statistics is necessary to prove this ; as the late Mr. Ramsay Macdonald put it, "it is not a matter of opinion, it is a fact." "Half the agricultural population of India to-day do not know from one half-year's end to another what it is to have a full meal," said Sir Charles Elliot ; while Mr. G. K. Gokhale, a member of the Viceroy's Executive Council, said, "From 60 to 70 million of the people in India do not know what it is to have their hunger fully satisfied even once in a year." There is no reason, therefore, to be the least surprised when Mr. W. R. Robertson says "The condition of labourers in India is a disgrace to any country calling itself civilised." The problem of unemployment in India is, therefore, not a problem of adjustment but one that calls for sweeping reconstruction. It is not a problem that has shot up yesterday but is a problem which has existed in this country for decades and which has become all the more deep-rooted through neglect.

Some ten years back, Sir Basil Blackett in his analysis of India's impoverishment said that it was all due to the fundamental conservatism and the 'unrepentantly medieval' ways of the people. He also found fault with 'the Hindu social system, in the Doctrine of Karma' and also with the crude and compartmental social system. Far be it from us to minimise the import of any drawback that clogs the wheels of progress and, while admitting that the Indian people are unaspiring, uneducated and unenterprising, we would like to probe below the surface. It is my firm conviction that Indians are no whit inferior to any of their brethren in the west and for their lack of education there is none more responsible than the government. "In several Indian provinces literacy was more widespread before the British took possession than it is now after a century and a half of British control" says Will Durant, an American savant. That it is the considered policy of the government to keep the Indian people illiterate is not difficult to prove. Parker Thomas Moon, Professor of Economics, at the Columbia University says, "In fact the total expenditure on education in India is less than one half the educational expenditure in New York state alone," and this is so even when the military budget runs into several crores. I agree with Mr. E. Holton James when he says, "The hand that takes our money, and keeps us ignorant, keeps us also in slavery to the elephant and the monkey god." There is no power which changes nations which is more powerful than the power of education. This we are denied. No wonder the people of India are religion-ridden. In fact the uneconomic outlook of the Indian people results from ignorance and, while we agree with the government that our people are unrepentantly medieval, we also emphasize that it is solely due to the abject lack of education for which we hold the government alone responsible. "We have denied to the people of the country all that can raise them in society, all that could elevate them as men" says Mr. Malcolm Sewin. What the Indian people need is education, and that of the proper kind, and not words of pessimism which dub them in season and out of season as unfit. They have all the qualities that make a great race, what they need is opportunity and education. A small beginning has been made by the Congress ministries with their literacy drives and in the course of time it should bear good fruits.

Another excuse that finds favour with the official section of the country is that India is over-populated. It is indeed evident on the very face of it that as the things exist India is unable to ensure decent living for her sons and daughters. But if we dive below we will find that we will be nearer truth if we accept John Bright's dictum : "If a country be found possessing a most fertile soil and capable of bearing every variety of production, yet notwithstanding the people are in a state of extreme destitution and suffering, the chances are there is some fundamental error in the government of that country." The fact is that the country is over-populated simply because "manufactures are crippled, agriculture over taxed and a half of the revenue remitted out of the country." All things considered, it seems that Mahathma Gandhi was not far from right when he said "that over-population was only a superstition of the west" because the greater evil in this country is not excessive population but lack of industries and the heavy cost of administration. This poor country can ill-afford the high salaries that it is paying to its administrators, this poor country can ill-afford the heavy military budgets that she is forced to pay, and the fact that these high officers are invariably foreigners simply increases the dead-weight. As John Sullivan points out, "the system acts very much like a sponge, drawing up all the good things from the banks of the Ganges and squeezing them down on the banks of the Thames." More or less India is serving as the 'cattle-farm of England' and she is being made to pay for the Empire as well. The late Mr. Ramsay Macdonald himself confessed "We spend far too much of the income of India on Imperial purposes and far too little on Indian development." Sir Henry Campbell Bannerman strikes a particularly Indian note when he says "Famine stricken India is being bled white for the maintenance of England's world-wide Empire."

This inevitably necessitates heavy taxation and further cripples industries and reduces the purchasing power of the people. "Taxation is not merely actually but relatively far heavier" says Mr. Hyndman, while even Sir William Hunter confesses, "The government assessment does not leave enough food to the cultivator to support himself and his family throughout the year." The fact that a major portion of this goes out of the country, never to return, only intensifies the problem. Prof. K. T. Shah estimates that out of the total tax collection of 400 crores nearly 200 crores never bring any real return to the people of India. Mr. R. C. Dutt strikes the same note when he lays down, "One-half of what we here in India pay every year in taxes goes out of the country and is of no service to those who have paid this tax." When we are told that it is for the efficient administration we are reminded of the words of Lord Morley. "The usual excuse of those who do evil to others is that their object is to do them good," If we are to judge them by their fruits we must emphatically lay down that if this country is to be efficiently and cheaply governed it must be governed by its own countrymen and that the administrators must be paid only at the market rate of native labour ; for, Mr. F. J. Shore says "The grinding extortion of the English government has effected the impoverishment of the country and its people to an extent almost unparalleled."

Lastly, I must refer to the the lack of industries. This country is so happily situated and has such resources that if it chooses it has all the means to be self-supporting. The industrialization of the country will not only bring prosperity to its people but may also supply the world with cheaply manufactured goods. But in her remaining a backward country I easily smell the bad part that the step-motherly government is forced to play. In this country there is a complete lack of state aid to any industry or enterprise and such favouritism as exists is for Lancashire and foreign products. Nay, more than this, the home industries that existed in this country have been wilfully destroyed by what Mr. W. H. Hunter terms 'the arm of political injustice'. I ask those who have eyes to see to note that the muslin of Dacca, silk of Murshidabad, inlay metal work of Bidar, shawl weaving of Amritsar, brass-work of Benares, carpet weaving of Mirzapur, horn manufacture and silver filigree work of Katak, and wood carving and bronze work of Madras have all been crushed and killed. Embroidery of Ahmedabad, enamelling of Delhi and Lucknow, Indian paper the manufactures of. Kashmir and the cloth printing of Brindaban have all vanished, with the result that India is getting poorer and poorer day by day. Her people have been snatched from their cottage industries. The charkha has, however, been a god-sent gift.

In the final analysis, we find that if India is to escape from the claws of starving and hunger she must educate herself. In the twentieth century there is no use for the people who still live in the eighteenth. India must keep abreast of the times. Her second need is to reduce her civil and military expenditure. If the good of the Indian people be at the heart of the government the time has come to save her from economic depression and the ever present unemployment problem.

And lastly, rapid strides must be made to industrialise the country and to provide her people with some cottage industries as is done in Switzerland. India is passing through uneasy times and any delay will be dangerous. The time has come when India can wait no longer and her sons must be assured of their bread.

RAO SAHIB C.S.SRINIVASACHARI

M. A.

Professor and Head of History and Politics
Annamalai University
Annamalainager

Professor Srinivasachari, who was born in 1890, graduated with distinction from the Madras University in 1910. Since graduating and until 1931 he was the Professor of History at the Pachaipappa's College, Madras from whence he joined his present appointment. During his career the Professor has edited *The Empire in India* and jointly edited *The Journal of India History* and as an author he has published '*A History of Ginges*', '*A college History of India*', '*The History and Institutions of the Pallavas*' and '*A History of the City of Madras from its begining to the present day*'.

In selecting some aspects South India culture in the past as the basis of an article for *What India Thinks*, Professor Srinivasachari has been guided by the historical and cultural interest of his subject and also its usefulness in this present age of renaissance and we feel sure that our readers will agree that all interested in present day Indian social and economical reconstruction can learn a great deal from the historical aspects of India's ancient institutions.

SOME ASPECTS OF SOUTH INDIAN CULTURE IN THE PAST

IT is now a well-accepted fact that the genius of the ancient peoples of South India shone very prominensly, and with a special individuality of its own in the various fields of culture like political and administrative institutions, local autonomy and organisation, the temple as a centre of social life and the maintenance of trade and external contact. The filiations of early Dravidian culture with the civilization of Mohenjo-Daro are coming to be recognised to an increasing extent by great scholars.

It is proposed in this paper to give a few points bearing on early South Indian culture that will very clearly illustrate the peculiarities and noteworthy features it developed, and it is hoped that this will lead to a more just and better deserved understanding of South India by the intelligensia of the country and by learned opinion outside. The points to be dealt with are

(1) rural democracy that prevailed in the past, markedly in the Tamil country and that is essentially modern in many respects ;

(2) the temple which developed into a centre of civic life and cultural promotion. This may be contrasted with the present status of the temple as a mere place of ritualistic worship ;

and (3) the communal harmony that prevailed in the land.

VILLAGE DEMOCRACY

In the days of Chola and Pallava rule, in the matter of local administration, power was vested in the hands of the following assemblies.

(i) The district assembly, or Nattar—a body which met when subjects touching the interests of the whole district were discussed or when there were no *sabhas for* the villages with the district.

(ii) Members of commerce—*Nagarattar*,

(iii) Village assembly, or *Oorar*—the general body of the residents of a village ; and

(iv) Another assembly of the village—the *sabha* or the *mahasabha*—which was composed wholly of Brahmins.

The jurisdiction of this last body, the village sabha, extended over what was called in ancient times a *chaturvedimangalam*, which consisted of a central village with a number of hamlets and minor villages, called *padagai* and *cheri* ; as well as streets, all situated within a radius of ten miles.

COMMITTEES

The chief committees of the assembly were four ; the committee of annual supervision, that of tank supervision, that of garden supervision, and that for the supervision of justice. Other committees were also chosen for field supervision, gold supervision, ward supervision and the Panchavara-variyam.

As regards the appointment of accountants, who were the chief servants of the assembly, they were required to be choosen from among "arbitrators and those who have earned their wealth by honest means." One who had been an accountant was not be appointed to that office again until he should have properly submitted his accounts for the period of his office, and declared to have been honest by the great men of the big committee, *i.e.*, the committee in charge of accountants. The accounts which accountant had been writing, he should submit himself, and other accountants should not be brought into close up his accounts. Accountants suspected of professional misconduct were asked to undergo the ordeal.

Members comprising the committees had to change every year. After the expiry of three years since one last held office, he became eligible normally for re-election ; and if elected he was made to serve on some other committee than the one in which he was before. The selection by lot and the normal change of office-bearers gave every qualified and deserving man an opportunity to get acquainted with the details of administration. All the villagers, young and old, had a knowledge of the village machinery and its working, watched over their interests jealously, and exercised a wholesome control over the doings of the various committees.

A HIGH MORAL STANDARD

Members of committees were always to keep up a very high standard of conduct ; and everyone had to give an account of his stewardship, probably to the village assembly, immediately before or after the expiry of his term of office. If he failed to do this, he was suspected of embezzlement, but, as a technical charge of this kind was difficult to prove, the defaulting member was deprived of his civic rights ; this punishment affected the prospects not only of the defaulter himself, but also of his remotest relations. Erratic committee members were dealt with more severely even than outcastes.

Such severe standards of conduct, the annual change of committee men, the vigilance that was expected of every householder who had a chance of occupying office himself, the exercise of wholesome control over the whole assembly should have realized a village democracy as perfect in its working and efficiency as the ideal of Periclean democracy in Athens. Casting lots was common in ancient India ; but among men possessing the same qualifications, it must in those tims have been very difficult to exercise choice. The presence of temple priests, on which special stress is laid, and the choice of a young lad to take out tickets from the pot, were evidently meant to eliminate, as much as possible, the human element and to introduce that of divine choice.

THE CONSTITUTION

The corporate and permanent character of the assemblies was a well-founded fact admitted even by hostile kings. The constituents of a *sabha* were usually the big men of the village (the elders), the *bhattas* (learned men), the *visishtas* (the very highly pious and upright men), and the temple priests. Often enough, and on stated occasions, the merchants (nagarattar), residents and professionals (oorar), and district representatives (nattar), also took their seats on the Brahmin assembly.

In most cases these bodies had their own separate meetings. The representatives of the king, the local officers and the agents of the parties interested in the business of the day, were also present at the meetings. No rules regulating the management of the other assemblies have come to light. Evidently all general qualifications for efficient membership, such as those that obtained in the Brahminical sabhas, must have been also in force, except, perhaps, the knowledge of the Vedas and the Mantrabrahmana. The tendency to corporate life extended, as already seen, to all aspects of temple activity.

PUBLIC WORKS

The assembly of the village sold or purchased lands on behalf of the temple. The assembly received deposits of money made by donors on behalf of the temple or from the temple itself, or again on account of other charities, and carried out the trust objects from the sums accruing regularly as interest year after year. These investments were evidently utilised by the assembly for carrying out the permanent public works of the village.

The *sabha* was empowered to attach and confiscate lands for arrears of revenue and sell them by public auction. No exception was made even if such lands happened to belong to the temple. Before public auction of such lands was resorted to, the procedure was adopted of advertising once, twice, and thrice, to know if there was any to purchase the land in question.

The assembly exercised all the powers of a regular administration in its own narrow sphere ; it possessed, sold, acquired and alienated corporate property ; it acted as the trustee of public charity of all kinds.

The *sabha* recognized the responsibility that lay upon it of maintaining the local institutions. The village corporation was liable also for the debts incurred by its employees. The relations between the *sabha* and the temple authorities were normally close and cordial. This was particularly the case when the village in question was either a *Devadana* or a *Brahmadesa*. The corporate and essentially vital character of the village assembly was a factor to be recognized even by other states and kings, as already noted. The relations subsisting between the village assembly and the king were close and important. The *sabha* seems to have possessed absolute authority over all the village lands subject to the payment of royal revenue. The members were generally untrammelled in the discharge of their duties by regulations imposed from above. Royal officers supervised the accounts of the *sabha* from time to time.

FULL CONTROL

In this connection one may doubt whether the status of these village *sva-rajes* was, to apply a modern notion, capable of complete self-determination. One is not fully certain whether these were certainly more than mere institutions of local government, enjoying rights and immunities only within the bounds of royal and imperial will : *viz.*, according to the grants of charters. The content of rural democracy in the Tamil country has been attempted to be described in a large measure in all its parts. In matters of internal administration, and to a certain extent even in matters relating to the relations of one village with other villages and external bodies, the *sabha* was largely free from royal control and direction. Local justice was within their competence. Even in cases of murder the assembly sat in judgment, and, what was more remarkable, exercised discretion in meting out punishments. In arriving at their decisions the assembly did not have ordinarily to refer the matter to the king or to his representative in the district.

This perfect organization of the village, the union of villages, the *nadu*, and in some cases the caste and the guild, must have had a very hoary origin to become so well-developed as it did in the centuries of the Chola imperial sway and after. The village organization of the Tamil country was certainly as old as, and probably much older than, the time of Nandivarman Pallavamalla whose Kasakudi Plates undoubtedly indicate some sort of a regular eighth century. Almost every village had its own temple or temples. The temple was in those times the busiest part of the town or village. At first temples should have been constructed in village groves.

THE TEMPLE

Royal and princely patronage in the Pallava, Chola and the later Pandya and Vijayanagara times led to the gradual extension of the size and the magnificence of our great temples adorned with covered and richly sculptured colonnades, huge *prakara* walls round the central shrine, towering *gopurams* at the gateways and high castellated walls, thousand-pillared mantapas, etc. Bound by agreement, a number of men who were in charge of the temple lands, money, livestock and other endowments, brought at the stated times their various offerings of ghee, oil, cleaned rice, vegetables, fruits, sandal-pastes, incense, musk, rose-water, etc. and promised never to fail in their duties. Persons who cultivated Devadana lands on lease had to bring to the temple courtyard at their own expense the stipulated quantities of grain and other produce. In the temples labour was efficiently performed and minutely divided.

Sometimes records speak of grants to temples for the maintenance of alms-houses, repairs of breaks or cracks in the temple structure, the supporting of temple servants and of Brahmins versed in the Vedas. In the temple-*mantapas*, the

Vedas were chanted and expounded ; while the Mahabharata, and Dharmasastras, the Puranas, grammar, rhetoric, logic, astrology, astronomy, medicine and other special sciences were taught to those that came to learn them. A temple in such places become the natural centre of both sacred and popular learning, and of hard, scientific and scholastic studies. One inscription makes a reference to the *Vyakarna-danamantapa* of a temple.

AN IMPORTANT CENTRE

Colonies of genuinely pious Brahmins were attached to temples. Sometimes the village assembly itself performed such educational work. Such culture-colonies were called *Gatiks*, *Agraharas* and *Brahmapuris*. The Mathas served, besides the temples, as centres of higher learning where advanced scholars gathered together and received generous patronage. In the *Ranga-mantapa* of the temples, dancing was usually practised and on special occasions dramas were also staged. The temple was also the principal feeding-house of the village. All strangers, ascetics, and men of learning were fed sumptuously at the temple. On festive occasions such feedings were specially prominent. The temple was also the place where kings performed their coronation, *tulabhara* and *hiranyagarbha* ceremonies. Rajaraja had his *tulabhara* performed in the Tiruvisalur temple ; Jatavarman Sundara Pandya (1251-75 A. D.) built several *tulapurusha-mantapas* in the Srirangam temple ; and in the Chidambaram temple Chola and Pandye rulers, of the thirteenth century especially, often were crowned victors.

Apart from the growth of the temple as a potent instrument of satisfying the religious impulse of the people, there grew up in the Chola times the *mathas*, presided over by Saiva Sanyasis, which have now spread their influence over a large portion of the country. A large number of records relates to the *mathas*, which grew in power and popularity under the Chola and Pandya kings. From about the tenth century onwards, it became a common feature to attach *mathas* to temples; and these wielded great influence and practically controlled the affairs of the temples ; while pilgrims found ready hospitally in them. They promoted learning, encouraged learned men, and served a double purpose being both teaching and disciplinary institutions. They provided for the teaching of the *Shastras*, the recital of the *Puranas*, and the promotion of devotional literature.

Agraharas, of culture colonies of Brahmins, were frequently founded in this, as even in later epochs.

DECAY

When the Vijaynagara monarchs spread their sway over the Tamil country, in the latter half of the fourteenth century, their imperial hierarchy of officials and the previous dislocation of society and its institutions, caused by the Mussalman invasions of the earlier part of the same century, de-vitalized to a dangerous extent the inherent vigour of the village constitution. They decayed very quickly and must have disappeared altogether by the beginning of the fifteenth century. Thus the village assemblies, which were powerful local institutions during the Chola period, seem to have gradually died out and disappeared in little more than a century after the decline of the Chola Empire.

Thus we see that modern Indian social and economic reconstruction can learn a good a deal of value from the historical gleanings of our ancient institutions. Particularly in matters of village self-government and the management of temples and local affairs, the ancient village in South India and its executive commitee can serve as valuable models. The writer of this article will feel that his work has been of some value if it should be noted by publicists and social workers of the present day.

G. RAMESHWARA RAO

B.A., B.L., ADVOCATE

Was born on December 12, 1883 and educated at Madras X'ian and Law Colleges. Is a Director of the District Central Co-operative Bank, Cuddapah and of the Madras Provincial Co-operative Bank Ltd., was elected member for Anantapur in the Legislative Council, Madras, 1923-1926 ; and again M. L. C., from 1934 onwards ; Elected President, Peace Memorial Association, Anantapur, for a term ; Director & Executive Committee Member, District Co-operative Central Bank, Anantapur ; President Andhra Homeopathic Conference, Coconada, 1935 ; Member & Provincial Secretary, All-India Homeopathic Association ; Opened a free Homeopathic Dispensary of his own at Anantapur. Takes a keen interest in the depressed classes and peasants ; Director, Commercial Bank and Trust Ltd., Publications : Bulletins on Homeopathy.

PUBLIC HEALTH AND HOMOEOPATHY

THE vital statistics for London show that within the last fifty years, the death rate has fallen from 18 to 12 per 1000 (and this from all causes put together). The figures for longevity indicate that a man can now expect to live till 58 years of age as opposed to 40 fifty years ago. Similarly the average life of a woman has increased from 44 to 64. The death rate for children under one year has dropped from 141 to 60 per 1000 children born alive.

How do figures in India compare with those of London which is the busiest and most populous city in the world ? Unfortunately our public health reports, either Provincial or Indian, do not give us a comparative idea to estimate the longevity of a man or a woman in our country but in all conventional talk it is understood that one generation means 25 years. What a short span of life especially when we remember that the majority of Indians live in villages—which are certainly much more healthy than towns and cities! The Public Health Department in India admits that the death rate in villages is far less than that in towns and cities, and yet, one generation means only 25 years—the average life of an Indian person! Coming to infantile mortality, the latest census report shows that in British India it varies from 180 to 190 per 1000 of live births and in the Madras Presidency the rate varies from 170 to 185 ; the figures for 1937 being 170 per 1000.

The Administration Report of the Public Health Department of Madras for the year 1937 makes two significant admissions. The first is that "*the infantile mortality rates in India are very high when compared with rates in the West.*" The second admission relates to the death rates as a whole and the Report says "*that it had been steady for the last 37 years in the Madras Presidency.*" The population of the Presidency for the year 1937 is 44,182,017. Out of these, the largest number of deaths from one single cause appears to be 286,700 and that is from fevers. Next in order are respiratory diseases which account for 95,900 deaths. The third cause, diarrhoea and dysentry, claims 84276 lives, while deaths due to unclassified causes are 532,750. (I am here omitting figures relating to epidemics such as cholera, smallpox and plague.) Does it not show that there is much to be done for the improvement of public health, as the figures above give a fair idea of public health in India taken as a whole ?

INDIGENOUS MEDICINES

Local autonomy in the department of public health has been obtaining in all the provinces for nearly 30 years and yet no marked improvement has been found. Till thirty years ago, this subject was in charge of a government not responsive to, nor responsible for, public opinion ; but now things have changed yet with no effect. This shows that the individual in charge is not a material factor ; but all that really matters is his zeal based on culture and an outlook free from any prejudice. It is no doubt true that greater impetus has been given, of late, to what are called the indigenous systems of medicines and in this class are included the Ayurvedic, the Siddha and the Unani systems. Whether indigenous medicines include only these three systems and whether all these three are really indigenous is a debatable point.

For instance, if Muhammadans are not indigenous to India, neither is the Unani system. If Muhammadans have been with us for a long time and therefore their system may be taken as indigenous, the same argument might apply to Europeans and allopathy also may be put down in the same category. If the period of stay of any particular community in India is to be the test, an arbitrary period may be fixed at 500 or 1000 years, but there would be no logic behind it. Therefore there is no rational basis for mentioning only these three systems as indigenous and excluding others.

India, being predominantly Hindu in population, and inasmuch as all Hindus accept the Sanskrit culture as essentially theirs apart from the sciences and arts stored in Dravidian literature, one may state that systems of medicine dealt with by Sanskrit writers may be taken as indigenous. These systems were absolutely scientific and not empirical. If the scientific basis is forgotten or ignored at present, it is because there are no savants to continue research on the ancient lines and develop them in the light of modern knowledge and experience. Stagnancy is no ground for discarding any Indian system as unscientific. But the question of questions is whether the ancient method of diagnosis is still the working basis or whether it has been yielding to other methods. By feeling the pulse, the ancient Ayurvedic physicians were diagnosing all diseases. Alas! Their generation has come to an end and is fast decaying. Modern appliances, such as the thermometer and the stethoscope are coming into vogue among modern Ayurveds and the art of feeling the pulse is dying, if not already dead.

I am not disparaging the system at all; but I am only referring to the practice as it now obtains, to show that the fundamental principle of diagnosis is changing. All the same, God-given drugs have not changed their characteristics as much and their utility stands unchallenged. The environment in which the individual drug grows such as the soil, manure and the method of bringing it up, may make slight alterations in its effects, but the essential characteristics are still there and they are potent factors in effecting cures. There is a way of recognising the slight changes in their characteristics and that is by 'proving' them and conducting researches so that the drugs may be put to the best uses they can now yield. It is probable that this method of 'proving' was in vogue in ancient days when the ancient Sanskrit writers prepared their *Materia Medica* (Vastu Guna Deepika) for our guidance and it is a pity that this method of research by 'proving' drugs has been discontinued in India.

PROOF OF POTENCY

Now, there is a system which proves drugs—not on animals but on human beings. The results obtained by watching the effects of drugs on lower animals cannot be applied with any safety and precision to human beings. The results, as seen in experiments by the test tube, cannot well be expected to be exactly the same in the human stomach. Even among animals, the internal secretions are not exactly the same and so the response to a drug differs from animal to animal. For instance, an elephant can well feed on aconite and yet retain its health. But what other animal which after eating aconite, can retain it? A drug called *staphisagria* was tried on sheep, goats pigs and cows. With what effect? In one, it suppressed urine; in another it started polyuria! Yet again, in one it produced constipation, and in another diarrhoea! This is how different animals respond to the same drug. When this is so, how can we safely say that all drugs proved on lower animals are expected to act on human beings in exactly the same way and how can we be confident of the pathogenesis of a drug when applied to a human being? As Mr. Trotter said in the *British Medical Joarnal* (1930 p. 566) "*Experiment in man is the one wholly unexceptionable method available for the solutions of problems of human health and disease*".

Curative medicines should, therefore, be tested and proved on human beings before they can be administered to men with any confidence, and there is only one system that does it and that is homoeopathy. This system was prevalent in its rudiments among the ancient Indians but it was given to a Christian, Samuel Hahnemann, a German born in Meissin on 11-4-1755, to develope and give it a perfectly modern and scientific orientation.

Homoeopathy is a system of cures by similars—*similia similibus curantur.* It is not a cure by contraries—*contra contraris curantur.* Let me explain. When a man is suffering with very high temperature, ice is applied to the head and cold wraps are applied to the body to reduce the temperature. This is a method of cure by contraries and is the way of treatment acording to allopathy. The other method is treating by similars i. e., when a man is feeling hot, give him something which makes him hotter and this is done on the principle of *ushnam ushnena seethalam*—heat becomes cold by further application of heat. This may be paradoxical but yet true and this is the method of treatment in homoeopathy. On the same lines, we see in our literature *sarpa dashtam vishakrantam sarpena nyana damsayat, —dashtans sadyaiya jievathi.* If one is bitten by a snake and is suffering from its poison, get him bitten by another snake ; the latter snake dies at once and the man bitten will soon recover. This principle must have been of such common knowledge in ancient India that we find it mentioned in a book dealing with Advita philosophy. *"Dirt is washed off with dirt by those who know the art of cleansing,* (just as) *a missile is warded off by another missile and poison is counteracted by another poison".* Similarly, Rwami Rama Thirtha, lecturing in San francisco on 18th January 1903 said ; *"It is imagination and current of ideas in the wrong direction that bind you. It is imagination directed in the right channels which liberates you...similia similibus curantur".* This is said when he was speaking of *Samathi shatka sampathi,* i. e., self-control.

HISTORY

Thus we see that the Hindus were quite familiar with the principles of homœopathy which must have been a part of common knowledge among the educated in the olden days and that is why we find the references quoted above in our sanskrit literature. This makes us pause and ponder 'Is homœopathy indigenous then' ? The inevitable answer is 'yes'. When the principle is found in medical literature, when it is freely in vogue in common parlance, when it is found in general literature and books on Hindu philosophy, the necessary conclusion is that the system is indigenous and not foreign.

If the system has been developed by Hahnemann, a German, it is because local talent was not applied to it and hence a foreigner came in to emphasise and expound a hidden doctrine in the Hindu system. Why then was this not included in the indigenous systems by the Government of our country? It is mere ignorance of the history of the system and nothing but that.

Regarding the history of modern homœopathy in India, the writer said, in his speech on 8-8-1935 in the Madras Legislative Council:

> "The history of this system in India begins in the year 1839 when Maharaja Ranjit, in his last throes of agony and when all available means had failed, consulted Dr. John Martin Honigberger who only was able to give him any relief. But homœopathy was little known in our country at that time. Some time later it began to draw the attention of the public in Bengal, and mention can be made of Sir John Litler, a Deputy Governor of Bengal, Mr. Ironside, a Sessions Judge and Dr. Fabre who did much towards the establishment of hospitals, and charitable dispensaries and helping associations in many places. Further on, Mr. Rajendra Lal Dutta, a notable Bengalee gave a great impetus to the system. Again, another gentleman, Dr. Sarkar, at first the Secretary and later the Vice-president of the British Medical Assosiation of Calcutta, became a convert to homœopathy and he gave it the very best impetus that was possible in those days. This system has been in vogue in India to a lesser or higher degree from the year 1839 onwards, i. e., for about a century."

All this had to be stated with a view to impress on the Goverment that the system was not new to India, for on 21-3-1935 the minister in charge of medicine had said: *"I am afraid it will be necessary for my friend ... ... to carry on a great deel of propaganda to persuade the Government or the Council to adopt that system (Homœopathy)."*

Attempts were made all over India to dispel the ignorance in our administrators. As a result the Government of India said, in answer to an interpellation that they saw no objection to any doctor, (including one in Government service) practising homœopathy privately or in Government hospitals. It is a relief to find that in Bengal, which generally leads the rest of India, the Government appointed a committee in April 1939 for drafting statutes for a proposed general council and state facultiy of homœopathic medicine in Bengal. It is hoped that other provincial governments will also fall in line.

"*Having eyes ye see not ; having ears ye hear not*" is generally true of governments and it applies to the Madras Government in particular. The Government was not in a mood to gather information from Indian states like Indore and Travancore regarding their experience of homœopathy nor did it condescend to verify the immense popularity this system had gained in Bengal, nor the usefulness of so many homœopathic schools and dispensaries in that province. Similarly, it did not make enquiries about similar institutions and hospitals in England, Europe and America. Even the fact that homœopaths are patronised by the royal household in England and are resorted to by members of the royal family did not appeal to the Madras Government. My honorable colleague who seconded my resolution in the Madras Legislative Council is a member of the Madras Cabinet now. Yet the Madras Government wishes neither to hear nor to see the true excellence of homœopathy.

The word 'Homœopathy' is of Greek origin ; (*Homœo*=similar and *pathy*=treatment) and means treatment by similars, as contrasted with the opposite method of treatment by contraries. Let us examine the good points in this system of cure.

CLASSIFICATION

This is a scientific system in the truest sense of the word. It is developed by proving the drugs on healthy human beings and symptoms developed in the provers have been noted and classified in what is called '*schema*' on a basis of a regional division of the human body. Drugs having been tested on men, women and children of various types, they lend themselves to a rational classification. More than all, the subjective symptoms are given greater prominence than the mere objective, pathological or other morbid changes in the functioning and anatomy. It has been discovered that mental indisposition starts first, a sort of malaise, as a beginning of all disease and then comes on the disfunctioning of various organs and last of all are exhibited the pathological changes. Provings on healthy persons can be carried on only up to a certain stage so as not to endanger the prover and so cases of poisioning come in handy for further study of poisonous drugs. In other cases, drugs given to sufferers in an advanced stage of disease cure advanced pathological changes and so clinical experiences supply another source for the study of symptomatology of the drug. These are the sources of study and methods of research for the construction of the homœopathic *Materia Medica* and the results arrived at are infallible. The homœopath has no pet theories of an ephemeral nature changing with the times and his principles, being based on immutable natural laws, are axiomatic truths, abiding and permanent for all time. By proving more and more drugs, we go on adding to the fund of knowledge. We find in our pharmacopea medicines from mineral, vegetable and animal kingdoms and the more we explore these regions, the greater will be our capacity to cure diseases.

The homœopath believes that the root of every disease is in the mind. When the mind is functioning normally, the body must be in harmony with the vital force animating the body and normal health is enjoyed. The moment we see an aberration or an abnormality in the mind, it is the seed of the disease and disease is then starting though it takes some time to exhibit itself in the body, first by affecting the proper functioning of the organs and later by developing lesions and producing other pathological changes. These later exhibitions are only the resulting manifestations of the disease and the homœopath believes that these cannot be eradicated (*cured* in the proper sense of the term) unless the mental aberration also is set right. This, the homœopath professes to do. He takes the subjective symptoms in the *schema* as developed in the proving of a drug and endeavours to compare them with the mental symptoms of the patient. Similarly, he takes the physical symptoms next such as general symptoms and local symptoms. He then takes the sensations of the patient and his sensitiveness (technically called modalities) as to how the patient reacts to changes in the seasons, to heat and cold, to hot air and cold air, hot drinks and cold drinks and also whether he likes to be alone or in company and his likes and aversions to music and journeys, to certain kinds of foods and to friends and relations. Having noted all these in the patient, he turns to the *schema* to compare these symptoms with those of a proved drug and when he finds a perfect match, he cries '*Eureka*'—I have got the *similimum*—the most similar drug or the exact drug suitable to the patient. That is to say, the drug, which, when given to a healthy person produces the very symptoms that are found in the particular patient. When this drug is administered, the patient soon responds and quickly recovers both in mind and body, if the dose is of the right potency. Thus we see that totality of the symptoms is the test in the selection of the drug. The theory of potency is explained below.

EXPERIMENTS

The drug to be given to a patient for a disease is the one which produces the same disease in a healthy man. A sick person answering to such a disease is cured by the very drug that is capable of producing the same disease in a healthy individual. This wonderful law of nature was demonstrated by Hahnemann in his own life. While translating Cullen's *Materia Medica,* he came across a sentence to the effect that a Peruvian bark given to a healthy person produces chills and temperature. Being himself a notable physician, he was astounded at this statement as Peruvian bark (*chincona*) was the usual remedy for malaria and now he was told that it produced malaria when given to a healthy person ! He was a great scientist and had 150 publications on scientific subjects to his credit including some on chemistry. With a view to verifying this statement, he tried it on himself and promptly got malaria. The correctness of the statement was thus proved to his satisfaction. Then he began to dream the dreams of a research scholar.

If *chincona* acts like this, he argued, by curing in the sick what it is capable of producing in the healthy, what about other drugs known to the *Materia Medica* which are used in curing certain other diseases ? He tried them slowly and steadily one after another on himself, on his relations and on a select group of trusted colleagues in the field of medicine and on an ever increasing scale and satisfied himself that all drugs behaved as *chincona* did and thus he constructed his monumental *Materia Medica Pura.* The wiseacres of those days who knew nothing of his researches and who did not care to know about them (but who had the ears of the government) managed to get him expelled from state to state for his heretical medical doctrines and their persecution knew no bounds. That however is another history.

This is the great seer who immortalised himself by giving Homœopathy to the world. His '*Organon*' is the *Veda* and the Bible of homœopathy and is the fountain source of the theory of the science.

DILUTION

How was the discovery applied in practice ? The recognised massive doses in vogue did not appeal to him in his experience. So he began to reduce the dose of a drug and with a view to going further in this direction, he began to dissolve them and proceed with a systematic process of progressive dilution. By so doing, he was able to reduce the quantity of a drug in a dose and enunciated the excellence of the theory of dilution. He found by experimentation that the drugs in dilution were more effective in curing diseases and he demonstrated it in his practice. The word "dilution" was found to give rise to a misconception as regards the curative effects and it was therefore changed to 'potentisation' to signify the idea that the curative effect of a drug went on increasing with the increase in dilution and drugs came to be used in 'potencies' by homœopaths. These potencies have no toxic effects whatever and the cures effected by them are miraculous, especially when the potencies are matched with the plane of the disease i.e., according to the acuteness of the disease. By this process of dilution or potentisation, the dynamic energy in the crude drug is released and its curative effects increased in proportion. Modern physics show that the energy in an atom, when suddenly released, is enough to explode the whole world. What applies in physics is equally applicable in medicine.

Those who have no knowledge of the theory or the practice of potencies condemn the system on the ground that homœopathy is a faith cure, based on dietetics : This criticism was knocked on the head, when Boenninghausen treated pigs and sheep in epidemics, on mere statements of their owners regarding the symptoms of the disease, by sending some pills. He said that the animals did not see him and so the theory of faith did not come in. He did not direct any change in the normal food of the animals and so the theory of dietetics does not find a place in explaining the cures effected. Hence it is positively certain that it is the potency of the diluted drug that is responsible for the cures and nothing else.

The theory of the potencies is that the potency chosen must be just enough to set up a reaction in the body metabolism to enable nature to assert herself and fight the disease. The stimulus given must not be too great as the reaction would be too great and the weakened patient may not have enough vitality to withstand medicinal reaction. This is the principle of regulating the dosage and this is the bed rock of homœopathic therapeutics. Having chosen the right drug and the right potency, the doctor is sure to cure any given case unless the vitality of the patient is so low that he is not able to react to the drug. Treatment on these lines has resulted in a marvel in the proportion of cures, as statistics show, when compared with other systems of treatment. Figures in my hands show that in a cholera epidemic in my district, 99% were cured even by laymen who acted according to the instructions given and administered selected drugs according to the symptoms seen in the patients at the various stages of the disease.

MENTAL CASES

As stated above, the subjective symptoms play a great part in the right choice of a drug, and it is claimed for homœopathy that it can set right mental aberrations. Let us see the logical results of this claim. If a child is looked after by a homœopath from its first entry into this world, it cannot be below par in its physique or intellect. The problems of idiocy or lunacy are solved. If a case of suspected idiocy or lunacy comes into the care of a homœopath at its inception, the mental defect would promptly be checked and mental equilibrium restored. There are several cases of children exhibiting a tendency to tell a lie, thieve, or to be cruel to their neighbours or to animals or birds. These abnormal idiosyncracies can well be brought under control in early life and when the child grows into manhood, his character will in no way be below the average. Intellect and character can both be developed by recourse to homœcpathic treatment. Nervousness and sensitiveness can be replaced by grit and stamina to stand the ordinary shocks of life. National character and national stamina can both improve and with the improvement in character the problem of crime is also solved as criminal tendencies can be brought under control. It has been rightly said by the Very Rev: W. R. Inge D. D. that: "*Abnormal proclivities are often more like disease than crime.*" Therefore it is the duty of the state to give the best protection possible to boys and girls to develop them into the pick of manhood.

In addition to all the above advantages, the cheapness of homœopathic medicines is a factor which must arrest the attention of anyone aware of the poverty of an average Indian. He cannot afford to seek the aid of the prohibitively costly allopathic treatment, and homœopathic medicines are cheapest when compared with other medicine. A dram phial contains about 200 doses of medicine and costs only one anna and three pies in the ordinary potencies. Even in the highest potencies, a dram costs only about Rs. 5 for about 200 doses. For poor India, when Government and local bodies in charge of public health are complaining of want of funds and when public health is showing no signs of improvement, wisdom should dictate that this cheap system of treatment deserves the first attention of our administrators. As a science, this is nearest perfection; as a live science, researches are proceeding in the unexplored fields of mineral, vegetable and animal kingdoms; as a curative art, it is *par excellence* and as an economic problem, this beats everything else. Only ignorance and conservatism are standing in the way of its advancement. Let us not throw away nature's gifts nor discard the results of modern science. May God give us the insight to view everything in its right perspective and evaluate things on their own merits after a fair and unbiassed trial.

"Truth crushed to Earth will rise again
The eternal years of God are hers
Error, stung, writhes in pain
And dies, amidst her worshippers."

K. VISWANATHAN

B. SC.

Born early in this century (December 1903) he had his childhood education under private tutors and then graduated from Ferguson College. He is the first B. Sc., from his community and is a keen student of science, mathematics, English literature, Sanskrit, comparative religion and philosophy. Takes a keen interest in sports and games hiking, reading, photography, stamp and coin collecting. Has been teaching science, Sanskrit, English and Mathematics for over 10 years. Under 40, he has made a study of comparative religion and philosophy for over 15 years.

Has contributed articles on education, religion, social topics and the like to papers and journals; submitted papers to the First All Asia Education and other conferences, and has been a delegate to many conferences. Has edited and translated original Sanskrit works, and still has a lot to publish. His essay on *The Cattle Problem of India* will be published shortly.

He desires India to be one, each one of her inhabitants following his own religion, social customs and other private affairs, but politically one. Wishes swaraj for India as any other, but thinks that it can be got, not by fasting, but by constitutional means; believing the rule that in Nature nothing is useless, tolerates all, though he may not like some.

THE RELIGION OF THE HINDUS

IF religion be the teaching of the relation between man and his Maker, then certainly the Hindus have one of the best religions in the world ; because at every step in the Hindu's acts, words and thoughts, the Maker comes. It is religion that forms the stronghold and life-blood of the Hindu nation. Apart from religion the Hindu cannot exist and Hindu society has no existence. In fact the Hindu has no existence even in a dream without his Maker ; so much so that it has been said that "*the Hindu thinks religiously, talks religiously, eats religiously, walks religiously, worships religiously, marries religiously, learns religiously, and even procreates religiously.*"

The Hindu makes no difference between religion, philosophy, and theology ; to him, science, hygiene, physiology, religion, philosophy all come under one head '*Dharma*' and for authority and guidance in everything he looks to the '*sastras*,'...whether it is the death ceremony, marraige, birth, pilgrimage, or enjoyment, sin or merit, learning or punishment, inheritance or charity. In the course of time, due to a variety of causes, this has divided into different branches and different religious practices rose up.

DIFFERING ROADS

According to P. N. Bose. "*Hinduism is rather a collective name for a group of religions. The path pointed by Vaishnavism is different from the path pointed by Saivism ; both of these again, differ from the path pointed out by Vedantism. Yet all who follow these and other paths are Hindus. There is probably no religion in the world which allows so much freedom of religious conviction and the literature of which is so many-sided as Hinduism. Educated Hindus whether they be pantheists, monotheists, agnostics, or positivists, whether they seek for salvation in the path of knowledge, of faith, or love, can find light and guidance in some part or other of the rich literature of their anscestors which has now been placed within their reach by the labours of Sanskrit scholars.*" (A History of Hindu Civilisation duing the British Rule p 87)

On the surface it may appear that Hindus are pantheistic, but that the Hindu religion is monotheistic can be amply proved. The sentence "*The One exists, sages call it many*" should be sufficient. The *Upanisads* are the apothesis of all religious and philosophical literature of the Hindus and they treat of the Secondless Supreme One. But different paths are pointed for different grades of intellects in different stations in life carrying on different profession, just as children are taught the same subject in one way, the adult in a different way.

THOUGHT, WORD & DEED

Karma is threefold—thought, word and deed—and each *karma*, virtuous or vicious, produces a corresponding effect. The relative importance attached to the different *karmas* and the methods of performing them differ in different countries and these differences are determined by the situation and the climate of the country, the temperament, mental calibre and the aspirations, material and spiritual, of the people, and other causes. Rules of conduct, social customs, food, etc. depend on conditions and climate. Climate and the products have been the law-giver in many cases.

There are two kinds of evolution—material and spiritual. The Hindu considers the limitations of matter, however refined they may be, as bondage and will never rest satisfied until the spirit which is unlimited by matter is reached. The Hindu wants to go to the very source of his Self.

THE VEDAS

The *Vedas* are the pristine source of all that the Hindu does or believes in. For everything sanction must be found therein. We need not go into the various denominations of the Hindus. Such denominations are bound to be found in every religion of the world, by the very nature of the followers being not all of the same mental calibre, nor advanced to the same spiritual level. The *Arya Samaj* "*not only defends the Vedic Rishis from all imputations of Pantheism and Polytheism, but finds in their writings numerous indications of an accurate acquaintance with the fact of science. It holds that cremation, vegetarianism and abstinence from spirituous liquors are inculcated by the Vedas and inculcated to a large extent on purely scientific grounds. It holds that the great religious rite of the Vedic times, the Agnihotra or home sacrifice, is instituted with a view to rendering air and water wholesome and subservient to health, and because it plays a prominent part in putting a stop to the prevalence of epidemics and the scarcity of rainfall! It is convinced that the latest discoveries of science such as those of electricity and evolution, were perfectly well-known to the seers who were inspired to write the Vedas."* (P. N. Bosé. *op. cit.* p 99). All the sects follow the Vedic and the *Upanishadic* teachings in some form or other.

AN IDEAL

The caste system has been variously viewed by many. There is no Hinduism without caste. Hinduism without caste is Buddhism; and caste added to Buddhism is Hinduism. The Brahmin is an ideal. According to the latest Western teachings, the soul takes birth in a family which it finds congenial for its growth and development. Similarly the soul is born in a family for its growth and development on its previous inclinations and as a result of its *Karma*. One quotation is enough. Writing of Aryan civilisation E. B. Havell says:

> "But the rigidity and exclusiveness of the caste system, as we know it, were largely the product of medieval conditions and did not exist either in the time of the Buddha or for many centuries afterwards. Neither is it right to suppose that the rigour of caste was imposed upon India by the craft and sublety of an unscrupulous priesthood bent upon self-aggrandisement. It was rather an inevitable consequence of the peculiar conditions and circumstances which produced Aryan civilisation in India. It be assumed that a certain race, few in numbers and surrounded by a vast population of aliens, had by profound insight or by divine revelation obtained a knowledge of the laws of life far above that of their fellow-men, it would obviously be for the advantage of the community at large that the purity of the race should

be maintained by strict marriage laws and that the utmost care should be taken to hand down to posterity a tradition so pregnant with human happiness. The Aryans believed themselves to be in possession of this precious knowledge, and lest it should be perverted or made a weapon in the hands of unscrupulous adversaries, by common consent it was guarded as a national palladium and entrusted to the custody of a class specially selected and trained for the purpose. Caste laws were laws of spiritual eugenics, designed to promote the evolution of a higher race. It was also by a process of natural selection, or survival of the fittest, that the Brahmans, originally only attendants at the tribal sacrifices who chanted the accompanying hymns and had charge of the sacred vessels, gradually obtained precedence over the Kshatriyas, who in Vedic times combined priestly functions with their military profession and were the representatives of the purest Aryan stock. The marriage laws, the strict rules of seclusion, and the severe penalities for injuries caused to Brahmans by any one of the lower orders were, in the social conditions which obtained in India, a necessary protection for those who were the especial custodians of the honour and traditions of the Aryan race, and who by the nature of their calling did not usually bear arms for self defence—(The History of Aryan Rule in India pp 17, 19).

THE CASTE SYSTEM

That the caste system is scientific and natural has been proved and accepted by many. Classification is bound to be found in all places as all men are not equal ; if not caste, there is class. The world over there is no place where such division of mankind is not found ; it may be according to profession, natural bent, intelligence, social grade, or any other.

Much has been made of social tyrrany, but is appears only on the surface. The quintuplication of the five main castes—*brahmin, kshatriya, vasiya, sudra* and *samkara*—gives us 25 castes such as *brahmin-brahmin, brahamin-kshatriya, brahmin-vaisya, barhmin-sudra, brahmin-samkara etc.* Of these the *brahmin-samkara* is said to be worse than or inferior to the *samkara-brahmin.* Or the fallen brahmin is worse than the lowest born who has improved. In fact evolution to a higher stage has been the aim of the Hindu all along. Examples can be found in plenty where a low-class man has taken precedence over the high-class one by his spirituality.

As said previously social customs are not religious, but are the outcome of the climate, products, etc of the country, and are the result of the economic, eugenic, and other conditions under which the people have to live. After ages they assume a religious character, Some accretions have resulted in Hindu religion as found today, but they need neither be praised nor decried. It is bound to be so. It is at least not wisdom to discuss about one's clothing and praise or decry it, but a waste of time and energy. Time will make the needed adjustment automatically. Hinduism, as it exists today, needs changes here and there, but moral suasion and example of advanced persons in the community will bring about the desired ends,—the abuses and misuses will vanish as they creep in.

MR. SADGOPAL
M.SC., (TECH.)

DIWAN BAHADUR KRISHNALAL MOHANLAL JHAVERI

M A., LL.B., J.P.,

Is an Ex-Judge of the High Court, Bombay and a retired Chief Judge, Presidency Court of Small Causes of the same city. Fellow and Syndic, Bombay University; Judical Adviser, Palanpur State.

He was born in December 30, 1868 and educated at Surat, Broach; and Bhavnagar and Elphinstone Colleges, Bombay. He is a Gold Medallist and Dakshina Fellow, Elphinstone College.

Lectured on Persian in 1890-92. Practised on Appellate Side, High Court of Bombay 1893-1905; Judge and Chief Judge, Presidency Court of Small Causes, Bombay, 1905-1917 and 1918-1928; Puisne Judge, High Court of Bombay 1927; Fellow and Syndic, University of Bombay, 1928. Has written a number of Gujarati, English and Persian Books on literary and historical subjects.

GUJARATI LANGUAGE AND LITERATURE

GUJARAT at present includes Cutch and Kathiawar, where the Gujarati language is spoken. In older times, its linguistic boundaries were wider and different. Part of the present Rajputana in the north, and right up to the region of Lat in the south, a common language was spoken and written. Due, however, to politics, changes came over the spoken and written language: Rajputana or rather Marward Rajasthan, preserved its old Western Rajasthani language and the language in current use in Gujarat underwent several changes till it assumed its present form, which is about two centuries old.

The origin of the language is traced to Sanskrit, like that of all other principal modern Indian languages, such as Bengali, Hindi and Marathi. Pali succeeded Puranic Sansktit as the spoken language, and was replaced by the Prakrits the spoken dialects of the peoples of various parts of India. Four distinct dialects of Prakrit prevalent about 1000 A. D., are thus described in old works : Maharashtri, Saurseni, Paishachi, and Magadhi. Out of these Saurseni was prevalent in the Doab, with Mathra as its centre. Its subdivisions comprised Gujarati, western Rajputani and Eastern Rajputani, Maharashtri. Gaurjari or Gujarati underwent several changes, till it assumed its present form. These changes can be traced backwards. The nearest approch to the present form of the language is called Apabramsha and it has preceded old Gujarati. Examples of Apabramsha are found in books written so early as Vikram Samvat year 875. By about the 10th century of the Christian era, it had established itself as a literary language.

EVOLUTION

Roughly speaking, therefore, there are three or rather four stages through which the language passed before it assumed its present form : (I) the pre-Apabramsha stage, (II) Apabramsha or old Gujarati stage, (III) the middle Gujarati stage, and (IV) the modern or new Gujarati stage dating from the seventeenth century onwards.

Gujarati characters are borrowed from Sanskrit, with slight modifications and with the top lines removed. At present attempts are being made to change some of them to make them approximate to the original Sanskrit, and also to be written in such a way as to present the least difficulty to readers of sister-derived-language like Bengali, Marathi and Hindi, so as to make a uniform script for India possible. Broadly speaking in syntax and grammar Gujarati resembles Bengali and Hindi, many of the spoken and written words are common because of having a common derivation. The idea behind the scheme of the common script is to facilitate the evolution of one national language for India.

FLOWING & FORCEFUL

The language is easy and does not present many obstacles to the student. As a conversational language, it is concise, simple and well adapted for social and domestic intercourse, Though not possessing a large vocabulary it is flowing and forceful. To express abstruse metaphysical and scientific disquisitions, it has to borrow largely from Sanskrit. The conjugations of its verbs are few and less complex than those of English, Sanskrit and Arabic ; and it is not overloaded with auxiliaries. articles, prepositions and adverbs (*Milestones in Gujarati Literature p. 8.).*

Gujarat was for a long time under Mahomedan rule and Persian being the court language, there is a large admixture of Persian words in modern Gujarati. Persian words are found in works written four or five hundred years ago. They have for all practical purposes become indigenous, and assumed the form of household words in every day use. English words also have crept in due to the same cause ; *viz.*, British rule over the province.

DARK DAYS

The early state of literature in Gujarat shows that during the period it was ruled by Rajputs, say about the 8th and 9th centuries of the Christian era, works were written on various subjects in Sanskrit. Then came the turn of the Apabramsha and Rasas were written in that language in praise of the rulers by Bhats and Charans (bards) and stories and poems in praise of wealthy persons by Jain Sadhus. Sanskrit was thus displaced. Jains and Brahmins both contributed their share, but the largest was contributed by Jain Sadhus and Acharyas, who kept the torch of learning alight during the dark days of chaos in the early political history of Gujarat. Pali and Magadhi which were being used by Baudh and Jain writers as learned languages gave way to Prakrit. The use of Prakrit was, however, considered vulgar by the Brahmins, and Prakrit works were, therefore translated into Sanskrit. However by the 9th century, everything was levelled down and Apabramsha took its place amongst the cultured Prakrit languages of India, like Vraj and Hindi. During the Musalman period of rule Prakrit or Apabramsha remained in vogue, but Sanskrit was not neglected. These were dark days politically but somehow or other Jain Sadhus continued their literary activities. The output was mostly, not wholly, religious.

The seeds of early Gujarati literature were sown in about the fourteenth century, and therefore, poets both Jain and non Jain *i. e.*, Brahmins, Banias, artisans even and later, women, came in quick succession. Even Parsis took a hand in it. Bhakti Marga, furnished the staple food to Vaishanav poets, praises of Mahavir and Tirthankars to the Jains. The Parsis translated their religious books from Pehelavi into Sanskrit and from Sanskrit into Prakrit (Gujarati).

A GLORIOUS PERIOD

Miran Bai—the well known devotee of Krishna, a Princess and poetess, and Narsinh Mehta are the outstanding personalities amongst non Jains of the fifteenth century. Their songs and poems are still recited by the inhabitants of Gujarat wherever they are, and some of Narsinh Mehta's verses have become such favourites of Mahatma Gandhi that he hardly misses any occasion to have them sung, when he requires some special inspiration.

The next century witnessed an innovation and story writing, though still in verse, was taken up both by Jain and non Jain writers. Prose writing which till then was neglected, also came into vogue, amongst both communities. The century following (the 17th) was a glorious period of old Gujarat literature, Akha the philosopher poet, Premanand the popular bard who popularised Akhyanas and Mythology and Samal, the best story writer dominate the period, and their works are still very popular. A crowd of lesser poets, both Jains and non Jains wrote verses on various subjects, Parsis did not fall behind, and some of their best Nanehs (chronicles) were written at this time.

A SWEET SINGER

The eighteenth century does not boast of work of any high quality and whatever it was, it was sectarian. The cult of the goddess—the female element in nature found its followers singing the praises of the Mata (Mother) in effective language. Allegorical poems were also written.

The first half of the nineteenth century, with which the period of early Gujarati literature closes, cast up poetesses and

Bhagats, who wrote on the fleeting nature of mundane matters and allied subjects. The rear was brought up by Dayaram, a lyrical poet, a towering personality, and a sweet singer, whose verses and Garbis are sung with great feeling by the men and women of Gujarat, even today.

After Dayarm we enter upon the modern period of Gujarati literature. The earliest exponents of it were Narmadashankar and Dalpatram. The former has written more prose than poetry still he is popularly known as a poet. He was a free-lance compared to Dalpatram who was sober and conservative in thought and expression. Education given in High Schools and colleges in English moulded the thought and ideas of young men all over the country in the latter half of the nineteenth century, and Gujarat naturally came under its sway. Poetry, which till now flowed into the old channel, that of religion and mythology, left it for a new one, and the styles of Shelley, Tennyson, and Keats were imitated. Narsinhrao Divatia set the ball rolling and others followed. New avenues were opened, fiction and novels, dramas and plays, history, biography and works on science, dictionaries and humorous writings, slowly made their way among readers and writers, till now *i.e.*, within a period of one hundred years we find the whole face of the literature changed. Monotony has given place to variety, and all due to the spread of English education ; a result which is common to other modern Indian languages like Bengali, Marathi, Hindi, and Urdu. Shakespeare attracted some Parsi and Hindu writers, who either translated or imitated his plays. Other branches of literature, even such abstruse subjects as metaphysics and philosophy, have deep attention paid to them. Scientific works are being produced in popular style, and altogether a new spirit is moving the young alumni of the university. This phase of activity is also not peculair to Gujarat : it runs all over the country.

A HEARTENING FEATURE

Till now Mahomedan Gujaratis had not played a prominent part in the development of the literature of the Province. Strange to say, however, some of the Khoja Mahomedans of the past generation had taken very kindly to Vedant philosophy and discussed it with as much intimacy with the subject as any

Hindu savant. A couple of such Khoja Mahomedan gentlemen are still to be found in Kathiawad. But apart from such singularities, a band of Muslim youths has girded up their loins to do all they can for the development of the literature of their motherland. Due to several causes they have to take to Urdu, but it must be said to their credit that because of that they do not look askance at their mother tongue Gujarati ; on the other hand they try to enrich Gujarati literature through the medium of all that is best in Urdu. It is a heartening feature.

A noted Indian, himself a poet and a literature, Sir Abdul Kadir has thus described the trend of modern literature (*The Indian World*, February 1939) "Urdu poetry is now finding fresh fields in poems describing the beauties of nature or singing the songs of patriotism or promulgating the best thought of modern philosophy. In prose this literature has made great advances. Besides numerous translations from English and other Western literature it now possesses a large number of works of fiction, of history, of travel and biography." The causes of development and expansion mentioned by him and summarised as follows apply equally to the other languages :—Contact with Western literature through the medium of the English language, the growing desire to have a medium of exchange of ideas between different parts of India within the sphere of Indian languages. The increasing attention paid to indigenous literature by the educated youth of the country.

A STEADY ADVANCE

The onward march has been steady, and all communities residing in Gujarat have given their quota. The share of the Musalmans has already been mentioned. Parsis have all throughout the process of evolution and development stuck to it. At one time they were dominated by the literature of Iran, and they rejoiced in imitating the style of Iranian writers and translating books written by them. Later they crossed over to English literature and followed the same procedure there. Of late many of them have produced work which can be compared with the best work turned out by their Hindu brethren ; *e. g.*, the poem of the late Mr. Malabarior those of Mr. Khabardar one of the finest writers of Gujarati verse.

Christian missionaries in all provinces of India, Bengal, the Deccan, Madras, have from the very start of the foundation of their missions toiled in this field. Carey has left a name in Bengal, Candy in the Deccan, Pope in Madras. Similarly the late Rev. Dr. Taylor, the late Rev. Dr. Scott to mention a few out of those who are dead and the Rev. W. Graham Mulligan M. A., of the Irish Presbyterian Mission at Ahmedabad, not only applied themselves closely to the study of the language of those who were under their pastoral charge, but have written books which will endure, *e. g.*, Dr. Taylor's *Grammars* (large and small) of the Gujarati language. Conversions to christianity are imperceptibly but slowly taking place in increasing numbers. There are large colonies of such converts in Gujarat. The converts naturally ask for the spiritual fare to be given in their own language. This necessitated the writing of books in Gujarati bearing on the Christian religion. The output in this direction has lately became a feature of the literature of the province which cannot be ignored.

RESEARCH

Hindus, both Jain and non Jain, predominate. They are keen on research work also. A large number of old Mss. is being rescued from hiding places in Bhandars and published. A movement is on foot also to build suitable buildings at a large cost and house them there.

Recently the Bombay University decided that answers can at certain examinations be written in the mother language of the student. The study of modern Indian languages is improved and speeded up for Degree Examinations. The Government is also devising means for imparting higher edncation in the mother tongue of the pupil. This measure cannot but eventuate in improving the chances of Gujarati literature having a bright future in front of it.

THE GANDHI SCHOOL

A few years ago, Hindu scholars were in the habit of eschewing the use of words whose origin cannot be traced to Sanskrit. They had Sanskritised the style and mode of writing so much that their writings savoured of Sanskrit written in Gujarati syntax. The Parsis were furious at it. The ordinarily educated Hindu not conversant with Sanskrit disliked and avoided it. Thanks however, to Mahatma Gandhi and his school, who have freed the style from the stigma of Sanskriticism and taken it back to the simplicity of the older writers, simplicity of language, such as would enable a peasant even to understand what is written is the ideal of his school, and writers like Mahadev Desai and Narhari Parikh have successfully tackled the problem, both in journalism and books. In fact books on abstruse complicated and scientific subjects have been written in an exemplary simple and understandable style. The school has filled up a number of gaps in the literature and still adhered to simplicity of style.

A number of Sahitya Sabhas, and Sahitya Mandals, journals published by schools and colleges, and various other literary activities, prophesy a bright future for Gujarati literature. The province is astir : it is humming with the exertions of young writers : along with good work a lot of trash is also coming out : but that is inevitable. In the refinery of public opinion, dross is eliminated hence only sterling gold will abide : that gold is found in large quantities.

PARIPURNANAND VARMA SHASTRI

Was born on February 7, 1907. He boycotted school during the Non-Co-operation Movement and joined the National University, Kashi Vidyapith, and graduated (Shastri) in History, Economics and Politics. In 1926 he married Miss Sita of Bilaspur, C. P. He has been Professor of English and Economics in Premmaha Vidyalaya of Raja Mahendra Pratap, (Brindaban) ; and joint editor "*Prema*" of Brindaban, "*Sanik*" of Agra, and the Daily "*Lokmat*" of Jubbulpore. He was Editor of "*Sandesh*", Benares and Special Correspondent to certain foreign and Indian journals.

His publications include one in English, 12 biographies, three text books and others on history etc.

WE MUST KNOW OUR FINANCIAL POSITION

I AM an humble worker for the cause of my country and I consider freedom, complete independence, to be the panacea of all the ills from which our Motherland is suffering. So long as the fight is going on, we cannot afford to sit idle for every minute is precious in the life of a person and a nation too.

Thus, to bring our country into line with the most advanced nations of the world, an herculean attempt is needed. Poverty is the first thing to be fought and if we eradicate this, India will be soon the guide and leader of the world. Poverty is a curse which brings on all the evils in the universe.

It is gratifying that our leaders are devoting attention to this aspect of our necessity and under the able guidance of Pandit Jawaharlal Nehru, the Industrial Planning Commission has begun to tackle the problem of our industrialisation and other matters seriously.

But, at this stage, I wish to lay certain points before my countrymen for their consideration. I have stressed the same issue before the second session of the All India Statistical Conference, held at Lahore as a delegate of the Federation of the Indian Chambers of Commerce and Industry. My thesis had a country-wide reception and my standpoint was appreciated. I am thus emboldened to beat the same drum.

Without raising national income, no country can prosper. Therefore, the ideal before every planning commission should be to raise our national income. The best way of doing this is by fostering production. The situation should be studied with a view to identify those branches which yield the highest fiscal returns, and which therefore, from that point of view, are most deserving of encouragement even at the cost of temporary losses of revenue and government aid. There persists an excessive disparity in the distribution of wealth as between province and province, which leads to fiscal pressure now being concentrated in a few provinces.

How can we know what production is necessary and what steps need be taken ? Is industrial planning possible without good statistical data ? Can a province rise to the standard without this data ?

Let me submit my case in clearer terms. After the inauguration of Provincial Automony and the augmentation of industrial enterprises in several provinces under popular government, it becomes imperative for all wishers of financial growth to prepare an adequate accurate and up-to-date trade balance and economic census of every province, and on its basis to devise a definite plan of industrial renaissance. The development of the modern world is on a mathematical basis. The growth of industry, commerce, trade and wealth, depend on a calculated statistical movement No progress is possible without the recognition of this important factor. The cleverer a businessman is in the realm of statistics, the more fitted is he for piloting the ship of his business through the troubled waters of time.

The total percentage of British imports from India in relation to its imports from the world, according to Col. IV, 1936 of the "*Trade of the United Kingdom*" was 5.76% *i,e.,* roughly speaking when the total import from the world amounted to

Rs. 975,21,83,773 it was only Rs. 56,13,63,973 from India. World exports to Britain and India were respectively Rs. 5,96,30,51,573 and Rs. 49,61,92,907 *i.e.*, 8.3% was the percentage of our country. Now, friends, these figures exclude treasure and are for the year 1934.

The total for world oxport in treasure to the British was was Rs. 18,83,485,720/- and for India it amounted to Rs. 1,05, 95,733/- *i.e.* 0.56%, while import in treasure from the world and India amounted to Rs. 3,795,600,693/- and Rs. 54,37,49,107/- respectively, *i.e.* the Indian shars was 14.33%. To be brief, so far as India is concerned, her trade balance in merchandise was about 5 million pounds in her favour while as regards treasure she loses by 40 million pounds. Still, the financial pundits of the Government of India, have the tenacity to go on repeating that the present exchange ratio has been extremely favourable to our country. This sort of financial jugglery can only be exposed by a statistician and, therefore, we need a regular army of statisticians.

THE NECESSITY OF AN ECONOMIC CENSUS

If we want to improve the financial and economical position of our provinces, we must first know where we stand. We must realise the shortcomings and requirements of each province ; what industry is needed ; in what sphere of business there is weakness ; the actual drainage of its wealth ; its trade-balance and etc. These are questions which must be answered by provincial administrators, if they want to improve the lot of their government and the governed. Without an accurate economic census, no provincial administration can understand where it actually stands. With weakness in the economic structure of the provinces, provincial autonomy can never successfuly be worked and if provincial administrations are faulty, the centre can never thrive.

The Bowlley Committee advised such economic censuses. News appeared in 1938 that the Economic Advisor to the Government of India, Dr. Gregory, had undertaken the collection and analysis of commercial and other information in relation to the joint benefit of the government and the people interested in the business condition of the country. His activities were to be on a province-wide division basis. Inter-provincial divisions and important municipalities are to be asked to supply their octroi and other tax figures and to calculate the total amount of trade carried in to the city. After arriving at these figures, the actual trade-balance of a province has to be worked out.

I was immensely pleased to receive this news because I thought it would help me in the preparation of a trade-balance and of effecting the economic census of my Province (U. P.)

THE DIFFICULTIES

But the more I tried to go into the matter deeply and to obtain help from the Government of India, the Government of United Provinces, State Railways, the Railway Companies and even the co-operative societies, the more I found, to my utter disappointment, that there was neither connected thought nor disconnected information available on the subject, nor that the Government were contemplating moving ahead in the matter. The Hon'ble Minister for Industires (U. P.) Dr. Kailashnath Katju has been kind enough to assure me of every assistance from his department, but even the Government statistician had to confess that help from his department will have to be meagre.

We wrote to the Minister for Industries that mere assumptions in preparation of a trade-balance will be very harmful and that steady and staple research in the line was necessary. We have absolutely no data and means by which to reach actual figures and gain the knowledge of our financial status.

For the preparation of a trade-balance and economic census the following are the minimum requirements :

(a) Statistics relating to the imports to provinces from foreign countries and other provinces in India.

(b) Exports from a province to other provinces and abroad. (It will facilitate matters a great deal if a differentiation between urban and rural requirements and also a classification of raw materials and finished products and articles of merchandise are given).

(c) Aggregate value of the crops produced in a province, its consumption, export of the surplus and foodstuff imported from outside.

(d) Agricultural implements and cattle etc. imported by a province, and also sold to outsiders. Figures for purchases from outside or travelling salemen may be lacking, but octroi duties imposed on such transmission by the municipalities may be helpful.

(e) Provincial income from Income-Tax, rebate allowed on such taxes due to other provincial charges.
(f) Freight paid in the province on others.
(g) Refunds paid on merchandise and other taxable goods.
(h) Excise duty on matches and sugar and other such duties.
(i) Banking statistics.
(j) Provincial debts and interest and approximate circulation of currency.

AVAILABLE MATERIAL

It transpired that information relating to the irrigated area under improved varities of crops, consumption of artificical manure, imports of machinery, mileage of railways and roads, consumption of iron, steel and cement, expenditure of municipalities on water and sanitary works, capital expenditure on hydro-electric and other electrical undertakings etc. may be anticipated to be found although vigourous attempts are needed. Secondly figures for rice, wheat, linseed, sugar, textile, textile mills, handlooms, co-operation etc. are available and also for the quantity of the main commodities exported and imported by the U. P.

Even the publishers of these figures do not claim them to be authoritative and the difficulty of analysing the last item is the greatest.

GENERALISATION OF THE FIGURES

The quantity of the articles supplied relates to main cities only and is no indication whether the same city consumes or re-exports to the other towns of the province. Secondly, the figures stand for certain towns and not for the whole province. Hence they are not complete. Thirdly, they are given in terms of maunds and to evaluate them is an impossibility. Even the *Indian Finance Year Book* on its page 159 (35-36 edition) leaves the task in despair. It considers it "*Impossible for purposes of those acounts to work out the corresponding figures of value and experience in the past has shown that on whatever basis the values are assigned to the quantity figures recorded they are in most cases liable to make only a very vague approximation to the truth and should more often that not afford no basis for working out a correct balance of trade for the different provinces involved.*"

The Statistical Department of the U. P. has prepared a book on agricultural prices but it is not very helpful for the purpose. The Director of Agriculture for the U. P. was approached and he also could not do much in the matter. The Director of Statistics for the U. P. informed me that the heads of statistics specified no doubt cover a broad field and *"I am afraid reliable information may not be availabe under all heads in the form desired."* When I wrote about agricultural figures to the Imperial Council of Agricultural Research they referred me to the Director of Agriculture who in his turn, as I have already written, could not help me. Practically, everybody referred me to the *Trade Journal* accounts relating to the inland (rail and river borne) and raw cotton trade statistics. Some esteemed authorities confused the trade-balance with the economic census. Figures for rural indebtedness were to be obtained from the Banking Enquiry Committee but I wonder if any one can get serious help in this matter. On account of the lack of information there was always an evasive procrastination and no definite reply could be received. Municipal blue books to which I have referred for octroi figures are incomplete in the sense that there is uo specification of those figures which either do, or do not, contain refunds, most of the income is from articles received from villages in the same districts to the town and *vice versa.*

One of the very important items of information necessary for the province is the trade movements through the railways of a particular province. On writing to the agents of the E. I., the G. I. P. and the B. N. W. railways, the former two found it impossible for their office even to allow the facility for the figures to be copied from their office. The Director of the Railway Board intimated that the E. I. R. obtained from municipalites and other local bodies such statistics of road-borne traffic as may be required by them from time to time. This information they gave us in view of our pointing out to them "that a company of your organization is not maintaining the records of inland-trade passing through your railways in the Province of U. P. when your company, is evidently anxious, to bear the road vehicle competition and even B. N. W. R. services, how can you formulate by the diversion unless a data is prepared.'

The advice given in this connection by the Indian Statistical Institute is quite valuable, but all the advice gathered together amounts to one thing; that unless the Provincial Government itself undertakes the job and realises the importance .of the thing, it will be impossible to do anything really useful and worthwhile in the matter.

ADVICE

The total expense of the central government on statistical work in the year 34-35 was Rs. 5,44,497/-only, and inclusive of provinces it rose to Rs. 5,99,193/-out of which the Government of Madras spent Rs. 7,777/-on gazetteers and statistical memoirs (and no other province on this item); the same Government spent Rs. 10,730/-; Bombay Rs. 1,635/-Bengal Rs. 260/- Bihar Rs. 6,000/-, N. W. F. P. Rs. 849/-; Assam Rs. 799/-only on provincial statistics. Burma's expenses are ideal and may, of course, be due to its separation necessitating a comprehensive survey. In British India, Madras has an ideal figure, although too small for a province of its size. My purpose in pointing out these figures is to show that while out of their total "miscellaneous income" of Rs. 1,08,14,745/-the Government of India is spending 5.03% on statistical work, the Government of U. P. has spent 7.37% (its miscellaneous income is Rs. 91,871/- only) which is better than the Governmant of India; I also find that out of its total revenue (34-53) of Rs. 1,21,31,33,295/- only the Government of India's expenses are ·044%, only on statistical working, the U.P. Government's ratio comes to .0061 p. c. on its revenne of Rs. 11,02,73,980/- only. The position is appaling in both cases, the U. P. 's expenses are only 1.11 p. c. on the total statistical expenditure are not very graceful. Unless provincial administrations know the position of the administered, they can neither improve on finances from revenue or expenditure side of the government, nor solve the many problems facing the subjects.

Thus, it is absolutely impossible for any province to raise its economical status and improve its financial condition, until and unless a trade balance of the province is prepared. It is important to keep a good statistical chart of the province; a comprehensive and the detailed document is the thing we need today.

The Gregory Committee, instituted by the Government of India, is now trying to evolve a framework in the collection of trade statistics for the country.

In the end, I submit that any talk of economic planning for any government, the more so for our Congress Government, will be a farce and should be taken as a farce without knowing where we stand.

With the best wishes in the world, we cannot progress much and let me submit further that it will be sailing too near the wind of industrial backwardness if we are not vigilent enough to point out to our provincial governments what we need.

PANDIT G. KRISHNA SASTRI

Born on the 5th February 1863 in Malabar, S. India of a distinguished and well-known orthodox Brahman family. He was the editor and publisher of *Arya Siddhanta Chandrika* (Malayalama), the *Hindu Heritage* (English) and the *Madras Chronicle* (English tri-weekly) and was closely associated with Col. H. S. Olcott of the Theosophical Society until his death in the organisation of the now famous Adyar Library.

Came in contact with the great Appayacharya, the latest Vedanta Bhashyakara and the resuscitator of the synthetic system of Sankhya-Yoga of the 108 Upanishads, in 1892 and entrusted by him with the diffusion of the doctrines of Anubhavadvaita has been steadily working towards it ever since. Brought out in 1901 *Sri Rama Gita* (Sanskrit text, 1000 verses with English translation), the Bible of the Anubahavadvaita system, and he is the author of Democratic Hinduism.

He founded the O. P. C. L in Madras in 1904 for publishing the literature pertaining to this system. Later founded the Vedic Mission in 1909. He has brought out more than 100 publications, chief among them being those in the Arya Siddhanta Chandrika series, Bharati series, Vedic lore and Vedic Academy series. He is now chiefly concerned with the silent work of the Vedic Academy and devotes his whole time, energy, resources and enthusiasm to carry on the work of his Acharya in the future.

VEDIC RELIGION AND PHILOSOPHY

JUST as in mathematics the "fourth dimension of matter," though difficult of comprehension, is by constant study and practice, realised by means of Hinton's blocks and other methods, even so in our religious philosophy "the Fourth dimension of spirit" is realised by means of the various methods taught in our books of knowledge. meditation and work, into which the 108 Upanishads are divided.

Mundaka speaks of the spiritual evolution thus: "As from a blazing fire sparks, being like unto fire, fly forth a thousand fold, thus are various beings brought forth from the imperishible, my friend, and return thither also."

Mahopanishad says : "The *Jivas* attached to *samsara* have originated from *cit.* Those that have formerly come into existence together with the forms created by *Brahman* in lakhs and crores like minute particles of water that break forth from a spring are endless in number. Similarly those that now come and those that will hereafter be ushered into existence are also endless in number. Some among these had one birth, some have had more than a hundred births, some have had numberless births. Some had two or three births".

We are mainly concerned with the evolution and involution of the divine element (or the divine spirit in us) and not of matter and mind which are but the outer aspects of the spirit. In the heart of everything is the divine spirit or spark, technically termed the *Pratyagatman.* This *Pratyagatman* is the Son and Paramatman is the Father. The realisation "I and my father are one" is possible only when the fourth dimension of spirit is comprehended.

The Upanishads graphically describe how the divine sparks (the sons) strayed away from the eternal source (the Father), how they became entangled and enmeshed in flesh and how they are stranded in the ocean of matter and how they might, if they choose, extricate themselves therefrom and go back to their Father, by living the religious life recommended in the three books of knowledge, meditation and work.

Although *Brahman* is all-pervading like the ether, yet, a fourth part (of it) is pervaded by its *Mulaprakriti* (or root-matter). This Mulaprakriti possesses the inherent *Vijatiya* differences (or differences pertaining to various species), known as *Avarana Sakti, (Sukshma), Vikshepa Sakti,* and *Sthula* (*Vikshepa*) *Sakti,* and *Sthula* (*Vikshepa*) *Sakti,* and is therefore, the seed of all the universe, We come to understand from the *Purusha Sukta* (passage quoted below) that the *Jivas* that come out like sparks from fire fall on the said *Mulaprakriti.*

"All the universe (together with all that was and will be) is but a manifestation of the glory (and power) of the said *Purusha.* His real nature is greater than this glory. For, all living beings (in all the three periods of time) are but a quarter of Him, while, three-fourths remain immortal and changeless in His own Self-Effulgence."

Then when these Jivas, like those in deep sleep, remained stagnant, immersed in ignorance, the all generous Supreme Lord, for the purpose of their acquiring knowledge and experience, made them first enter the subtle bodies (created by Himself), and then those gross bodies (created through Brahma). On entering those bodies, they became entitled to all the knowledge that might be acquired from the world, sciences, etc.

The *Jiva* (the *Pratyagatman*) who is a part of *Para Brahman* and who is naturally untainted, becomes thus attached to the effects of *Prakriti*, suffers various kinds of pains pertaining to *Samsara*, and remains attached to worldly actions, because, through the influence of the Supreme Lord's *Maya*, he believes, along with those others with whom he associates, that the greatest enjoyment of senses in the world is the highest *Summum bonum*. Even though *Jivas* be, in the manner aforesaid, attached to worldly actions, one in a crore will, through the effect of his uselfish meritorious deeds, aspire for liberation. When such a desire crops up, what he ought to study is the science of self taught in the 108 *Upanishads.*

The abstract of what is taught in these three books (called Jnana, Upasanı and Karma Kandas) which teach us how to become liberated from the thraldom of matter and how to realise our "native blissfulness," in our everyday life, is given below.

I. "That endless Nirguna Brahman which has the privative attributes of Sat, Chit and Ananda, as opposed to non-existence, non-intelligence, and non-blies ; which is the source of Jivas ; which is back of the universe and its Lord (Saguna Brahman) ; and which is below that nirgunatita Brahman which is beyond the reach of speech and mind, should be known as the One Being which is back of all, without a second. No state is attributed to it beyond the three states (of waking, dreaming and dreamless sleep). Being the witness of the three kinds of Jiva, it is said to be no Jiva. Being devoid of the three bodies, it is said to be bodiless. Being full of knowledge, it is said to be devoid of ignorance. A portion of that Brahman alone having become Jiva, always thinks and grieves, that "I am the doer, I am the enjoyer." All the rest which are the creations (or rather, emanations) of Maya and Avidya, including the universe and its Lord, are non-eternal. He who, by means of his past virtues, knows thus ; who is possessed of discrimination and non-attachment ; and who has seen the self within the body, is entitled to hear more about the Self. He should take instructions from a good teacher regarding the formula "That thou art". The word "That" denotes the Lord who is joined to Maya, but aims at that Nirguna Brahman whose attributes are truth, knowledge and beauty—symmetry or harmony. The word "Thou" denotes the Jiva who is subject to Avidya, but aims at that Kutastha (or supreme one) who is Nirguna, and subtle in his nature, and who is known as Pratyagatman. The word "art" while denoting the identity of Jiva and Isa, virtually aims at that of Kutastha and Brahman. By hearing this from his teacher one frees himself from the ignorance of the self. By means of discriminative knowledge produced by constant reflection on these teachings, he frees himself from doubts, and then through the world of Brahma, gradually attains moksha which knows no rebirth. He enjoys comfort after he has known that "I am the Pratyagatman who is the witness of the body Indriyas, Manas, Budhi and the Void ; and who is free from decay." When the superimposition of Self on the body is known by means of the knowledge of the identity of Self and Brahman, he enters Brahman through the sun and enjoys bliss. Only when one knows the decayless and deathless Self whose nature is Sat, Chit and Ananda, is he saved from sinking in the ocean of Samsara, subject to decay and death. Knowledge is extolled, and study of the Vedas and Vedantas, and the the performance of various ceremonies, sacrifices, devotion, pilgrimage, siddhis. etc, are said to be useless without the dawn of Self-knowledge. Desires which are worldly and heavenly, are said to linger in the minds of men and *devas* only until the dawn of the knowledge of Brahman. After acquiring the knowledge "I am Brahman", one is freed from ignorance and doubt, and also from all Sanchita karma. He then becomes pure. He who knows that he is not Annamaya, not Pranamaya, not Manomaya, not Vijnanamaya, not even the fifth one which is Anandamaya, in the state of deep sleep ; but that he is the sixth one who is the Brahmic Self, full of bliss, (such a man) at his death, reaches through the path of the Devas, the seat of Brahman, even though he might only lead an ordinary life in this world. One should kuow that he is not the elements or their qualities, but he is that Sat, Chit, Ananda which is back of all effects and causes."

11. "The Jnana Kanda ends with Sravana and Manana (*i.e* with hearing and reflection). The aspirant should practise meditations (or Nididhyasana) after obtaining the discriminative knowledge, "I am Brahman" by means of Manana (or reflection). Upasana is nothing but constant meditation on the identity of Self and Brahman. This meditation called Nididhyasana entirely removes Viparyaya (*i.e.* obstructions, errors, or misconceptions). As intensely and rapidly as meditation is practised in the manner herein taught, so intensely and rapidly does the Light (or Jyotis) manifest. According as the manifestation of Light, so is the removal of veils. On the entire removal of veils, the aspirant gets a complete view of the Supreme Light, and experiences full bliss after overcoming all sorrows. Owing to the identity of the thing meditated upon and himself, the aspirant attains liberation in life, being freed from Sanchita and Agami Karmas. Just as knowledge is enforced in the Sruti by means of commandments, even so is Upasana, undoubtedly, enforced in the Srutis. This Upasana, coupled with Jnana, being the seventh stage of Yoga, the wise do not see any difference between the meditator and that meditated upon. That Nirguna Brahman which is the source of Maya and all other effects, and which is the final peace, is verily said by the Srutis to be the Only Being to be medidtated upon. He is liberated who meditates thus : "I am that non-dual Brahman which supports all, which needs no other support, and which is centred in Pranava. Just as Brahman, which was originally devoid of parts, or differentiation, ultimately became Jiva by the process of evolution, even so does the differentiated Jiva become Brahman by means of this Yoga (or Upasana). This very same Upasana or the highest meditation on the identity of the Self and the Supreme, is taught by means of Gayatri and other mighty mantras. That meditation whereby the identity of the meditator and the thing meditated upon is accomplished, is the only means of Self-experience. The Vedanta holds that he who knows Brahman perfectly well, is the only one who is

entitled to practise this meditation. The method, or process, by which this meditation is carried on, is also given in full detail. During meditation, the mind, on account of its previous impressions, will run after external objects. The wise man should then repeatedly meditate upon Brahman by controlling the mind by means of arguments and non-attachment. He will not feel the practice tiresome as he will soon experience bliss. When by the practice of such meditation, Jiva is absorbed in Brahman, then the Pranas which support the Jiva are agitated. When Pranas are absorbed, the Nadis, which support the Pranas are agitated. When Nadis are absorbed, the body which supports the Nadis is agitated. Just as when a pole firmly fixed in the ground is agitated, the ground also shakes, even so is the body shaken and exhausted. But such indications are seen only in those practitioners who are slow and middling. Whereas in the case of the practitioners of the highest order, no such indications are seen because they do not need great efforts in controlling the mind. If the practitioner meditate upon Paramatman by conceiving Him as bright as the midday sun, then he becomes capable of pervading everything like the all-pervading ether. The Srutis and Smritis teach this very idea in the words "as one wills so he becomes." Let one hear the meanings of Mahavkyas constantly and let him also intensely reflect upon those meanings continually, he can never hope for liberation without this Upasana. By the knowledge of the identity of Self and Brahman, the mind can never be absorbed (or annihilated), but it can, by means of this meditaton (or Upasana), be asbsorbed with the Pranas and Indriyas along with it. By this meditation on the Self as the Brahman which is back of the universe, the Self will naturally take the form of the undivided bliss, and the veil of darknes will be removed, as self-effulgence will then begin to spread itself on all sides. Let it not be doubted that that Nirguna which is beyond the reach of speech and mind can be conceived of by the mind. We are not speaking here about that Nirgunatita which is formless and which is back of the Nirguna, because it can never be grasped by the mind. The Nirgunatita is the one which even transcends the Moksha State. We speak of that Nirguna alone which is non-dual and sat-chit-ananda by nature, and which is the seat of Moksha itself. If this Nirguna Brahman be meditated upon as directed, with a pure mind, then by that, the knot of the heart will be entirely broken. No amount of hearing about the non-dual nature of the Self and no amount of reflection will ever enable any one to realise the said Brahman without this meditation on Brahman. Hundreds of Srutis and Smrits proclaim the necessity of Brahma-dhyana. Then how can one directly cognise Brahman by mere argumentation? Deplorable indeed is the ignorance of people who profess to follow the Vedantic teachings which pre-eminently urge the necessity of meditation, and who, at the same time, contend that knowledge alone is sufficient for Moksha. By this Upasana alone can one destroy the various kinds of distractions and veils, and by it alone can one annihilate the mind, and attain Jivanmukti. Even some, among those who know this perfectly well, are deluded. They think that after the dawn of knowledge, nothing more has to be done. After duly considering what is secondary and what is essential, the wise have came to the conclusion that knowledge is secondary and Upasana is essential. If one will not admit that knowledge is secondary to Upasana, then surely will his Indriyas become wayward. Owing to such waywardness, many sins will be committed. What is the use of his knowledge when he commits all sorts of sins? If knowledge is considered secondary, then it is used for purposes of Upasana by means of which the waywardness of Indriyas can be arrested. In the Srutis it is declared : That the disciple ought to hear the teacher only after beholding (the Self), that he should then reflect on those teachings, and then alone should Nididhyasana (or abstract meditation) be practised". When such is the declared order, how can one say that Sravana or hearing is the last thing? The knowledge necessary for Kram amukti is obtained by Sravana. The perfect knowledge necessary for Jivanmukti is obtained by Upasana. The best among the wise, who alone know the method of realising the Self in the Sastraic way, attain Jivanmukti by their practice, and not others who cheat the world. They are cheats who say that the formless Brahman which is beyond the reach of speech and mind, can be reached by words, that it is endowed with privative attributes, that it should be known by those who desire Mokha ; and who also say that that Brahman, whose form is intelligence (or Light) is Saguna and that it is, on that account alone, fit to be meditated upon. Those who thus discourse upon the Arupa Brahman, having lost their intelligence are sure to fall into miseries owing to their waywardness. The Jivanmukta who meditates upon the identity of Self and Brahman, reaches that Arupa, on the loss of his Praraboha body. The wise man shall, therefore, with the idea "I am Brahman", meditate upon that Nirguna Brahman whose form is intelligence, and who is the object of perfect knowledge. That Brahman which is recommended to be known should alone be meditated upon. That which is not recommended to be meditated upon is the one which cannot be known."

I11. "In the Srutis and Smritis are mentioned three kinds of Karmas (or religious practices), *viz*, Nitya (obligatory), Naimittika (occasional), and Karmya (optional or those performed with motives). Out of them, the Karmya karmas are to be rejected altogether by those who desire Moksha. Naimittika karmas ought to be performed even by Yogis who are Jivanmuktas, and the Nitya karmas ought to be performed either for the good of the world or for one's own good. Agnihotra and others are Nityakarmas, and they ought to be performed for preserving one's own Asrama or order of life. Until the Jivanmukta reaches the state of Ativarnasramin (*i. e.* one who has risen above the castes and orders of life), and until he attains Videhamukti, he ought to perform Nityakarmas. Because the hightest liberation called Videhamukti depends upon the performance of Nityakarmas, it follows that that Mukti is born of Karma. Or because that Mukti is attained by means of Niavikalpa and other Samadhis, it is said that it is born of karmas. That Samadhi which should be performrd by a Jivanmukta and which is even superior to Upasana is a mental Karma. What will Jnanins attain if they will neither practise Dhyana nor that Samadhi which removes samsara ? The Upasakas too, without considering their own downfall, neglect the Karmas pertaining to their respective order of life. Nityakarmas etc are the external Karmas, and Samadhi the last internal Karma that should be performed for the sake of Videhamukti. He who does not perform his Nityakarmas loses his caste status, and he who has no such status is not entitled to Mukti, even nominally. Only he who belongs to his Asrama or order of life is allowed to under go Sarvana, Manana and Dhyana, but not the sinner who is devoid of any discipline. Those who, on account of their delusion, do what they like of their own account after neglecting the observance of duties pertaining to their order of life, are said to be violators of Vedic injunctions. Even though one has attained Jivanmukti, he has to meet with sorrows.

To remedy those sorrows he is ordained to follow the observances pertaining to his order of life to the very end of his life. By merely following the observances pertaining to the order of life to which one belongs, sorrows cannot be remedied. They can only be remedied by Samadhi, and Samadhi is impossible without the help of some Asrama. Even a Jivanmukta should always perform Samadhi along with his Asramachara for the sake of attaining Videhamukti. Whether he be student, house-holder, hermit, or ascetic, one should, until he forgets his body, diligently perform the Karmas pertaining to his Asrama. All those that do not perform the unselfish deeds that are ordained by the Srutis and Smritis are sinners. It is not right to say that because a Jivanmukta does not desire to secure Videhamukti, his observing the Karmas is useless. Even if such a Jivanmukta neglect his karmas, he will become wayward, will meet with downfall, and will then become the chief among the violators of Vedic injunctions. If you hold that it is reasonable to say that ignorance is the cause of bondage, and knowledge that of release, but that it is not reasonable to say that Karma is the cause of both bondage and release, then hear the reply. The cause of bondage is the action done with desire or motive; the cause of release is the desireless action which is never to be deprecated. By the Upasana spoken of before, one becomes the knower of Brahman (or Brahmavid). For attaining the condition of Brahmavidvara, Brahmavidvariya and Brahmavidvarishtha, one should, with Vairagya, perform the higher Samadhis known as Nirvikalpa, Nissamkalpa and Nirvrittika respectively. He who thus reaches the condition of Varishtha and remains in the seventh stage (or Bhumi) will in a short time attain the Nirvasana state. That is the Nirvasana state which is beyond the reach of all speech and mind, which is devoid of all pairs of opposites, and which can only be described by negations. Of what use is the unknowable and unknown to the hearer now, when it is impossible to describe it by authorities or reasoning. One should therefore understand that Brahman alone which can be directly cognised by means of Samadhis, which is truth, knowledge and bliss, and by which Moksha is attained. He whose mind is absorbed in that Brahman, whose form is one undivided bliss, and which is motionless, is, undoubtedly, liberated. The Videhamukta enjoys permanent Self-bliss by means of the highest Samadhi. He does not experience anything else than Self-bliss. By the experience of Self-bliss alone that Muni (silent man) attains supreme peace and rests extended on the ground like Ajagara (a huge snake), having reached the condition of Varishtha. Then having attained Videhamukti, he gives up even his previous behaviour (like a child a mad man, a ghost etc) and becomes motionless. That is a great man in this world who has so forgotten his body as not to feel the effect of Prarabdha which is being completely worked out. By Karma is Karma generated, by Karma is Karma destroyed, and by Karma is attained Akarma (or absence of Karma) by means of which is attained bliss which is due to no Karma whatever. Some Karmas are to be re-rejected, some are to be accepted and some are such as are not to be accepted or rejected. The seed of Akarma is Karma, and the seed of Karma is Akarma, hence the wise man should always depend upon both. When Jiva who is the doer is totally lost by means of Samadhis, in Brahman which is pure Intelligence (or Light) which is devoid of doubts (or volitions) and which is eternal, then whatever may be the effects of merits and demerits of the doer, all of them become extinct. There is no doubt of this. Thoughts, devotions, yogas, meditations, bodies, samsara, indriyas, manas, pranas, avaranas, nescience, intelligence, matter, animal species, men, devas, Brihaspati, Brahma, Vishnu, Siva, Prakriti, and the whole universe are due to Karma alone. He is liberated who, fully knowing this, avoids Karma by depending upon Karma. Karma is capable of releasing him who is bound to this samsara by Karma, in the same manner as the elephant which has fallen into the pit can be raised by another elephant. What is the use of Vedantic knowledge to him who is subjected to samsaric pains, and who yet will disregard Samadhis, as mere Self. To those who diligently perform obligatory rites such as Agnihotra etc and who also perform the internal Karma called Samadhi, there will be no decay whatever.

He who has reached the condition of Jivanmukti shall perform, untill his death, the obligatory rites, and Samadhi Karma. If that wise one desires to attain Videhamukti, let him constantly perform Samadhi by depending upon the hundred and eight Upanishads.

DR. NARAYAN SUBRAO HARDIKAR

M. C. P. S. (CAL) M. SC. (U.S.A.)

Was educated at Hubli, Calcutta and in the U. S. A. where he stayed for eight years taking his Master's degree in Public Health from the State University of Michigan. He kept terms for Ph. D., in the Illinois University but left to join Lala Lajpat Rai at the end of 1916. Joined the Swadeshi Boycott Movement, 1905 ; on the Staff, "*Kannada Kesari*" (A Weekly) 1908. He was the General Secretary of the Home Rule League of America in 1917-21 ; and Editor of "*Young India*", started by Lala Lajpat Rai in New York. Returning to India in 1921 he joined the Non Co-Operation Movement and was the General Secretary Karnatak Provincial Congress Committee : acted as Dir. Karnatak Prov. Volunteer Bd. Founder, Karnatak Vast Prasarak Sangh ; Bhagini Mandal, Tilak Grantha Sangh, and other Institutions ; Founded Hindustani Seva Dal, 1923, and acted as its Secretary General up to 1931, and then as its Organizing Secretary under the Congress Working Committee. Editor of the "*Volunteer*" Sentenced to one year's R. I. in the Nagpur Satyagraha 1923 ; Member, Congress Working Committee, during the first Satyagraha Movement, 1930 ; Sentenced twice in Salt Satyagraha ; Detenue, 1932, and sentenced for one year and six months after the 1932 Satyagraha Movement. Founded the Indian Messenger System, 1932 ; His publications include "*Bharateeya Rashtra Dhwaja*" in Hindi, Marathi, Kanarese, Gujrati and other languages.

INTERNATIONAL HAPPENINGS AND THEIR REPURCUSSIONS ON INDIA

WAR clouds in Europe are very intense. The humidity may burst at any moment and inundate all through. It is only a matter of days if not hours. To whatever side we turn we hear the talk of war.

As such it will be necessary to have a paid survey of the international situation and the causes that led to the present European crisis before one can presage the repurcussions outside Europe in the event of any conflagration. As it is, in Europe there are different conflicting ideologies ; democracy, dictatorship and socio-communism. It is difficult however to say how the countries would range themselves in the case of a general conflagration.

It may bs said that the pressnt situation in Europe is more an outcome of the Treaty of Versailles than of any intention of one's supremacy over the other though of late some countries in Central Europe are responsible for the threatened conflagration on account of their economic interests.

At the end of the Great War the Treaty of Versailles was drafted in France in November 1918. The drafting Committee, after many withdrawals consisted of three powers represented by Wilson (America), Lloyd George (Gt. Britain) and Clemanceau (France). Clemanceau wanted to crush France's old enemy and neighbour Germany and humble her in every way so that she would not be able to raise her head again. The Treaty was drawn with the aid of Lloyd George to the dertriment of Germany and she was forced to sign it. As a result Germany was not only injured but also insulted. In addition to heavy reparation, Germany's colonies were distributed among the allies, England getting the choicest morsel. Germany was multilated in Europe. Her resources were crippled. Ever since Hitler came to power he has been trying for Germany's territorial expansion. He began to declare openly that the Treaty of Versailles was a dictated one and therefore the Germany of his time could not be bound by it. Taking advantage of the dormant League of Nations he began to rearm Germany. Italy, too, was one of the disgruntled nations. When Mussolini came to power, like Hitler, he wanted to expand Italian territory, but conld not have his way in Europe, As a result of the Laval-Mussolini Pact of 1935 he had a free hand in Africa. Italy wanted to test her strength and measure the attitude of the other powers in Europe so Abyssinia was made the victim. None in Europe came to the rescue of Abyssinia but only helped Italy by pacts and committees. The League of Nations, of which Abyssinia was a member, did not lift a finger in defence of its member but betrayed her by sweet speeches and useless committees. Italy's strength was tested and the two Fascist powers, Germany and Italy, joined together and commenced to impose supermacy over other parts of Europe.

First they aimed at Spain. Their object in winning over Spain was clear. Britain was too powerful in naval force and has the key of the sea routes. In the event of a major conflict between Germany and Britain or Italy and Britain or in any case, with Gibralter and the Suez Canal under her control Britain could create an economic blockade of Italy which would be disastrous to the latter. So, if Spain was won over, Gibralter could be brought under control and be a check to Britain. Germany and Italy therefore staked their men and money, created a civil war in Spain, took sides with Franco—the Rebel leader—and finally brought Republican Spain under control. Here it is needless to repeat the part played by the so-called democracies, especially the arms embargo against the recognised Government of Spain. Trade agreements have now been concluded the new Spain under France, Italy and Germany. Portugal is a minor Fascist State revolving on the Rome-Berlin axis. Thus the Fascist powers have under their control strategic places.

Germany repudiated the Treaty of Versailles and as a token occupied Rhineland in 1936. Gaining self confidence Hitler made a clear walk over Austria and even without spilling a drop of blood annexed the territory. His claim is that all Germans should be under the German Reich wherever they may be. Even in the Austrian invasion Hitler had a free hand.

Then came the Sudeten land of Czecho-Slovakia. Because there were a greater number of Germans than Czechs in the Sudeten territory Germany should exercise control over the portion. This was the plea of Hitler. Chamberlain and Daladier found force in Hitler's argument and abetted him in occupying the province and it came under Germany. This was not enough. Hitler knew the weakness of Britain and France. He knows too that Britain and France, besides being phrase-mongers, could not take direct action against anybody under the present world circumstances. The whole of Czecho-Slovakia was the next target. That country also fell a prey to Hitler when she realised that she could depend more on Hitler than on either Britain or France. Poland is refusing to cooperate with Germany. Germany is merely mocking at the peace parleys of Britain and France. Hitler has definitely stated in a speech that he is not going to avoid war if need be. This indicates that other tiny nations in Central Europe may be swallowed up at any time. Rumania is likely to be the next to be brought under control. After thus strengthening its own hands Germany and Italy may together strike at those who are frowning at her to-day. Germany would have struck at France or Britain direct earlier had it not been for Russia and the U. S. A. Anyway, it seems that it is only a matter of days for a major conflict in Europe.

In Asia, Japan wanted economic expansion as her land was limited. She had the promise and backing of the Fascist powers and she launched her offensive in China thinking that China would yield easily. At the beginning, with the help of the Fascist powers, Japan gained some portion of China, though she has been forced to recede to-day But help could not be afforded by the fascist powers to Japan as they have to concentrate their energy and force in Europe in case of a sudden outbreak of war. Besides, China has organised herself much better than on a previous occasion and she is now in a position to inflict defeat after defeat on Japan. The resources of Japan have now become exhausted and she has learnt to her cost that she should not have interfered with China. The ultimate course for Japan would be to conclude some settlement with China and revive the lost industries and markets which were set back on account of this conflict.

A world war seems to be imminent in view of the unabated adventures of the fascist powers and the passivity of Britain and France. How will that affect us in India? Are we to take sides in a war? Now that with the help of the Muslim League Party, the Government of India has got the Army Recruitment Bill passed, those who advise others not to be recruited to the British army may be taken to task by the Non-Congress provinces. Are we to keep quiet? No! the anxiety of Whitehall to alter the 1935 Act to cope with emergencies of war is quite revealing considering their statesmen's boast that the Act cannot be altered at any cost.

From the available figures of steel by different powers it may be seen that countries smaller in territory and with less resource than India are able to produce much more than India. Why then should not India strain her nerves, organise the industries and be self sufficient in every way? The Great War of 1914 helped Japan to organize and improve her industries and commerce and taking full advantage of the dislocation of trade during that War, Japan developed her resources. With the growth of Japanese industry and commerce grew their political power also and they were able to occupy a prominent seat in the Concert of Nations. Why can India not develop her industries in the given circumstances.

Instead of depending upon Norway and Canada for paper, glassware from Japan, glass bangles from Czecho-Slovakia sugar from Java and so many other necessaries from outside countries, India can manufacture her own requirements and be self-sufficient. Necessities and luxuries such as motor cars and aeroplanes may be manufactured with the help of experts. India, being predominantly an agricultural country it need not be assumed that cottage industries are in conflict with large scale industries can be utilized for heavy manufactures to facilitate trade and commerce outside and cottage industries may be developed alongside. Even in agriculture, there are methods and methods by means of which modern science can be made to help in increasing the output instead of diminishing it. Where the small scale industries cannot cope with requirements the large scale industries may be substituted. There is a vast market for Indian produce. Why need cotton be sent outside? Is it not being taken at ridiculously low prices and returned as finished products with heavy increases in price? Why need rice be imported from abroad when every necessary of life is grown in abundance in India? All these may be protected. Therefore, it is most opportune for India to equip herself with all necessaries without depending on outside help. When there is economic self sufficiency political bondage will automatically vanish.